AF478060

Baptist Hymnal

Baptist Hymnal

(1975 EDITION)

CONVENTION PRESS
Nashville, Tennessee

The Scripture quotations in this hymnal, except where otherwise noted, are from the King James Version.

Those marked RSV are from the *Revised Standard Version Bible,* copyrighted 1946, 1952, and © 1971 by the Division of Christian Education of the National Council of the Churches of Christ in the U.S.A. Used by permission.

Those marked NASB are from the *New American Standard Bible,* © The Lockman Foundation, 1960, 1962, 1968, 1971, 1972. Used by permission.

Those marked TEV are from the *Today's English Version* of the New Testament and Psalms, © Copyright American Bible Society 1966 and 1970, and *Wisdom for Modern Man,* © Copyright American Bible Society, 1972. Used by permission.

Preface

During the dynamic days of the sixties and seventies the stream of Christian music has been joined by many new rivulets. The sounds of haunting folk melodies with biblically based texts join the stately grandeur of traditional hymns. The surge of new rhythmic sounds contrasts with more familiar gospel songs, bringing new dimensions to proclamation.

Celebration of the work and love of Christ is a key thought in contemporary worship. Nostalgia for the old has brought back to the fore many of the hymns and gospel songs of another generation. The music used in worship in our churches will run the gamut. This is a new age of singing in a time that emphasizes participation. What a time for a new hymnbook!

This collection is being issued during an era of unparalleled richness in musicology and hymnology. The variety of music used and performed in our churches is undoubtedly the greatest in our history. The need is clear for a new collection that provides for the wide ranging needs of the young and the mature, the musician and the musically unskilled, and the varying tastes of those who worship within our congregations.

Baptist Hymnal is brought to you with the belief that it will honor Christ, reflect scriptural truth, and meet the needs of our churches. It is our prayer that this hymnal will contribute to the enrichment of worship of almighty God. It should provide an aid to more effective congregational singing in all of our churches.

Thus, for the glory of God, the enriching of worship, the proclamation of the gospel, and the building of the churches, we joyfully present this hymnal.

Grady C. Cothen
President
Sunday School Board
Southern Baptist Convention

Introduction

Christian song is dynamic, slowly changing with the passing of time. Each generation adds to its heritage its own responses to God, its relevant expressions of praise to God, and its witness to the gospel of Jesus Christ and the presence and power of the Holy Spirit. In this way Christian song is enlarged and enriched as followers of Christ sing of God, God's world, God's work, and God's will with the spirit and the understanding. This hymnal, designed to be used by the people called Baptists, seeks to bring together a significant body of songs for congregational singing in this day and in the decades ahead.

Congregational singing has not always been a common practice in Baptist churches. Some churches in both England and America in the seventeenth century offered vigorous opposition to "promiscuous singing" (the singing of believers and unbelievers together) and the singing of "set forms" (the metrical versions of the psalms because they were "man made"). However, congregational singing prevailed and continues to be a vital force in Christian worship and fellowship among Baptists.

Because each Baptist congregation is autonomous, each is free to sing any songs and to use any compilation it chooses: there is no authorized or required denominational hymnal. Thus, during the past two centuries, at least two hundred different hymnals have been published by or for Baptist congregations in America. Most of the early collections were initiated and compiled by individuals, usually pastors. The first one, simply titled *Hymns and Spiritual Songs,* was published in Newport, Rhode Island, in 1766, by an unknown compiler.

The Philadelphia Baptist Association published a hymnal for the churches of its fellowship in 1790, and the Dover Baptist Association did likewise in 1828. Many individuals—on their own initiative and sometimes at their own expense—have produced collections of hymns for Baptists. Among these are Andrew Broaddus, Jesse Mercer, David Benedict, Starke Dupuy, James Winchell, Staunton S. Burdett, Basil Manly, Jr., Baron Stow, Samuel Francis Smith, J. M. D. Cates, Sidney Dyer, J. R. Graves, W. E. Penn, and Robert H. Coleman.

In the last half of the nineteenth century the publishing of hymnals by Baptist denominational publishing houses, both in the North and the South, became increasingly significant. The Southern Baptist Publication Society, established in Charleston, South Carolina, in 1847, published *Baptist Psalmody* (1850). The American Baptist Publication Society in Philadelphia published *The Baptist Hymn and Tune Book* (1871), and *The Baptist Hymnal* (1883). The Sunday School Board of the Southern Baptist Convention, established in Nashville, Tennessee, in 1891, published *The Baptist Hymn and Praise Book* (1904). *The New Baptist Hymnal* (1926), published jointly in Philadelphia and Nashville, was designed to be an updating of the 1882 hymnal.

While *The Broadman Hymnal* (1940), published by the Sunday School Board in 1940 under the Broadman Press imprint, did not bear the name Baptist, it was the first hymnal to be widely accepted by Southern Baptist churches. *Baptist Hymnal* (1956) has been used even more extensively and has provided a common ground for congregational singing in the churches during a period of extraordinary growth and emphasis on church music. This 1975 hymnal, in the tradition of these earlier hymnals, retains the name *Baptist Hymnal,* and takes its place in the forward march of congregational song.

The Hymnal Committee, representing the many facets of Southern Baptist life, strove diligently to provide a book of hymns appropriate in every respect for the needs of the churches. The committee adopted the basic criterion of congregational usefulness in content selection, which automatically removed from consideration songs designed specifically for choirs, soloists, or special groups.

A research survey of current hymn-singing practices in the churches brought unusual insight to the committee. To replace hymns no longer widely used in the churches, the committee searched many sources of Christian song—music of older traditions and more recent decades, the contemporary songs of the gospel, and new songs yet unknown. With prayerful hearts and objective minds the committee pursued the task of compilation, enriched by the great diversity of the group, yet fused to oneness by the unanimity of spirit. To the well-known and dearly loved hymns the committee has added new songs of the Spirit, incorporating contemporary expressions and vocabulary—both poetic and musical. The result is a happy blending of the old and the new, of the familiar and the unfamiliar.

This hymnal reflects the biblical emphasis of Baptist tradition. Hymn texts were critically examined for theological accuracy and doctrinal soundness. Since congregational singing is a musical experience, much attention needs to be focused on the tunes. In its search for new and unfamiliar material, the committee sought singable tunes with strength and character, avoiding awkwardness, difficulty, and dullness. The wide variety of tunes chosen reflects the basic concern for musical values. To strengthen the musical experience of congregational singing, more tunes for unison singing have been included, some tunes have been lowered to more comfortable keys, and, in some instances, alternate tunes have been suggested to give more variety.

The organization of the hymnal reflects a theocentric, or God-centered, rationale for the book. The hymns are arranged logically and sequentially in four sections: God, God speaks, God's work, and God's people. The balance and proportion in these major divisions provide material for congregational singing in the life of the church—worship, fellowship, witness, evangelism, missions—and the many experiences of the Christian life. The detail of the organization is seen in the listing of contents. No indication of specific categories is given on the hymn pages, thus providing greater flexibility and allowing wider use of the hymns without specific identification with only one category.

The following distinctive features are identified regarding the format of the hymn pages:

1. First lines are used as titles of the hymns except where another title is more commonly known.

2. The scriptural basis for the hymn is given if indicated by the author or obvious from the content of the hymn.

3. The author, composer, and/or source of the words and tune, and the tune name are given below the hymn. The date given is that of the writing or the publication, if this is known.

4. The metrical forms of the tunes are not furnished on the page but may be found in the alphabetical index of tunes.

5. Asterisks appearing within the stanzas of a hymn indicate an explanatory scripture reference or notation below the hymn.

6. Brackets above the music indicate a suggested introduction for the accompanist.

7. If a tune is used more than once, opportunity is provided for a change in the key. Where this occurs, reference is made below the hymn to the number of the tune in a higher or lower key.

8. Reference is made below a number of hymns to alternate tunes that may be used with the hymn text.

The Hymnal Committee commends to the churches this compilation with the prayer that it will find full and extensive use in the churches, and that its songs might resound from those who know redemption and the abundant life through Jesus Christ our Lord.

THE HYMNAL COMMITTEE
William J. Reynolds, *Chairman and General Editor*

Subcommittee I: Content Organization

Donald C. Brown	Earl Holloway	Shelden H. Russell
Ural C. Clayton	Warren C. Hultgren	Charles Storey
Russell H. Dilday	Alma Hunt	Steve A. Taylor
Harry Eskew	LeRoy McClard,	James D. Whitmire
Alta C. Faircloth	*Chairman*	

Subcommittee II: Scripture Readings

Elmer F. Bailey	J. Loyd Landrum	Ed Seabough
J. M. Crowe	Bill F. Leach,	Doyal Spence
Robert J. Hastings	*Chairman*	Evelyn Marney Phillips
Donald C. Howell	Robert J. Norman	Ronald K. Wells

Subcommittee III: Theological and Doctrinal Evaluation

John H. Buchanan	Charles R. Livingstone,	Cecil E. Sherman
Allen B. Comish	*Chairman*	William H. Souther
W. A. Criswell	Hugh T. McElrath	James L. Sullivan
Raoul Cunningham	John McKay	James D. Woodward
William L. Hendricks	W. B. Mitcham	

Subcommittee IV: New Material

Cliff Barrows	Emma M. McCall	Thad Roberts, Jr.
Larry Black	Gerald B. Ray	Joe Ann Shelton
James W. Clark	Buryl Red	Gordon Stoker
Donald P. Hustad	William J. Reynolds,	Claude H. Rhea, Jr.
Sharron Lyon	*Chairman*	

Subcommittee V: Promotion and Interpretation

James C. Allcock, Jr.	Frank G. Charton	S. W. Prestidge, Jr.
Gene Bartlett	Dan C. Hall	Eugene F. Quinn
Paul R. Bobbitt, Jr.	Ervin Keathley	Paul H. Stewart
Allen R. Brown	Rod Latta	Joseph O. Stroud
John R. Chandler,	Carroll Lowe	Thomas H. Westmoreland
Chairman	Paul McCommon	Bob Woolley

x

Contents

Let the word of Christ dwell in you richly in all wisdom; teaching and admonishing one another in psalms and hymns and spiritual songs, singing with grace in your hearts to the Lord.

Colossians 3:16

Holy, Holy, Holy 1

1. Ho - ly, ho - ly, ho - ly! Lord God Al - might - y!
2. Ho - ly, ho - ly, ho - ly! all the saints a - dore thee,
3. Ho - ly, ho - ly, ho - ly! tho the dark - ness hide thee,
4. Ho - ly, ho - ly, ho - ly! Lord God Al - might - y!
Ear - ly in the morn - ing our song shall rise to thee;
Cast - ing down their gold - en crowns a - round the glass - y sea;
Tho the eye of sin - ful man thy glo - ry may not see;
All thy works shall praise thy name, in earth, and sky, and sea;
Ho - ly, ho - ly, ho - ly, mer - ci - ful and might - y!
Cher - u - bim and ser - a-phim fall - ing down be - fore thee,
On - ly thou art ho - ly; there is none be - side thee,
Ho - ly, ho - ly, ho - ly; mer - ci - ful and might - y!
God in three Per - sons, bless - ed Trin - i - ty!
Who wert, and art, and ev - er - more shalt be.
Per - fect in pow'r, in love, and pu - ri - ty.
God in three Per - sons bless - ed Trin - i - ty! A -MEN.

Revelation 4:8-11. Words, Reginald Heber, 1826. Tune NICAEA, John B. Dykes, 1861.

2 Come, Thou Almighty King

1. Come, thou Al - might - y King, Help us thy
2. Come, thou In - car - nate Word, Gird on thy
3. Come, Ho - ly Com - fort - er, Thy sa - cred
4. To thee, great One in Three, The high - est

name to sing, Help us to praise: Fa - ther! all -
might - y sword, Our prayer at - tend! Come, and thy
wit - ness bear In this glad hour! Thou, who al -
prais - es be, Hence ev - er - more; Thy sov - 'reign

glo - ri - ous, O'er all vic - to - ri - ous, Come, and reign
peo - ple bless, And give thy word suc - cess: Spir - it of
might - y art, Now rule in ev - 'ry heart And ne'er from
maj - es - ty May we in glo - ry see, And to e -

o - ver us, An - cient of Days.
ho - li - ness, On us de - scend.
us de - part, Spir - it of pow'r.
ter - ni - ty Love and a - dore. A - MEN.

Words, Anonymous, 1757. Tune ITALIAN HYMN, Felice de Giardini, 1769.

God, Our Father, We Adore Thee 3

1. God, our Fa - ther, we a - dore thee! We, thy chil - dren, bless thy name!
2. Son E - ter - nal, we a - dore thee! Lamb up - on the throne on high!
3. Ho - ly Spir - it, we a - dore thee! Par - a - clete and heav'n-ly guest!
4. Fa - ther, Son, and Ho - ly Spir - it, Three in One! we give thee praise!

Cho - sen in the Christ be - fore thee, We are "ho - ly, with-out blame."
Lamb of God, we bow be - fore thee, Thou hast bro't thy peo - ple nigh!
Sent from God and from the Sav - ior, Thou hast led us in - to rest.
For the rich - es we in - her - it, Heart and voice to thee we raise!

We a - dore thee! we a - dore thee! Ab - ba's prais - es we pro - claim!
We a - dore thee! we a - dore thee! Son of God, who came to die!
We a - dore thee! we a - dore thee! By thy grace for - ev - er blest:
We a - dore thee! we a - dore thee! Thee we bless thro' end-less days!

We a - dore thee! we a - dore thee! Ab-ba's prais - es we pro-claim!
We a - dore thee! we a - dore thee! Son of God, who came to die!
We a - dore thee! we a - dore thee! By thy grace for - ev - er blest.
We a - dore thee! we a - dore thee! Thee we bless thro' end-less days! A - MEN.

Words, st. 1, 2, 4, George W. Frazer, 1904; st. 3, Alfred S. Loizeaux, 1953. Tune BEECHER, John Zundel, 1870.

4 Glory Be to the Father

Glo-ry be to the Fa-ther, and to the Son, and to the Ho - ly Ghost; As it
was in the be-gin-ning, is now, and ev-er shall be, world without end. A-men, A-men.

Words, Anonymous, 4th Century. Tune GLORIA PATRI (Meineke), Charles Meineke, 1844.

5 Glory Be to the Father

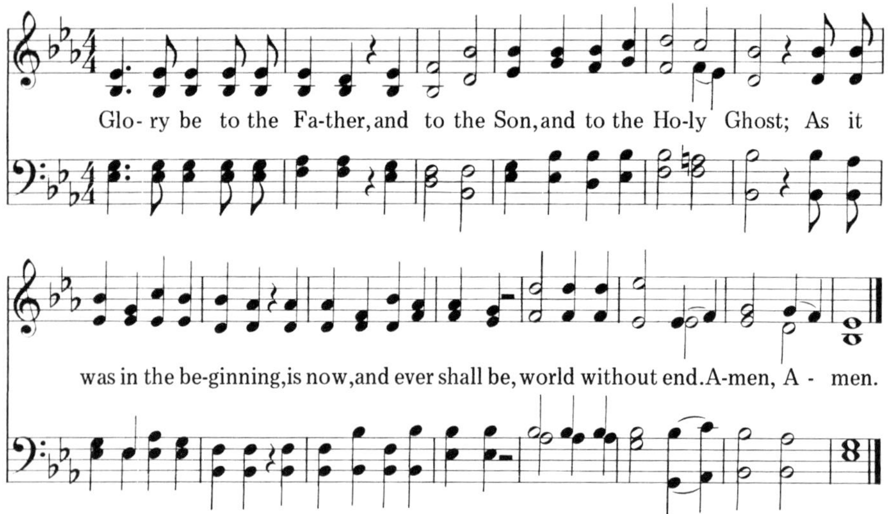

Glo- ry be to the Fa-ther, and to the Son, and to the Ho-ly Ghost; As it
was in the be-ginning, is now, and ever shall be, world without end. A-men, A - men.

Words, Anonymous, 4th Century. Tune GLORIA PATRI (Greatorex), from Henry W. Greatorex' *Collection*, 1851.

Praise God, from Whom All Blessings Flow 6

Praise God, from whom all bless-ings flow;Praise him, all crea-tures here be-low;
Praise him a-bove, ye heav'nly host; Praise Fa-ther, Son, and Ho-ly Ghost. A - MEN.

Words, Thomas Ken, 1695. Tune OLD 100TH (altered), *Genevan Psalter*, 1551.

Praise God, from Whom All Blessings Flow 7

Praise God, from whom all bless-ings flow;Praise him all crea-tures here be - low;
Praise him a-bove, ye heav'n-ly host;Praise Fa-ther, Son, and Ho-ly Ghost. A-MEN.

Words, Thomas Ken, 1695. Tune OLD 100TH (original), *Genevan Psalter*, 1551.

8 Praise, My Soul, the King of Heaven

Unison

1. Praise, my soul, the King of heav-en, To his feet thy
2. Praise him for his grace and fa-vor To our fa-thers
3. Frail as sum-mer's flow'r we flour-ish; Blows the wind and
4. An-gels in the height, a - dore him; Ye be-hold him

trib-ute bring; Ran-somed, healed, re-stored, for-
in dis-tress; Praise him, still the same as
it is gone; But, while mor-tals rise and
face to face; Saints tri-um-phant, bow be-

giv-en, Ev-er-more his prais-es sing; Al-le-lu-ia!
ev-er, Slow to chide, and swift to bless; Al-le-lu-ia!
per-ish, God en-dures un-chang-ing on: Al-le-lu-ia!
fore him; Gath-ered in from ev-'ry race; Al-le-lu-ia!

Al-le-lu-ia! Praise the ev-er-last-ing King.
Al-le-lu-ia! Glo-rious in his faith-ful-ness.
Al-le-lu-ia! Praise the high e-ter-nal one.
Al-le-lu-ia! Praise with us the God of grace. A-MEN.

Psalm 103. Words, Henry F. Lyte, 1834. Tune LAUDA ANIMA (Andrews), Mark Andrews, 1931. Copyright 1931, Renewed 1959 G. Schirmer, Inc. Used by permission. Alternate tune REGENT SQUARE, No. 87.

All Creatures of Our God and King 9

Unison
1. All crea-tures of our God and King, Lift up your voice and with us
2. Thou rush-ing wind that art so strong, Ye clouds that sail in heav'n a-
3. And all ye men of ten-der heart, For-giv-ing oth-ers, take your
4. Let all things their Cre-a-tor bless, And wor-ship him in hum-ble-
sing Al-le-lu-ia! Al-le-lu-ia! Thou burn-ing sun with gold-en
long, O praise him! Al-le-lu-ia! Thou ris-ing morn, in praise re-
part, O sing ye! Al-le-lu-ia! Ye who long pain and sor-row
ness, O praise him! Al-le-lu-ia! Praise, praise the Fa-ther, praise the
beam, Thou sil-ver moon with soft-er gleam! O praise him, O
joice, Ye lights of eve-ning, find a voice! O praise him, O
bear, Praise God and on him cast your care! O praise him, O
Son, And praise the Spir-it, Three in One! O praise him, O
praise him! Al-le-lu-ia! Al-le-lu-ia! Al-le-lu-ia! A-MEN.

10 Praise to the Lord, the Almighty

1. Praise to the Lord, the Al-might-y, the King of cre-a - tion!
2. Praise to the Lord, who o'er all things so won-drous-ly reign-eth,
3. Praise to the Lord, who doth pros-per thy work and de-fend thee;
4. Praise to the Lord, O let all that is in me a-dore him!

O my soul, praise him, for he is thy health and sal-va - tion!
Shel-ters thee un-der his wings, yea, so gent-ly sus-tain-eth!
Sure-ly his good-ness and mer-cy here dai-ly at-tend thee.
All that hath life and breath, come now with prais-es be-fore him.

All ye who hear, Now to his tem-ple draw near;
Hast thou not seen How thy de-sires e'er have been
Pon-der a - new What the Al-might-y can do,
Let the A - men Sound from his peo-ple a - gain,

Praise him in glad ad-o-ra - tion.
Grant-ed in what he or-dain - eth?
If with his love he be-friend thee.
Glad-ly for aye we a-dore him. A - MEN.

Psalm 103:1-6; Psalm 150. Words, German Hymn, Joachim Neander, 1680; translated, Catherine Winkworth, 1863, alt. Tune LOBE DEN HERREN, from *Stralsund Gesangbuch*, 1665; harmonized, W. Sterndale Bennett, 1863.

Praise the Lord! Ye Heavens, Adore Him 11

1. Praise the Lord! ye heav'ns, a - dore him; Praise him, an - gels, in the height;
2. Praise the Lord! for he is glo - rious; Nev - er shall his prom - ise fail;
3. Wor - ship, hon - or, glo - ry, bless-ing, Lord, we of - fer un - to thee;
Sun and moon, re - joice be - fore him; Praise him, all ye stars of light.
God hath made his saints vic - to - rious; Sin and death shall not pre - vail.
Young and old, thy praise ex - press - ing, In glad hom-age bend the knee.
Praise the Lord! for he hath spo - ken; Worlds his might - y voice o - beyed;
Praise the God of our sal - va - tion! Hosts on high, his pow'r pro-claim;
All the saints in heav'n a - dore thee. We would bow be - fore thy throne;
Law which nev-er shall be bro - ken For their guid-ance hath he made.
Heav'n and earth and all cre - a - tion Laud and mag - ni - fy his name.
As thine an - gels serve be-fore thee, So on earth thy will be done. A - MEN.

Psalm 148. Words, st. 1, 2, Anonymous, c. 1801; st. 3, Edward Osler, 1836. Tune HYFRYDOL, Rowland H. Prichard, 1830.

12 Come, Thou Fount of Every Blessing

1. Come, thou Fount of ev - 'ry bless - ing, Tune my heart to
2. Here I raise mine *Eb - en - e - zer; Hith - er by thy
3. O to grace how great a debt - or Dai - ly I'm con-

sing thy grace; Streams of mer - cy, nev - er ceas - ing,
help I'm come; And I hope by thy good plea - sure
strained to be! Let thy grace, Lord, like a fet - ter,

Call for songs of loud - est praise.
Safe - ly to ar - rive at home. I am bound for the king-dom,
Bind my wan - d'ring heart to thee.

Will you go to glo - ry with me? Hal - le - lu - jah, praise the Lord.

Words, Robert Robinson, 1758. Tune WARRENTON, *The Sacred Harp*, 1844; arranged, John Drakestone, 1956. © Copyright 1957 Broadman Press. All rights reserved. *1 Samuel 7:12.

Come, Thou Fount of Every Blessing 13

1. Come, thou Fount of ev - 'ry bless - ing, Tune my heart to sing thy grace;
2. Here I raise mine *Eb - en - e - zer; Hith - er by thy help I'm come;
3. O to grace how great a debt -or Dai - ly I'm con-strained to be!
Streams of mer - cy, nev - er ceas - ing, Call for songs of loud - est praise:
And I hope, by thy good pleas-ure, Safe- ly to ar - rive at home:
Let thy grace, Lord, like a fet - ter, Bind my wan-d'ring heart to thee:
Teach me some me - lo - dious son - net, Sung by flam - ing tongues a - bove;
Je - sus sought me when a stran-ger, Wand'ring from the fold of God;
Prone to wan - der, Lord, I feel it, Prone to leave the God I love;
Praise the mount! I'm fixed up-on it, Mount of thy re - deem- ing love.
He, to res - cue me from dan - ger, In - ter-posed his pre-cious blood.
Here's my heart, Lord, take and seal it, Seal it for thy courts a - bove.

Words, Robert Robinson, 1758. Tune NETTLETON, Wyeth's *Repository of Sacred Music, Part Second*, 1813.
*1 Samuel 7:12.

14 Praise the Lord

Unison

1. Praise the Lord! Praise, O ser-vants of the Lord! Praise the
2. Praise the Lord! Thanks and prais-es sing to God! Day by
3. Praise the Lord! Praise and glo-ry give to God! Who is
4. Praise the Lord! Praise, O ser-vants of the Lord! Praise the

name of the Lord! Bless-ed be the name of the Lord!
day to the Lord! High a - bove the na-tions is God,
like un-to him? Rais-ing up the poor from the dust,
love of the Lord! Giv-ing to the home-less a home,

Bless-ed be the name of the Lord From this time
High a - bove the na-tions is God, His glo-ry
Rais-ing up the poor from the dust, He makes them
Giv-ing to the home-less a home, He fills their

forth and for-ev-er - more! Praise the Lord! Praise the Lord!
high o-ver earth and sky! Praise the Lord! Praise the Lord!
dwell in his heart and home. Praise the Lord! Praise the Lord!
hearts with new hope and joy! Praise the Lord! Praise the Lord!

Words, st. 1, Psalm 113:1, 2; st. 2-4, Marjorie Jillson, 1971. Tune CARPENTER 1970, Heinz Werner Zimmermann, 1970. From *Five Hymns* by Heinz Werner Zimmermann, copyright 1973 by Concordia Publishing House. Used by permission.

We Praise Thee, O God, Our Redeemer 15

1. We praise thee, O God, our Re - deem - er, Cre - a - tor,
2. We wor - ship thee, God of our fa - thers, we bless thee;
3. With voic - es u - nit - ed our prais - es we of - fer,

In grate - ful de - vo - tion our trib - ute we bring.
Thro' life's storm and tem - pest our Guide hast thou been.
To thee, great Je - ho - vah, glad an - thems we raise.

We lay it be - fore thee, we kneel and a - dore thee,
When per - ils o'er - take us, thou wilt not for - sake us,
Thy strong arm will guide us, our God is be - side us,

We bless thy ho - ly name, glad prais - es we sing.
And with thy help, O Lord, our bat - tles we win.
To thee, our great Re - deem - er, for - ev - er be praise. A - MEN.

Words, Julia Cady Cory, 1902. Tune KREMSER, Netherlands Folk Song; arranged, Edward Kremser, 1877.

16 God Himself Is with Us

1. God him-self is with us: Let us now a-dore him,
2. God him-self is with us: Whom an-gel-ic le-gions
3. Lord, come dwell with-in us; While on earth we tar-ry;

And with awe ap-pear be-fore him. God is in his
Serve with awe in heav-'nly re-gions. "Ho-ly, Ho-ly,
Make us your blest sanc-tu-ar-y. Grant us now your

tem-ple, All with-in keep si-lence, And be-fore him
Ho-ly," Sing the hosts of heav-en, Praise to God be
pres-ence, Un-to us draw near-er, And re-veal your-

bow with rev-'rence. Him a-lone, God we own;
ev-er giv-en. O give ear To us here:
self still clear-er. Where we are, Near or far,

Words, Gerhard Tersteegen, 1729; translation, composite. Tune ARNSBERG, Joachim Neander, 1680.

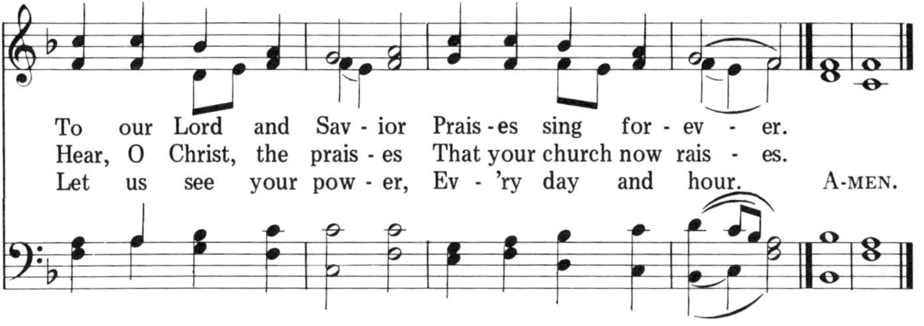

To our Lord and Sav - ior Prais - es sing for - ev - er.
Hear, O Christ, the prais - es That your church now rais - es.
Let us see your pow - er, Ev - 'ry day and hour. A-MEN.

All People That on Earth Do Dwell 17

1. All peo - ple that on earth do dwell, Sing to the
2. The Lord, ye know, is God in - deed, With - out our
3. O en - ter then his gates with praise, Ap - proach with
4. For why? the Lord our God is good, His mer - cy

Lord with cheer - ful voice; Him serve with fear, his
aid he did us make; We are his folk, he
joy his courts un - to; Praise, laud, and bless his
is for - ev - er sure: His truth at all times

praise forth - tell; Come ye be - fore him and re - joice.
doth us feed, And for his sheep he doth us take.
name al - ways, For it is seem - ly so to do.
firm - ly stood, And shall from age to age en - dure. A-MEN.

Psalm 100. Paraphrased, William Kethe, 1561. Tune OLD 100TH, *Genevan Psalter*, 1551.

18 Praise Him, O Praise Him

Unison
1. Praise him, O praise him, Praise the Lord for all his bless - ings; Praise him, O praise him, Sing a joy - ful song be - fore him; Praise him, O praise him, Sing a joy - ful, ju - bi - lant song.
2. Glo - ry and hon - or, Glo - ry be to God the Fa - ther; Glo - ry and hon - or To the Son and Ho - ly Spir - it;
1.
2.
*A-MEN.

O Gracious Lord, Accept Our Praise 19

Unison
1. O gra-cious Lord, ac - cept our praise; We bow be-fore thy throne;
2. Lord, we would tru-ly wor-ship thee, And serve thee day by day,
3. Dear Lord, we bring our grate-ful hearts, And place them in thy hand;
Pro-claim thro' us thy love for man; Thy will for all make known.
That oth-ers may thy grace re-ceive, And walk thy ho-ly way.
O use our lives to show the world Thy great sal-va-tion plan.
Thy prais-es, Lord, we sing to thee Now and for-ev-er-more;
Our songs shall thy great name re-sound, And ring from shore to shore.

20 God of Earth and Outer Space

Unison

1. God of earth and out - er space, God of love and
2. God of at - mo - sphere and air, God of life and
3. God of man's ex - plor - ing mind, God of wis - dom,
4. God of earth and out - er space, God who guides the

God of grace, Bless the as - tro - nauts who fly
plan - ets bare, Use man's cour - age and his skill
God of time, Launch us from com - pla - cen - cy
hu - man race, Guide the lives of seek - ing youth

As they soar be - yond the sky. God who flung the stars in space,
As he seeks your ho - ly will. God of depth and God of height
To a world in need of thee. God of pow - er, God of might
In their search for heav - 'nly truth. God who reigns be - low, a - bove,

God who set the sun a - blaze, Fling the space - craft
God of dark - ness, God of light, As man walks in
God of rock - ets fir - ing bright. Hearts ig - nite and
God of u - ni - ver - sal love, Love that gave Na -

Words, Thad Roberts, Jr., 1970. From *The Hymn*, Copyright 1970 by The Hymn Society of Americ
Used by permission. Tune ABERYSTWYTH, Joseph Parry, 1879.

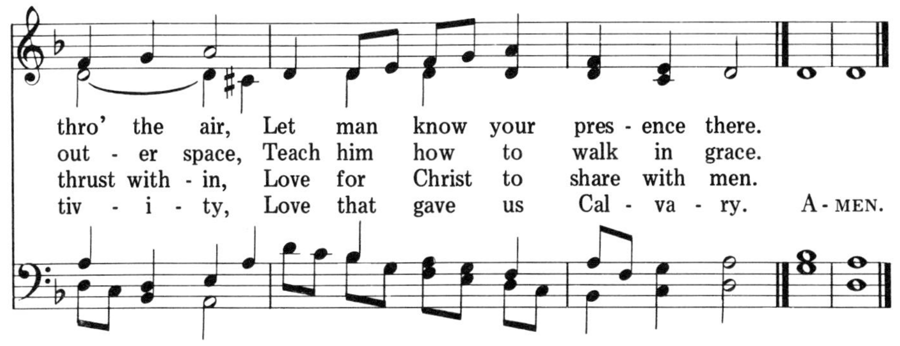

thro' the air, Let man know your pres - ence there.
out - er space, Teach him how to walk in grace.
thrust with - in, Love for Christ to share with men.
tiv - i - ty, Love that gave us Cal - va - ry. A - MEN.

O Come, Loud Anthems Let Us Sing 21

1. O come, loud an - thems let us sing, Loud
2. In - to his pres - ence let us haste, To
3. The depths of earth are in his hand, Her
4. O let us to his courts re - pair, And

thanks to our Al - might - y King; For we our voic - es
thank him for his fa - vors past; To him ad - dress, in
se - cret wealth at his com - mand; The strength of hills that
bow with ad - o - ra - tion there; Down on our knees, de -

high should raise, When our sal - va - tion's Rock we praise.
joy - ful songs, The praise that to his name be - longs.
reach the skies, Sub - ject - ed to his em - pire lies.
vout - ly all, Be - fore the Lord, our Mak - er, fall.

Psalm 95:1-6. Words, Tate and Brady's *New Version*, 1696. Tune HERR JESU CHRIST, *Cantionale Germanicum*, Dresden, 1628.

22 Sing Praise to God Who Reigns Above

1. Sing praise to God who reigns a-bove, The God of all cre-
2. What God's al-might-y pow'r hath made His gra-cious mer-cy
3. The Lord is nev-er far a-way, But, thro' all grief dis-
4. Thus all my toil-some way a-long I sing a-loud his

a - tion, The God of pow'r, the God of love, The God of our
keep-eth, By morn-ing glow or eve-ning shade His watch-ful eye
tress-ing, An ev-er-pres-ent help and stay, Our peace and joy
prais-es, That men may hear the grate-ful song My voice un-wea-

sal - va - tion; With heal-ing balm my soul he fills, And
ne'er sleep-eth; With-in the king-dom of his might, Lo!
and bless-ing; As with a moth-er's ten-der hand He
ried rais - es; Be joy-ful in the Lord, my heart! Both

ev - 'ry faith-less mur-mur stills: To God all praise and glo - ry!
all is just and all is right: To God all praise and glo - ry!
leads his own, his cho-sen band: To God all praise and glo - ry!
soul and bod - y bear your part: To God all praise and glo - ry!

Deuteronomy 32:3. Words, Johann J. Schütz, 1675; translated, Frances E. Cox, 1864. Tune MIT FREUDEN ZART, Bohemian Brethren's *Kirchengesänge*, 1566.

Praise the Lord Who Reigns Above 23

1. Praise the Lord who reigns a-bove, And keeps his court be-low;
2. Cel - e - brate th'e - ter - nal God With harp and psal - ter - y,
3. Him, in whom they move and live, Let ev - 'ry crea - ture sing,

Praise the ho - ly God of love, And all his great - ness show;
Tim - brels soft and cym - bals loud In his high praise a - gree;
Glo - ry to their Mak - er give, And hom - age to their King.

Praise him for his no - ble deeds, Praise him for his match - less pow'r;
Praise him ev - 'ry tune - ful string; All the reach of heav'n - ly art,
Hal - lowed be his name be - neath, As in heav'n on earth a - dored;

Him from whom all good pro-ceeds Let earth and heav'n a - dore.
All the pow'rs of mu - sic bring, The mu - sic of the heart.
Praise the Lord in ev - 'ry breath, Let all things praise the Lord. A-MEN.

Psalm 150. Words, Charles Wesley, 1743. Tune AMSTERDAM, *Foundery Collection,* 1742.

24 Let All the World in Every Corner Sing

Unison
1. Let all the world in ev - 'ry cor - ner sing: My God and King!
2. Let all the world in ev - 'ry cor - ner sing: My God and King!
The heav'ns are not too high, His praise may thith - er fly; The
The church with psalms must shout, No door can keep them out; But,
earth is not too low, His prais - es there may grow. Let
more than all, the heart Must bear the long - est part. Let
all the world in ev - 'ry cor - ner sing: My God and King!
all the world in ev - 'ry cor - ner sing: My God and King! A - MEN.

Words, George Herbert, 1633. Tune ALL THE WORLD, Robert G. McCutchan, 1934. Music copyright renewal 1962 assigned to Abingdon Press. All rights reserved. Used by permission.

The God of Abraham Praise 25

1. The God of A - braham praise, All prais - ed be his name,
2. His spir - it flow - eth free, High surg - ing where it will;
3. He hath e - ter - nal life Im - plant - ed in the soul;
Who was, and is, and is to be, For aye the same!
In proph-et's word he spoke of old, He speak - eth still.
His love shall be our strength and stay While a - ges roll.
The one e - ter - nal God, Ere aught that now ap - pears;
Es - tab - lished is his law, And change - less it shall stand,
Praise to the liv - ing God! All prais - ed be his name,
The First, the Last: be - yond all tho't His time - less years!
Deep writ up - on the hu - man heart, On sea or land.
Who was, and is, and is to be, For aye the same! A - MEN.

Words, Daniel ben Judah Dayyan, *c.* 1400; translated, Newton Mann and W. C. Gannett, 1884-85, alt.
Tune LEONI, Traditional Hebrew Melody; transcribed, Meyer Lyon, *c.* 1770.

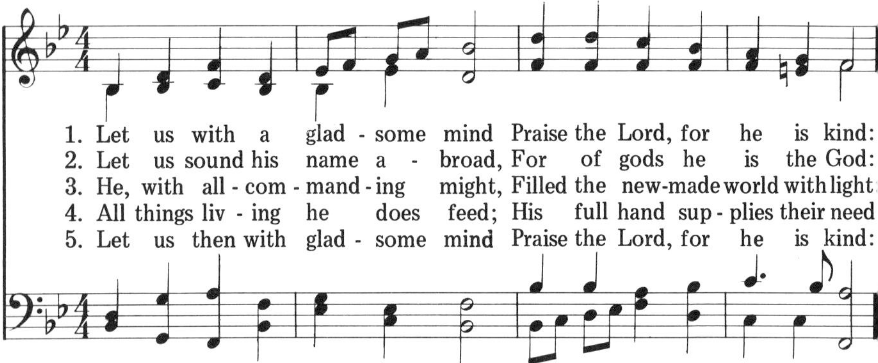

26 Stand Up and Bless the Lord

1. Stand up and bless the Lord, Ye peo - ple of his choice;
2. Tho high a - bove all praise, A - bove all bless - ing high,
3. O for the liv - ing flame From his own al - tar brought,
4. God is our strength and song, And his sal - va - tion ours;
5. Stand up and bless the Lord; The Lord your God a - dore;

Stand up and bless the Lord your God With heart and soul and voice.
Who would not fear his ho - ly name, And laud and mag - ni - fy?
To touch our lips, our minds in - spire, And wing to heav'n our thought!
Then be his love in Christ proclaimed With all our ran-somed pow'rs.
Stand up and bless his glo - rious name, Henceforth for - ev - er - more.

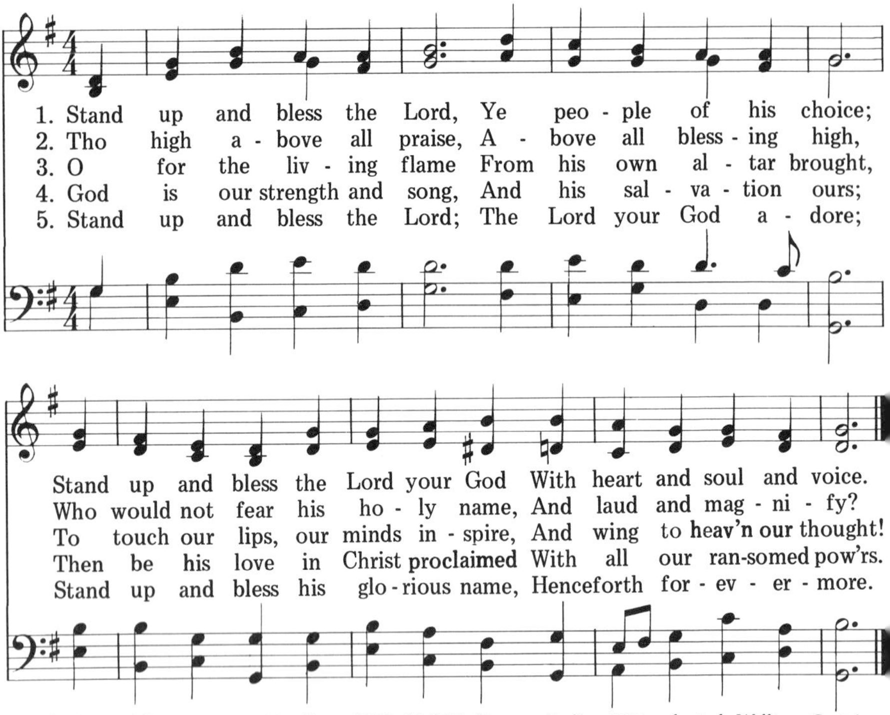

Words, James Montgomery, 1824. Tune OLD 134TH, *Genevan Psalter*, 1551; adapted, William Crotch, 1836.

27 Let Us with a Gladsome Mind

1. Let us with a glad - some mind Praise the Lord, for he is kind:
2. Let us sound his name a - broad, For of gods he is the God:
3. He, with all - com - mand - ing might, Filled the new-made world with light:
4. All things liv - ing he does feed; His full hand sup - plies their need:
5. Let us then with glad - some mind Praise the Lord, for he is kind:

Psalm 136:1,2,7,25. Paraphrased, John Milton, 1623. Tune MONKLAND, John Antes, *c.* 1790; arranged, John B. Wilkes, 1861.

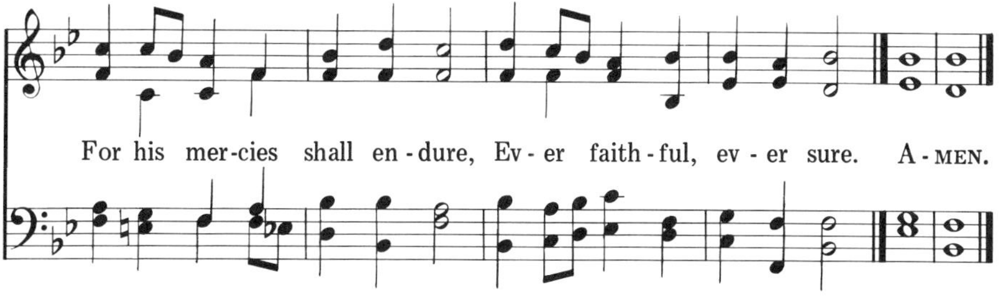

For his mer-cies shall en-dure, Ev-er faith-ful, ev-er sure. A-MEN.

Rejoice, Ye Pure in Heart 28

1. Re - joice, ye pure in heart, Re - joice, give thanks and sing
2. Bright youth and snow-crowned age, Strong men and maid - ens fair,
3. Yes, on thro' life's long path, Still sing - ing as ye go;
4. Still lift your stand - ard high, Still march in firm ar - ray,

Be - neath the stand - ard of your God, The cross of Christ your King.
Raise high your free, ex - ult - ing song, God's won-drous praise de - clare.
From youth to age, by night and day, In glad - ness and in woe.
As war - riors thro' the dark - ness toil Till dawns the gold - en day.

Re - joice, re - joice, Re - joice, give thanks and sing.
Re - joice, re - joice,

Psalm 20:4, Philippians 4:4. Words, Edward H. Plumptre, 1865. Tune MARION, Arthur H. Messiter, 1883.

29 We Believe in One True God

1. We be-lieve in one true God, Fa-ther, Son, and Ho-ly Ghost,
2. We be-lieve in Je-sus Christ, Son of God and Ma-ry's Son,
3. We con-fess the Ho-ly Ghost, Who from both for-e'er pro-ceeds,

Ev - er - pre-sent help in need, Praised by all the heav'n-ly host,
Who de-scend-ed from his throne And for us sal - va - tion won,
Who up-holds and com-forts us In all tri - als, fears, and needs.

By whose might-y pow'r a - lone All is made and wrought and done.
By whose cross and death are we Res - cued from sin's mis - er - y.
Blest and ho - ly Trin - i - ty, Praise for - ev - er be to thee!

Words, Tobias Clausnitzer, 1668; translated, Catherine Winkworth, 1863. Tune SPANISH HYMN, arranged, Benjamin Carr, 1825.

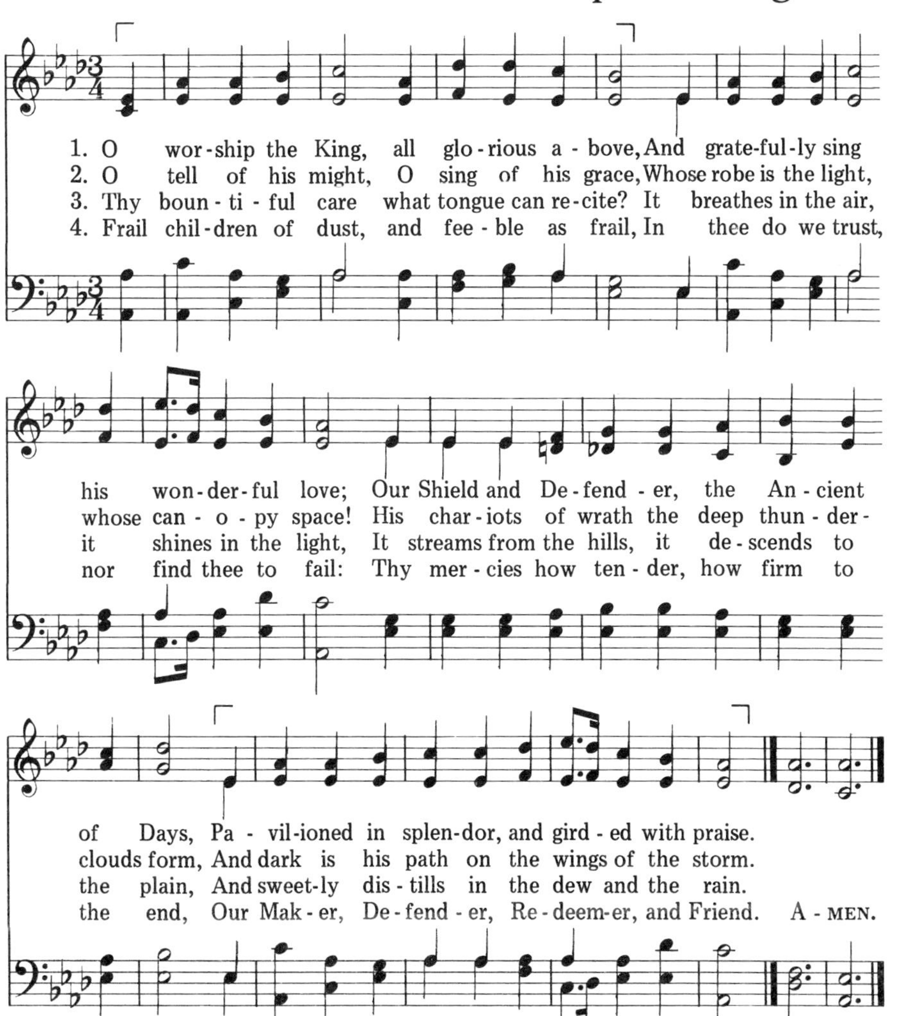
1. O wor-ship the King, all glo-rious a-bove, And grate-ful-ly sing
2. O tell of his might, O sing of his grace, Whose robe is the light,
3. Thy boun-ti-ful care what tongue can re-cite? It breathes in the air,
4. Frail chil-dren of dust, and fee-ble as frail, In thee do we trust,

his won-der-ful love; Our Shield and De-fend-er, the An-cient
whose can-o-py space! His char-iots of wrath the deep thun-der-
it shines in the light, It streams from the hills, it de-scends to
nor find thee to fail: Thy mer-cies how ten-der, how firm to

of Days, Pa-vil-ioned in splen-dor, and gird-ed with praise.
clouds form, And dark is his path on the wings of the storm.
the plain, And sweet-ly dis-tills in the dew and the rain.
the end, Our Mak-er, De-fend-er, Re-deem-er, and Friend. A-MEN.

Psalm 104. Words, Robert Grant, 1833 Tune LYONS, attr. to Johann Michael Haydn, in William Gardiner's *Sacred Melodies*, 1815.

31 Joyful, Joyful, We Adore Thee

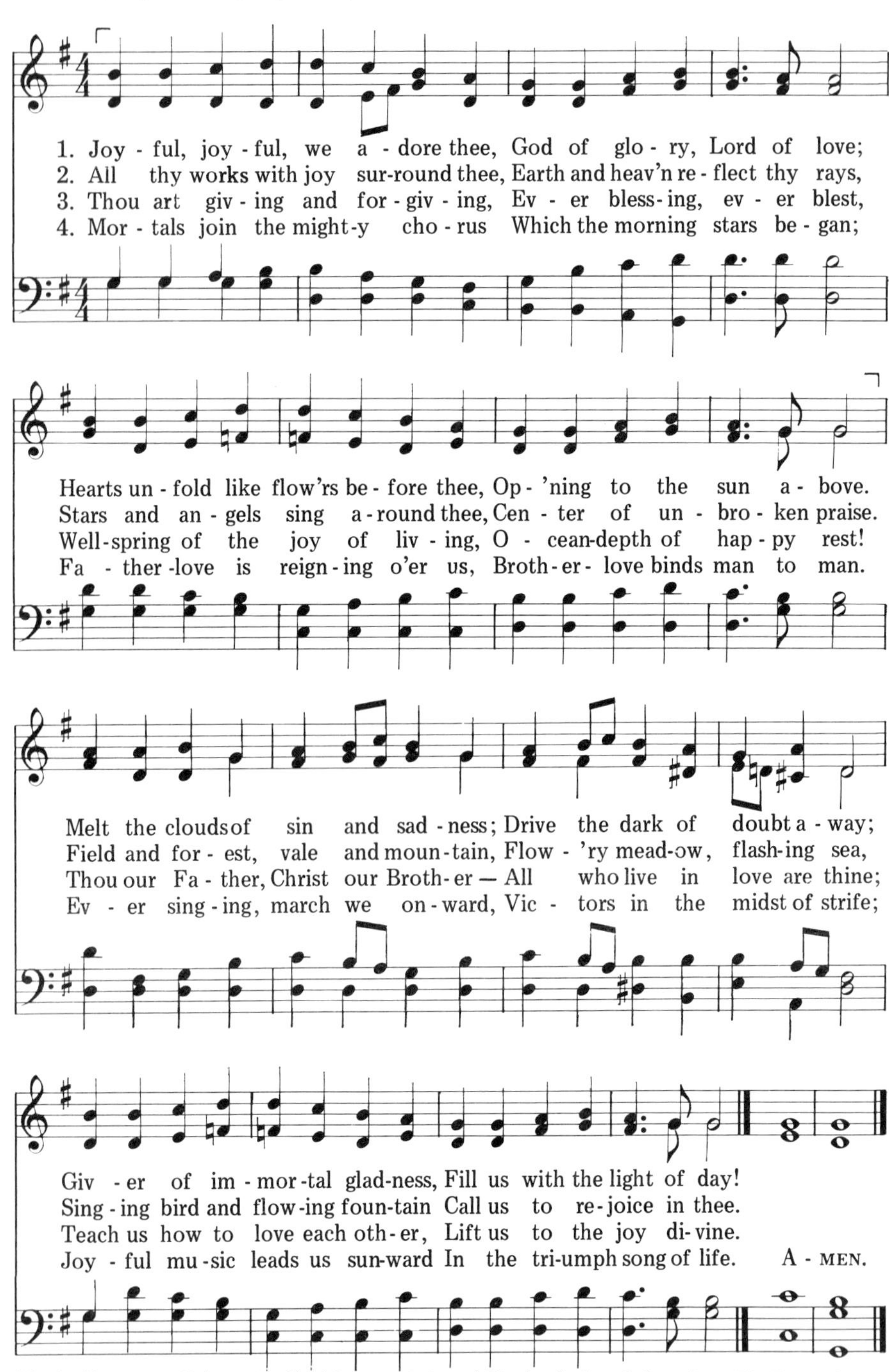

1. Joy - ful, joy - ful, we a - dore thee, God of glo - ry, Lord of love;
2. All thy works with joy sur-round thee, Earth and heav'n re - flect thy rays,
3. Thou art giv - ing and for - giv - ing, Ev - er bless-ing, ev - er blest,
4. Mor - tals join the might-y cho - rus Which the morning stars be - gan;
Hearts un - fold like flow'rs be - fore thee, Op- 'ning to the sun a - bove.
Stars and an - gels sing a - round thee, Cen - ter of un - bro - ken praise.
Well-spring of the joy of liv - ing, O - cean-depth of hap - py rest!
Fa - ther -love is reign - ing o'er us, Broth-er- love binds man to man.
Melt the clouds of sin and sad - ness; Drive the dark of doubt a - way;
Field and for - est, vale and moun-tain, Flow - 'ry mead-ow, flash-ing sea,
Thou our Fa - ther, Christ our Broth-er — All who live in love are thine;
Ev - er sing-ing, march we on-ward, Vic - tors in the midst of strife;
Giv - er of im - mor-tal glad-ness, Fill us with the light of day!
Sing - ing bird and flow-ing foun-tain Call us to re-joice in thee.
Teach us how to love each oth-er, Lift us to the joy di-vine.
Joy - ful mu-sic leads us sun-ward In the tri-umph song of life. A - MEN.

Words, Henry van Dyke, 1907. Used by permission of Charles Scribner's Sons from *The Poems of Henry van Dyke*. Copyright 1911 Charles Scribner's Sons; renewal copyright 1939 Tertius van Dyke. Tune HYMN TO JOY, Ludwig van Beethoven, 1824.

This tune in a lower key, No. 275.

Immortal, Invisible, God Only Wise 32

1. Im - mor - tal, in - vis - i - ble, God on - ly wise,
2. Un - rest - ing, un - hast - ing, and si - lent as light,
3. To all, life thou giv - est to both great and small;
4. Great Fa - ther of glo - ry, pure Fa - ther of light,

In light in - ac - ces - si - ble hid from our eyes,
Nor want - ing, nor wast - ing, thou rul - est in might;
In all life thou liv - est, the true life of all;
Thine an - gels a - dore thee, all veil - ing their sight;

Most bless - ed, most glo - rious, the An - cient of Days,
Thy jus - tice like moun - tains high soar - ing a - bove,
We blos - som and flour - ish as leaves on the tree,
All praise we would ren - der; O help us to see

Al - might - y, vic - to - rious, thy great name we praise.
Thy clouds which are foun - tains of good - ness and love.
And with - er and per - ish — but naught chang - eth thee.
"Tis on - ly the splen - dor of light hid - eth thee! A - MEN.

1 Timothy 1:17. Words, Walter Chalmers Smith, 1867. Tune ST. DENIO, Welsh Hymn Tune.

33 To God Be the Glory

1. To God be the glo - ry, great things he hath done; So loved he the
2. O per - fect re - demp - tion, the pur - chase of blood, To ev - 'ry be-
3. Great things he hath taught us, great things he hath done, And great our re-
world that he gave us his Son, Who yield-ed his life an a -
liev - er the prom - ise of God; The vil - est of - fend - er who
joic - ing thro' Je - sus the Son; But pur - er, and high - er, and
tone-ment for sin, And o-pened the life-gate that all may go in.
tru - ly be-lieves, That mo-ment from Je - sus a par-don re-ceives.
great - er will be Our won-der, our vic - t'ry, when Je - sus we see.
Praise the Lord, praise the Lord, Let the earth hear his voice! Praise the Lord,

Words, Fanny J. Crosby, 1875. Tune TO GOD BE THE GLORY, William H. Doane, 1875.

praise the Lord, Let the peo-ple re-joice! O come to the Fa-ther, thro'
Je-sus the Son, And give him the glo-ry, great things he hath done. A-MEN.

O My Soul, Bless God the Father 34

1. O my soul, bless God the Fa-ther; All with-in me bless his name;
2. Who for-giv-eth thy trans-gres-sions, Thy dis-eas-es all who heals;
3. Far as east from west is dis-tant, He hath put a-way our sin;
4. As it was with-out be-gin-ning, So it lasts with-out an end;
5. Un-to such as keep his cov'-nant And are stead-fast in his way;
6. Bless the Fa-ther, all his crea-tures, Ev-er un-der his con-trol,

Bless the Fa-ther, and for-get not All his mer-cies to pro-claim.
Who re-deems thee from de-struc-tion, Who with thee so kind-ly deals.
Like the pit-y of a fa-ther Hath the Lord's com-pas-sion been.
To their chil-dren's chil-dren ev-er Shall his right-eous-ness ex-tend:
Un-to those who still re-mem-ber His com-mand-ments, and o-bey.
All thro'-out his vast do-min-ion: Bless the Fa-ther, O my soul.

Psalm 103. Paraphrased in *The Book of Psalms*, 1871. Tune STUTTGART, Christian F. Witt, 1715; adapted, Henry Gauntlett, 1861.

35 How Great Thou Art

1. O Lord my God! When I in awe-some won-der Con-sid-er
2. When thro' the woods and for-est glades I wan-der, And hear the
3. And when I think that God, his Son not spar-ing, Sent him to
4. When Christ shall come with shout of ac-cla-ma-tion, And take me
all the*worlds thy hands have made, I see the stars, I hear the
birds sing sweet-ly in the trees; When I look down from loft-y
die, I scarce can take it in; That on the cross, my bur-den
home, what joy shall fill my heart! Then I shall bow in hum-ble
*roll-ing thun-der, Thy pow'r thro'-out the u-ni-verse dis-played,
moun-tain gran-deur, And hear the brook and feel the gen-tle breeze;
glad-ly bear-ing, He bled and died to take a-way my sin;
ad-o-ra-tion, And there pro-claim, my God, how great thou art!
Then sings my soul, my Sav-ior God to thee;

Words, Carl Boberg, 1886; translated, Stuart K. Hine, 1949. Tune O STORE GUD, Swedish Folk Melody; arranged, Stuart K. Hine, 1949. © Copyright 1953 by Stuart K. Hine, assigned to Manna Music, Inc. © Copyright 1955 by Manna Music, Inc. 2111 Kenmere Ave., Burbank, CA 91504. International copyright secured. All rights reserved. Used by permission. *Author's original words are "works" and "mighty."

How great thou art, how great thou art! Then sings my soul, my
Sav - ior God to thee; How great thou art, how great thou art!

God Is Love, His Mercy Brightens 36

1. God   is love; his mer - cy bright-ens All   the path   in which we rove;
2. Chance and change are bus - y   ev - er; Man   de - cays and   a - ges move;
3. E'en   the hour that dark-est seem-eth Will   his change-less good - ness prove;
4. He   with earth - ly   cares en - twin - eth Hope and com - fort from   a - bove;

Bliss   he wakes and   woe   he   light - ens: God   is   wis - dom, God   is   love.
But   his   mer - cy   wan - eth   nev - er: God   is   wis - dom, God   is   love.
Thro'   the gloom his   bright-ness stream-eth: God   is   wis - dom, God   is   love.
Ev - 'ry-where his   glo - ry   shin - eth: God   is   wis - dom, God   is   love.

Words, John Bowring, 1825. Tune STUTTGART, Christian Friedrich Witt, 1715; arranged,
Henry Gauntlett, 1861.

37 A Mighty Fortress Is Our God

1. A might-y for-tress is our God, A bul-wark nev-er
2. Did we in our own strength con-fide, Our striv-ing would be
3. And tho this world, with dev-ils filled, Should threat-en to un-
4. That word a-bove all earth-ly pow'rs, No thanks to them, a-

fail - ing; Our help-er he, a - mid the flood
los - ing; Were not the right Man on our side,
do us, We will not fear, for God hath willed
bid - eth; The Spir - it and the gifts are ours

Of mor - tal ills pre - vail - ing: For still our an-cient foe
The Man of God's own choos - ing: Dost ask who that may be?
His truth to tri-umph thro' us: The Prince of Dark-ness grim,
Thro' him who with us sid - eth: Let goods and kin-dred go,

Doth seek to work us woe; His craft and pow'r are great,
Christ Je - sus, it is he; Lord Sa - ba - oth, his name,
We trem - ble not for him; His rage we can en - dure,
This mor - tal life al - so; The bod - y they may kill:

Psalm 46. Words, Martin Luther, 1529; translated, Frederick H. Hedge, 1853. Tune EIN' FESTE BURG, Martin Luther, 1529.

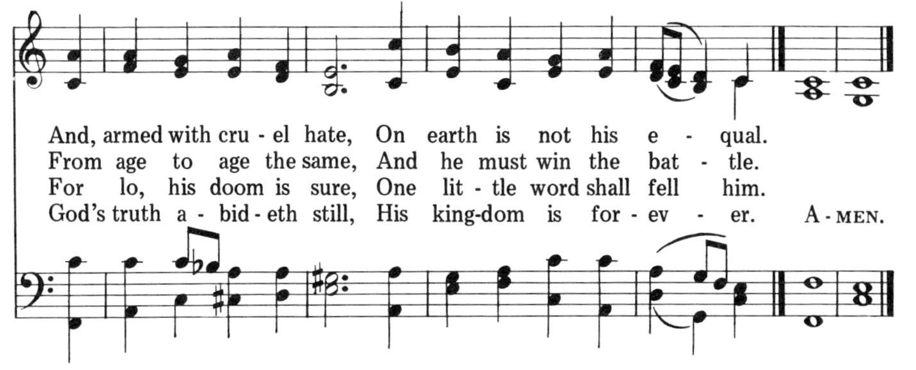

And, armed with cru - el hate, On earth is not his e - qual.
From age to age the same, And he must win the bat - tle.
For lo, his doom is sure, One lit - tle word shall fell him.
God's truth a - bid - eth still, His king-dom is for - ev - er. A - MEN.

Jesus Lives and Jesus Leads 38

1. Je - sus lives and Je - sus leads, Tho the way be drear - y;
2. All the words he ev - er spoke Still to us he speak - eth;
3. Je - sus lives, but Je - sus died, Love to death con - signed him;
4. Je - sus lives, and ev - 'ry grace Comes be - cause he giv - eth;

Morn to dark - est night suc - ceeds, Cour - age, then, ye wea - ry:
All the bread he ev - er broke Still for us he break - eth:
Death the might - y love re - signed, Could not hold or bind him:
Life and love in ev - 'ry place Live, for Je - sus liv - eth:

Still the faith - ful shep-herd feeds, Je - sus lives and Je - sus leads.
Still the faith - ful shep-herd feeds, Je - sus lives and Je - sus leads.
There-fore still he meets our needs, Je - sus lives and Je - sus leads.
All our thoughts his love ex - ceeds, Je - sus lives and Je - sus leads.

Words, Edwin Paxton Hood, 1873. Tune VARNDEAN, Erik R. Routley, 1950. Used by permission of the composer.

39 All Glory, Laud, and Honor

1. All glo - ry, laud, and hon - or, To thee, Re - deem - er, King,
2. The com - pa - ny of an - gels Are prais-ing thee on high,
3. To thee, be - fore thy pas - sion They sang their hymns of praise;

To whom the lips of chil - dren Made sweet ho - san - nas ring:
And mor - tal men and all things Cre - at - ed make re - ply:
To thee, now high ex - alt - ed, Our mel - o - dy we raise:

Thou art the King of Is - ra - el, Thou Da - vid's roy - al Son,
The peo - ple of the He - brews With palms be - fore thee went;
Thou didst ac - cept their prais - es; Ac - cept the praise we bring,

Who in the Lord's name com - est, The King and bless - ed One.
Our praise and pray'r and an - thems Be - fore thee we pre - sent.
Who in all good de - light - est, Thou good and gra - cious King.

Words, Theodulph of Orleans, *c.* 820; translated, John Mason Neale, 1851. Tune ST. THEODULPH, Melchior Teschner, 1615.

All Hail the Power of Jesus' Name 40

1. All hail the pow'r of Je - sus' name! Let an - gels pros-trate fall;
2. Ye cho- sen seed of Is - rael's race, Ye ran-somed from the fall,
3. Let ev - 'ry kin- dred, ev - 'ry tribe, On this ter - res - trial ball,
4. O that with yon- der sa - cred throng We at his feet may fall!
Bring forth the roy - al di - a - dem,
Hail him who saves you by his grace,
To him all maj - es - ty as - cribe,
We'll join the ev - er - last - ing song,
And crown him Lord of all; Bring forth the roy - al
And crown him Lord of all; Hail him who saves you
And crown him Lord of all; To him all maj - es -
And crown him Lord of all; We'll join the ev - er -
di - a - dem, And crown him Lord of all.
by his grace, And crown him Lord of all.
ty as - cribe, And crown him Lord of all.
last - ing song, And crown him Lord of all. A - MEN.

Words, st. 1, 2, Edward Perronet, 1779; st. 3, 4, John Rippon, 1787. Tune CORONATION, Oliver Holden, 1793.

41 All Hail the Power of Jesus' Name

1. All hail the pow'r of Je - sus' name! Let an - gels
2. Ye cho - sen seed of Is - rael's race, Ye ran - somed
3. Let ev - 'ry kin - dred, ev - 'ry tribe, On this ter -
4. O that with yon - der sa - cred throng We at his

pros - trate fall, Let an - gels pros - trate fall; Bring forth the
from the fall, Ye ran - somed from the fall; Hail him who
res - trial ball, On this ter - res - trial ball, To him all
feet may fall, We at his feet may fall! We'll join the

roy - al di - a - dem,
saves you by his grace,
maj - es - ty as - cribe,
ev - er - last - ing song,

And crown
And crown him, crown him,

him, crown him,
crown him, crown him,

crown

Words, st. 1, 2, Edward Perronet, 1779; st. 3, 4, John Rippon, 1787. Tune DIADEM, James Ellor, 1838.

crown him, crown him, And crown him Lord of all. A-MEN.
him,

All Hail the Power of Jesus' Name 42

1. All hail the pow'r of Je - sus' name! Let an - gels
2. Ye cho - sen seed of Is - rael's race, Ye ran - somed
3. Let ev - 'ry kin - dred, ev - 'ry tribe, On this ter -
4. O that with yon - der sa - cred throng We at his

pros - trate fall; Bring forth the roy - al di - a - dem,
from the fall, Hail him who saves you by his grace,
res - trial ball, To him all maj - es - ty as - cribe,
feet may fall! We'll join the ev - er - last - ing song,

And crown him, crown him, crown him, crown him Lord of all.
And crown him, crown him, crown him, crown him Lord of all.
And crown him, crown him, crown him, crown him Lord of all.
And crown him, crown him, crown him, crown him Lord of all. A-MEN.

Words, st. 1, 2, Edward Perronet, 1779; st. 3, 4. John Rippon, 1787. Tune MILES LANE, William Shrubsole, 1779.

43 All Praise to Thee

Unison

1. All praise to thee, for thou, O King di - vine,
2. Thou cam'st to us in low - li - ness of thought;
3. Let this mind be in us which was in thee,
4. Where - fore, by God's e - ter - nal pur - pose, thou
5. Let ev - 'ry tongue con - fess with one ac - cord

Didst yield the glo - ry that of right was thine,
By thee the out - cast and the poor were sought,
Who wast a ser - vant that we might be free,
Art ex - alt - ed o'er all crea - tures now,
In heav'n and earth that Je - sus Christ is Lord;

That in our dark - ened hearts thy grace might shine:
And by thy death was God's sal - va - tion wrought:
Hum - bling thy - self to death on Cal - va - ry:
And giv'n the name to which all knees shall bow:
And God the Fa - ther be by all a - dored:

Philippians 2:5-11. Words, F. Bland Tucker, 1938. Used by permission of the Church Pension Fund.
Tune SINE NOMINE, Ralph Vaughan Williams, 1906. From *The English Hymnal* by permission of Oxford University Press.
This tune in a higher key, No. 144.

Al - le - lu - ia! Al - le - lu - ia! A - MEN.

When Morning Gilds the Skies 44

1. When morn - ing gilds the skies, My heart a - wak - ing cries,
2. The night be - comes as day, When from the heart we say,
3. Ye na - tions of man - kind, In this your con - cord find:
4. In heav'n's e - ter - nal bliss The love - liest strain is this,

May Je - sus Christ be praised! A - like at work and prayer,
May Je - sus Christ be praised! The pow'rs of dark - ness fear,
May Je - sus Christ be praised! Let all the earth a - round
May Je - sus Christ be praised! Let earth, and sea, and sky

To Je - sus I re - pair; May Je - sus Christ be praised.
When this sweet song they hear, May Je - sus Christ be praised.
Ring joy - ous with the sound: May Je - sus Christ be praised.
From depth to height re - ply, May Je - sus Christ be praised. A - MEN.

Words, *Katholiches Gesangbuch,* Wurzburg, 1828; translated, St. 1, 2, 4, Edward Caswall, 1854; St. 3, Robert Bridges, 1899. Tune LAUDES DOMINI, Joseph Barnby, 1868.

45 We Praise Thee with Our Minds, O Lord

Unison

1. We praise thee with our minds, O Lord, Kept sharp to think thy thought;
2. We praise thee thro' our bod - ies, Lord, Kept strong to do thy will;
3. We praise thee in our hearts, O King, Kept pure to know thy ways;

Come, Ho - ly Ghost with grace out-poured, To teach what Christ hath taught.
Thy Spir - it's tem - ples, which af - ford A means to praise thee still.
And raise to thee a hymn to sing E - ter - nal - ly thy praise.

In all our learn - ing may we seek That wis - dom from a - bove
We give our-selves, a sac - ri - fice, To live as un - to thee;
Al - tho a - dor - ing hearts will bow As age on a - ges roll;

Which comes to all: the brave, the meek, Who ask in faith and love.
For thou a - lone hast paid the price To bring sal - va - tion free.
We praise thee in our be - ings now, Mind, bod - y, heart, and soul.

Praise the Lord, the King of Glory 46

1. Praise the Lord, the King of glo-ry, Gra-cious Son of God is he;
2. Bless-ed be the Lord of glo-ry, Sun of righ-teous-ness and grace;
3. Might-y is the King of glo-ry, His great works the heav'ns proclaim;

Long fore-told by proph-ets ho-ly, Great in pow'r and maj-es-ty.
Sing, O earth, the won-drous sto-ry; Christ re-deems the fall-en race.
Full of maj-es-ty, and ho-ly, Lord of Sab-a-oth his name.

With the Fa-ther thro' cre-a-tion, Heav'n and earth doth tell his fame;
Praise him for his great sal-va-tion, Pre-cious Lamb of God a-dore;
Myr-iad tongues in joy-ful cho-rus Sing his praise with sweetest chords;

Hope and joy of ev-'ry na-tion, Life and light are in his name.
Lord and light of all cre-a-tion, Laud and serve him ev-er-more.
In our hearts he reign-eth o'er us, King of kings and Lord of lords!

47 Declare, O Heavens, the Lord of Space

Unison
1. De - clare, O heav'ns, the Lord of space; Re - ply, broad lands in
2. Launch forth, O man, and bold - ly rise; Be - yond our plan - et
3. Yet see this world with prob - lems filled; Earth longs for life the
4. O Lord, whose pow'r all space ex - tols, Draw near our lives, en -
ev - 'ry place; Tell his splen - dor! Al - le - lu - ia! New realms we find
pierce the skies; Bound - less ven - ture! Al - le - lu - ia! No soar - ing flight
Mas - ter willed; Light its dark - ness! Al - le - lu - ia! Reach out all bro -
large our souls; Dwell with - in us! Al - le - lu - ia! Stir deeds of grace
he first hath made; All be - ing is his pow'r dis - played;
can e'er out - run Truth God has shown us in his Son;
ken lives to mend, In Christ win peace no war will end;
to serve thy plan; Wake joy the morn - ing stars be - gan;
Al - le - lu - ia! Al - le - lu - ia! Al - le -

Words, Robert Lansing Edwards, 1962. Copyright 1962 by The Hymn Society of America. Used by permission. Tune LASST UNS ERFREUEN, *Geistliche Kirchengesäng*, 1623; arranged, Ralph Vaughan Williams. Music from *The English Hymnal*; used by permission of Oxford University Press.

lu - ia! Al - le - lu - ia! Al - le - lu - ia! A - MEN.

Fairest Lord Jesus 48

1. Fair - est Lord Je - sus, Rul - er of all na - ture,
2. Fair are the mead - ows, Fair - er still the wood - lands,
3. Fair is the sun - shine, Fair - er still the moon - light
4. Beau - ti - ful Sav - ior, Lord of all na - tions,

O thou of God and man the Son; Thee will I cher-ish,
Robed in the bloom - ing garb of spring; Je - sus is fair - er,
And all the twin - kling, star - ry host; Je - sus shines bright-er,
Son of God and Son of man! Glo - ry and hon - or,

Thee will I hon-or, Thou, my soul's glo - ry, joy, and crown.
Je - sus is pur - er, Who makes the woe-ful heart to sing.
Je - sus shines pur - er Than all the an - gels heav'n can boast.
Praise, ad - o - ra - tion, Now and for - ev - er - more be thine! A - MEN.

Words, Anonymous German Hymn, *Münster Gesangbuch,* 1677; translated, st. 1-3, Source Unknown, 1850; st. 4, Joseph A. Seiss, 1873. Tune CRUSADERS' HYMN, *Schlesische Volkslieder,* 1842; arranged, Richard S. Willis, 1850.

49 For the Beauty of the Earth

Harmony
Christ our God, to thee we raise This our hymn of grate-ful praise.

Unison
1. For the beau - ty of the earth, For the glo - ry
2. For the won - der of each hour Of the day and
3. For the joy of hu - man love, Broth - er, sis - ter,

of the skies, For the love which from our birth O - ver
of the night, Hill and vale and tree and flow'r, Sun and
par - ent, child, Friends on earth, and friends a - bove, For all

and a - round us lies, O - ver and a - round us lies.
moon, and stars of light, Sun and moon, and stars of light.
gen - tle thoughts and mild, For all gen - tle thoughts and mild.

Words, Folliott S. Pierpoint, 1864. Tune RAYMER, Buryl Red, 1971. © Copyright 1971 Broadman Press.

Blessed Be the Name 50

1. O for a thou-sand tongues to sing, Bless-ed be the name of the Lord!
2. Je - sus, the name that calms my fears, Bless-ed be the name of the Lord!
3. He breaks the pow'r of can - celed sin, Bless-ed be the name of the Lord!
4. I nev - er shall for - get that day, Bless-ed be the name of the Lord!
The glo -ries of my God and King, Bless -ed be the name of the Lord!
'Tis mu - sic in the sin - ner's ears, Bless -ed be the name of the Lord!
His blood can make the foul -est clean, Bless -ed be the name of the Lord!
When Je - sus washed my sins a - way, Bless-ed be the name of the Lord!
Bless -ed be the name, Bless-ed be the name, Bless-ed be the name of the Lord!
Bless-ed be the name, Bless-ed be the name, Bless-ed be the name of the Lord.

Words, Charles Wesley, 1739, alt.; Refrain, Ralph E. Hudson, 1887. Tune BLESSED NAME, Anonymous; arranged, Ralph E. Hudson, 1887.

51 Great Redeemer, We Adore Thee

1. Great Re-deem-er, we a-dore thee, God of mer - cy, love, and grace;
2. Great Re-deem-er, we im-plore thee, Drive our doubts and fears a - way;
3. Life and love from thee are beam-ing, Sin and sor-row melt a-way;
4. When we see thee in thy beau - ty, As thou art, so we shall be;

Warm our hearts with thine own be - ing, May we see thy kind-ly face!
Cause thy face to smile up - on us, Shine on us thy light to-day!
King of kind - ness, God of glo - ry, Fill us with thy - self to-day!
In thy im - age thou hast made us, Great Re-deem-er, we love thee!

Great Re-deem-er, we a - dore thee, God's great love to man thou art;
Great Re-deem-er, we a - dore thee, High-est hills pro-claim thy fame;
Great Re-deem-er, we a - dore thee, Life and lib - er - ty are thine;
Great Re-deem-er, we a - dore thee, In thy like-ness we shall be;

We a-dore thee, Great Redeemer, Reign supreme in ev - 'ry heart.
We a-dore thee, Great Redeemer, Men and an-gels praise thy name.
We a-dore thee, Great Redeemer, Fill us with thy love di -vine.
We a-dore thee, Great Redeemer, God of life e - ter - nal- ly. A - MEN.

Words, John Roy Harris, 1934. Tune REDENTORE, Paolo Conte, 1936. From *The Broadman Hymnal.*
Copyright 1940. Renewal 1968. Broadman Press. All rights reserved.

Crown Him with Many Crowns 52

1. Crown him with man - y crowns, The Lamb up - on his throne;
2. Crown him the Lord of life, Who tri - umphed o'er the grave,
3. Crown him the Lord of peace, Whose pow'r a scep - ter sways
4. Crown him the Lord of love; Be - hold his hands and side,

Hark! how the heav'n - ly an - them drowns All mu - sic but its own:
And rose vic - to - rious in the strife For those he came to save;
From pole to pole, that wars may cease, And all be pray'r and praise:
Those wounds, yet vis - i - ble a - bove, In beau - ty glo - ri - fied:

A - wake, my soul, and sing Of him who died for thee,
His glo - ries now we sing Who died, and rose on high,
His reign shall know no end, And round his pierc - ed feet
All hail, Re - deem - er, hail! For thou hast died for me:

And hail him as thy matchless King Thro' all e - ter - ni - ty.
Who died e - ter - nal life to bring, And lives that death may die.
Fair flow'rs of par - a - dise ex - tend Their fra - grance ev - er sweet.
Thy praise and glo - ry shall not fail Thro'- out e - ter - ni - ty. A - MEN.

Words, st. 1, 3, 4, Matthew Bridges, 1851; st. 2, Godfrey Thring, 1874. Tune DIADEMATA,
George J. Elvey, 1868.
This tune in a lower key, No. 406.

53 I Will Sing the Wondrous Story

1. I will sing the won-drous sto-ry Of the Christ who
2. I was bruised, but Je-sus healed me; Faint was I from
3. He will keep me till the riv-er Rolls its wa-ters

died for me. How he left his home in glo-ry For the
man-y a fall; Sight was gone, and fears pos-sessed me, But he
at my feet; Then he'll bear me safe-ly o-ver, Where the

cross of Cal-va-ry. I was lost, but Je-sus found me,
freed me from them all. Days of dark-ness still come o'er me,
loved ones I shall meet. Yes, I'll sing the won-drous sto-ry

Found the sheep that went a-stray, Threw his lov-ing
Sor-row's paths I of-ten tread, But the Sav-ior
Of the Christ who died for me, Sing it with the

Words, Francis H. Rowley, 1886. Tune HYFRYDOL, Rowland H. Prichard, c. 1830.

arms a - round me, Drew me back in - to his way.
still is with me; By his hand I'm safe - ly led.
saints in glo - ry, Gath - ered by the crys - tal sea.

For the Beauty of the Earth 54

1. For the beau - ty of the earth, For the glo - ry of the skies,
2. For the won - der of each hour Of the day and of the night,
3. For the joy of hu - man love, Broth - er, sis - ter, par - ent, child,
4. For thy church that ev - er - more Lift - eth ho - ly hands a - bove,
5. For the joy of ear and eye, For the heart and mind's de - light,
6. For thy - self, best Gift Di - vine! To our race so free - ly giv'n;

For the love which from our birth O - ver and a - round us lies:
Hill and vale, and tree and flow'r, Sun and moon, and stars of light:
Friends on earth, and friends a - bove, For all gen - tle thoughts and mild:
Of - f'ring up on ev - 'ry shore Her pure sac - ri - fice of love:
For the mys - tic har - mo - ny Link - ing sense to sound and sight:
For that great, great love of thine, Peace on earth, and joy in heav'n:

Christ our God, to thee we raise This our hymn of grate - ful praise. A - MEN.

Words, Folliott S. Pierpoint, 1864. Tune DIX, Conrad Kocher, 1838; adapted, William H. Monk, 1861.

55 I Will Sing the Wondrous Story

1. I will sing the wondrous sto - ry Of the Christ who died for me,
2. I was lost, but Je - sus found me, Found the sheep that went a-stray,
3. I was bruised, but Je - sus healed me; Faint was I from man-y a fall;
4. Days of dark - ness still come o'er me, Sor - row's paths I of-ten tread,
5. He will keep me till the riv - er Rolls its wa - ters at my feet;

How he left his home in glo - ry For the cross of Cal - va - ry.
Threw his lov - ing arms a - round me, Drew me back in - to his way.
Sight was gone, and fears pos-sessed me, But he freed me from them all.
But the Sav - ior still is with me; By his hand I'm safe - ly led.
Then he'll bear me safe - ly o - ver, Where the loved ones I shall meet.

Yes, I'll sing the won-drous sto - ry,
Yes, I'll sing the won-drous sto - ry,

Of the Christ who died for me,
Of the Christ who died for me,

Words, Francis H. Rowley, 1886. Tune WONDROUS STORY, Peter P. Bilhorn, 1886.

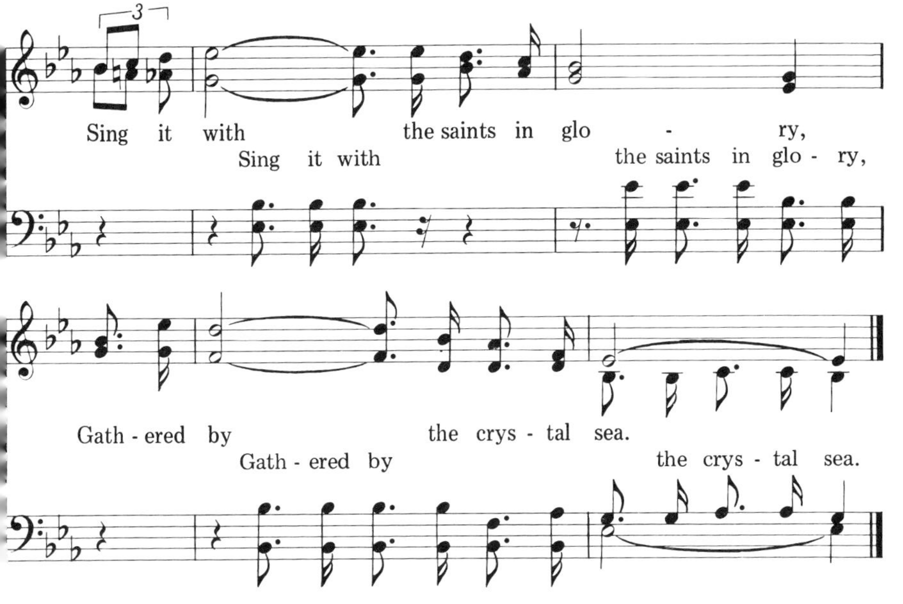

Sing it with the saints in glo - ry,
Sing it with the saints in glo - ry,
Gath - ered by the crys - tal sea.
Gath - ered by the crys - tal sea.

"Man of Sorrows," What a Name 56

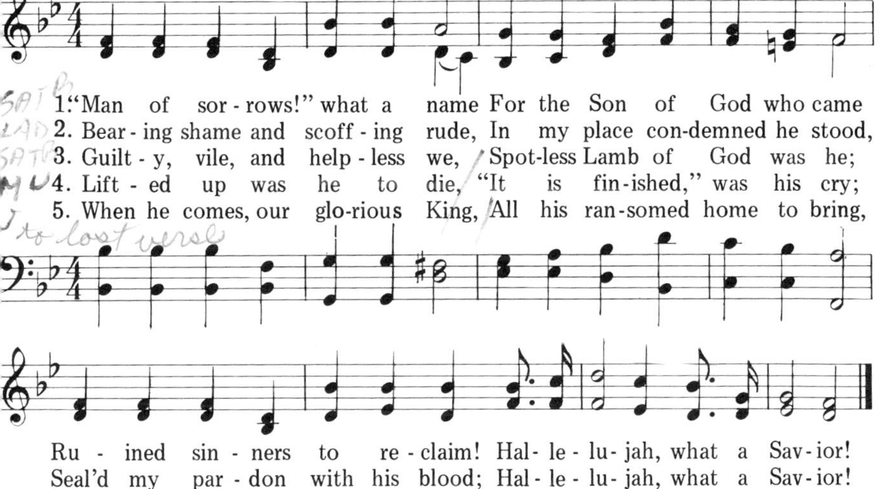

1. "Man of sor - rows!" what a name For the Son of God who came
2. Bear - ing shame and scoff - ing rude, In my place con-demned he stood,
3. Guilt - y, vile, and help - less we, Spot-less Lamb of God was he;
4. Lift - ed up was he to die, "It is fin-ished," was his cry;
5. When he comes, our glo-rious King, All his ran-somed home to bring,

Ru - ined sin - ners to re - claim! Hal - le - lu - jah, what a Sav - ior!
Seal'd my par - don with his blood; Hal - le - lu - jah, what a Sav - ior!
Full a - tone-ment! can it be? Hal - le - lu - jah, what a Sav - ior!
Now in heav'n ex - alt - ed high, Hal - le - lu - jah, what a Sav - ior!
Then a - new this song we'll sing, Hal - le - lu - jah, what a Sav - ior!

Words and tune HALLELUJAH! WHAT A SAVIOR, Philip P. Bliss, 1875.

57 My God, I Love Thee

1. My God, I love thee, not be-cause I hope for heav'n there-by,
2. And griefs and tor-ments num-ber-less, And sweat of ag - o - ny;
3. Not with the hope of gain-ing aught, Not seek-ing a re-ward,
Nor yet for fear that lov-ing not I might for-ev-er die;
E'en death it-self, and all for man, Who was thine en-e-my.
But as thy-self hast lov-ed me, O ev-er-lov-ing Lord!
But for that thou didst all man-kind Up-on the cross em-brace;
Then why, most lov-ing Je-sus Christ, Should I not love thee well?
E'en so I love thee, and will love, And in thy praise will sing,
For us didst bear the nails and spear, And man-i-fold dis-grace;
Not for the sake of win-ning heav'n, Nor an-y fear of hell;
Sole-ly be-cause thou art my God And my e-ter-nal King!

Words, attr. to Francis Xavier; translated, Edward Caswall, 1849. Tune KINGSFOLD, Traditional English Melody collected by Lucy Broadwood; arranged, Ralph Vaughan Williams, 1906. Words from *Enlarged Songs of Praise*, and music from *The English Hymnal* by permission of Oxford University Press.

Love Divine, All Loves Excelling 58

1. Love di-vine, all loves ex-cell-ing, Joy of heav'n, to earth come down;
2. Breathe, O breathe thy lov-ing Spir-it In-to ev-'ry trou-bled breast!
3. Come, Al-might-y to de-liv-er, Let us all thy grace re-ceive;
4. Fin-ish, then, thy new cre-a-tion; Pure and spot-less let us be;

Fix in us thy hum-ble dwell-ing; All thy faith-ful mer-cies crown.
Let us all in thee in-her-it, Let us find the prom-ised rest;
Sud-den-ly re-turn, and nev-er, Nev-er more thy tem-ples leave.
Let us see thy great sal-va-tion Per-fect-ly re-stored in thee:

Je-sus, thou art all com-pas-sion, Pure, un-bound-ed love thou art;
Take a-way our bent to sin-ning; *Al-pha and O-me-ga be;
Thee we would be al-ways bless-ing, Serve thee as thy hosts a-bove,
Changed from glo-ry in-to glo-ry, Till in heav'n we take our place,

Vis-it us with thy sal-va-tion; En-ter ev-'ry trem-bling heart.
End of faith, as its be-gin-ning, Set our hearts at lib-er-ty.
Pray, and praise thee with-out ceas-ing, Glo-ry in thy per-fect love.
Till we cast our crowns be-fore thee, Lost in won-der, love, and praise. A-MEN.

Words, Charles Wesley, 1743. Tune BEECHER, John Zundel, 1870. *Revelation 1:8.

59 Glorious Is Thy Name

1. Bless - ed Sav - ior, we a - dore thee, We thy love and grace pro-claim;
2. Great Re-deem - er, Lord and Mas - ter, Light of all e - ter - nal days;
3. From the throne of heav-en's glo - ry To the cross of sin and shame,
4. Come, O come, im - mor - tal Sav - ior, Come and take thy roy - al throne;
Thou art might- y, thou art ho - ly, Glo-rious is thy match-less name!
Let the saints of ev - 'ry na - tion Sing thy just and end - less praise!
Thou didst come to die a ran-som, Guilt-y sin - ners to re -claim!
Come, and reign, and reign for - ev - er, Be the king - dom all thine own!
Glo - ri-ous, Glo - ri -ous,
Glo-rious is thy name, O Lord! Glo-rious is thy name, O Lord!
Glo-rious is thy name, O Lord! Glo - ri - ous,
Glo-rious is thy name, O Lord!

Glo - ri-ous, Glo-rious is thy name, O Lord! A - MEN.
Glo-rious is thy name, O Lord!

Ask Ye What Great Thing I Know 60

1. Ask ye what great thing I know That de - lights and
2. What is faith's foun - da - tion strong? What a - wakes my
3. Who is life in life to me? Who the death of
4. This is that great thing I know; This de - lights and

stirs me so? What the high re - ward I win? Whose the name I
lips to song? He who bore my sin - ful load, Pur - chased for me
death will be? Who will place me on his right With the count - less
stirs me so: Faith in him who died to save, Him who tri - umphed

glo - ry in? Je - sus Christ, the cru - ci - fied.
peace with God, Je - sus Christ, the cru - ci - fied.
hosts of light? Je - sus Christ, the cru - ci - fied.
o'er the grave, Je - sus Christ, the cru - ci - fied. A - MEN.

1 Corinthians 2:2; Galatians 6:14. Words, Johann C. Schwedler, 1741; translated, Benjamin H. Kennedy, 1863. Tune HENDON, Henri A. C. Malan, 1823.

61 Come, Christians, Join to Sing

1. Come, Chris-tians, join to sing   Al - le - lu - ia!   A - men!
2. Come, lift your hearts on high;   Al - le - lu - ia!   A - men!
3. Praise yet our Christ a - gain;   Al - le - lu - ia!   A - men!
Loud praise to Christ our King;   Al - le - lu - ia!   A - men!
Let prais - es fill the sky;   Al - le - lu - ia!   A - men!
Life shall not end the strain;   Al - le - lu - ia!   A - men!
Let all, with heart and voice,   Be - fore his throne re - joice;
He is our guide and friend;   To us he'll con - de - scend;
On heav - en's bliss - ful shore   His good - ness we'll a - dore,
Praise is his gra - cious choice: Al - le - lu - ia!   A - men!
His love shall nev - er end: Al - le - lu - ia!   A - men!
Sing - ing for - ev - er - more, "Al - le - lu - ia!   A - men!"

Words, Christian H. Bateman, 1843. Tune MADRID, arranged, Benjamin Carr, 1826; harmonized, David Evans, 1927.

Unison

1. Of the Fa-ther's love be-got-ten, Ere the worlds be-gan
2. O ye heights of heav'n a-dore him; An-gel hosts, his prais-
3. Christ, to thee with God the Fa-ther, And, O Ho-ly Ghost,

to be, He is *Al-pha and O-me-ga, He the source, the
es sing; Pow'rs, do-min-ions, bow be-fore him, And ex-tol our
to thee, Hymn and chant and high thanks-giv-ing And un-wea-ried

end-ing he, Of the things that are, that have been,
God and King; Let no tongue on earth be si - lent,
prais-es be: Hon-or, glo-ry, and do-min - ion,

And that fu-ture years shall see, Ev-er-more and ev-er-more!
Ev-'ry voice in con-cert ring, Ev-er-more and ev-er-more!
And e-ter-nal vic-to-ry, Ev-er-more and ev-er-more! A - MEN.

Words, Aurelius Clemens Prudentius, 4th Century; translated, John Mason Neale, 1851, and
Henry W. Baker, 1859. Tune DIVINUM MYSTERIUM, 13th Century Plainsong Melody; arranged,
C. Winfred Douglas, 1940. Used by permission The Church Pension Fund. *Revelation 1:8.

63 I Stand Amazed in the Presence

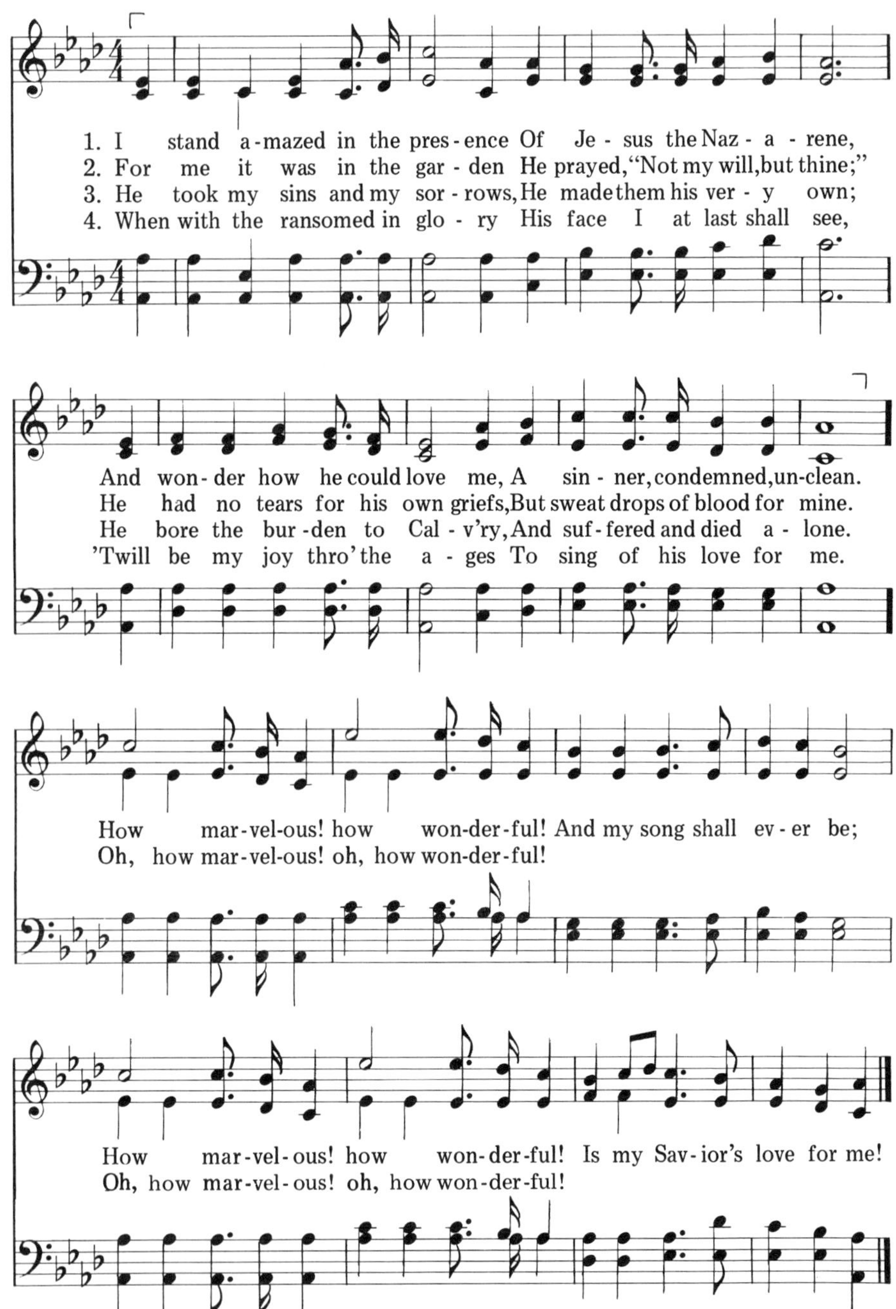
1. I stand a-mazed in the pres-ence Of Je-sus the Naz-a-rene,
2. For me it was in the gar-den He prayed,"Not my will,but thine;"
3. He took my sins and my sor-rows,He made them his ver-y own;
4. When with the ransomed in glo-ry His face I at last shall see,
And won-der how he could love me, A sin-ner,condemned,un-clean.
He had no tears for his own griefs,But sweat drops of blood for mine.
He bore the bur-den to Cal-v'ry,And suf-fered and died a-lone.
'Twill be my joy thro'the a-ges To sing of his love for me.
How mar-vel-ous! how won-der-ful! And my song shall ev-er be;
Oh, how mar-vel-ous! oh, how won-der-ful!
How mar-vel-ous! how won-der-ful! Is my Sav-ior's love for me!
Oh, how mar-vel-ous! oh, how won-der-ful!

Words and tune MY SAVIOR'S LOVE, Charles H. Gabriel, 1905.

Jesus! What a Friend for Sinners 64

1. Je - sus! what a friend for sin - ners! Je - sus! lov - er of my soul;
2. Je - sus! what a strength in weak - ness! Let me hide my - self in him;
3. Je - sus! what a help in sor - row! While the bil - lows o'er me roll,
4. Je - sus! what a guide and keep - er! While the tem - pest still is high,
5. Je - sus! I do now re - ceive him, More than all in him I find,
Friends may fail me, foes as - sail me, He, my Sav - ior, makes me whole.
Tempt - ed, tried, and some - times fail - ing, He, my strength, my vic - t'ry wins.
E - ven when my heart is break - ing, He, my com - fort, helps my soul.
Storms a - bout me, night o'er - takes me, He, my pi - lot, hears my cry.
He hath grant - ed me for - give - ness, I am his, and he is mine.
Hal - le - lu - jah! what a Sav - ior! Hal - le - lu - jah! what a friend!
Sav - ing, help - ing, keep - ing, lov - ing, He is with me to the end.

65 Savior, Again to Thy Dear Name

1. Sav - ior, a - gain to thy dear name we raise,
2. Grant us thy peace up - on our home - ward way;
3. Grant us thy peace, Lord, through the com - ing night,
4. Grant us thy peace through - out our earth - ly life,
With one ac - cord our part - ing hymn of praise;
With thee be - gan, with thee shall end the day:
Turn thou for us its dark - ness in - to light;
Our balm in sor - row, and our stay in strife;
We stand to bless thee ere our wor - ship cease,
Guard thou the lips from sin, the hearts from shame,
From harm and dan - ger keep thy chil - dren free,
Then, when thy voice shall bid our con - flict cease,
And still our hearts to wait thy word of peace.
That in this house have called up - on thy name.
For dark and light are both a - like to thee.
Call us, O Lord, to thine e - ter - nal peace. A - MEN.

Words, John Ellerton, 1866. Tune ELLERS, Edward J. Hopkins, 1869.
This tune in a lower key, No. 266.

There Is a Name I Love to Hear 66

1. There is a name I love to hear, I love to sing its worth;
2. It tells me of a Sav-ior's love, Who died to set me free;
3. It tells me what my Fa-ther hath In store for ev-'ry day,
4. It tells of One whose lov-ing heart Can feel my deep-est woe,

It sounds as mu-sic in mine ear, The sweetest name on earth.
It tells me of his pre-cious blood, The sin-ner's per-fect plea.
And though I tread a dark-some path, Yields sun-shine all the way.
Who in each sor-row bears a part, That none can bear be-low.

Oh, how I love Je-sus, Oh, how I love Je-sus,

Oh, how I love Je-sus, Be-cause he first loved me.

Words, Frederick Whitfield, 1855. Tune O HOW I LOVE JESUS, Anonymous, 19th Century.

67 Praise Him! Praise Him!

1. Praise him! praise him! Je-sus, our bless-ed Re-deem-er! Sing, O
2. Praise him! praise him! Je-sus, our bless-ed Re-deem-er! For our
3. Praise him! praise him! Je-sus, our bless-ed Re-deem-er! Heav'n-ly
Earth, his won-der-ful love pro-claim! Hail him! hail him! high-est arch-
sins he suf-fered and bled and died; He our Rock, our hope of e-
por-tals loud with ho-san-nas ring! Je-sus, Sav-ior, reign-eth for-
an-gels in glo-ry, Strength and hon-or give to his ho-ly name!
ter-nal sal-va-tion, Hail him! hail him! Je-sus the cru-ci-fied:
ev-er and ev-er; Crown him! crown him! proph-et and priest and King!
Like a shep-herd, Je-sus will guard his chil-dren; In his arms he
Sound his prais-es! Je-sus who bore our sor-rows, Love un-bound-ed,
Christ is com-ing, o-ver the world vic-to-rious, Pow'r and glo-ry

Words, Fanny J. Crosby, 1869. Tune JOYFUL SONG, Chester G. Allen, 1869.

car - ries them all day long:
won - der - ful, deep, and strong: Praise him! praise him! tell of his
un - to the Lord be - long:

ex -cel -lent great -ness! Praise him! praise him! ev - er in joy -ful song!

This Is the Day the Lord Hath Made 68

1. This is the day the Lord hath made; He calls the hours his own;
2. To - day he rose and left the dead, And Sa - tan's em - pire fell;
3. Ho - san - na to th 'a-noint - ed King, To Da - vid's ho - ly Son:
4. Blest be the Lord, who comes to men With mes - sag - es of grace;

Let heav'n re - joice, let earth be glad, And praise sur-round the throne.
To - day the saints his triumph spread, And all his won-ders tell.
Help us, O Lord! de-scend and bring Sal - va - tion from thy throne.
Who comes, in God his Fa-ther's name, To save our sin - ful race. A-MEN.

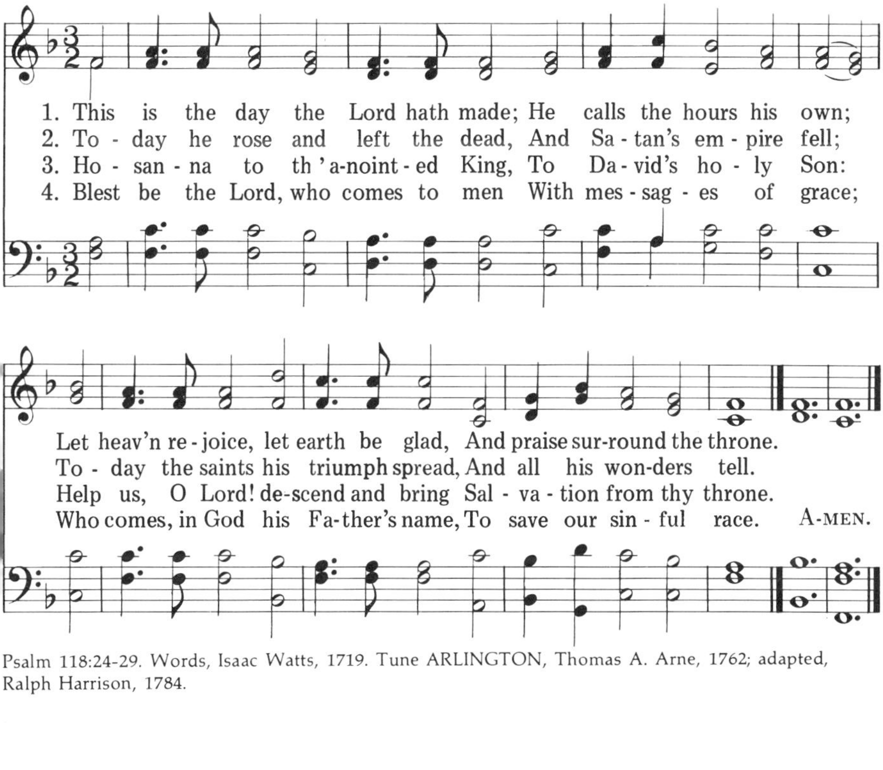

Psalm 118:24-29. Words, Isaac Watts, 1719. Tune ARLINGTON, Thomas A. Arne, 1762; adapted, Ralph Harrison, 1784.

69 O for a Thousand Tongues to Sing

1. O for a thou-sand tongues to sing My great Re-deem-er's praise,
2. My gra-cious Mas-ter and my God, As-sist me to pro-claim,
3. Je-sus, the name that calms my fears, That bids my sor-rows cease;
4. He breaks the pow'r of can-celed sin, He sets the pris-'ner free;

The glo-ries of my God and King, The tri-umphs of his grace!
To spread thro' all the earth a-broad The hon-ors of thy name.
'Tis mu-sic in the sin-ner's ears; 'Tis life and health and peace.
His blood can make the foul-est clean, His blood a-vailed for me. A-MEN.

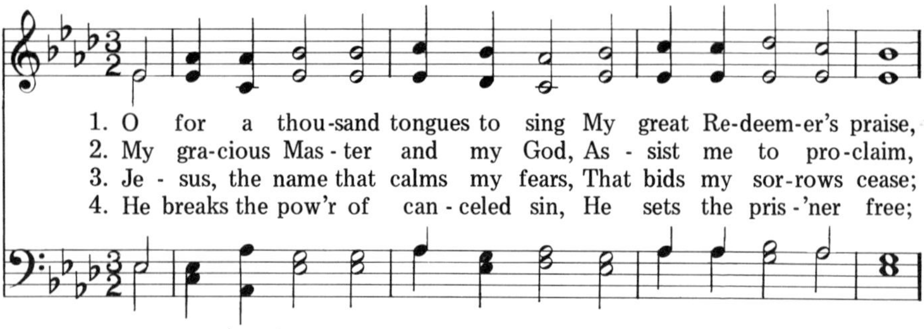

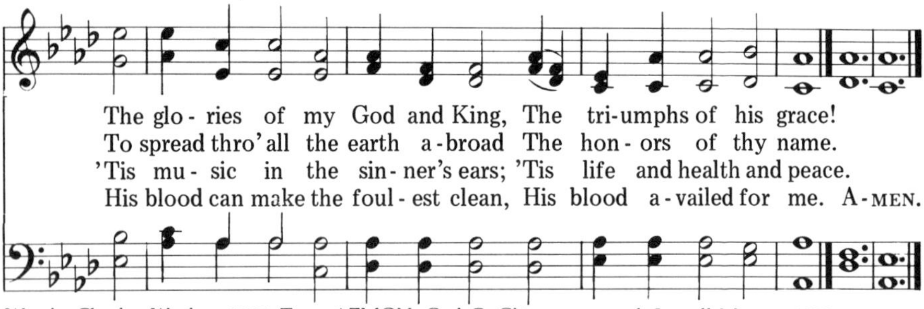

Words, Charles Wesley, 1739. Tune AZMON, Carl G. Gläser; arranged, Lowell Mason, 1839.
This tune in a lower key, No. 450.

70 In the Cross of Christ I Glory

1. In the cross of Christ I glo-ry, Tow'r-ing o'er the wrecks of time,
2. When the woes of life o'er-take me, Hopes de-ceive and fears an-noy,
3. When the sun of bliss is beam-ing Light and love up-on my way,
4. Bane and bless-ing, pain and plea-sure, By the cross are sanc-ti-fied;

All the light of sa-cred sto-ry Gath-ers round its head sub-lime.
Nev-er shall the cross for-sake me: Lo! it glows with peace and joy.
From the cross the ra-diance streaming Adds new lus-ter to the day.
Peace is there that knows no mea-sure, Joys that thro' all time a-bide.

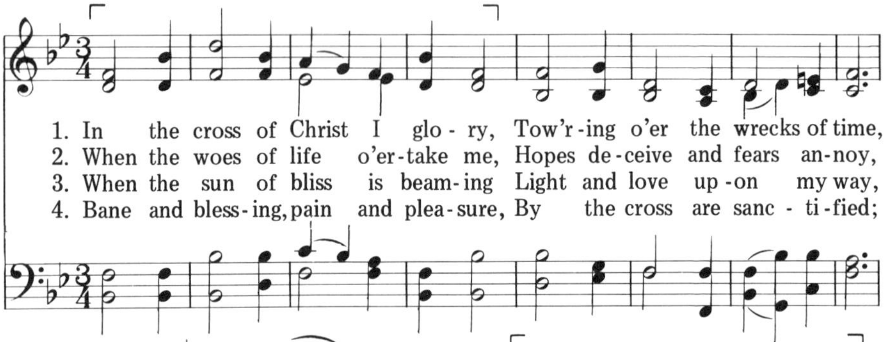

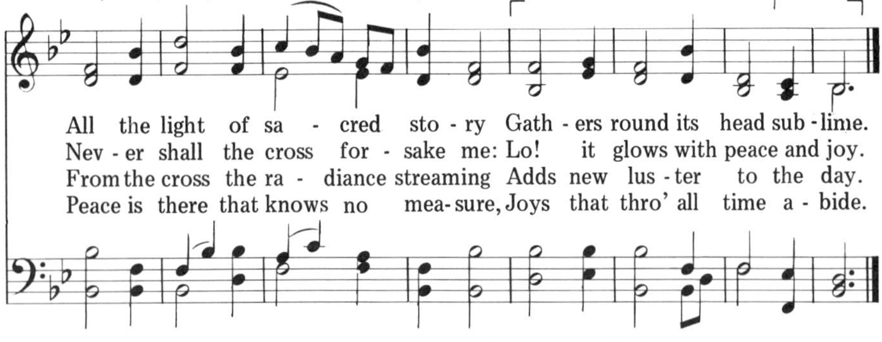

Galatians 6:14. Words, John Bowring, 1825. Tune RATHBUN, Ithamar Conkey, 1849.

His Name Is Wonderful 71

His name is Won-der-ful, His name is Won-der-ful,
He is the might-y King, Mas-ter of ev-'ry-thing,
His name is Won-der-ful, Je-sus, my Lord;
Je-sus, my Lord.
He's the great Shep-herd, the Rock of all a-ges, Al-might-y
God is he; Bow down be-fore him, Love and a-
dore him, His name is Won-der-ful, Je-sus, my Lord.

72 Jesus, Thou Joy of Loving Hearts

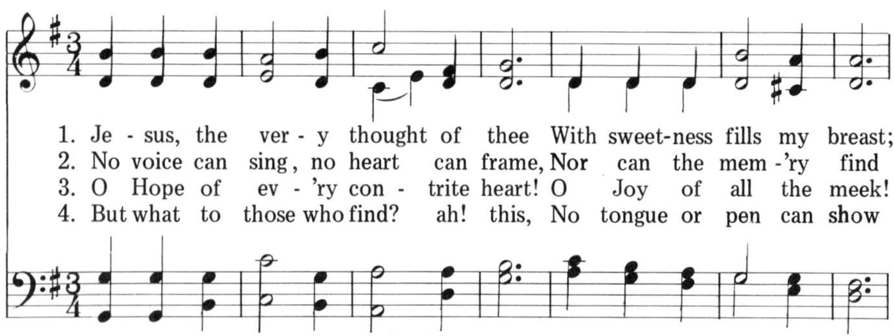

1. Je - sus, thou joy of lov - ing hearts, Thou fount of life,
2. Thy truth un-changed hath ev - er stood; Thou sav - est those
3. O Je - sus, ev - er with us stay, Make all our mo -

thou light of men, From the best bliss that earth im - parts,
who on thee call; To them who seek thee, thou art good,
ments calm and bright; Chase the dark night of sin a - way,

We turn un - filled to thee a - gain.
To them who find thee, all in all.
Shed o'er the world thy ho - ly light. A - MEN.

Words, Latin Hymn, 12th Century; translated, Ray Palmer, 1858. Tune QUEBEC, Henry Baker, 1854.

73 Jesus, the Very Thought of Thee

1. Je - sus, the ver - y thought of thee With sweet-ness fills my breast;
2. No voice can sing, no heart can frame, Nor can the mem -'ry find
3. O Hope of ev - 'ry con - trite heart! O Joy of all the meek!
4. But what to those who find? ah! this, No tongue or pen can show

Words, Latin Hymn, 12th Century; translated, Edward Caswall, 1849. Tune ST. AGNES,
John B. Dykes, 1866.
This tune in a lower key, No. 133.

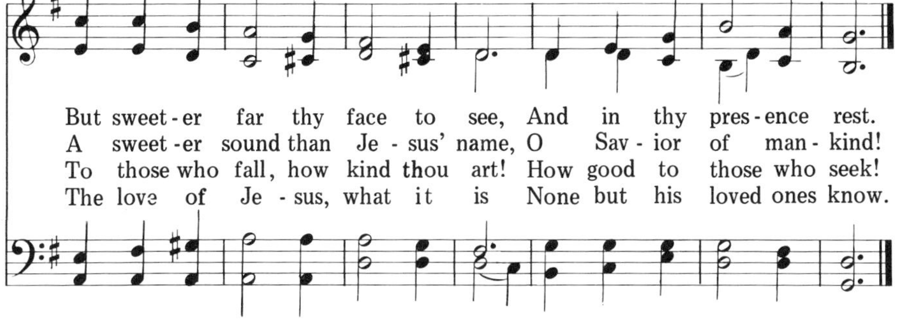

But sweet-er far thy face to see, And in thy pres-ence rest.
A sweet-er sound than Je-sus' name, O Sav-ior of man-kind!
To those who fall, how kind thou art! How good to those who seek!
The love of Je-sus, what it is None but his loved ones know.

Jesus! Name of Wondrous Love 74

Unison

1. Je-sus! Name of won-drous love, Name all oth-er names a-bove,
2. Je-sus! Name of price-less worth To the fall-en sons of earth,
3. Je-sus! On-ly name that's giv'n Un-der all the might-y heav'n
4. Je-sus! Name of won-drous love, Hu-man name of God a-bove:

Un-to which must ev-'ry knee Bow in deep hu-mil-i-ty.
For the prom-ise that it gave, "Je-sus shall his peo-ple save."
Where-by man, to sin en-slaved, Bursts his fet-ters and is saved.
Plead-ing on-ly this we flee, Help-less, O our God, to thee.

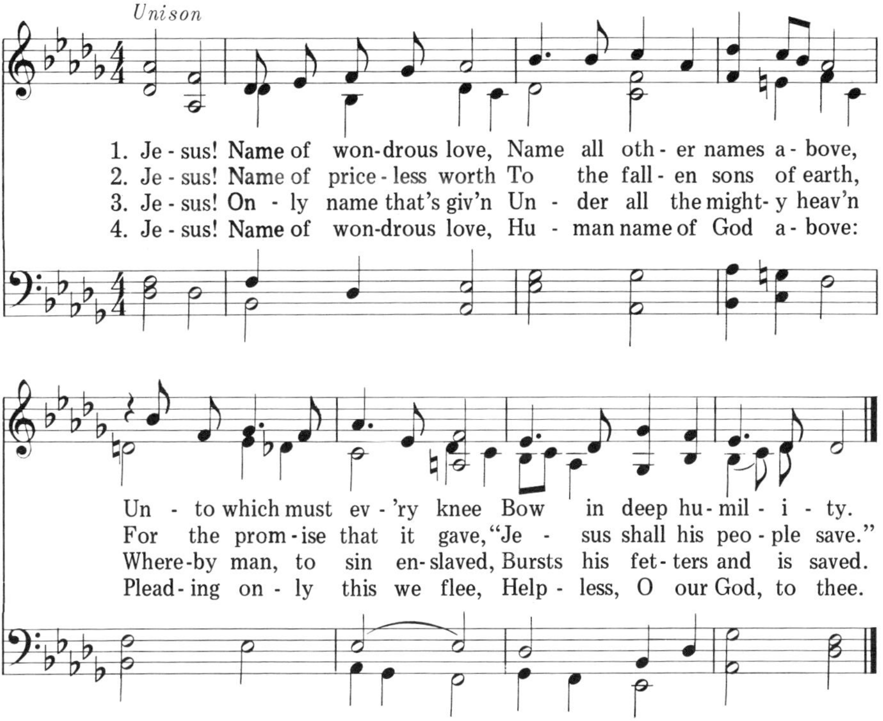

Philippians 2:9,10. Words, William Walsham How, 1854. Tune CARLSON, Everett Titcomb, 1947.

75 I Love Thee

1. I love thee, I love thee, I love thee, my Lord;
2. I'm hap-py, I'm hap-py, oh, won-drous ac-count!
3. O Je-sus, my Sav-ior, with thee I am blest,
4. Oh, who's like my Sav-ior? he's *Sa-lem's bright King;

I love thee, my Sav-ior, I love thee, my God:
My joys are im-mor-tal, I stand on the mount:
My life and sal-va-tion, my joy and my rest:
He smiles and he loves me and helps me to sing:

I love thee, I love thee, and that thou dost know;
I gaze on my trea-sure and long to be there,
Thy name be my theme, and thy love be my song;
I'll praise him, I'll praise him with notes loud and clear,

But how much I love thee my ac-tions will show.
With Je-sus and an-gels and kin-dred so dear.
Thy grace shall in-spire both my heart and my tongue.
While riv-ers of plea-sure my spir-it shall cheer.

Words and tune I LOVE THEE, Anonymous, Jeremiah Ingalls' *Christian Harmony*, 1805. *Hebrews 7:2.

My Jesus, I Love Thee 76

1. My Je - sus, I love thee, I know thou art mine,
2. I love thee be - cause thou hast first lov - ed me,
3. In man - sions of glo - ry and end - less de - light

For thee all the fol - lies of sin I re - sign;
And pur - chased my par - don on Cal - va - ry's tree;
I'll ev - er a - dore thee in heav - en so bright;

My gra - cious Re - deem - er, my Sav - ior art thou;
I love thee for wear - ing the thorns on thy brow;
I'll sing with the glit - ter - ing crown on my brow,

If ev - er I loved thee, my Je - sus, 'tis now.
If ev - er I loved thee, my Je - sus, 'tis now.
If ev - er I loved thee, my Je - sus, 'tis now.

Words, William R. Featherston, *c.* 1862. Tune GORDON, Adoniram J. Gordon, 1876.

77 Comfort, Comfort Ye My People

1. Com-fort, com-fort ye my peo-ple, Speak ye peace, thus saith our God;
2. Hark, the voice of one that cri-eth In the des-ert far and near,
3. Make ye straight what long was crook-ed, Make the rough-er plac-es plain;

Com-fort those who sit in dark-ness, Mourn-ing 'neath their sor-rows' load.
Bid-ding all men to re-pent-ance Since the king-dom now is here.
Let your hearts be true and hum-ble, As be-fits his ho-ly reign.

Speak ye to Je-ru-sa-lem Of the peace that waits for them;
O that warn-ing cry o-bey! Now pre-pare for God a way;
For the glo-ry of the Lord Now o'er earth is shed a-broad;

Tell her that her sins I cov-er, And her war-fare now is o-ver.
Let the val-leys rise to meet him, And the hills bow down to greet him.
And all flesh shall see the to-ken That his word is nev-er bro-ken. A-MEN.

Isaiah 40:1-8. Words, Johannes Olearius, 1671; translated, Catherine Winkworth, 1863. Tune PSALM 42, *Genevan Psalter*, 1551.

O Come, O Come, Emmanuel 78

May be sung in unison
1. O come, O come, Em - man - u - el, And ran - som cap - tive
2. O come, thou Day-spring, come and cheer Our spir - its by thine
3. O come, thou Wis - dom from on high, And or - der all things,
4. O come, De - sire of na - tions, bind All peo - ples in one
Is - ra - el, That mourns in lone - ly ex - ile here, Un -
ad - vent here; Dis - perse the gloom - y clouds of night, And
far and nigh; To us the path of knowl-edge show, And
heart and mind; Bid en - vy, strife, and quar - rels cease; Fill
til the Son of God ap - pear.
death's dark shad - ows put to flight.
cause us in her ways to go.
the whole world with heav - en's peace.
Re - joice! Re - joice! Em -
man - u - el Shall come to thee, O Is - ra - el! A-MEN.

Words, Latin Hymn, *Psalteriolum Cantionum Catholicarum,* 1710; st. 1, 2, John Mason Neale, 1851;
st. 3, 4, Henry Sloane Coffin, 1916. Tune VENI EMMANUEL, adapted from Plainsong by
Thomas Helmore, 1854.

79 Come, Thou Long-Expected Jesus

1. Come, thou long - ex - pect - ed Je - sus, Born to set thy
2. Born thy peo - ple to de - liv - er, Born a child, and
peo - ple free; From our fears and sins re - lease us;
yet a King, Born to reign in us for - ev - er,
Let us find our rest in thee. Is - rael's strength and con - so -
Now thy gra - cious king-dom bring. By thine own e - ter - nal
la - tion, Hope of all the earth thou art; Dear de - sire of
spir - it Rule in all our hearts a - lone; By thine all - suf -

Words, Charles Wesley, 1744. Tune HYFRYDOL, Rowland H. Prichard, c. 1830.

ev - 'ry na - tion, Joy of ev -'ry long - ing heart.
fi - cient mer - it, Raise us to thy glo - rious throne. A-MEN.

Away in a Manger 80

1. A - way in a man - ger, no crib for a bed, The lit - tle Lord
2. The cat - tle are low - ing, the Ba - by a - wakes, But lit - tle Lord
3. Be near me, Lord Je - sus, I ask thee to stay Close by me for-

Je - sus laid down his sweet head; The stars in the sky looked
Je - sus, no cry - ing he makes; I love thee, Lord Je - sus! look
ev - er, and love me, I pray; Bless all the dear chil - dren in

down where he lay, The lit - tle Lord Je - sus, a - sleep on the hay.
down from the sky, And stay by my cra - dle till morn - ing is nigh.
thy ten - der care, And fit us for heav - en to live with thee there. A - MEN.

Words, st. 1, 2, Anonymous, 1885; st. 3, Anonymous, 1892. Tune MUELLER, James R. Murray, 1887.

81 O Come, All Ye Faithful

1. O come, all ye faith-ful, joy-ful and tri-um-phant, O come ye, O
2. Sing, choirs of an-gels, sing in ex-ul-ta-tion, O sing, all ye
3. Yea, Lord, we greet thee, born this hap-py morn-ing, Je-sus, to
come ye to Beth-le-hem! Come and be-hold him, born the King of
bright hosts of heav'n a-bove! Glo-ry to God, all glo-ry in the
thee be all glo-ry giv'n; Word of the Fa-ther, now in flesh ap-
an-gels!
high-est! O come, let us a-dore him, O come, let us a-dore him,
pear-ing!
O come, let us a-dore him, Christ the Lord!

Words, Latin hymn; ascribed to John Francis Wade, c. 1743; translated, Frederick Oakeley, 1841, and others. Tune ADESTE FIDELES, John Francis Wade, 1743.

Go, Tell It on the Mountain 82

Unison
Go, tell it on the moun-tain, O-ver the hills and ev-'ry-where;
Fine
Go, tell it on the moun-tain That Je-sus Christ is born!
Harmony
1. While shep-herds kept their watch-ing O'er si-lent flocks by night,
2. The shep-herds feared and trem-bled When lo! a-bove the earth
3. Down in a low-ly man-ger The hum-ble Christ was born,
D.C. al Fine
Be-hold through-out the heav-ens There shone a ho-ly light.
Rang out the an-gel cho-rus That hailed our Sav-ior's birth.
And God sent us sal-va-tion That bless-ed Christ-mas morn.

Words, John W. Work, Jr., 1907. Tune GO TELL IT, Negro Spiritual; harmonized, John W. Work II, 1940. Words and harmonization used by permission Mrs. John W. Work III.

83 Hark! The Herald Angels Sing

1. Hark! the her - ald an - gels sing, "Glo - ry to the new - born King;
2. Christ, by high - est heav'n a - dored, Christ, the ev - er - last - ing Lord:
3. Hail the heav'n-born Prince of Peace! Hail the Sun of righ - teous - ness!
Peace on earth, and mer - cy mild; God and sin - ners rec - on - ciled."
Late in time, be - hold him come, Off-spring of a vir - gin's womb.
Light and life to all he brings, Ris'n with heal - ing in his wings.
Joy - ful, all ye na - tions, rise, Join the tri - umph of the skies;
Veiled in flesh the God-head see, Hail th'in - car - nate De - i - ty!
Mild he lays his glo - ry by, Born that man no more may die,
With an - gel - ic hosts pro -claim, "Christ is born in Beth - le - hem!"
Pleased as man with men to dwell, Je - sus our Im - man - u - el.
Born to raise the sons of earth, Born to give them sec - ond birth.

Words, Charles Wesley, 1739, alt. Tune MENDELSSOHN, Felix Mendelssohn, 1840; arranged,
William H. Cummings, 1855.

Hark! the her-ald an-gels sing, "Glo - ry to the new-born King."

Child in the Manger 84

Unison

1. Child in the man - ger, In - fant of Ma - ry; Out - cast and
2. Once the most ho - ly Child of sal - va - tion Gent - ly and
3. Proph - ets fore - told him In - fant of won - der; An - gels be-

strang - er, Lord of all; Child who in - her - its All our trans-
low - ly Lived be - low; Now as our glo - rious Might - y Re-
hold him On his throne; Wor - thy our Sav - ior Of all our

gres - sions, All our de - mer - its On him fall.
deem - er, See him vic - to - rious O'er each foe.
prais - es; Hap - py for - ev - er Are his own.

Words, Mary Macdonald; translated, Lachlan Macbean, 1888. Used by permission *The Fifeshire Advertiser,* Ltd. Tune BUNESSAN, Gaelic Melody.

85 O Little Town of Bethlehem

1. O lit - tle town of Beth - le - hem, How still we see thee lie!
2. For Christ is born of Ma - ry, And gath - ered all a - bove,
3. How si - lent - ly, how si - lent - ly The won - drous gift is giv'n!
4. O ho - ly Child of Beth - le - hem! De - scend to us, we pray;
A - bove thy deep and dream-less sleep The si - lent stars go by;
While mor - tals sleep, the an - gels keep Their watch of won-d'ring love.
So God im - parts to hu - man hearts The bless - ings of his heav'n.
Cast out our sin, and en - ter in, Be born in us to - day!
Yet in thy dark streets shin - eth The ev - er - last - ing Light; The
O morn-ing stars, to - geth - er Pro - claim the ho - ly birth, And
No ear may hear his com - ing, But in this world of sin, Where
We hear the Christ-mas an - gels The great glad tid - ings tell; O
hopes and fears of all the years Are met in thee to - night.
prais - es sing to God the King, And peace to men on earth!
meek souls will re - ceive him, still The dear Christ en - ters in.
come to us, a - bide with us, Our Lord Im-man - u - el!

Words, Phillips Brooks, 1868. Tune ST. LOUIS, Lewis Redner, 1868.

It Came upon the Midnight Clear 86

1. It came up-on the mid-night clear, That glo-rious song of old,
2. Yet with the woes of sin and strife The world has suf-fered long,
3. All ye, be-neath life's crush-ing load, Whose forms are bend-ing low,
4. For lo! the days are has-t'ning on, By proph-et bards fore-told,
From an-gels bend-ing near the earth, To touch their harps of gold:
Be-neath the an-gel strain have rolled Two thou-sand years of wrong;
Who toil a-long the climb-ing way With pain-ful steps and slow,
When with the ev - er - cir-cling years Comes round the age of gold;
"Peace on the earth, good will to men," From heav'n's all-gra-cious King.
And man, at war with man, hears not The love song which they bring:
Look now! for glad and gold-en hours Come swift-ly on the wing:
When peace shall o - ver all the earth Its an - cient splendors fling,
The world in sol - emn still-ness lay, To hear the an-gels sing.
O hush the noise, ye men of strife, And hear the an-gels sing!
O rest be-side the wea-ry road, And hear the an-gels sing!
And the whole world give back the song Which now the an-gels sing.

Words, Edmund H. Sears, 1849. Tune CAROL, Richard S. Willis, 1850.

87 Angels, from the Realms of Glory

1. An - gels, from the realms of glo - ry, Wing your flight o'er
2. Shep - herds, in the fields a - bid - ing, Watch - ing o'er your
3. Sag - es, leave your con - tem - pla - tions, Bright - er vi - sions
4. Saints, be - fore the al - tar bend - ing, Watch - ing long in

all the earth; Ye who sang cre - a - tion's sto - ry,
flocks by night, God with man is now re - sid - ing,
beam a - far; Seek the great De - sire of na - tions,
hope and fear, Sud - den - ly the Lord, de - scend - ing,

Now pro - claim Mes - si - ah's birth: Come and wor - ship,
Yon - der shines the in - fant Light: Come and wor - ship,
Ye have seen the In - fant's star: Come and wor - ship,
In his tem - ple shall ap - pear: Come and wor - ship,

come and wor - ship, Wor - ship Christ, the new - born King!
come and wor - ship, Wor - ship Christ, the new - born King!
come and wor - ship, Wor - ship Christ, the new - born King!
come and wor - ship, Wor - ship Christ, the new - born King!

Words, James Montgomery, 1816. Tune REGENT SQUARE, Henry Smart, 1867.

Joy to the World! The Lord Is Come 88

1. Joy to the world! the Lord is come; Let earth re - ceive her King;
2. Joy to the earth! the Sav - ior reigns; Let men their songs em - ploy;
3. No more let sins and sor - rows grow, Nor thorns in - fest the ground;
4. He rules the world with truth and grace, And makes the na - tions prove

Let ev - 'ry heart pre - pare him room,
While fields and floods, rocks, hills, and plains
He comes to make his bless - ings flow
The glo - ries of his righ - teous - ness,

And heav'n and na - ture sing, And heav'n and na - ture sing,
Re - peat the sound-ing joy, Re - peat the sound-ing joy,
Far as the curse is found, Far as the curse is found,
And won-ders of his love, And won-ders of his love,

1. And heav'n and na-ture sing,

1. And heav'n and na-ture sing, And heav'n and na-

And heav'n, and heav'n and na - ture sing.
Re - peat, re - peat the sound - ing joy.
Far as, far as the curse is found.
And won - ders, won - ders of his love.

ture sing,

Psalm 98. Words, Isaac Watts, 1719. Tune ANTIOCH, arranged from George Frederick Handel by Lowell Mason, 1839.

89 Silent Night, Holy Night

1. Si - lent night, ho - ly night, All is calm, all is bright
2. Si - lent night, ho - ly night, Dark - ness flies, all is light;
3. Si - lent night, ho - ly night, Son of God, love's pure light
4. Si - lent night, ho - ly night, Won - drous Star, lend thy light;
Round yon vir - gin moth-er and child! Ho - ly In - fant so
Shep - herds hear the an - gels sing, "Al - le - lu - ia!
Ra - diant beams from thy ho - ly face, With the dawn of re -
With the an - gels let us sing Al - le - lu - ia
ten - der and mild, Sleep in heav - en - ly
hail the King! Christ the Sav - ior is
deem - ing grace, Je - sus, Lord, at thy
to our King; Christ the Sav - ior is
peace, Sleep in heav - en - ly peace.
born, Christ the Sav - ior is born."
birth, Je - sus, Lord, at thy birth.
born, Christ the Sav - ior is born.

Words, German Hymn, Joseph Mohr, 1818; translated, st. 1, 3, John Freeman Young, 1863; st. 2, 4, Anonymous. Tune STILLE NACHT, Franz Gruber, 1818.

Good Christian Men, Rejoice 90

1. Good Chris - tian men, re - joice With heart and soul and voice!
2. Good Christ - tian men, re - joice With heart and soul and voice!
3. Good Christ - tian men, re - joice With heart and soul and voice!
Give ye heed to what we say: Je - sus Christ is born to - day.
Now ye hear of end - less bliss: Je - sus Christ was born for this.
Now ye need not fear the grave: Je - sus Christ was born to save;
Man and beast be - fore him bow, And he is in the man - ger now:
He hath o - pened heav-en's door, And man is blest for - ev - er-more.
Calls you one and calls you all, To gain his ev - er - last - ing hall.
Christ is born to - day, Christ is born to - day!
Christ was born for this, Christ was born for this!
Christ was born to save, Christ was born to save!

Words, Medieval Latin Carol, 14th Century; translated, John Mason Neale, 1853. Tune IN DULCI JUBILO, Traditional German Carol, 14th Century.

91 The First Nowell the Angel Did Say

1. The first Now-ell the an-gel did say, Was to cer-tain poor
2. For all to see there was a star Shin-ing in the
3. And by the light of that same star The Wise Men
4. Then let us all with one ac-cord Sing prais-es

shep-herds in fields as they lay; In fields where they lay
east, be-yond them far, And to the earth it
came from coun-try far; To seek for a king was
to our heav-en-ly Lord Who hath made heav'n and

keep-ing their sheep, On a cold win-ter's night that was so deep.
gave great light, And so it con-tin-ued both day and night.
their in-tent, And to fol-low the star wher-ev-er it went.
earth of naught, And with his blood man-kind hath bought.

Now-ell, Now-ell, Now-ell, Now-ell, Born is the King of Is-ra-el.

Words and tune THE FIRST NOWELL, Traditional English Carol.

1. Hark to the sto-ry an-gels are tell-ing Of the birth
2. Shep-herds a-keep-ing watch on the hill-side Heard the won-
3. Come, all ye peo-ple, come to the man-ger, Wor-ship and
of Je-sus, Born in a man-ger mid cat-tle low-ly
drous sto-ry, Knelt down in won-der, gazed at the glo-ry
a-dore him; Sing as the an-gels, kneel as the shep-herds,
Is the Babe most ho-ly.
Sud-den-ly ap-pear-ing. Sing, all ye an-gels, Sing, all
To the Christ our Sav-ior.
ye shep-herds! Sing to the lit-tle Babe in the man-ger; Sing a soft
ho-san-na, Sing a loud ho-san-na, Je-sus Christ is born to-day.

93 There's a Song in the Air

Unison

1. There's a song in the air! There's a star in the sky!
2. There's a tu - mult of joy O'er the won - der - ful birth,
3. In the light of that star Lies re - demp - tion un - furled;
4. We re - joice in the light And we ech - o the song

There's a moth - er's deep prayer And a ba - by's low cry!
For the vir - gin's sweet boy Is the Lord of the earth.
And that song from a - far Has swept o - ver the world.
That comes down thro' the night From the heav - en - ly throng.

And the star rains its fire while the beau - ti - ful sing,
And the star rains its fire while the beau - ti - ful sing,
Ev - 'ry hearth is a - flame, and the beau - ti - ful sing
And we shout to the love - ly *e - van - gel they bring,

For the man - ger of Beth - le - hem cra - dles a King!
For the man - ger of Beth - le - hem cra - dles a King!
In the homes of the na - tions that Je - sus is King!
And we greet in his cra - dle our Sav - ior and King!

Words, Josiah G. Holland, c. 1874. Tune KOHOUTEK, attr. to B. F. White in *The Sacred Harp*, 1844; arranged, Carlton R. Young, 1966. © Copyright 1967 Broadman Press. All rights reserved. *Good news.

Infant Holy, Infant Lowly   94
1. In - fant ho - ly, In - fant low - ly, For his bed a cat - tle stall;
2. Flocks were sleeping Shep-herds keeping Vig - il till the morn-ing new
Ox - en low - ing, Lit - tle knowing Christ the Babe is Lord of all.
Saw the glo - ry, Heard the sto - ry, Ti - dings of a gos - pel true.
Swift are wing - ing An - gels sing - ing, No - els ring - ing,
Thus re - joic - ing, Free from sor - row, Prais - es voic - ing
Ti - dings bring - ing: Christ the Babe is Lord of all.
Greet the mor - row: Christ the Babe was born for you!

95 Angels We Have Heard on High

1. An - gels we have heard on high, Sweet - ly sing - ing o'er the plains:
2. Shepherds, why this ju - bi - lee? Why your joy - ous strains pro - long?
3. Come to Beth - le - hem, and see Him whose birth the an - gels sing;
4. See him in a man - ger laid, Whom the choirs of an - gels praise;
And the moun - tains in re - ply, Ech - o - ing their joy - ous strains.
What the glad - some ti - dings be Which in - spire your heav'n - ly song?
Come, a - dore on bend - ed knee Christ the Lord, the new - born King.
Ma - ry, Jo - seph, lend your aid, While our hearts in love we raise.
Glo - ri - a in ex - cel - sis De - o!
Glo - ri - a in ex - cel - sis De - o!

Words, Traditional French Carol; translated, Source Unknown, 1862, alt. Tune GLORIA, Traditional French Carol; arranged, Warren M. Angell, 1956.

Awake, My Soul, Awake, My Tongue 96

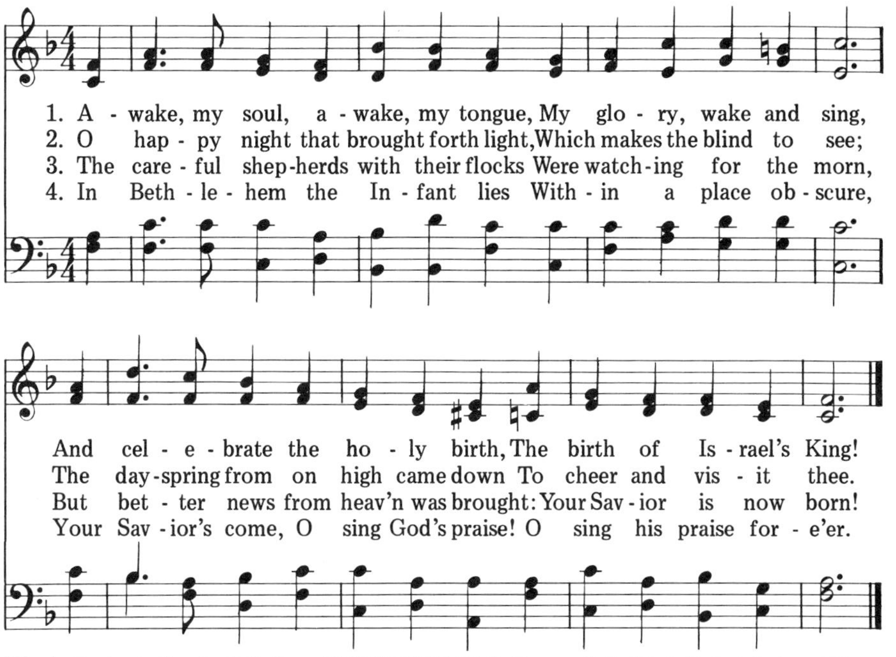

1. A - wake, my soul, a - wake, my tongue, My glo - ry, wake and sing,
2. O hap - py night that brought forth light, Which makes the blind to see;
3. The care - ful shep-herds with their flocks Were watch-ing for the morn,
4. In Beth - le - hem the In - fant lies With - in a place ob - scure,
And cel - e - brate the ho - ly birth, The birth of Is - rael's King!
The day-spring from on high came down To cheer and vis - it thee.
But bet - ter news from heav'n was brought: Your Sav - ior is now born!
Your Sav - ior's come, O sing God's praise! O sing his praise for - e'er.

Words, Benjamin Keach, 1696. Tune WINCHESTER OLD, Thomas Est's *Whole Book of Psalms*, 1592.

While Shepherds Watched Their Flocks 97

1

While shepherds watched their flocks by night,
  All seated on the ground,
The angel of the Lord came down,
  And glory shone around.

2

"Fear not!" said he; for mighty dread
  Had seized their troubled mind;
"Glad tidings of great joy I bring
  To you and all mankind.

3

"To you, in David's town, this day
  Is born of David's line
The Savior, who is Christ the Lord;
  And this shall be the sign:

4

"The heavenly Babe you there shall find
  To human view displayed,
All gently wrapped in swaddling clothes,
  And in a manger laid."

5

Thus spake the seraph, and forthwith
  Appeared a shining throng
Of angels praising God, who thus
  Addressed their joyful song:

6

"All glory be to God on high,
  And to the earth be peace;
Good will henceforth from heav'n to men
  Begin and never cease!"

Luke 2:8-14. Words, paraphrased, Nahum Tate, 1700. Tune WINCHESTER OLD, Thomas Est's *Whole Book of Psalms*, 1592.

98 We Would See Jesus; Lo! His Star

Unison

1. We would see Je - sus; lo, his star is shin - ing
2. We would see Je - sus; Ma - ry's Son most ho - ly,
3. We would see Je - sus; on the moun - tain teach - ing,
4. We would see Je - sus; in the ear - ly morn - ing,

A - bove the sta - ble while the an - gels sing;
Light of the vil - lage life from day to day;
With all the lis - t'ning peo - ple gath - ered round;
Still as of old he call - eth "Fol - low me";

There in a man - ger on the hay re - clin - ing;
Shin - ing re - vealed thro' ev - 'ry task most low - ly;
While birds and flow'rs and sky a - bove are preach - ing
Let us a - rise, all mean - er ser - vice scorn - ing;

Haste, let us lay our gifts be - fore the King.
The Christ of God, the life, the truth, the way.
The bless - ed - ness which sim - ple trust has found.
Lord, we are thine, we give our - selves to thee.

Words, J. Edgar Park, 1913. Tune MORA PROCTOR, William J. Reynolds, 1974. © Copyright 1975 Broadman Press. All rights reserved.

1. O sing a song of Beth-le-hem, Of shep-herds watch-ing there,
2. O sing a song of Naz-a-reth, Of sun-ny days of joy,
3. O sing a song of Gal-i-lee, Of lake and woods and hill,
And of the news that came to them From an-gels in the air.
O sing of fra-grant flow-ers' breath And of the sin-less Boy;
Of him who walked up-on the sea And bade its waves be still;
The light that shone on Beth-le-hem Fills all the world to-day;
For now the flow'rs of Naz-a-reth In ev-'ry heart may grow;
For tho like waves on Gal-i-lee, Dark seas of trou-ble roll,
Of Je-sus' birth and peace on earth The an-gels sing al-way.
Now spreads the fame of his dear name On all the winds that blow.
When faith has heard the Mas-ter's word, Falls peace up-on the soul.

Words, Louis F. Benson, 1899. Tune KINGSFOLD, Traditional English Melody collected by Lucy Broadwood; arranged, Ralph Vaughan Williams, 1906. Music from The English Hymnal; used by permission of Oxford University Press.

100 Jesus, Friend of Thronging Pilgrims

Unison

1. Je - sus, friend of throng - ing pil - grims, As of those who
2. Thou didst know the mar - ket plac - es And the streets in
3. Send thy ser - vants to the high - ways Where are heard the
4. By thy pow'r be streets trans - fig - ured, Haunts of sin be

walk a - lone, Look up - on our crowd - ed cit - ies
days of yore; Thou couldst see be - neath the plea - sures
dole - ful cries; Call a - gain the hun - gry mass - es
pur - i - fied; Rich and poor be found in con - cord,

With com - pas - sion from thy throne; Lov - ing Shep - herd,
Bro - ken hearts and spir - its sore; Gra - cious Heal - er,
To the feast that sat - is - fies; For the sup - per,
Zi - on's courts their hope and pride; Lord of cit - ies,

Lov - ing Shep - herd, Move a - mong us as thine own.
Gra - cious Heal - er, How we need thy touch once more!
For the sup - per Now is spread be - fore their eyes.
Lord of cit - ies, Here make heal - ing peace a - bide.

Words, W. Nantlais Williams, 1954. From *Five City Hymns,* Copyright 1954 by The Hymn Society of America. Used by permission. Tune ERIN, Paul Langston, 1974. Music © Copyright 1975 Broadman Press. All rights reserved.

Strong, Righteous Man of Galilee 101

1. Strong, righ - teous Man of Gal - i - lee, Robed with thy
2. Firm, peace - ful Man of Gal - i - lee, Girt with thy
3. Calm, suf - f'ring Man of Gal - i - lee, Clad in thy
4. God's peace - ful Man of Gal - i - lee, Love's tri - umph,

peace we fol - low thee: In tem - ple court, thy cleans - ing rod;
strength we fol - low thee: Not to re - venge, but heal and pray,
grace we fol - low thee: Love at the well, share Mar - tha's loss,
we shall fol - low thee: To crum - ble ev - 'ry boun - d'ry wall,

On Phar - i - sees, the scorn of God. Robed with thy
To turn the cheek and trib - ute pay: Girt with thy
For - give the nails, and take the cross. Clad in thy
Build high - ways to the hearts of all. Love's tri - umph,

peace we fol - low thee, Strong, righ - teous Man of Gal - i - lee.
strength we fol - low thee, Firm, peace - ful Man of Gal - i - lee.
grace we fol - low thee, Calm, suf - f'ring Man of Gal - i - lee.
we shall fol - low thee, God's peace - ful Man of Gal - i - lee.

Words, Harry Webb Farrington, 1921. Tune MELITA, John B. Dykes, 1861.

102 The Great Physician

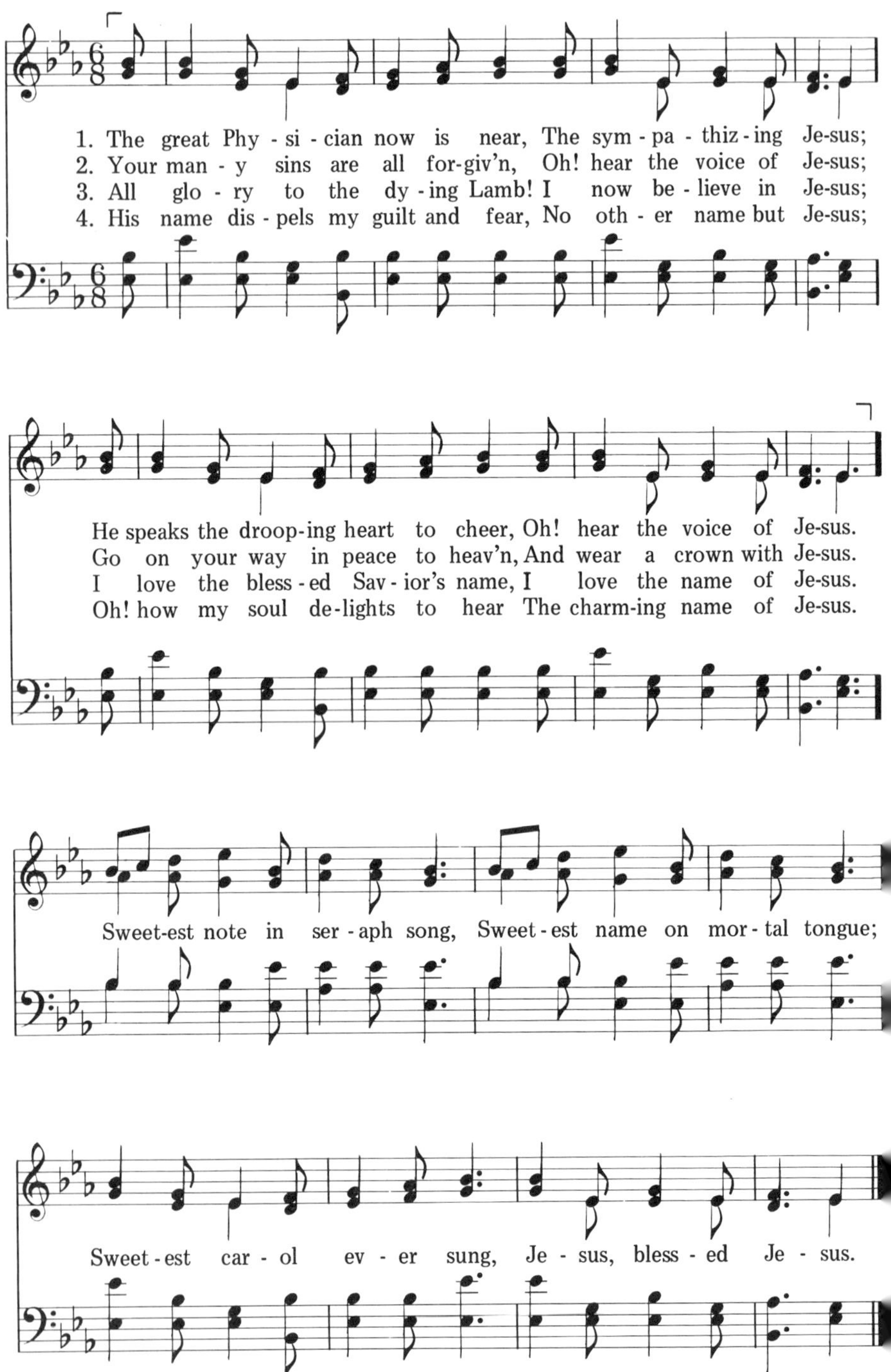

1. The great Phy - si - cian now is near, The sym - pa - thiz - ing Je-sus;
2. Your man - y sins are all for-giv'n, Oh! hear the voice of Je-sus;
3. All glo - ry to the dy - ing Lamb! I now be - lieve in Je-sus;
4. His name dis - pels my guilt and fear, No oth - er name but Je-sus;

He speaks the droop-ing heart to cheer, Oh! hear the voice of Je-sus.
Go on your way in peace to heav'n, And wear a crown with Je-sus.
I love the bless - ed Sav - ior's name, I love the name of Je-sus.
Oh! how my soul de-lights to hear The charm-ing name of Je-sus.

Sweet-est note in ser - aph song, Sweet-est name on mor - tal tongue;

Sweet - est car - ol ev - er sung, Je - sus, bless - ed Je - sus.

Words, William Hunter, 1859. Tune GREAT PHYSICIAN, John H. Stockton, 1869.

My Master Was So Very Poor 103

Unison

1. My Mas-ter was so ver-y poor, A man-ger was his cra-dling place;
2. My Mas-ter was so ver-y poor, And with the poor he broke the bread;
3. My Mas-ter was so ver-y poor, They nailed him na-ked to a cross;

So ver-y rich my Mas-ter was, Kings came from far to gain his grace.
So ver-y rich my Mas-ter was, That mul-ti-tudes by him were fed.
So ver-y rich my Mas-ter was, He gave his all and knew no loss.

Words, Harry Lee, c. 1927. Tune DUNWODY, Alta C. Faircloth, 1964. Music © Copyright 1964 Broadman Press. All rights reserved.

Glory Be to God on High 104

Unison

1. Christ was born in Beth-le-hem, Al-le-lu - ia,
2. He grew up an earth-ly child, Al-le-lu - ia,
3. Je-sus died at Cal-va-ry, Al-le-lu - ia,
4. He will cleanse us from our sin, Al-le-lu - ia,
5. We will live with him one day, Al-le-lu - ia,
Glo-ry be to God on high, Al-le-lu - ia,

D.C. for Refrain

Son of God and Son of man, Al-le-lu - ia.
Of the world, but un-de-filed, Al-le-lu - ia.
He a-rose tri-um-phant-ly, Al-le-lu - ia.
If we put our trust in him, Al-le-lu - ia.
And for-ev-er with him stay, Al-le-lu - ia.
Glo-ry be to God on high, Al-le-lu - ia.

Words, Anonymous. Tune MICHAEL, Traditional Folk Tune.

105 O Sacred Head, Now Wounded

1. O sa - cred Head, now wound - ed, With grief and shame weighed down,
2. What thou, my Lord, hast suf - fered Was all for sin - ners' gain:
3. What lan - guage shall I bor - row To thank thee, dear - est Friend,
Now scorn - ful - ly sur - round - ed With thorns, thine on - ly crown;
Mine, mine was the trans - gres - sion, But thine the dead - ly pain;
For this thy dy - ing sor - row, Thy pit - y with - out end?
How pale thou art with an - guish, With sore a - buse and scorn!
Lo, here I fall, my Sav - ior! 'Tis I de - serve thy place;
O make me thine for - ev - er, And should I faint - ing be,
How does that vis - age lan - guish Which once was bright as morn!
Look on me with thy fa - vor, Vouch-safe to me thy grace.
Lord, let me nev - er, nev - er Out - live my love to thee. A-MEN.

Words, Paul Gerhardt, 1656, based on a Medieval Latin poem; translated, James W. Alexander, 1830.
Tune PASSION CHORALE, Hans Leo Hassler, 1601; harmonized, J. S. Bach, 1729.

What Wondrous Love Is This 106

Unison

1. What won-drous love is this, O my soul, O my soul! What
2. When I was sink-ing down, sink-ing down, sink-ing down, When
3. To God and to the Lamb I will sing, I will sing, To
4. And when from death I'm free, I'll sing on, I'll sing on, And

won-drous love is this, O my soul! What won-drous love is
I was sink-ing down, sink-ing down, When I was sink-ing
God and to the Lamb I will sing, To God and to the
when from death I'm free, I'll sing on, And when from death I'm

this That caused the Lord of bliss To bear the dread-ful curse
down Be - neath God's righ-teous frown, Christ laid a - side his crown
Lamb Who is the great "I Am," While mil-lions join the theme,
free, I'll sing and joy-ful be, And thro' e-ter-ni-ty

for my soul, for my soul, To bear the dread-ful curse for my soul.
for my soul, for my soul, Christ laid a - side his crown for my soul.
I will sing, I will sing, While mil-lions join the theme, I will sing.
I'll sing on, I'll sing on, And thro' e-ter-ni-ty I'll sing on.

Words, American Folk Hymn. Tune WONDROUS LOVE, William Walker's *Southern Harmony*, 1843.

107 There Is a Fountain

1. There is a foun-tain filled with blood Drawn from Im-man - uel's veins;
2. The dy - ing thief re-joiced to see That foun-tain in his day;
3. Dear dy - ing Lamb, thy pre-cious blood Shall nev - er lose its pow'r
4. E'er since by faith I saw the stream Thy flow-ing wounds sup - ply,

And sin - ners, plunged be-neath that flood, Lose all their guilt - y stains:
And there may I, though vile as he, Wash all my sins a - way:
Till all the ran-somed church of God Be saved, to sin no more:
Re - deem-ing love has been my theme, And shall be till I die:

Lose all their guilt - y stains, Lose all their guilt - y stains;
Wash all my sins a - way, Wash all my sins a - way;
Be saved, to sin no more, Be saved, to sin no more;
And shall be till I die, And shall be till I die;

And sin - ners, plunged be-neath that flood, Lose all their guilt - y stains.
And there may I, though vile as he, Wash all my sins a - way.
Till all the ran-somed church of God Be saved, to sin no more.
Re - deem-ing love has been my theme, And shall be till I die.

Zechariah 13:1. Words, William Cowper, *c.* 1771. Tune CLEANSING FOUNTAIN, Early American Melody.

1. Were you there when they cru - ci - fied my Lord? Were you
2. Were you there when they nailed him to the tree? Were you
3. Were you there when they laid him in the tomb? Were you
there when they cru - ci - fied my Lord?
there when they nailed him to the tree? Oh!
there when they laid him in the tomb?
Some - times it caus - es me to trem - ble, trem - ble, trem - ble.
Were you there when they cru - ci - fied my Lord?
Were you there when they nailed him to the tree?
Were you there when they laid him in the tomb?

Words and tune WERE YOU THERE, Traditional Negro Spiritual; adapted, John W. Work, Jr., and Frederick J. Work, 1907.

109 Blessed Redeemer

1. Up Cal-vary's moun-tain one dread-ful morn, Walked Christ my Sav-ior,
2. "Fa-ther, for-give them!" thus did he pray, E'en while his life-blood
3. O how I love him, Sav-ior and Friend, How can my prais-es

wea-ry and worn; Fac-ing for sin-ners death on the cross,
flowed fast a-way; Pray-ing for sin-ners while in such woe—
ev-er find end! Thro' years un-num-bered on heav-en's shore,

That he might save them from end-less loss.
No one but Je-sus ev-er loved so. Bless-ed Re-deem-er!
My tongue shall praise him for-ev-er-more.

pre-cious Re-deem-er! Seems now I see him on

Cal-va-ry's tree; Wound-ed and bleed-ing, for sin-ners

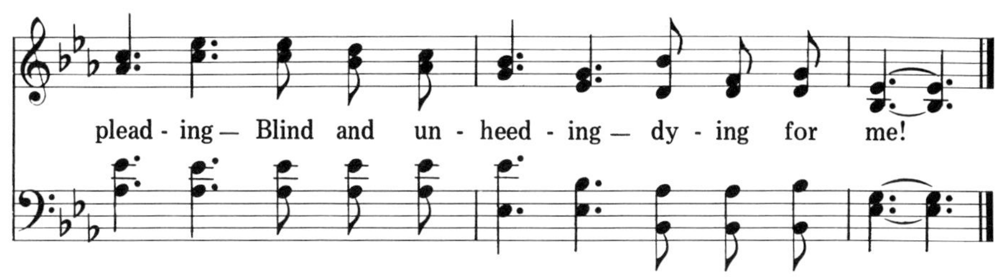

plead-ing— Blind and un-heed-ing— dy-ing for me!

For Me 110

1. Un - der an east - ern sky, A - mid a rab-ble's cry,
2. Thorn-crowned his bless - ed head, Blood-stained his ev - 'ry tread;
3. Pierc - ed his hands and feet, Three hours o'er him did beat
4. Thus wert thou made all mine; Lord, make me whol-ly thine;
5. In tho't and word and deed, Thy will to do, O lead

A Man went forth to die, For me (For me), for me.
Cross - lad - en, on he sped For me (For me), for me.
Fierce rays of noon - tide heat, For me (For me), for me.
Grant grace and strength di - vine To me (To me), to me.
My soul, e'en tho it bleed, To thee (To thee), to thee.

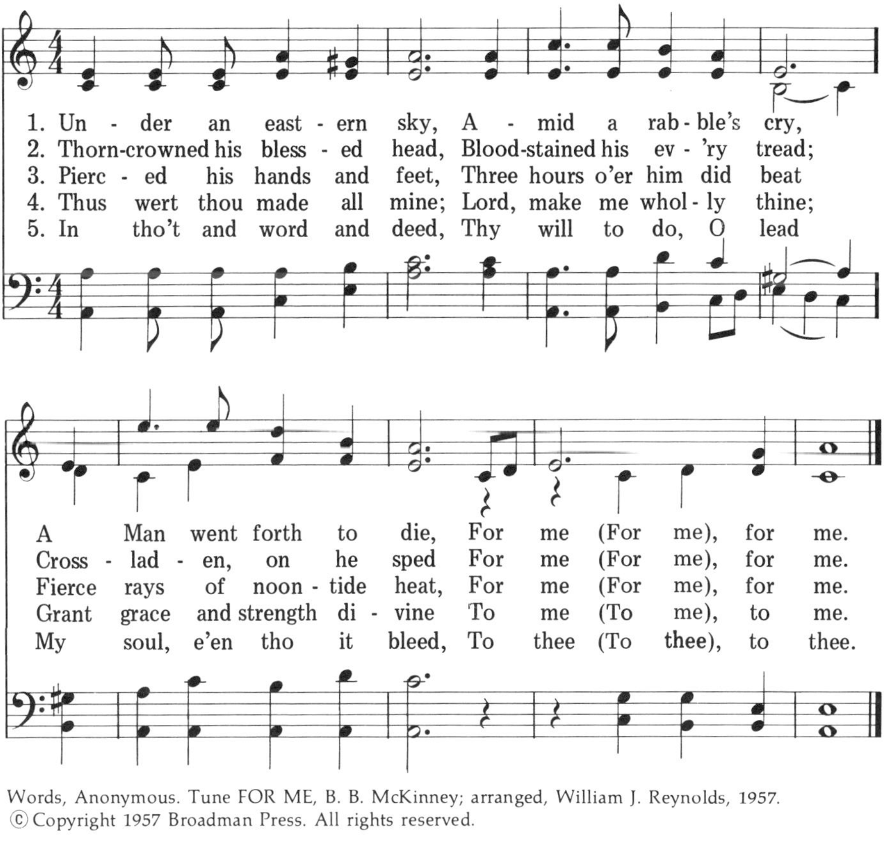

111 When I Survey the Wondrous Cross

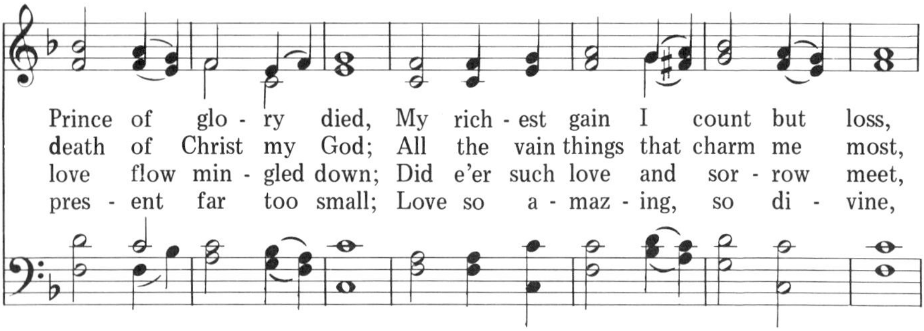

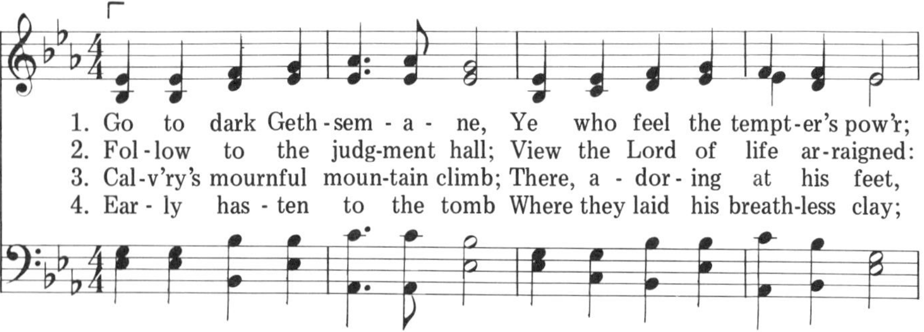

1. When I sur - vey the won - drous cross, On which the
2. For - bid it, Lord, that I should boast, Save in the
3. See, from his head, his hands, his feet, Sor - row and
4. Were the whole realm of na - ture mine, That were a

Prince of glo - ry died, My rich - est gain I count but loss,
death of Christ my God; All the vain things that charm me most,
love flow min - gled down; Did e'er such love and sor - row meet,
pres - ent far too small; Love so a - maz - ing, so di - vine,

And pour con - tempt on all my pride.
I sac - ri - fice them to his blood.
Or thorns com - pose so rich a crown.
De - mands my soul, my life, my all. A - MEN.

Galatians 6:14. Words, Isaac Watts, 1707. Tune HAMBURG, Lowell Mason, 1824.

112 Go to Dark Gethsemane

1. Go to dark Geth - sem - a - ne, Ye who feel the tempt-er's pow'r;
2. Fol-low to the judg-ment hall; View the Lord of life ar-raigned:
3. Cal-v'ry's mournful moun-tain climb; There, a - dor - ing at his feet,
4. Ear - ly has - ten to the tomb Where they laid his breath-less clay;

Words, James Montgomery, 1822. Tune REDHEAD 76, Richard Redhead, 1853. *Lamentations 3:19.

Your Re-deem-er's con-flict see; Watch with him one bit-ter hour;
O the*worm-wood and the gall! O the pangs his soul sus-tained!
Mark that mir-a-cle of time, God's own sac-ri-fice com-plete:
All is sol-i-tude and gloom; Who hath tak-en him a-way?

Turn not from his griefs a-way; Learn of Je-sus Christ to pray.
Shun not suf-f'ring, shame, or loss; Learn of him to bear the cross.
"It is fin-ished!" Hear the cry; Learn of Je-sus Christ to die.
Christ is ris'n! He meets our eyes: Sav-ior, teach us so to rise. A-MEN.

Alas, and Did My Savior Bleed 113

1. A-las, and did my Sav-ior bleed And did my Sov-'reign die?
2. Was it for crimes that I had done He groaned up-on the tree?
3. Well might the sun in dark-ness hide, And shut his glo-ries in,
4. Thus might I hide my blush-ing face While Cal-v'ry's cross ap-pears,
5. But drops of grief can ne'er re-pay The debt of love I owe;

Would he de-vote that sa-cred head For sin-ners such as I?
A-maz-ing pit-y, grace un-known, And love be-yond de-gree!
When Christ the might-y Mak-er died For man, the crea-ture's sin.
Dis-solve my heart in thank-ful-ness, And melt mine eyes to tears.
Here, Lord, I give my-self a-way, 'Tis all that I can do.

Words, Isaac Watts, 1707. Tune AVON, Hugh Wilson, 1825.

114 Christ the Lord Is Risen Today

1. Christ the Lord is ris'n to-day, Al - le - lu - ia!
2. Lives a-gain our glo-rious King, Al - le - lu - ia!
3. Love's re-deem-ing work is done, Al - le - lu - ia!
4. Soar we now where Christ has led, Al - le - lu - ia!
Sons of men and an-gels say, Al - le - lu - ia!
Where, O Death, is now thy sting? Al - le - lu - ia!
Fought the fight, the bat-tle won, Al - le - lu - ia!
Fol - l'wing our ex - alt-ed Head, Al - le - lu - ia!
Raise your joys and tri-umphs high, Al - le - lu - ia!
Dy - ing once he all doth save, Al - le - lu - ia!
Death in vain for - bids him rise, Al - le - lu - ia!
Made like him, like him we rise, Al - le - lu - ia!
Sing, ye heav'ns, and earth, re - ply, Al - le - lu - ia!
Where thy vic - to - ry, O Grave? Al - le - lu - ia!
Christ hath o - pened Par - a - dise, Al - le - lu - ia!
Ours the cross, the grave, the skies, Al - le - lu - ia! A-MEN.

Words, Charles Wesley, 1739. Tune EASTER HYMN, *Lyra Davidica*, 1708.

1. Je - sus Christ is ris'n to - day, Al - le - lu - ia!
2. Hymns of praise then let us sing, Al - le - lu - ia!
3. But the pains which he en - dured, Al - le - lu - ia!
4. Sing we to our God a - bove, Al - le - lu - ia!
Our tri - um - phant ho - ly day, Al - le - lu - ia!
Un - to Christ, our heav'n - ly King, Al - le - lu - ia!
Our sal - va - tion have pro - cured; Al - le - lu - ia!
Praise e - ter - nal as his love; Al - le - lu - ia!
Who did once, up - on the cross, Al - le - lu - ia!
Who en - dured the cross and grave, Al - le - lu - ia!
Now a - bove the sky he's King, Al - le - lu - ia!
Praise him, all ye heav'n - ly host, Al - le - lu - ia!
Suf - fer to re - deem our loss, Al - le - lu - ia!
Sin - ners to re - deem and save, Al - le - lu - ia!
Where the an - gels ev - er sing: Al - le - lu - ia!
Fa - ther, Son, and Ho - ly Ghost, Al - le - lu - ia!

Words, st. 1, 14th Century Latin Hymn; translated in *Lyra Davidica*, 1708; st. 2, 3, Arnold's *Compleat Psalmodist*, 1749; st. 4, Charles Wesley, 1740. Tune LLANFAIR, Robert Williams, 1817.

116 Rejoice, All Ye People

1. Re - joice, all ye peo - ple, your might - y an - thems raise;
2. De - spised and re - ject - ed, the Lamb for sin - ners slain;
3. Lord Je - sus, be near us, thy pres - ence we would know;
The Sav - ior, vic - to - rious, is wor - thy of your praise.
Sin's death he has con - quered by suf - fer - ing death's pain.
Thy face shine up - on us wher - e'er our feet may go.
All glo - rious Lord, thy tri - umph we pro - claim,
But now he lives to reign e - ter - nal - ly,
Show us thy love, to fol - low and a - dore,
Who from the grave has ris - en, O praise his name!
An - gel - ic choirs re - ech - o with songs of joy.
That we may see thy glo - ry for - ev - er - more.

Words, Anonymous; translated, Esther Bergen. Used by permission of the translator. Tune
METHFESSEL, Albert G. Methfessel, c. 1840.

1. Al - le - lu - ia! Al - le - lu - ia! Hearts to heav'n and voic - es raise;
2. Now the i - ron bars are bro - ken, Christ from death to life is born,
3. Al - le - lu - ia! Al - le - lu - ia! Glo - ry be to God on high;

Sing to God a hymn of glad - ness, Sing to God a hymn of praise.
Glo - rious life, and life im - mor - tal, On this res - ur - rec - tion morn;
Al - le - lu - ia to the Sav - ior, Who has won the vic - to - ry;

He who on the cross as Sav - ior For the world's sal - va - tion bled,
Christ has tri - umphed, and we con - quer By his might - y en - ter - prise,
Al - le - lu ia to the Spir - it, Fount of love and sanc - ti - ty;

Je - sus Christ, the King of Glo - ry, Now is ris - en from the dead.
We with him to life e - ter - nal By his res - ur - rec - tion rise.
Al - le - lu - ia! Al - le - lu - ia! To the Tri-une Maj - es - ty. A-MEN.

Words, Christopher Wordsworth, 1862, alt. Tune HYMN TO JOY, Ludwig van Beethoven, 1824; adapted, Edward Hodges, 1864.
This tune in a lower key, No. 275.

118 Low in the Grave He Lay

1. Low in the grave he lay, Je-sus my Sav-ior! Wait-ing the com-ing day,
2. Vain-ly they watch his bed, Je-sus my Sav-ior! Vain-ly they seal the dead,
3. Death can-not keep his prey, Je-sus my Sav-ior! He tore the bars a-way,
Je-sus my Lord! Up from the grave he a-rose,
he a-rose,
With a
might-y tri-umph o'er his foes;
he a-rose!
He a-rose a vic-tor from the
dark do-main, And he lives for-ev-er with his saints to reign. He a-
rose! He a-rose! Hal-le-lu-jah! Christ a-rose!
He a-rose! He a-rose!

Words and tune CHRIST AROSE, Robert Lowry, 1874.

1. They rolled a stone be - fore the door, As in the grave he lay;
2. The birds that sang, the flow'rs that bloomed, They brought no joy that spring,
3. All earth is dressed in green this day, To greet our ris - en Lord;

God raised him up, our liv - ing Lord, And made the first Lord's Day.
Till Christ was raised from death to be Our liv - ing Lord and King.
We praise him, for he lives a - gain, He keeps his prom - ised word.

We sing for joy, we sing for joy, With lov - ing thanks we say:

"God raised him up, our liv - ing Lord, And made the first Lord's Day."

120 Rejoice, the Lord Is King

1. Re - joice, the Lord is King: Your Lord and King a - dore!
2. Je - sus, the Sav - ior, reigns, The God of truth and love;
3. His king - dom can - not fail, He rules o'er earth and heav'n;
4. Re - joice in glo - rious hope! Our Lord and judge shall come

Re - joice, give thanks and sing, And tri - umph
When he had purged our stains, He took his
The keys of death and hell Are to our
And take his ser - vants up To their e -

ev - er - more: Lift up your heart, lift up your voice!
seat a - bove: Lift up your heart, lift up your voice!
Je - sus given: Lift up your heart, lift up your voice!
ter - nal home: Lift up your heart, lift up your voice!

Re - joice, a - gain I say, re - joice!
Re - joice, a - gain I say, re - joice!
Re - joice, a - gain I say, re - joice!
Re - joice, a - gain I say, re - joice! A- MEN.

Philippians 4:4. Words, Charles Wesley, 1744. Tune DARWALL, John Darwall, 1770.

Look, Ye Saints! The Sight Is Glorious 121

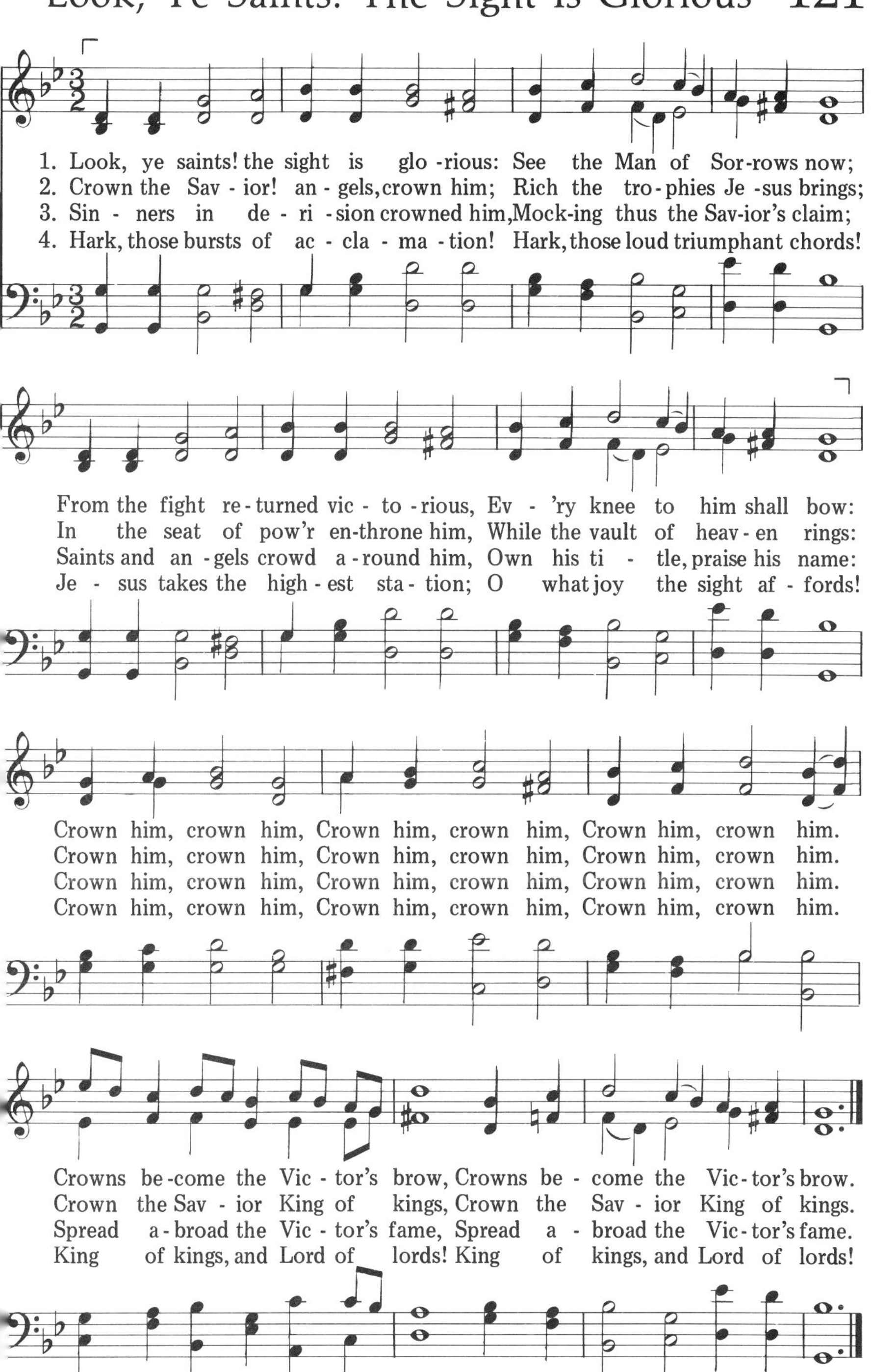

1. Look, ye saints! the sight is glo-rious: See the Man of Sor-rows now;
2. Crown the Sav-ior! an-gels, crown him; Rich the tro-phies Je-sus brings;
3. Sin-ners in de-ri-sion crowned him, Mock-ing thus the Sav-ior's claim;
4. Hark, those bursts of ac-cla-ma-tion! Hark, those loud triumphant chords!

From the fight re-turned vic-to-rious, Ev-'ry knee to him shall bow:
In the seat of pow'r en-throne him, While the vault of heav-en rings:
Saints and an-gels crowd a-round him, Own his ti-tle, praise his name:
Je-sus takes the high-est sta-tion; O what joy the sight af-fords!

Crown him, crown him, Crown him, crown him, Crown him, crown him.
Crown him, crown him, Crown him, crown him, Crown him, crown him.
Crown him, crown him, Crown him, crown him, Crown him, crown him.
Crown him, crown him, Crown him, crown him, Crown him, crown him.

Crowns be-come the Vic-tor's brow, Crowns be-come the Vic-tor's brow.
Crown the Sav-ior King of kings, Crown the Sav-ior King of kings.
Spread a-broad the Vic-tor's fame, Spread a-broad the Vic-tor's fame.
King of kings, and Lord of lords! King of kings, and Lord of lords!

Revelation 11:15. Words, Thomas Kelly, 1809. Tune BRYN CALFARIA, William Owen, c. 1890. Alternate tune REGENT SQUARE, No. 87.

122 I Know that My Redeemer Liveth

1. I know that my Re-deem-er liv-eth, And on the
2. I know his prom-ise nev-er fail-eth, The word he
3. I know my man-sion he pre-par-eth, That where he

earth a-gain shall stand; I know e-ter-nal life he giv-eth,
speaks, it can-not die; Tho cru-el death my flesh as-sail-eth,
is there I may be; O won-drous tho't, for me he car-eth,

That grace and pow'r are in his hand.
Yet I shall see him by and by.
And he at last will come for me.

I know, I know
I know, I know

that Je-sus liv-eth, And on the earth a-gain shall
And on the earth

stand; I know, I know that life he
I know, I know

Job 19:25. Words, Jessie Brown Pounds, 1893. Tune HANNAH, James H. Fillmore, 1893.

giv - eth, That grace and pow'r   are in his hand.
That grace and pow'r

Good Christian Men, Rejoice and Sing 123

1. Good Chris-tian men, re-joice and sing! Now is the tri-umph
2. The Lord of life is ris'n for aye; Bring flow'rs of song to
3. Praise we in songs of vic-to-ry That love, that life which
4. Thy name we bless, O ris-en Lord, And sing to-day with

of our King! To all the world glad news we bring:
strew his way; Let all man-kind re-joice and say:
can-not die, And sing with hearts up-lift-ed high:
one ac-cord The life laid down, the life re-stored:

Al - le - lu - ia!   Al - le - lu - ia!   Al - le - lu - ia!

Words, Cyril A. Alington, 1925. Used by permission of the Proprietors of *Hymns Ancient and Modern.*
Tune GELOBT SEI GOTT, Melchior Vulpius, 1609.

124 This Joyful Eastertide

1. This joy-ful Eas-ter-tide, What need is there for griev - -
Cast all your cares a - side And be not un-be-liev - -
2. Now put your trust in Christ, In wak-ing or in sleep - -
His grace on earth suf-ficed; He'll nev-er quit his keep - -
- ing.
- ing.
- ing.
- ing.
Come, share our Eas - ter joy That death could
not im-pris - on, Nor an - y pow'r de - stroy
Our Christ, who is a-ris - en, a-ris - en, a-
ris - en, a-ris - - - - - en.

Words, F. Pratt Green. Words © Oxford University Press. Used by permission. Tune VREUCHTEN, Dutch Melody, 17th Century.

The Head That Once Was Crowned 125

1. The head that once was crowned with thorns Is crowned with glo-ry now;
2. The joy of all who dwell a-bove, The joy of all be-low,
3. To them the cross, with all its shame, With all its grace, is giv'n;
4. The cross he bore is life and health, Tho shame and death to him,

A roy-al di-a-dem a-dorns The might-y Vic-tor's brow.
To whom he man-i-fests his love, And grants his name to know.
Their name an ev-er-last-ing name, Their joy the joy of heav'n.
His peo-ple's hope, his peo-ple's wealth, Their ev-er-last-ing theme.

Hebrews 2:10. Words, Thomas Kelly, 1820. Tune ST. MAGNUS, Jeremiah Clark, 1707.

Come, Let Us Join Our Cheerful Songs 126

1. Come, let us join our cheer-ful songs With an-gels round the throne;
2. "Wor-thy the Lamb who died," they cry, "To be ex-alt-ed thus!"
3. Je-sus is wor-thy to re-ceive The hon-or, pow'r di-vine;
4. The whole cre-a-tion join in one, To bless the sa-cred name

Ten thou-sand thou-sand are their tongues, But all their joys are one.
"Wor-thy the Lamb," our lips re-ply, "For he was slain for us."
And bless-ings, more than we can give, Be, Lord, for-ev-er thine!
Of him who sits up-on the throne, And to a-dore the Lamb!

Revelation 5:11-13. Words, Isaac Watts, 1707. Tune NATIVITY, Henry Lahee, 1855.

127 One Day

1. One day when heav-en was filled with his prais-es, One day when
2. One day they led him up Cal-va-ry's mountain, One day they
3. One day they left him a-lone in the gar-den, One day he
4. One day the grave could con-ceal him no long-er, One day the
5. One day the trum-pet will sound for his com-ing, One day the

sin was as black as could be, Je-sus came forth to be
nailed him to die on the tree; Suf-fer-ing an-guish, de-
rest-ed, from suf-fer-ing free; An-gels came down o'er his
stone rolled a-way from the door; Then he a-rose, o-ver
skies with his glo-ries will shine; Won-der-ful day, my be-

born of a vir-gin, Dwelt a-mong men, my ex-am-ple is he!
spised and re-ject-ed: Bear-ing our sins, my Re-deem-er is he!
tomb to keep vig-il; Hope of the hope-less, my Sav-ior is he!
death he had conquered; Now is as-cend-ed, my Lord ev-er-more!
lov-ed One bring-ing; Glo-ri-ous Sav-ior, this Je-sus is mine!

Liv-ing, he loved me; dy-ing, he saved me; Bur-ied, he

car - ried my sins far a - way; Ris - ing, he jus - ti - fied
free - ly for - ev - er: One day he's com - ing— O glo - ri - ous day!

The Lord Will Come 128

1. The Lord will come and not be slow, His foot-steps can-not err;
2. Truth from the earth, like to a flow'r, Shall bud and blos-som then;
3. Rise, God, judge thou the earth in might, This wick-ed earth re-dress;
4. For great thou art, and won-ders great By thy strong hand are done:

Be - fore him righ-teous-ness shall go, His roy-al har-bin-ger.
And jus-tice, from her heav'n-ly bow'r, Look down on mor-tal men.
For thou art he who shall by right The na-tions all pos-sess.
Thou in thy ev-er-last-ing seat Re-main-est God a-lone.

Words, John Milton, 1648. Tune ST. MAGNUS, Jeremiah Clark, 1707.

129 What If It Were Today?

1. Je - sus is com - ing to earth a - gain, What if it were to - day?
2. Sa - tan's do - min - ion will then be o'er, O that it were to - day!
3. Faith - ful and true would he find us here If he should come to - day?
Com - ing in pow - er and love to reign, What if it were to - day?
Sor - row and sigh - ing shall be no more, O that it were to - day!
Watch - ing in glad - ness and not in fear, If he should come to - day?
Com - ing to claim his cho - sen Bride, All the re - deemed and puri - fied,
Then shall the dead in Christ a - rise, Caught up to meet him in the skies;
Signs of his com - ing mul - ti - ply, Morn - ing light breaks in eastern sky,
O - ver this whole earth scat - tered wide, What if it were to - day?
When shall these glo - ries meet our eyes? What if it were to - day?
Watch, for the time is draw - ing nigh, What if it were to - day?

Glo - ry, glo - ry! Joy to my heart 'twill bring,
Joy to my heart 'twill bring,
Glo - ry, glo - ry! When we shall crown him King;
When we shall crown him King;
Glo - ry, glo - ry! Haste to pre - pare the way;
Haste to pre - pare the way;
Glo - ry, glo - ry! Je - sus will come some day.

130 Pentecostal Power

1. Lord, as of old at *Pen - te - cost Thou didst thy pow'r dis - play,
2. For might - y works for thee, pre - pare And strength-en ev - 'ry heart;
3. All self con - sume, all sin de-stroy! With ear - nest zeal en - due
4. Speak, Lord! be - fore thy throne we wait, Thy prom - ise we be - lieve,

With cleans-ing, pu - ri - fy - ing flame, De - scend on us to - day.
Come, take pos - ses - sion of thine own, And nev - er - more de - part.
Each wait - ing heart to work for thee; O Lord, our faith re - new!
And will not let thee go un - til The bless - ing we re - ceive.

Lord, send the old-time power, the Pen - te-cos - tal power! Thy flood-gates of

bless-ing on us throw o-pen wide! Lord, send the old-time pow-er, the

Pen-te-cos-tal power, That sin-ners be con-vert-ed and thy name glo-ri-fied!

Breathe on Me 131

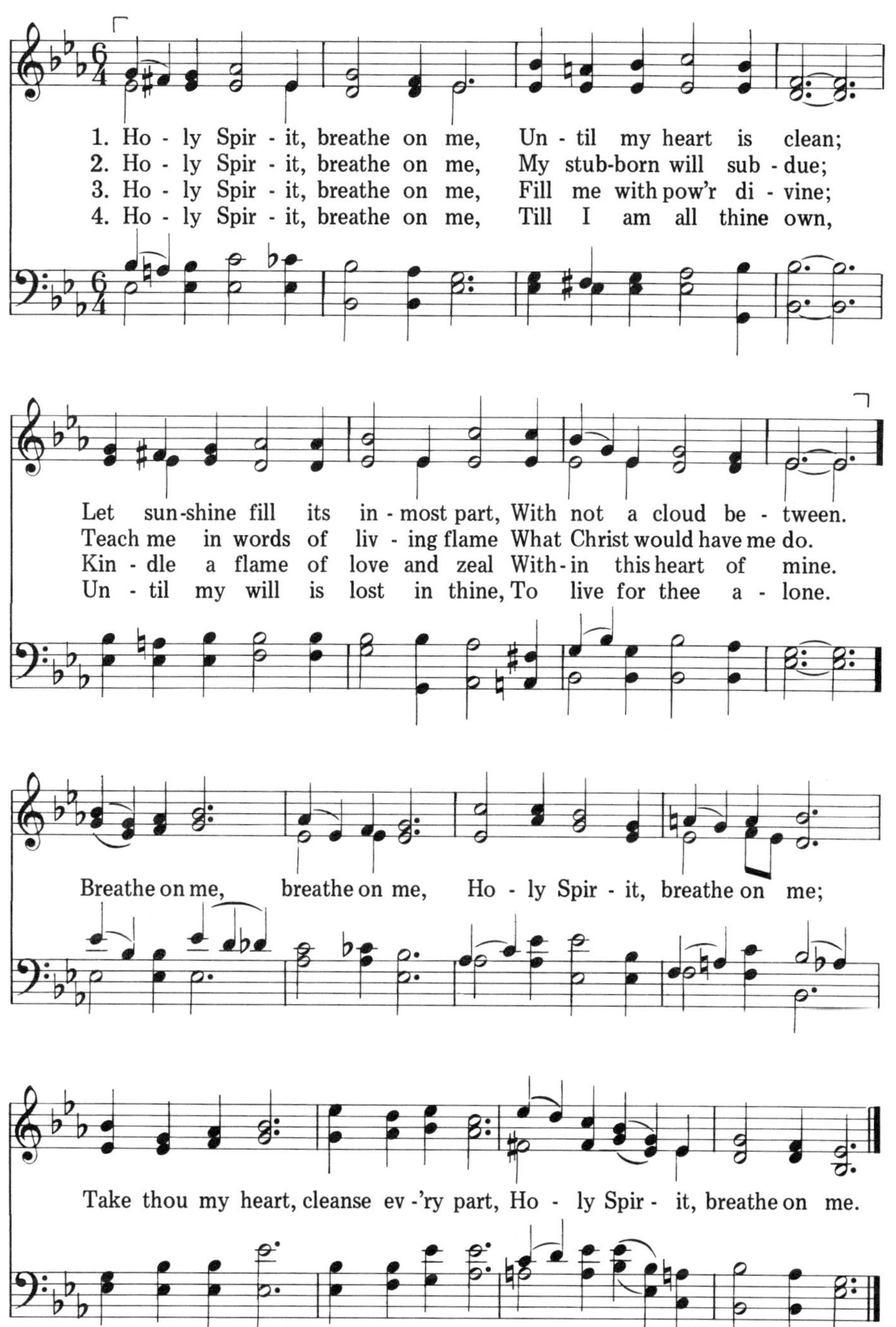

1. Ho - ly Spir - it, breathe on me, Un - til my heart is clean;
2. Ho - ly Spir - it, breathe on me, My stub-born will sub - due;
3. Ho - ly Spir - it, breathe on me, Fill me with pow'r di - vine;
4. Ho - ly Spir - it, breathe on me, Till I am all thine own,

Let sun-shine fill its in - most part, With not a cloud be - tween.
Teach me in words of liv - ing flame What Christ would have me do.
Kin - dle a flame of love and zeal With-in this heart of mine.
Un - til my will is lost in thine, To live for thee a - lone.

Breathe on me, breathe on me, Ho - ly Spir - it, breathe on me;

Take thou my heart, cleanse ev -'ry part, Ho - ly Spir - it, breathe on me.

John 20:22. Words, Edwin Hatch, 1878; adapted, B. B. McKinney, 1937. Tune TRUETT, B. B. McKinney, 1937.

132 Spirit of God, Descend upon My Heart

1. Spir - it of God, de - scend up - on my heart;
2. I ask no dream, no proph - et ec - sta - sies,
3. Teach me to feel that thou art al - ways nigh;
4. Teach me to love thee as thine an - gels love,

Wean it from earth; thro' all its puls - es move;
No sud - den rend - ing of the veil of clay,
Teach me the strug - gles of the soul to bear,
One ho - ly pas - sion fill - ing all my frame;

Stoop to my weak - ness, might - y as thou art,
No an - gel vis - i - tant, no o - p'ning skies;
To check the ris - ing doubt, the reb - el sigh;
The kin - dling of the heav'n - de - scend - ed Dove,

And make me love thee as I ought to love.
But take the dim - ness of my soul a - way.
Teach me the pa - tience of un - an - swered prayer.
My heart an al - tar, and thy love the flame. A - MEN.

Words, George Croly, 1854. Tune MORECAMBE, Frederick C. Atkinson, 1870.

Spirit of God, Our Comforter 133

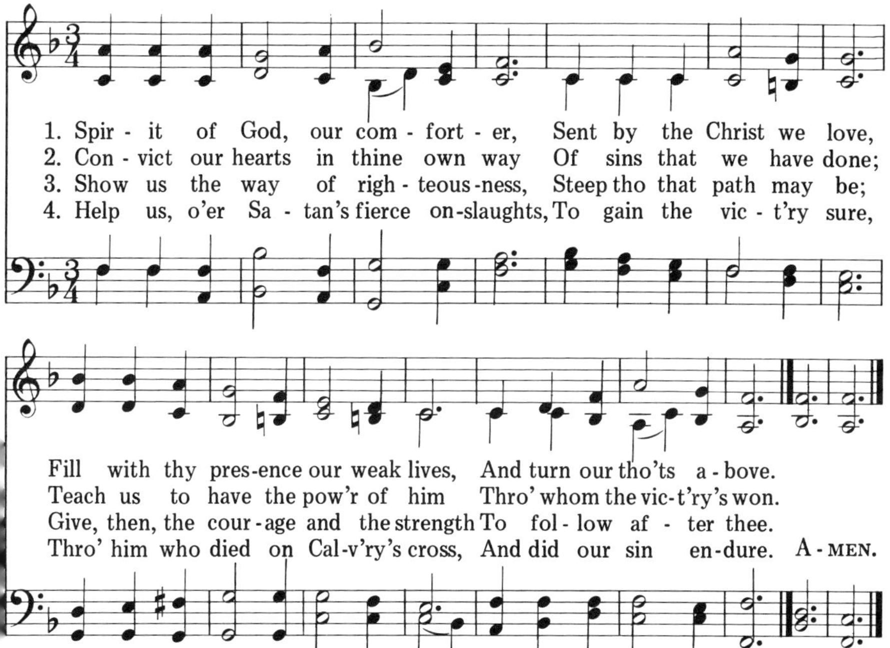

1. Spir - it of God, our com - fort - er, Sent by the Christ we love,
2. Con - vict our hearts in thine own way Of sins that we have done;
3. Show us the way of righ - teous-ness, Steep tho that path may be;
4. Help us, o'er Sa - tan's fierce on-slaughts, To gain the vic - t'ry sure,

Fill with thy pres-ence our weak lives, And turn our tho'ts a - bove.
Teach us to have the pow'r of him Thro' whom the vic-t'ry's won.
Give, then, the cour-age and the strength To fol - low af - ter thee.
Thro' him who died on Cal-v'ry's cross, And did our sin en-dure. A - MEN.

This tune in a higher key, No. 73.

Come, Holy Spirit, Heavenly Dove 134

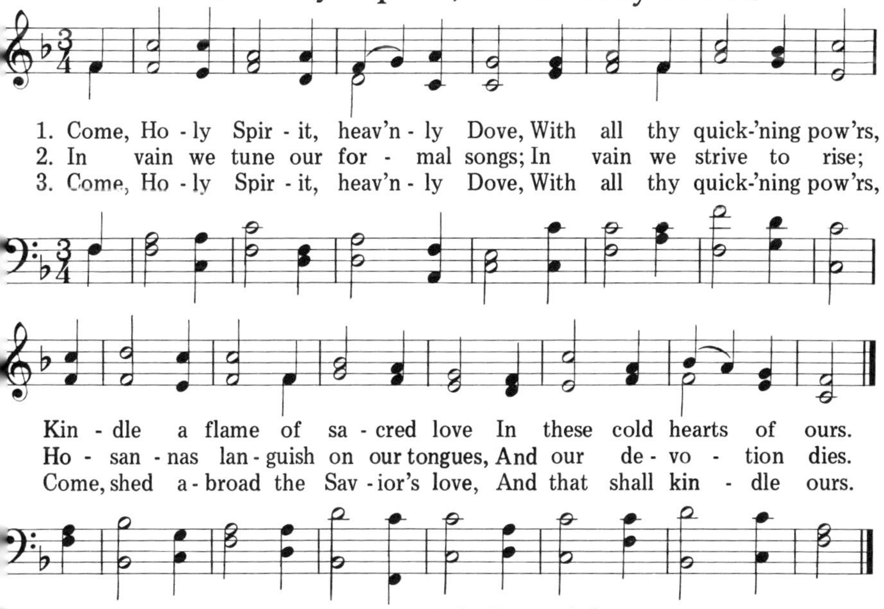

1. Come, Ho - ly Spir - it, heav'n - ly Dove, With all thy quick-'ning pow'rs,
2. In vain we tune our for - mal songs; In vain we strive to rise;
3. Come, Ho - ly Spir - it, heav'n - ly Dove, With all thy quick-'ning pow'rs,

Kin - dle a flame of sa - cred love In these cold hearts of ours.
Ho - san - nas lan - guish on our tongues, And our de - vo - tion dies.
Come, shed a - broad the Sav - ior's love, And that shall kin - dle ours.

Words, Isaac Watts, 1707. Tune MEAR, American Psalm Tune, 18th Century.

135 Holy Spirit, Light Divine

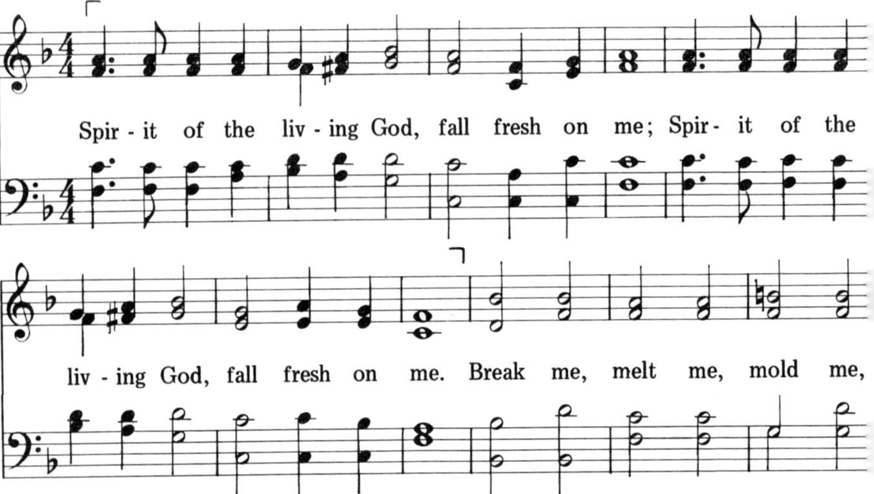

1. Ho - ly Spir - it, Light di - vine, Shine up - on this heart of mine;
2. Ho - ly Spir - it, Pow'r di - vine, Cleanse this guilt - y heart of mine;
3. Ho - ly Spir - it, Joy di - vine, Cheer this sad - dened heart of mine;
4. Ho - ly Spir - it, all di - vine, Dwell with - in this heart of mine;
Chase the shades of night a - way, Turn my dark - ness in - to day.
Long has sin, with - out con - trol, Held do - min - ion o'er my soul.
Bid my man - y woes de - part, Heal my wounded, bleed - ing heart.
Cast down ev - 'ry i - dol throne; Reign su - preme, and reign a - lone. A - MEN.

Words, Andrew Reed, 1817, alt. Tune MERCY, Louis M. Gottschalk, 1854; adapted, Edwin P. Parker c. 1880.

136 Spirit of the Living God

Spir - it of the liv - ing God, fall fresh on me; Spir - it of the liv - ing God, fall fresh on me. Break me, melt me, mold me,

Words and tune IVERSON, Daniel Iverson, 1926; arranged, B. B. McKinney, 1937.

fill me. Spir-it of the liv-ing God, fall fresh on me.

O Breath of Life 137

1. O Breath of Life, come sweep-ing thro' us, Re-vive thy
2. O Wind of God, come bend us, break us, Till hum-bly
3. O Breath of Love, come breathe with-in us, Re-new-ing
4. O Heart of Christ, once bro-ken for us, 'Tis there we
5. Re-vive us, Lord! Is zeal a-bat-ing While har-vest

church with life and pow'r; O Breath of Life, come, cleanse, re-
we con-fess our need; Then in thy ten-der-ness re-
thought and will and heart; Come, Love of Christ, a-fresh to
find our strength and rest; Our bro-ken, con-trite hearts now
fields are vast and white? Re-vive us, Lord, the world is

new us, And fit thy church to meet this hour.
make us, Re-vive, re-store, for this we plead.
win us, Re-vive thy church in ev-'ry part.
so-lace, And let thy wait-ing church be blest.
wait-ing, E-quip thy church to spread the light. A-MEN.

Words, Bessie Porter Head. Tune DET AR ETT FAST ORD, Joel Blomquist.

138 Break Thou the Bread of Life

1. Break thou the bread of life, Dear Lord, to me,
2. Bless thou the truth, dear Lord, To me, to me,
3. Thou art the bread of life, O Lord, to me,
4. O send thy Spir - it, Lord, Now un - to me,
As thou didst break the loaves Be - side the sea;
As thou didst bless the bread By Gal - i - lee;
Thy ho - ly Word the truth That sav - eth me;
That he may touch mine eyes, And make me see:
Be - yond the sa - cred page I seek thee, Lord;
Then shall all bond - age cease, All fet - ters fall;
Give me to eat and live With thee a - bove;
Show me the truth con - cealed With - in thy Word,
My spir - it pants for thee, O liv - ing Word.
And I shall find my peace, My all in all.
Teach me to love thy truth, For thou art love.
And in thy Book re - vealed I see thee, Lord. A - MEN.

John 6:35. Words, st. 1, 2, Mary A. Lathbury, 1877; st. 3, 4, Alexander Groves, 1913. Tune BREAD OF LIFE, William F. Sherwin, 1877.

Holy Bible, Book Divine 139

1. Ho - ly Bi - ble, Book di - vine,
2. Mine to chide me when I rove,
3. Mine to com - fort in dis - tress,
4. Mine to tell of joys to come,

Pre - cious trea - sure, thou art mine:
Mine to show a Sav - ior's love;
Suf - f'ring in this wil - der - ness;
And the reb - el sin - ner's doom:

Mine to tell me whence I came;
Mine thou art to guide and guard;
Mine to show, by liv - ing faith,
O thou ho - ly Book di - vine,

Mine to teach me what I am.
Mine to pun - ish or re - ward.
Man can tri - umph o - ver death.
Pre - cious trea - sure, thou art mine.

Words, John Burton, Sr., 1803. Tune ALETTA, William B. Bradbury, 1858.

140 O Word of God Incarnate

1. O Word of God In-car-nate, O Wis-dom from on high,
2. The church from thee, her Mas-ter, Re-ceived the gift di-vine,
3. It float-eth like a ban-ner Be-fore God's host un-furled;
4. O make thy church, dear Sav-ior, A lamp of pur-est gold,

O Truth un-changed, un-chang-ing, O Light of our dark sky:
And still that light she lift-eth O'er all the earth to shine:
It shin-eth like a bea-con A-bove the dark-ling world:
To bear be-fore the na-tions Thy true light as of old:

We praise thee for the ra-diance That from the hal-lowed page,
It is the sa-cred cas-ket, Where gems of truth are stored;
It is the chart and com-pass That o'er life's surg-ing sea,
O teach thy wan-d'ring pil-grims By this their path to trace,

A lan-tern to our foot-steps, Shines on from age to age.
It is the heav'n-drawn pic-ture Of thee, the liv-ing Word.
'Mid mists and rocks and quick-sands, Still guides, O Christ, to thee.
Till, clouds and dark-ness end-ed, They see thee face to face. A-MEN.

Psalm 119:105. Words, William W. How, 1867. Tune MUNICH, *Neuvermehrtes Gesangbuch*, 1693; adapted, Felix Mendelssohn, 1847.

Christian Men, Arise and Give 141

1. Chris - tian men, a - rise and give Words by which all
2. God's great Book is ours to share With all peo - ple
3. Share God's word — it is our task — An - sw'ring ques - tions
4. Stir your hearts now, let us give Words by which all

men can live. Give a sword to fight the wrong;
ev - 'ry - where. For con - fu - sion, give men light;
that men ask. Set be - fore them val - ues true;
men can live. Give the words that Je - sus taught;

Give for ev - 'ry day a song; Give the sto - ries
For their blind - ness, give them sight; Give the com - fort
With new truth their minds en - due; Give a guide to
Give a peace all men have sought. Word of God now

of the brave; Give the news that Christ can save.
of a Psalm; For our storm - y time, give calm.
point the way For the jour - ney of to - day.
let us share With all peo - ple ev - 'ry - where. A-MEN.

Words, Lois Horton Young, 1966. Copyright 1966 by The Hymn Society of America. Used by permission.
Tune DIX, Conrad Kocher, 1838; adapted, W. H. Monk, 1861.

142 Wonderful Words of Life

1. Sing them o - ver a - gain to me, Won-der-ful words of life;
2. Christ, the bless-ed One, gives to all Won-der-ful words of life;
3. Sweet - ly ech - o the gos - pel call, Won-der-ful words of life;
Let me more of their beau - ty see, Won-der-ful words of life;
Sin - ner, list to the lov - ing call, Won-der-ful words of life;
Of - fer par -don and peace to all, Won-der-ful words of life;
Words of life and beau - ty, Teach me faith and du - ty:
All so free - ly giv - en, Woo - ing us to heav - en:
Je - sus, on - ly Sav - ior, Sanc - ti - fy for - ev - er,
Beau - ti - ful words, won-der - ful words, Won-der - ful words of life;
Beau - ti - ful words, won-der - ful words, Won-der -ful words of life.

Words and tune WORDS OF LIFE, Philip P. Bliss, 1874.

Faith of Our Fathers 143

1. Faith of our fa - thers! liv - ing still In spite of dun - geon,
2. Faith of our fa - thers! we will strive To win all na - tions
3. Faith of our fa - thers! we will love Both friend and foe in

fire, and sword, O how our hearts beat high with joy
un - to thee, And through the truth that comes from God
all our strife, And preach thee, too, as love knows how

When - e'er we hear that glo - rious word! Faith of our fa - thers,
Man - kind shall then be tru - ly free: Faith of our fa - thers,
By kind - ly words and vir - tuous life: Faith of our fa - thers,

ho - ly faith! We will be true to thee till death.
ho - ly faith! We will be true to thee till death.
ho - ly faith! We will be true to thee till death.

Words, Frederick W. Faber, 1849. Tune ST. CATHERINE, Henri F. Hemy, 1864; arranged, James G. Walton, 1874.
This tune in a lower key, No. 326.

144 For All the Saints

Unison
1. For all the saints who from their la-bors rest, Who
2. Thou wast their Rock, their For-tress and their Might; Thou,
3. O may thy sol - diers, faith-ful, true, and bold,
4. And when the strife is fierce, the war-fare long,
5. From earth's wide bounds, from o-cean's far-thest coast, Thro'
thee by faith be - fore the world con-fessed, Thy
Lord, their cap - tain in the well-fought fight;
Fight as the saints who no - bly fought of old, And
Steals on the ear the dis - tant tri - umph song, And
gates of pearl streams in the count - less host, Sing -
name, O Je - sus, be for - ev - er blest.
Thou, in the dark - ness drear, their one true light.
win with them the vic - tor's crown of gold.
hearts are brave a - gain, and arms are strong.
ing to Fa - ther, Son, and Ho - ly Ghost,

Words, William W. How, 1864. Tune SINE NOMINE, Ralph Vaughan Williams, 1906. Music from *The English Hymnal* by permission of Oxford University Press.
This tune in a lower key, No. 43.

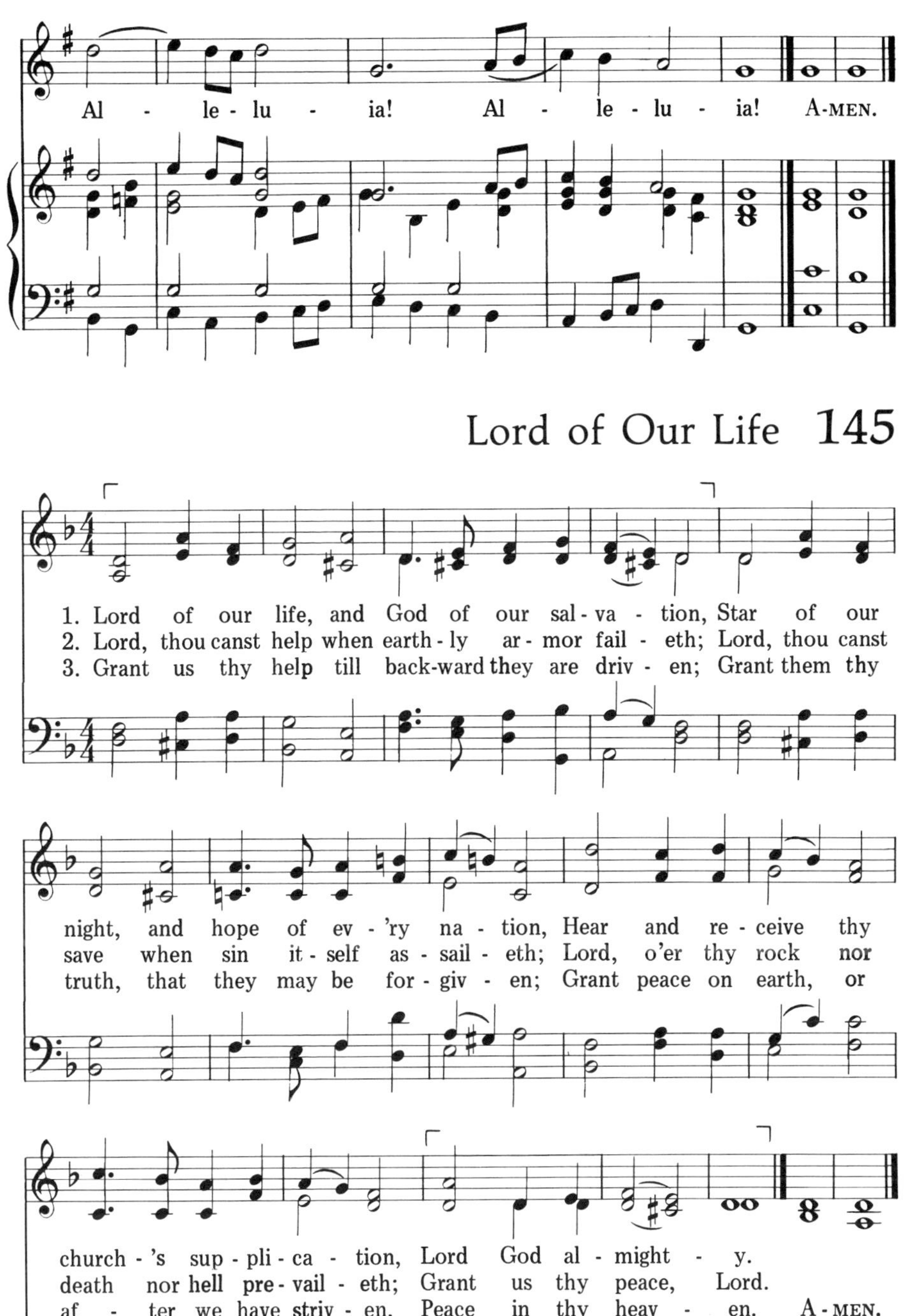

Al - le - lu - ia! Al - le - lu - ia! A-MEN.

Lord of Our Life 145

1. Lord of our life, and God of our sal - va - tion, Star of our
2. Lord, thou canst help when earth - ly ar - mor fail - eth; Lord, thou canst
3. Grant us thy help till back-ward they are driv - en; Grant them thy

night, and hope of ev - 'ry na - tion, Hear and re - ceive thy
save when sin it - self as - sail - eth; Lord, o'er thy rock nor
truth, that they may be for - giv - en; Grant peace on earth, or

church - 's sup - pli - ca - tion, Lord God al - might - y.
death nor hell pre - vail - eth; Grant us thy peace, Lord.
af - ter we have striv - en, Peace in thy heav - en. A-MEN.

Words, Philip Pusey, 1834, based on Matthäus von Löwenstern, 1644. Tune ISTE CONFESSOR (ROUEN), *Poitiers Antiphoner*, 1746.

146 Forward Through the Ages

1. For - ward through the a - ges, In un - bro - ken line,
2. Wid - er grows the king - dom, Reign of love and light;
3. Not a - lone we con - quer, Not a - lone we fall;

Move the faith - ful spir - its At the call di - vine:
For it we must la - bor Till our faith is sight:
In each loss or tri - umph Lose or tri - umph all:

Gifts in dif - f'ring mea - sure, Hearts of one ac - cord,
Proph - ets have pro - claimed it, Mar - tyrs tes - ti - fied,
Bound by God's far pur - pose In one liv - ing whole,

Man - i - fold the ser - vice, One the sure re - ward.
Po - ets sung its glo - ry, He - roes for it died.
Move we on to - geth - er To the shin - ing goal.

Words, Frederick L. Hosmer, 1908. Tune ST. GERTRUDE, Arthur S. Sullivan, 1871.

For - ward through the a - ges, In un - bro - ken line,
Move the faith - ful spir - its At the call di - vine.

We Are Climbing Jacob's Ladder 147

1. We are climb - ing Ja - cob's lad - der, We are climb - ing Ja - cob's
2. Ev - 'ry round goes high - er, high - er, Ev - 'ry round goes high - er,
3. Sin - ner, do you love my Je - sus? Sin - ner, do you love my
4. If you love him, why not serve him? If you love him, why not

lad - der, We are climb - ing Ja - cob's lad - der, Sol - diers of the cross.
high - er, Ev - 'ry round goes high - er, high - er, Sol - diers of the cross.
Je - sus? Sin - ner, do you love my Je - sus? Sol - diers of the cross.
serve him? If you love him, why not serve him? Sol - diers of the cross.

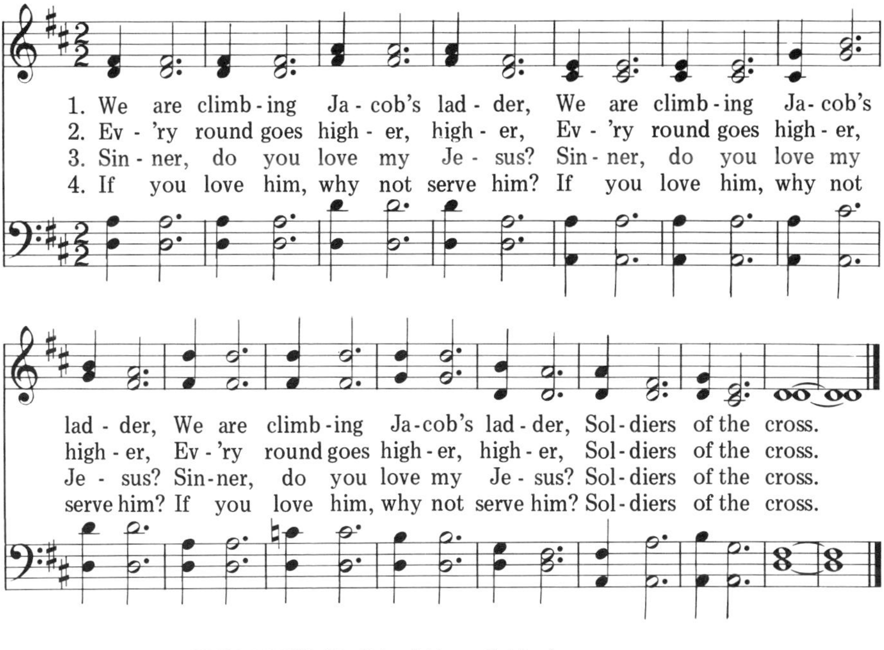

Words and tune JACOB'S LADDER, Traditional Negro Spiritual.

148 Word of God, Across the Ages

1. Word of God, a - cross the a - ges Comes thy mes-sage to our life;
2. Sto - ry of man's won-drous jour - ney From the shad-ows of the night;
3. In the tongues of all the peo - ples May the mes-sage bless and heal,

Source of hope for - ev - er pres - ent In our toil and fears and strife;
Gar - nered truth of sage and proph- et, Guid - ing for-ward in - to light;
As de -vout and pa - tient schol -ars More and more its depths re - veal;

Con - stant wit - ness to God's mer - cy, Still our grace what-e'er be - fall,
Words and deeds of Christ our Mas - ter, Point-ing to the life and way,
Bless, O God, to wise and sim - ple, All thy truth of age - less worth,

Guide un-fail - ing, strength e -ter - nal, Of - fered free - ly to us all.
Still ap-peal-ing, still in-spir-ing, 'Mid the strug - gles of to - day.
Till all lands re - ceive the wit - ness And thy knowl-edge fills the earth.

Words, Ferdinand Q. Blanchard, 1951. From *Ten New Hymns on the Bible,* copyright 1953 by The Hymn Society of America. Used by permission. Tune AUSTRIAN HYMN, Franz Joseph Haydn, 1797. This tune in a lower key, No. 405.

God of Our Fathers 149

(Trumpets before each stanza)
1. God of our fa - thers, whose al - might - y
2. Thy love di - vine hath led us in the
3. From war's a - larms, from dead - ly pes - ti-
4. Re - fresh thy peo - ple on their toil-some
hand Leads forth in beau - ty all the star - ry band
past, In this free land by thee our lot is cast;
lence, Be thy strong arm our ev - er sure de - fense;
way, Lead us from night to nev - er - end - ing day;
Of shin - ing worlds in splen - dor thro' the skies,
Be thou our rul - er, guard - ian, guide, and stay,
Thy true re - li - gion in our hearts in - crease,
Fill all our lives with love and grace di - vine,
Our grate - ful songs be - fore thy throne a - rise.
Thy Word our law, thy paths our cho - sen way.
Thy boun-teous good - ness nour - ish us in peace.
And glo - ry, laud, and praise be ev - er thine. A - MEN.

Words, Daniel C. Roberts, 1876. Tune NATIONAL HYMN, George W. Warren, 1876.

150 God, Who Stretched the Spangled Heavens

1. God, who stretched the span - gled heav - ens In - fi - nite in
2. We have con-quered worlds un-dreamed of Since the child-hood
3. As thy new ho - ri - zons beck - on, Fa - ther, give us

time and place, Flung the suns in burn - ing ra - diance Thro' the
of our race, Known the ec - sta - sy of wing - ing Thro' un -
strength to be Chil - dren of cre - a - tive pur - pose, Serv - ing

si - lent fields of space, We, thy chil - dren, in thy like - ness,
chart - ed realms of space, Probed the se - crets of the at - om,
man and hon - 'ring thee, Till our dreams are rich with mean - ing,

Share in - ven - tive pow'rs with thee, Great Cre - a - tor,
Yield - ing un - im - ag - ined pow'r, Fac - ing us with
Each en - deav - or thy de - sign, Great Cre - a - tor,

Words, Catherine C. Arnott, 1965. Used by permission of the author. Tune HYMN TO JOY, Ludwig van Beethoven, 1826; arranged, Edward Hodges, 1864.
This tune in a higher key, No. 31.

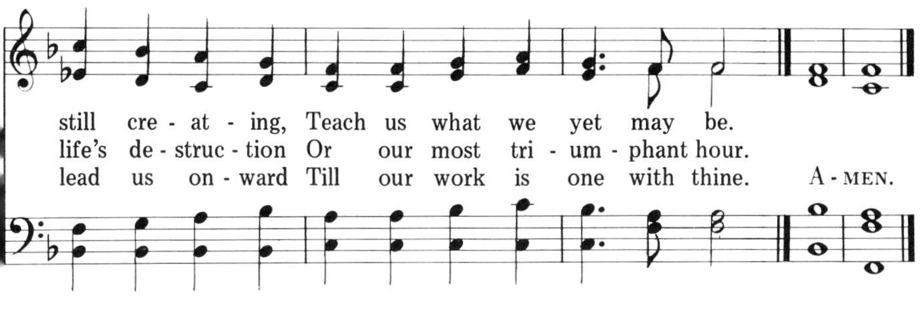

still cre - at - ing, Teach us what we yet may be.
life's de - struc - tion Or our most tri - um - phant hour.
lead us on - ward Till our work is one with thine. A - MEN.

Morning Has Broken 151

Unison

1. Morn - ing has bro - ken Like the first morn - ing, Black-bird has
2. Sweet the rain's new fall Sun - lit from heav - en, Like the first
3. Mine is the sun - light! Mine is the morn - ing Born of the

spo - ken Like the first bird. Praise for the sing - ing!
dew - fall On the first grass. Praise for the sweet - ness
one light E - den saw play! Praise with e - la - tion,

Praise for the morn - ing! Praise for them, spring - ing Fresh from the Word!
Of the wet gar - den, Sprung in com - plete - ness Where his feet pass.
Praise ev - 'ry morn - ing, God's re - cre - a - tion Of the new day!

Words, Eleanor Farjeon, 1931. Words copyright used by permission David Higham Associates, Ltd., London. Tune BUNESSAN, Traditional Gaelic Melody.

152 The Cattle on a Thousand Hills

1. The cat-tle on a thou-sand hills are his, How
2. The star-ry hosts in vel-vet skies are his, He
3. The wis-dom of the u-ni-verse is his, In
4. All praise and glo-ry to the Fa-ther God, All

rich our God a-bove. He knows and calls us
made them ev-'ry one. The light he gives for
him it all be-gan. And now the Spir-it
praise to Christ the Son. And to the Spir-it

each by name, How great our Fa-ther's love. How great our Fa-ther's
all our way Is Je-sus Christ the Son. Is Je-sus Christ the
of all truth Is giv-en to each one. Is giv-en to each
praise be giv'n, All hail, blest Three in One. All hail, blest Three in

love, How great our Fa-ther's love; He
Son, Is Je-sus Christ the Son; The
one, Is giv-en to each one; And
One, All hail, blest Three in One; We

knows and calls us each by name, How great our Fa - ther's love.
light he gives for all our way Is Je - sus Christ the Son.
now the Spir - it of all truth Is giv - en to each one.
lift our hearts with praise to sing, All hail, blest Three in One.

My God Is There, Controlling 153

Unison

1. We search the star - lit Milk - y Way, A mil - lion worlds
2. But as I grope from sphere to sphere, New won - ders crowd
3. We probe the at - oms for their cause, Ex - plore the earth
4. Each flash of fact from out the night, Each burst of truth

in rhyth - mic sway, Yet in our blind - ness some will say,
the eye, the ear, And faith grows firm - er ev - 'ry year:
for na - ture's laws, Yet sel - dom in our search - ing pause
up - on my sight That quick - ens awe or adds de - light,

"There is no God con - trol - ling, con - trol - ling!"
"My God is there, con - trol - ling, con - trol - ling!"
To think of God con - trol - ling, con - trol - ling.
Re - veals my God con - trol - ling, con - trol - ling.

154 I Sing the Almighty Power of God

1. I sing th'al-might-y pow'r of God, That made the moun-tains rise,
2. I sing the good - ness of the Lord, That filled the earth with food;
3. There's not a plant or flow'r be - low, But makes thy glo - ries known;
That spread the flow - ing seas a - broad, And built the loft - y skies.
He formed the crea - tures with his Word, And then pro-nounced them good.
And clouds a - rise, and tem - pests blow, By or - der from thy throne;
I sing the wis - dom that or - dained The sun to rule the day;
Lord, how thy won - ders are dis - played, Wher - e'er I turn my eye,
While all that bor - rows life from thee Is ev - er in thy care,
The moon shines full at his com-mand, And all the stars o - bey.
If I sur - vey the ground I tread, Or gaze up - on the sky!
And ev - 'ry-where that man can be, Thou, God, art pres - ent there.

Genesis 1. Words, Isaac Watts, 1715. Tune FOREST GREEN, Traditional English Melody; arranged, Ralph Vaughan Williams, 1906. From *The English Hymnal* by permission of Oxford University Press.

This Is My Father's World 155

1. This is my Fa - ther's world, And to my lis - t'ning ears,
2. This is my Fa - ther's world, The birds their car - ols raise;
3. This is my Fa - ther's world, O let me ne'er for - get

All na - ture sings, and round me rings The mus - ic of the spheres.
The morn - ing light, the lil - y white De - clare their Mak - er's praise.
That though the wrong seems oft so strong, God is the Rul - er yet.

This is my Fa - ther's world, I rest me in the thought Of
This is my Fa - ther's world, He shines in all that's fair; In the
This is my Fa - ther's world, The bat - tle is not done; Je -

rocks and trees, of skies and seas; His hand the won - ders wrought.
rust - ling grass I hear him pass, He speaks to me ev - 'ry - where.
sus who died shall be sat - is - fied, And earth and heav - en be one.

Words, Maltbie D. Babcock, 1901. Tune TERRA PATRIS, Franklin L. Sheppard, 1915.

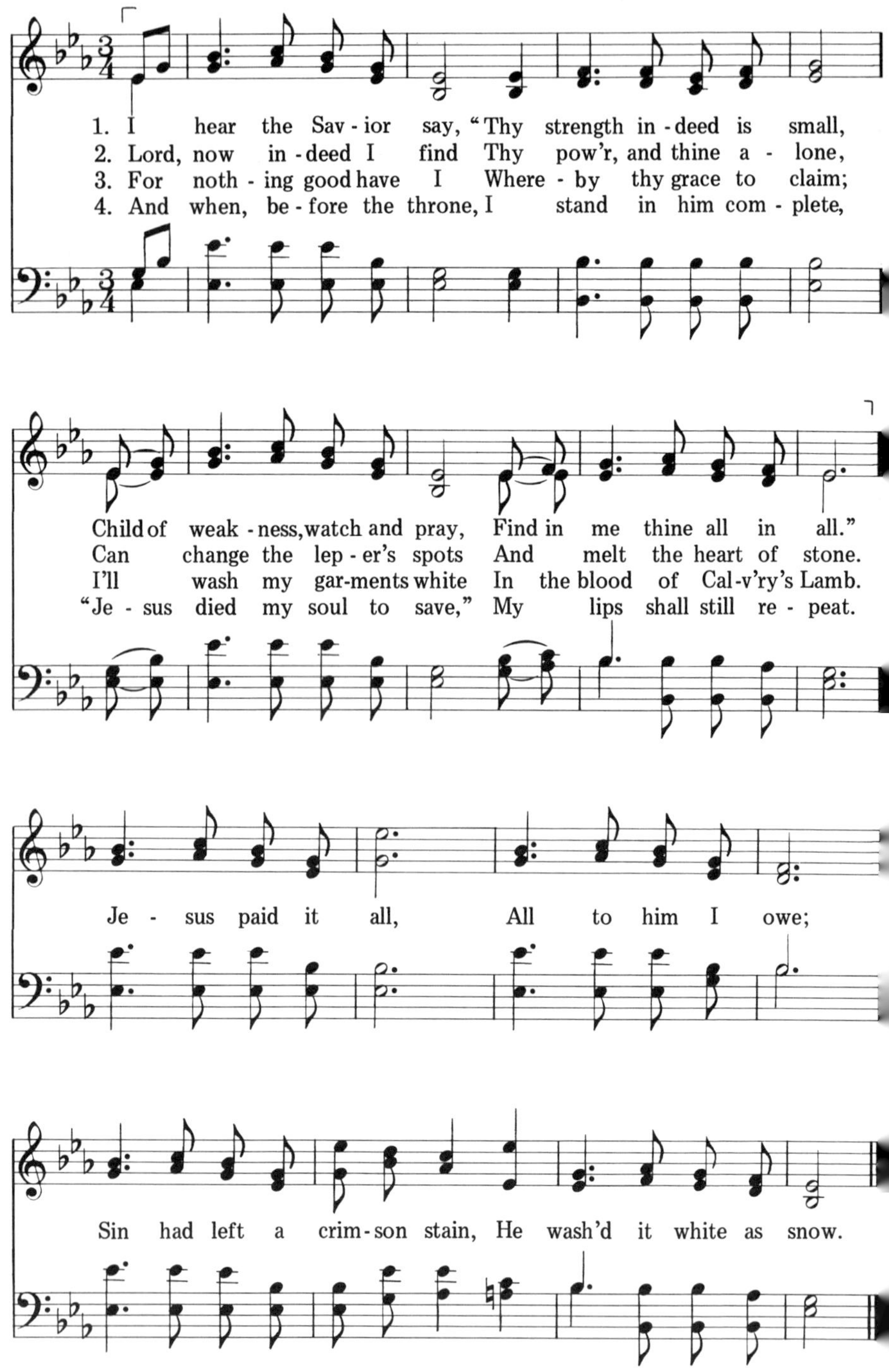

156 Jesus Paid It All

1. I hear the Sav-ior say, "Thy strength in-deed is small,
2. Lord, now in-deed I find Thy pow'r, and thine a-lone,
3. For noth-ing good have I Where-by thy grace to claim;
4. And when, be-fore the throne, I stand in him com-plete,

Child of weak-ness, watch and pray, Find in me thine all in all."
Can change the lep-er's spots And melt the heart of stone.
I'll wash my gar-ments white In the blood of Cal-v'ry's Lamb.
"Je-sus died my soul to save," My lips shall still re-peat.

Je - sus paid it all, All to him I owe;

Sin had left a crim-son stain, He wash'd it white as snow.

Words, Elvina M. Hall, 1865. Tune ALL TO CHRIST, John T. Grape, 1868.

1. A - las, and did my Sav - ior bleed, And did my Sov-'reign die?
2. Was it for crimes that I had done He groaned up - on the tree?
3. Well might the sun in dark - ness hide, And shut his glo - ries in,
4. But drops of grief can ne'er re - pay The debt of love I owe;

Would he de -vote that sa - cred head For sin - ners such as I?
A - maz - ing pit - y, grace un-known, And love be-yond de - gree!
When Christ the might - y Mak - er died For man, the crea-ture's sin.
Here, Lord, I give my - self a - way, 'Tis all that I can do.

At the cross, at the cross where I first saw the light, And the

bur - den of my heart rolled a - way (rolled away), It was there by faith

I re - ceived my sight, And now I am hap - py all the day!

Words, Isaac Watts, 1707; Refrain, Ralph E. Hudson, 1885. Tune HUDSON, Ralph E. Hudson, 1885.

158 Nothing but the Blood

1. What can wash a - way my sin? Noth-ing but the blood of Je - sus;
2. For my par - don this I see, Noth-ing but the blood of Je - sus;
3. Noth-ing can for sin a - tone, Noth-ing but the blood of Je - sus;
4. This is all my hope and peace, Noth-ing but the blood of Je - sus;
What can make me whole a - gain? Noth-ing but the blood of Je - sus.
For my cleans-ing, this my plea, Noth-ing but the blood of Je - sus.
Naught of good that I have done, Noth-ing but the blood of Je - sus.
This is all my righ-teous-ness, Noth-ing but the blood of Je - sus.
Oh! pre - cious is the flow That makes me white as snow;
No oth - er fount I know, Noth-ing but the blood of Je - sus.

Hebrews 9:22. Words and tune PLAINFIELD, Robert Lowry, 1876.

There Is Power in the Blood 159

1. Would you be free from the bur-den of sin? There's pow'r in the blood,
2. Would you be free from your pas-sion and pride? There's pow'r in the blood,
3. Would you be whit-er, much whit-er than snow? There's pow'r in the blood,
4. Would you do ser-vice for Je-sus your King? There's pow'r in the blood,
pow'r in the blood; Would you o'er e-vil a vic-to-ry win? There's
pow'r in the blood; Come for a cleans-ing to Cal-va-ry's tide; There's
pow'r in the blood; Sin stains are lost in its life-giv-ing flow; There's
pow'r in the blood; Would you live dai-ly his prais-es to sing? There's
won-der-ful pow'r in the blood. There is pow'r, pow'r, Wonder-working pow'r
there is
In the blood of the Lamb; There is pow'r, pow'r,
In the blood of the Lamb; there is
Won-der-work-ing pow'r In the pre-cious blood of the Lamb.

Words and tune POWER IN THE BLOOD, Lewis E. Jones, 1899.

160 Saved, Saved!

Unison
1. I've found a friend who is all to me, His
2. He saves me from ev - 'ry sin and harm, Se -
3. When poor and need - y and all a - lone, In
love is ev - er true; I love to tell how he
cures my soul each day; I'm lean - ing strong on his
love he said to me, "Come un - to me and I'll
lift - ed me, And what his grace can do for you.
might - y arm; I know he'll guide me all the way.
lead you home, To live with me e - ter - nal - ly."
Harmony
Saved by his pow'r di - vine, Saved to new life sub-lime!
Saved by his pow'r, Saved to new life,
Life now is sweet and my joy is com-plete, For I'm saved, saved, saved!

Words and tune RAPTURE, Jack P. Scholfield, 1911.

The Way of the Cross Leads Home 161

1. I must needs go home by the way of the cross,
2. I must needs go on in the blood - sprin - kled way,
3. Then I bid fare - well to the way of the world,

There's no oth - er way but this; I shall ne'er get sight
The path that the Sav - ior trod, If I ev - er climb
To walk in it nev - er - more; For my Lord says, "Come,"

of the gates of light, If the way of the cross I miss.
to the heights sub - lime, Where the soul is at home with God.
and I seek my home, Where he waits at the o - pen door.

The way of the cross leads home, The way of the cross leads home;
leads home, leads home;

It is sweet to know as I on-ward go, The way of the cross leads home.

Words, Jessie B. Pounds, 1906. Tune WAY OF THE CROSS, Charles H. Gabriel, 1906.

162 Are You Washed in the Blood

1. Have you been to Je-sus for the cleans-ing pow'r? Are you
2. Are you walk-ing dai-ly by the Sav-ior's side? Are you
3. When the Bride-groom com-eth will your robes be white? Are you
4. Lay a-side the gar-ments that are stained with sin, And be
washed in the blood of the Lamb? Are you ful-ly trust-ing
washed in the blood of the Lamb? Do you rest each mo-ment
washed in the blood of the Lamb? Will your soul be read-y
washed in the blood of the Lamb? There's a foun-tain flow-ing
in his grace this hour? Are you washed in the blood of the Lamb?
in the Cru-ci-fied? Are you washed in the blood of the Lamb?
for the man-sions bright, And be washed in the blood of the Lamb?
for the soul un-clean, O be washed in the blood of the Lamb?
Are you washed in the blood,
Are you washed in the blood,
In the
soul-cleans-ing blood of the Lamb? Are your garments spot-less?
of the Lamb?

Words and tune WASHED IN THE BLOOD, Elisha A. Hoffman, 1878.

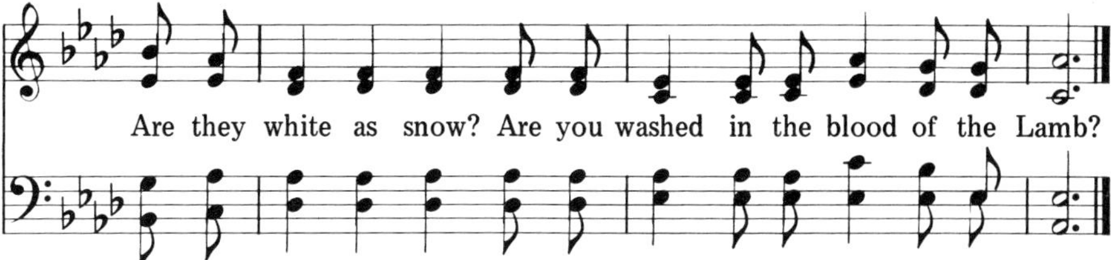
Are they white as snow? Are you washed in the blood of the Lamb?

Rock of Ages, Cleft for Me 163

1. Rock of A - ges, cleft for me, Let me hide my - self in thee;
2. Not the la - bors of my hands Can ful - fill thy law's de-mands;
3. While I draw this fleet- ing breath, When mine eyes shall close in death,

Let the wa - ter and the blood, From thy wound - ed side which flowed,
Could my zeal no res- pite know, Could my tears for - ev - er flow,
When I rise to worlds un-known, And be - hold thee on thy throne,

Be of sin the dou - ble cure, Save from wrath and make me pure.
All for sin could not a - tone; Thou must save, and thou a - lone.
Rock of A - ges, cleft for me, Let me hide my - self in thee. A - MEN.

Psalm 94:22. Words, Augustus M. Toplady, 1775, 1776. Tune TOPLADY, Thomas Hastings, 1832.

164 Grace Greater than Our Sin

1. Mar - vel - ous grace of our lov - ing Lord, Grace that ex - ceeds our
2. Dark is the stain that we can - not hide, What can a - vail to
3. Mar - vel - ous, in - fi - nite, match - less grace, Free - ly be - stowed on

sin and our guilt, Yon - der on Cal - va - ry's mount out - poured,
wash it a - way? Look! there is flow - ing a crim - son tide;
all who be - lieve; All who are long - ing to see his face,

There where the blood of the Lamb was spilt. Grace, grace,
Whit - er than snow you may be to - day.
Will you this mo - ment his grace re - ceive? Mar - vel - ous grace,

God's grace, Grace that will par - don and cleanse with - in; Grace,
in - fi - nite grace,
Mar - vel - ous

Words, Julia H. Johnston, 1910. Tune MOODY, Daniel B. Towner, 1910. Copyright 1910. Renewal 193
extended. Hope Publishing Co., owner. All rights reserved. Used by permission.

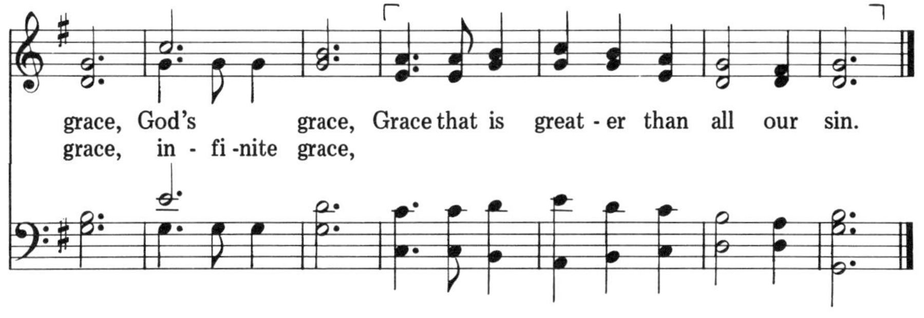

grace, God's grace, Grace that is great - er than all our sin.
grace, in - fi -nite grace,

Amazing Grace! How Sweet the Sound 165

1. A - maz - ing grace! how sweet the sound, That saved a wretch like me!
2. 'Twas grace that taught my heart to fear, And grace my fears re - lieved;
3. Thro' man - y dan - gers, toils, and snares, I have al - read - y come;
4. The Lord has prom - ised good to me, His word my hope se - cures;
5. When we've been there ten thou - sand years, Bright shin-ing as the sun,

I once was lost, but now am found, Was blind, but now I see.
How pre - cious did that grace ap - pear The hour I first be -lieved!
'Tis grace hath bro't me safe thus far, And grace will lead me home.
He will my shield and por - tion be As long as life en -dures.
We've no less days to sing God's praise Than when we first be-gun. A-MEN.

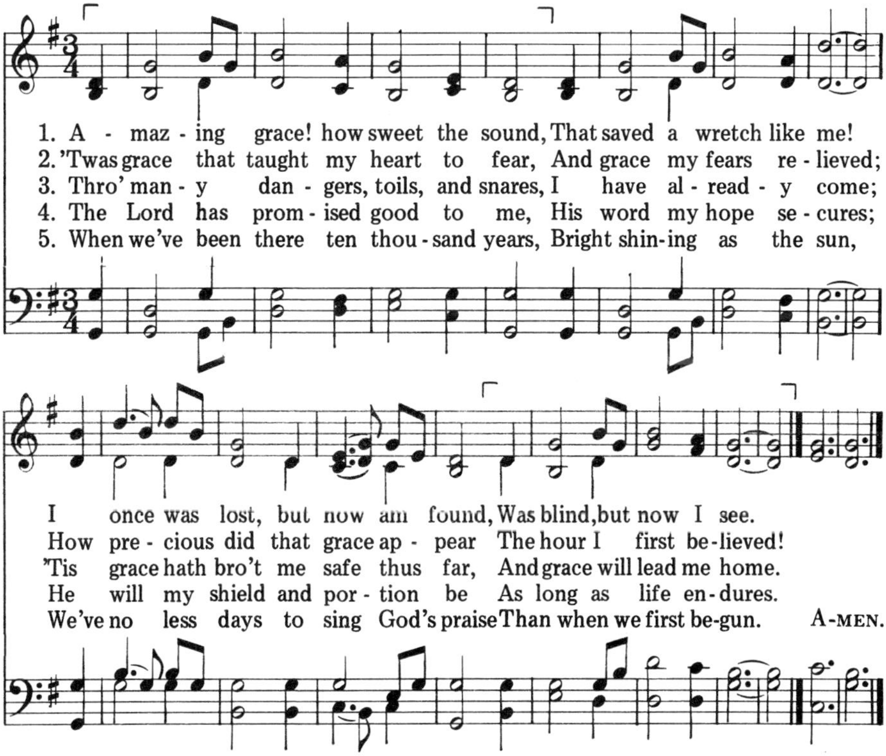

Words, st.1-4, John Newton, 1779; st. 5, Anonymous. Tune AMAZING GRACE, *Virginia Harmony*, 1831; arranged, Edwin O. Excell, 1900.

166 At Calvary

1. Years I spent in van - i - ty and pride, Car - ing not my Lord was
2. By God's Word at last my sin I learned; Then I trem-bled at the
3. Now I've giv'n to Je - sus ev - 'ry-thing, Now I glad - ly own him
4. Oh, the love that drew sal - va-tion's plan! Oh, the grace that bro't it

cru - ci - fied, Know-ing not it was for me he died On Cal - va - ry.
law I'd spurned, Till my guilt - y soul im - plor-ing turned To Cal - va - ry.
as my King, Now my rap-tured soul can on - ly sing Of Cal - va - ry.
down to man! Oh, the might-y gulf that God did span At Cal - va - ry.

Mer - cy there was great, and grace was free; Par - don there was mul - ti -

plied to me; There my bur-dened soul found lib - er - ty At Cal - va - ry.

Words, William R. Newell, 1895. Tune CALVARY, Daniel B. Towner, 1895.

Christ Receiveth Sinful Men 167

1. Sin - ners Je - sus will re - ceive: Sound this word of grace to all
2. Come, and he will give you rest; Trust him, for his word is plain;
3. Now my heart condemns me not, Pure be - fore the law I stand;
4. Christ re -ceiv -eth sin -ful men, E - ven me with all my sin;
Who the heav'n - ly path - way leave, All who lin - ger, all who fall.
He will take the sin - ful - est; Christ re - ceiv - eth sin - ful men.
He who cleansed me from all spot, Sat - is - fied its last de - mand.
Purged from ev - 'ry spot and stain, Heav'n with him I en - ter in.
Sing it o'er and o'er a - gain; Christ re-
Sing it o'er a-gain, Sing it o'er a-gain; Christ re-
ceiv - eth sin - ful men; Make the mes - sage
ceiv -eth sin-ful men, Christ re - ceiveth sin-ful men; Make the message plain,
clear and plain: Christ re - ceiv - eth sin - ful men.
Make the mes-sage plain:

Luke 15:1-7. Words, Erdmann Neumeister, 1718; translated, Emma F. Bevan, 1858. Tune NEUMEISTER, James McGranahan, 1883.

168 Free from the Law, O Happy Condition

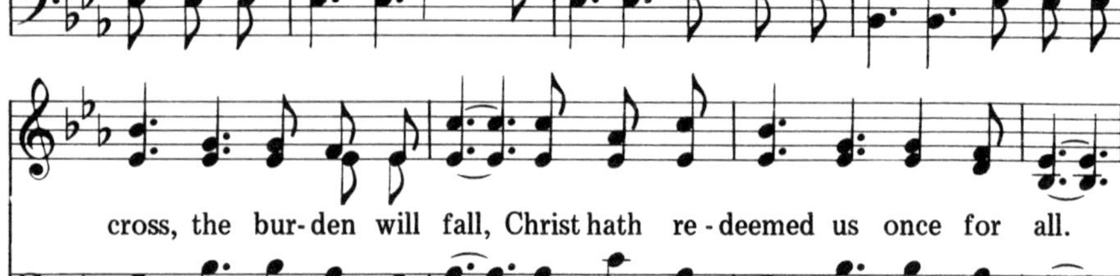

1. Free from the law, O hap-py con-di-tion, Je-sus hath
2. Now are we free, there's no con-dem-na-tion, Je-sus pro-
3. "Chil-dren of God," O glo-ri-ous call-ing, Sure-ly his

bled, and there is re-mis-sion; Cursed by the law and bruised by the
vides a per-fect sal-va-tion; "Come un-to me," O hear his sweet
grace will keep us from fall-ing; Pass-ing from death to life at his

fall, Grace hath re-deemed us once for all.
call, Come, and he saves us once for all. Once for all, O
call, Bless-ed sal-va-tion once for all.

sin-ner, re-ceive it, Once for all, O friend, now be-lieve it; Cling to the

cross, the bur-den will fall, Christ hath re-deemed us once for all.

Words and tune ONCE FOR ALL, Philip P. Bliss, 1873.

"Whosoever" Meaneth Me 169

1. I am hap-py to-day and the sun shines bright,
2. All my hopes have been raised, O his name be praised,
3. O what won-der-ful love, O what grace di-vine,

The clouds have been rolled a-way; For the Sav-ior said, who-so-
His glo-ry has filled my soul; I've been lift-ed up, and from
That Je-sus should die for me; I was lost in sin, for the

ev-er will May come with him to stay (to stay).
sin set free, His blood has made me whole(me whole)."Who-so-ev-er,"
world I pined, But now I am set free (set free).

sure-ly mean-eth me, Sure-ly mean-eth me, O sure-ly mean-eth me;

"Who-so-ev-er," sure-ly meaneth me, "Who-so-ev-er," mean-eth me.

170 He Included Me

1. I am so hap - py in Christ to - day,
2. Glad - ly I read, "Who - so - ev - er may
3. Ev - er God's Spir - it is say - ing, "Come!"
4. "Free - ly come drink," words the soul to thrill!
That I go sing - ing a - long my way; Yes, I'm so
Come to the foun - tain of life to - day"; But when I
Hear the Bride say - ing, "No long - er roam"; But I am
O with what joy they my heart do fill! For when he
hap - py to know and say, "Je - sus in - clud - ed me, too."
read it I al - ways say, "Je - sus in - clud - ed me, too."
sure while they're call - ing home, Je - sus in - clud - ed me, too.
said, "Who - so - ev - er will," Je - sus in - clud - ed me, too.
Je - sus in - clud - ed me, Yes, he in - clud - ed me, When the Lord said

Words, Johnson Oatman, Jr., 1909. Tune SEWELL, Hampton H. Sewell, 1909. Copyright 1914. Renewal 1942, John T. Benson, Jr. All rights reserved. Used by permission.

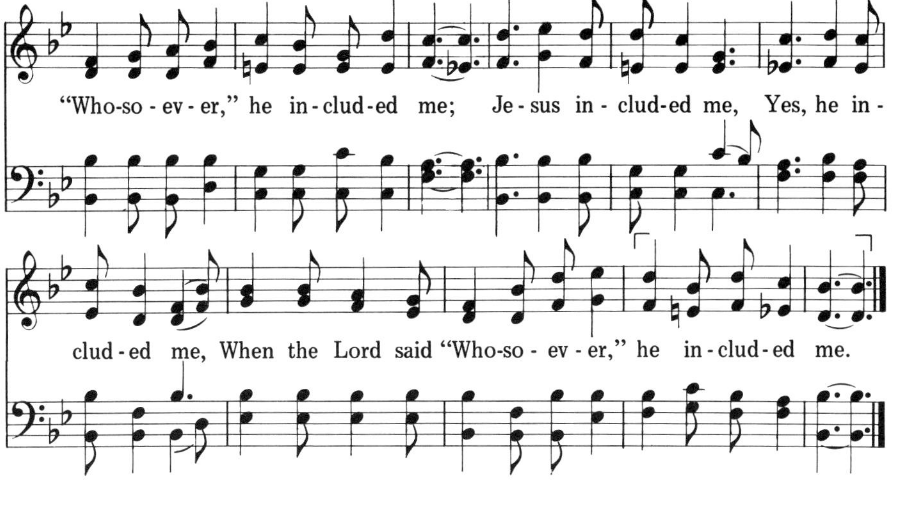

"Who-so - ev - er," he in-clud-ed me; Je - sus in - clud-ed me, Yes, he in -
clud - ed me, When the Lord said "Who-so - ev - er," he in - clud-ed me.

There's a Wideness in God's Mercy 171

1. There's a wide-ness in God's mer-cy, Like the wide- ness of the sea;
2. There is wel-come for the sin- ner, And more grac - es for the good;
3. But we make his love too nar-row By false lim - its of our own;
4. For the love of God is broad-er Than the mea - sure of man's mind;

There's a kind-ness in his jus-tice, Which is more than lib - er - ty.
There is mer-cy with the Sav-ior; There is heal-ing in his blood.
And we mag-ni - fy his strictness With a zeal he will not own.
And the heart of the E - ter-nal Is most won- der - ful-ly kind.

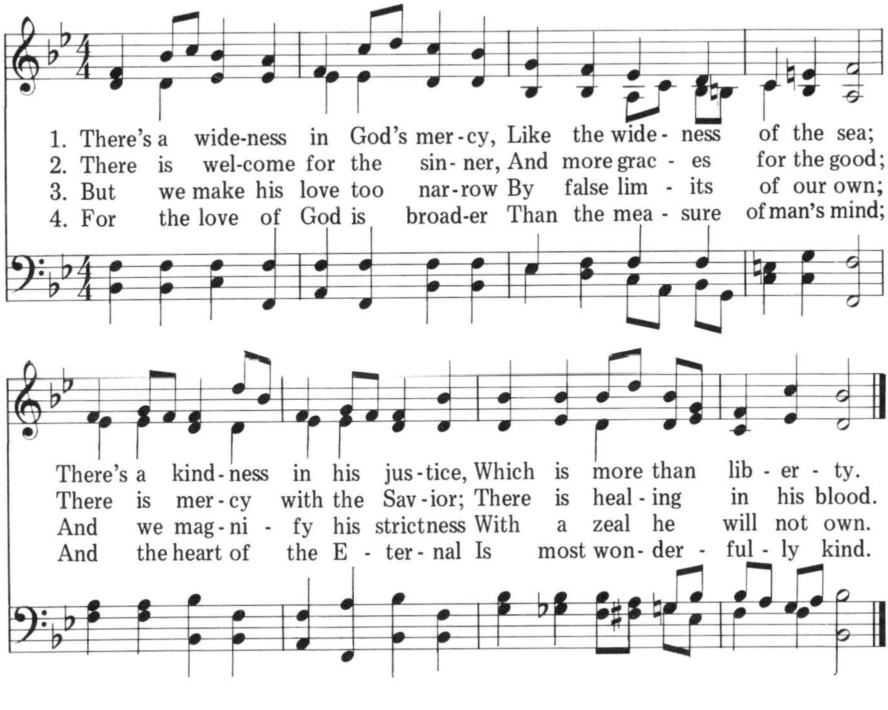

Words, Frederick W. Faber, 1862. Tune WELLESLEY, Lizzie S. Tourjee, 1878.

172 Jesus, Lover of My Soul

1. Je - sus, lov - er of my soul, Let me to thy bos - om fly,
2. Oth - er ref - uge have I none; Hangs my help-less soul on thee;
3. Thou, O Christ, art all I want; More than all in thee I find:
4. Plen-teous grace with thee is found, Grace to cov - er all my sin;
While the near - er wa - ters roll, While the tem - pest still is high:
Leave, O leave me not a - lone, Still sup-port and com - fort me:
Raise the fall - en, cheer the faint, Heal the sick and lead the blind:
Let the heal - ing streams a - bound; Make and keep me pure with - in:
Hide me, O my Sav - ior, hide, Till the storm of life is past;
All my trust on thee is stayed, All my help from thee I bring;
Just and ho - ly is thy name, I am all un - righteous - ness;
Thou of life the foun - tain art, Free - ly let me take of thee;
Safe in - to the ha - ven guide; O re - ceive my soul at last.
Cov - er my de - fense-less head With the shad - ow of thy wing.
False and full of sin I am, Thou art full of truth and grace.
Spring thou up with - in my heart, Rise to all e - ter - ni - ty.

Words, Charles Wesley, 1738. Tune MARTYN, Simeon B. Marsh, 1834. Alternate tune ABERYSTWYTH, No. 20.

No, Not Despairingly 173

1. No, not de-spair-ing-ly Come I to thee, No, not dis-
2. Ah! mine in-iq-ui-ty Crim-son hath been, In - fi - nite,
3. Lord, I con-fess to thee Sad - ly my sin; All I am
4. Faith-ful and just art thou, For-giv-ing all; Lov - ing and
5. Then all is peace and light This soul with - in; Thus shall I

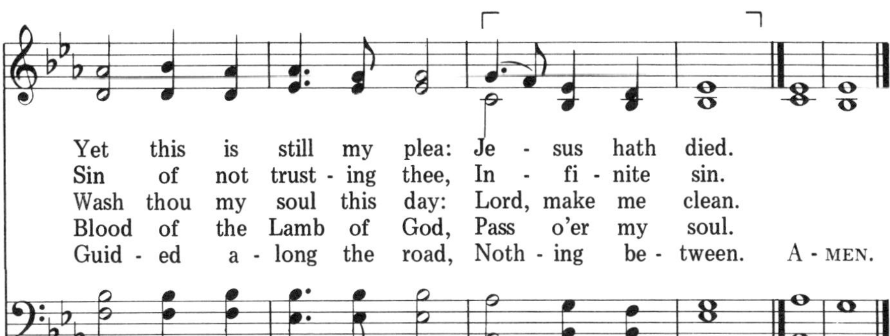

trust-ing-ly Bend I the knee: Sin hath gone o - ver me,
in - fi - nite Sin up - on sin: Sin of not lov-ing thee,
tell I thee, All I have been: Purge thou my sin a - way,
kind art thou When poor ones call: Lord, let the cleans-ing blood,
walk with thee, The loved Un - seen; Lean-ing on thee, my God,

Yet this is still my plea: Je - sus hath died.
Sin of not trust - ing thee, In - fi - nite sin.
Wash thou my soul this day: Lord, make me clean.
Blood of the Lamb of God, Pass o'er my soul.
Guid - ed a - long the road, Noth - ing be - tween. A - MEN.

Words, Horatius Bonar, 1866. Tune KEDRON, Ann B. Spratt.

174 Lord, I'm Coming Home

1. I've wan-dered far a - way from God, Now I'm com-ing home;
2. I've wast - ed man - y pre - cious years, Now I'm com-ing home;
3. I've tired of sin and stray - ing, Lord, Now I'm com-ing home;
4. My soul is sick, my heart is sore, Now I'm com-ing home;

The paths of sin too long I've trod, Lord, I'm com-ing home.
I now re - pent with bit - ter tears, Lord, I'm com-ing home.
I'll trust thy love, be - lieve thy word, Lord, I'm com-ing home.
My strength re - new, my hope re - store, Lord, I'm com-ing home.

Com - ing home, com - ing home, Nev - er - more to roam,

O - pen wide thine arms of love, Lord, I'm com-ing home.

Words and tune COMING HOME, William J. Kirkpatrick, 1892.

I Hear Thy Welcome Voice 175

1. I hear thy wel-come voice That calls me, Lord, to thee,
2. Tho com - ing weak and vile, Thou dost my strength as - sure;
3. 'Tis Je - sus calls me on To per - fect faith and love,
4. All hail! a - ton - ing blood! All hail! re - deem - ing grace!

For cleans-ing in thy pre-cious blood That flowed on Cal - va - ry.
Thou dost my vile-ness ful - ly cleanse, Till spot - less all, and pure.
To per - fect hope and peace and trust, For earth and heav'n a - bove.
All hail! the gift of Christ our Lord, Our strength and righ- teous-ness.

I am com - ing, Lord! Com - ing now to thee!

Wash me, cleanse me in the blood That flowed on Cal - va - ry!

Words and tune WELCOME VOICE, Lewis Hartsough, 1872.

176 Pass Me Not, O Gentle Savior

1. Pass me not, O gen - tle Sav - ior, Hear my hum - ble cry;
2. Let me at thy throne of mer - cy Find a sweet re - lief;
3. Trust - ing on - ly in thy mer - it, Would I seek thy face;
4. Thou the spring of all my com - fort, More than life to me,
While on oth - ers thou art call - ing, Do not pass me by.
Kneel - ing there in deep con - tri - tion, Help my un - be - lief.
Heal my wound - ed, bro - ken spir - it, Save me by thy grace.
Whom have I on earth be - side thee? Whom in heav'n but thee?
Sav - ior, Sav - ior, Hear my hum - ble cry;
While on oth - ers thou art call - ing, Do not pass me by.

Words, Fanny J. Crosby, 1868. Tune PASS ME NOT, William H. Doane, 1868.

1. I am re-solved no long-er to lin-ger, Charmed by the world's de-light;
2. I am re-solved to go to the Sav-ior, Leav-ing my sin and strife;
3. I am re-solved to fol-low the Sav-ior, Faith-ful and true each day;
4. I am re-solved to en-ter the kingdom, Leav-ing the paths of sin;
5. I am re-solved, and who will go with me? Come, friends, with-out de-lay,

Things that are high-er, things that are no-bler, These have al-lured my sight.
He is the true one, he is the just one, He hath the words of life.
Heed what he say-eth, do what he will-eth, He is the liv-ing way.
Friends may op-pose me, foes may be-set me, Still will I en-ter in.
Taught by the Bi-ble, led by the Spir-it, We'll walk the heav'n-ly way.

I will has-ten to him, Has-ten so glad and free,
I will has-ten, has-ten to him, Has-ten glad and free,

Je - sus, great-est, high-est, I will come to thee.
Je-sus, Je-sus,

Words, Palmer Hartsough, 1896. Tune RESOLUTION, James H. Fillmore, 1896.

178 Out of My Bondage, Sorrow, and Night

1. Out of my bondage, sor-row, and night, Je-sus, I come, Jesus, I come;
2. Out of my shameful fail - ure and loss, Je-sus, I come, Jesus, I come;
3. Out of un-rest and ar - ro-gant pride, Je-sus, I come, Jesus, I come;
4. Out of the fear and dread of the tomb, Je-sus, I come, Jesus, I come;

In - to thy freedom, gladness, and light, Je-sus, I come to thee; Out of my
In - to the glorious gain of thy cross, Je-sus, I come to thee; Out of earth's
In - to thy blessed will to a - bide, Je-sus, I come to thee; Out of my -
In - to the joy and light of thy home, Je-sus, I come to thee; Out of the

sick - ness in - to thy health, Out of my want and in - to thy wealth,
sor - rows in - to thy balm, Out of life's storms and in - to thy calm,
self to dwell in thy love, Out of de - spair in-to rap-tures a - bove,
depths of ru - in un - told, In - to the peace of thy shel-ter-ing fold,

Out of my sin and in - to thy - self, Je-sus, I come to thee.
Out of dis-tress to ju - bi-lant psalm, Je-sus, I come to thee.
Up-ward for aye on wings like a dove, Je-sus, I come to thee.
Ev - er thy glo-rious face to be-hold, Je-sus, I come to thee.

Words, William T. Sleeper, c. 1887. Tune JESUS, I COME, George C. Stebbins, 1887.

Let Jesus Come into Your Heart 179

1. If you are tired of the load of your sin, Let Je-sus come
2. If 'tis for pu-ri-ty now that you sigh, Let Je-sus come
3. If there's a tem-pest your voice can-not still, Let Je-sus come
4. If you would join the glad songs of the blest, Let Je-sus come
in-to your heart; If you de-sire a new life to be-gin,
in-to your heart; Foun-tains for cleans-ing are flow-ing near by,
in-to your heart; If there's a void this world nev-er can fill,
in-to your heart; If you would en-ter the man-sions of rest,
Let Je-sus come in-to your heart. Just now, your
doubt-ings give o'er; Just now, re-ject him no more; Just now, throw
o-pen the door; Let Je-sus come in-to your heart.

Words and tune MCCONNELSVILLE, Leila N. Morris, 1898.

 Ye Must Be Born Again

1. A rul-er once came to Je-sus by night To ask him the
2. Ye chil-dren of men, at-tend to the word So sol-emn-ly
3. O ye who would en-ter that glo-ri-ous rest, And sing with the
4. A dear one in heaven thy heart yearns to see, At the beau-ti-ful

way of sal-va-tion and light; The Mas-ter made an-swer in
ut-tered by Je-sus the Lord; And let not this mes-sage to
ran-somed the song of the blest, The life ev-er-last-ing if
gate may be watch-ing for thee, Then list to the note of this

words true and plain, *"Ye must be born a-gain.
you be in vain, "Ye must be born a-gain.
ye would ob-tain, "Ye must be born a-gain.
sol-emn re-frain, "Ye must be born a-gain.

Ye must be born a-gain, Ye must be born a-gain; I
a-gain, a-gain;

John 3. Words, William T. Sleeper, 1877. Tune BORN AGAIN, George C. Stebbins, 1877. *John 3: 7.

ver - i - ly, ver - i - ly say un - to thee, Ye must be born a - gain."

Who at My Door Is Standing 181

1. Who at my door is stand - ing, Pa - tient - ly draw - ing near,
2. All thro' the dark hours drea - ry, Knock - ing a - gain is he;
3. Door of my heart, I has - ten! Thee will I o - pen wide.

En - trance with - in de - mand - ing? Whose is the voice I hear?
Je - sus, art thou not wea - ry, Wait - ing so long for me?
Tho he re - buke and chas - ten, He shall with me a - bide.

If thou wilt heed my call - ing, I will a - bide with thee."

Sweet - ly the tones are fall - ing: "O - pen the door for me!

Words, Mary B. C. Slade, c. 1875. Tune EVERETT, Asa B. Everett, c. 1875.

182 The Savior Is Waiting

1. The Sav-ior is wait-ing to en-ter your heart, Why don't you
2. If you'll take one step t'ward the Sav-ior, my friend, You'll find his
let him come in? There's nothing in this world to keep you a-part,
arms o-pen wide; Re-ceive him, and all of your dark-ness will end,
What is your an-swer to him? Time af-ter time he has wait-ed be-
With-in your heart he'll a - bide.
fore, And now he is wait-ing a - gain To see if you're
will-ing to o-pen the door, Oh, how he wants to come in.

Only Trust Him 183

1. Come, ev - 'ry soul by sin op - pressed, There's mer - cy with the Lord,
2. For Je - sus shed his pre - cious blood Rich bless - ings to be - stow;
3. Yes, Je - sus is the truth, the way, That leads you in - to rest;
4. Come, then, and join this ho - ly band, And on to glo - ry go,

And he will sure - ly give you rest By trust - ing in his word.
Plunge now in - to the crim - son flood That wash - es white as snow.
Be - lieve in him with - out de - lay And you are ful - ly blest.
To dwell in that ce - les - tial land Where joys im - mor - tal flow.

On - ly trust him, on - ly trust him, on - ly trust him now;

He will save you, he will save you, he will save you now.

Words and tune STOCKTON, John H. Stockton, c. 1873.

184 "Whosoever Will"

1. "Who-so-ev-er hear-eth," shout, shout the sound! Spread the bless-ed ti-dings
2. Who-so-ev-er com-eth need not de-lay, Now the door is o-pen,
3. "Who-so-ev-er will" the promise is se-cure; "Who-so-ev-er will," for-

all the world a-round; Tell the joy-ful news wher-ev-er man is found,
en-ter while you may; Je-sus is the true, the on-ly Liv-ing Way:
ev-er must en-dure; "Who-so-ev-er will!" 'tis life for-ev-er-more;

"Who-so-ev-er will may come." "Who-so-ev-er will, who-so-ev-er will!"

Send the proc-la-ma-tion o-ver vale and hill; 'Tis a lov-ing

Fa-ther calls the wan-d'rer home: "Who-so-ev-er will may come."

John 3:16. Words and tune WHOSOEVER, Philip P. Bliss, 1869.

Whiter than Snow 185

1. Lord Je-sus, I long to be per-fect-ly whole; I want thee for-
2. Lord Je-sus, for this I most hum-bly en-treat; I wait, bless-ed
3. Lord Je-sus, thou know-est I pa-tient-ly wait; Come now, and with-

ev - er to ran-som my soul; Break down ev - 'ry i - dol, cast
Lord, at thy cru - ci - fied feet; By faith, for my cleans - ing I
in me a new heart cre - ate; To those who have sought thee, thou

out ev - 'ry foe: Now wash me, and I shall be whit - er than snow.
see thy blood flow: Now wash me, and I shall be whit - er than snow.
nev - er saidst No: Now wash me, and I shall be whit - er than snow.

Whit - er than snow, yes, whit - er than snow;

Now wash me, and I shall be whit - er than snow.

Psalm 51:7. Words, James Nicholson, 1872. Tune FISCHER, William G. Fischer, 1872.

186 Just As I Am

Unison
1. Just as I am, with-out one plea,
2. Just as I am, and wait-ing not
3. Just as I am, thy love un-known
But that thy
To rid my
Has bro - ken
blood was shed for me,
soul of one dark blot,
ev - 'ry bar - rier down;
And that thou
To thee whose
Now to be
bidd'st me come to thee,
blood can cleanse each spot,
thine, yea, thine a - lone,
O Lamb of God,
(after last stanza)
I come.
I come.

Just As I Am 187

1. Just as I am, with-out one plea, But that thy
2. Just as I am, and wait-ing not To rid my
3. Just as I am, tho tossed a-bout With man-y a
4. Just as I am, poor, wretch-ed, blind; Sight, rich-es,
5. Just as I am, thou wilt re-ceive, Wilt wel-come,
6. Just as I am, thy love un-known Hath bro-ken

blood was shed for me, And that thou bidd'st me
soul of one dark blot, To thee whose blood can
con-flict, many a doubt, Fight-ings with-in and
heal-ing of the mind, Yea, all I need in
par-don, cleanse, re-lieve, Be-cause thy prom-ise
ev-'ry bar-rier down; Now to be thine, yea,

come to thee, O Lamb of God, I come! I come!
cleanse each spot, O Lamb of God, I come! I come!
fears with-out, O Lamb of God, I come! I come!
thee to find, O Lamb of God, I come! I come!
I be-lieve, O Lamb of God, I come! I come!
thine a-lone, O Lamb of God, I come! I come!

Words, Charlotte Elliott, 1834. Tune WOODWORTH, William B. Bradbury, 1849.

188 Jesus Is Tenderly Calling

1. Je-sus is ten-der-ly call-ing thee home, Call-ing to-day,
2. Je-sus is call-ing the wea-ry to rest, Call-ing to-day,
3. Je-sus is wait-ing; O come to him now, Wait-ing to-day,
4. Je-sus is plead-ing; O list to his voice, Hear him to-day,

call-ing to-day; Why from the sun-shine of love wilt thou roam
call-ing to-day; Bring him thy bur-den and thou shalt be blest;
wait-ing to-day; Come with thy sins; at his feet low-ly bow;
hear him to-day; They who be-lieve on his name shall re-joice;

Far-ther and far-ther a-way?
He will not turn thee a-way. Call-ing to-day,
Come, and no long-er de-lay.
Quick-ly a-rise and a-way. Call-ing, call-ing to-day, to-day,

Call-ing to-day; Je-sus is
Call-ing, call-ing to-day, to-day; Je-sus is ten-der-ly

John 11:28. Words, Fanny J. Crosby, 1883. Tune CALLING TODAY, George C. Stebbins, 1883.

call - ing, Is ten-der-ly call-ing to - day.
call-ing to-day,

I'll Live for Him 189

1. My life, my love I give to thee, Thou Lamb of God who died for
2. I now be-lieve thou dost re-ceive, For thou hast died that I might
3. O thou who died on Cal - va - ry, To save my soul and make me
REF.—I'll live for him who died for me, How hap-py then my life shall

D.C. for Refrain

me; O may I ev - er faith-ful be, My Sav-ior and my God!
live; And now hence-forth I'll trust in thee, My Sav-ior and my God!
free; I'll con - se-crate my life to thee, My Sav-ior and my God!
be! I'll live for him who died for me, My Sav-ior and my God!

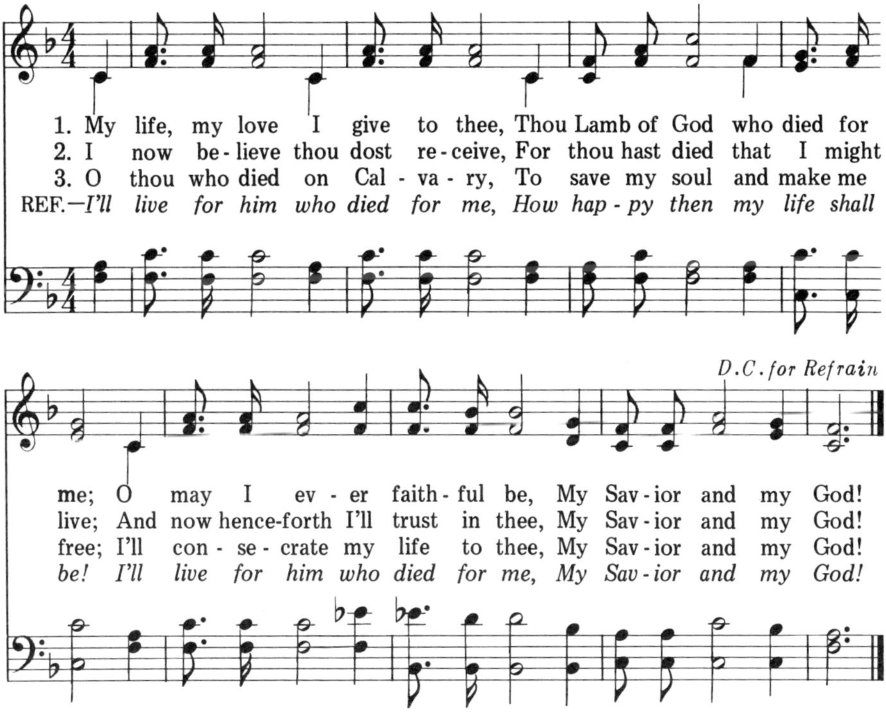

Words, Ralph E. Hudson, 1882. Tune DUNBAR, C. R. Dunbar, 1882.

190 Softly and Tenderly

1. Soft - ly and ten - der - ly Je - sus is call - ing, Call - ing for
2. Why should we tar - ry when Je - sus is plead - ing, Plead - ing for
3. Time is now fleet - ing, the mo - ments are pass - ing, Pass - ing from
4. Oh! for the won - der - ful love he has promised, Prom - ised for
you and for me; See, on the por - tals he's wait - ing and watching,
you and for me? Why should we lin - ger and heed not his mer - cies,
you and from me; Shad - ows are gath - er - ing, death-beds are com - ing,
you and for me; Tho we have sinned he has mer - cy and par - don,
Watch - ing for you and for me.
Mer - cies for you and for me? Come home, come home,
Com - ing for you and for me. Come home, come home,
Par - don for you and for me.
Ye who are wea - ry come home; Ear - nest - ly, ten - der - ly,

Words and tune THOMPSON, Will L. Thompson, 1880.

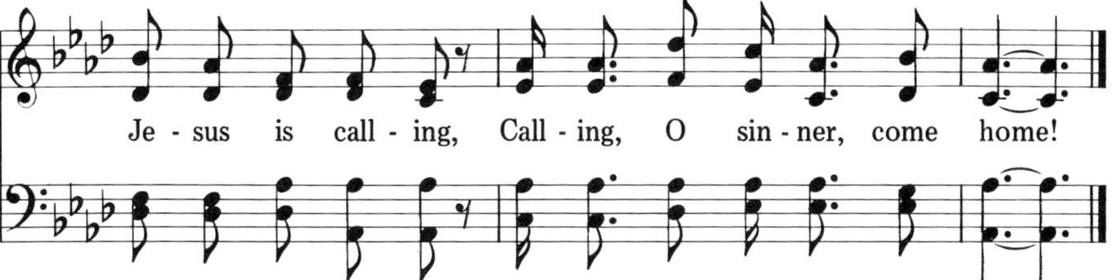

Je - sus is call - ing, Call - ing, O sin - ner, come home!

I Have Decided to Follow Jesus 191

1. I have de - cid - ed to fol - low Je - sus, I have de -
2. Tho none go with me I still will fol - low, Tho none go
3. My cross I'll car - ry till I see Je - sus, My cross I'll

cid - ed to fol - low Je - sus, I have de - cid - ed to fol - low
with me I still will fol - low, Tho none go with me I still will
car - ry till I see Je - sus, My cross I'll car - ry till I see

Je - sus, No turn - ing back, no turn - ing back.
fol - low, No turn - ing back, no turn - ing back.
Je - sus, No turn - ing back, I'll fol - low him.

Words, st. 1, 2, as sung by the Garo Christians; st. 3, John Clark. Tune ASSAM, Folk Song from India; arranged, William J. Reynolds, 1959. © Copyright 1959 Broadman Press. All rights reserved.

192 The Nail-Scarred Hand

1. Have you failed in your plan of your storm-tossed life?
2. Are you walk-ing a-lone thro' the shad-ows dim?
3. Would you fol-low the will of the ris-en Lord?
4. Is your soul bur-dened down with its load of sin?

Place your hand in the nail-scarred hand; Are you wea-ry and
Place your hand in the nail-scarred hand; Christ will com-fort your
Place your hand in the nail-scarred hand; Would you live in the
Place your hand in the nail-scarred hand; Throw your heart o-pen

worn from its toil and strife? Place your hand in the nail-scarred hand
heart, put your trust in him, Place your hand in the nail-scarred hand
light of his bless-ed Word? Place your hand in the nail-scarred hand
wide, let the Sav-ior in, Place your hand in the nail-scarred hand

Place your hand in the nail-scarred hand, Place your hand in the

nail - scarred hand; He will keep to the end, he's your
dear - est friend, Place your hand in the nail - scarred hand.

The Time Is Now 193

The time is now, the Lord is here, Won't you o - pen your heart while
he is near? His will o - bey, O don't de - lay, For sure-ly the time is now.

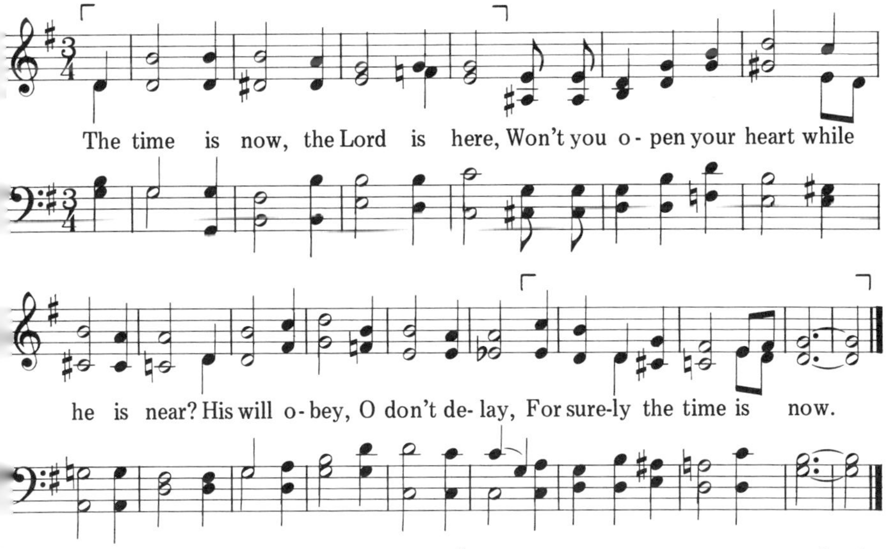

194 Room at the Cross

1. The cross up-on which Je-sus died Is a shel-ter in
2. Tho mil-lions have found him a friend, And have turned from the
3. The hand of my Sav-ior is strong, And the love of my

which we can hide; And its grace so free is suf-fi-cient for me,
sins they have sinned, The Sav-ior still waits to o-pen the gates,
Sav-ior is long; Thro' sun-shine or rain, thro' loss or in gain,

And deep is its foun-tain, as wide as the sea.
And wel-come a sin-ner be-fore it's too late. There's room at the
The blood flows from Cal-v'ry to cleanse ev-'ry stain.

cross for you, There's room at the cross for you; Tho mil-lions have come

There's still room for one, Yes, there's room at the cross for you.

1. There is a Rock in a wea-ry land, Its shad-ow falls on the
2. There is a Well in a des-ert plain, Its wa-ters call with en-
3. A great fold stands with its por-tals wide, The sheep a-stray on the
4. There is a cross where the Sav-ior died; His blood flowed out in a

burn-ing sand, In-vit-ing pil-grims as they pass, To seek a
treat-ing strain, "Ho, ev-'ry thirst-ing, sin-sick soul, Come, free-ly
moun-tain-side; The Shep-herd climbs o'er moun-tains steep; He's search-ing
crim-son tide, A sac-ri-fice for sins of men, And free to

shade in the wil-der-ness. Then why will ye die? O why will ye die?
drink, and thou shalt be whole." Then why will ye die? O why will ye die?
now for his wand'ring sheep. Then why will ye die? O why will ye die?
all who will en-ter in. Then why will ye die? O why will ye die?

When the shel-t'ring Rock is so near by, O why will ye die?
When the liv-ing Well is so near by, O why will ye die?
When the Shep-herd's fold is so near by, O why will ye die?
When the crim-son cross is so near by, O why will ye die?

Isaiah 32:2. Words and tune SHELTERING ROCK, W. E. Penn, 1887.

196 Come, Ye Sinners, Poor and Needy

1. Come, ye sin-ners, poor and need-y, Weak and wounded, sick and sore;
2. Let not conscience make you lin-ger, Nor of fit-ness fond-ly dream;
3. Saints and an-gels, joined in con-cert, Sing the prais-es of the Lamb;

Je-sus read-y stands to save you, Full of pit-y, love, and pow'r:
All the fit-ness he re-quir-eth Is to feel your need of him:
While the bliss-ful seats of heav-en Sweet-ly ech-o with his name:

He is a-ble, He is a-ble, He is will-ing, doubt no more;
This he gives you, This he gives you; 'Tis the Spir-it's glimm'ring beam;
Hal-le-lu-jah! Hal-le-lu-jah! Sin-ners here may do the same;

He is a-ble, He is a-ble, He is will-ing, doubt no more.
This he gives you, This he gives you; 'Tis the Spir-it's glim-m'ring beam.
Hal-le-lu-jah! Hal-le-lu-jah! Sin-ners here may do the same.

Words, Joseph Hart, 1759. Tune BEACH SPRING, *The Sacred Harp*, 1844; harmonized, James H. Wood, 1958.
This tune in a lower key and for unison singing, No. 362.

Come, Ye Sinners, Poor and Needy 197

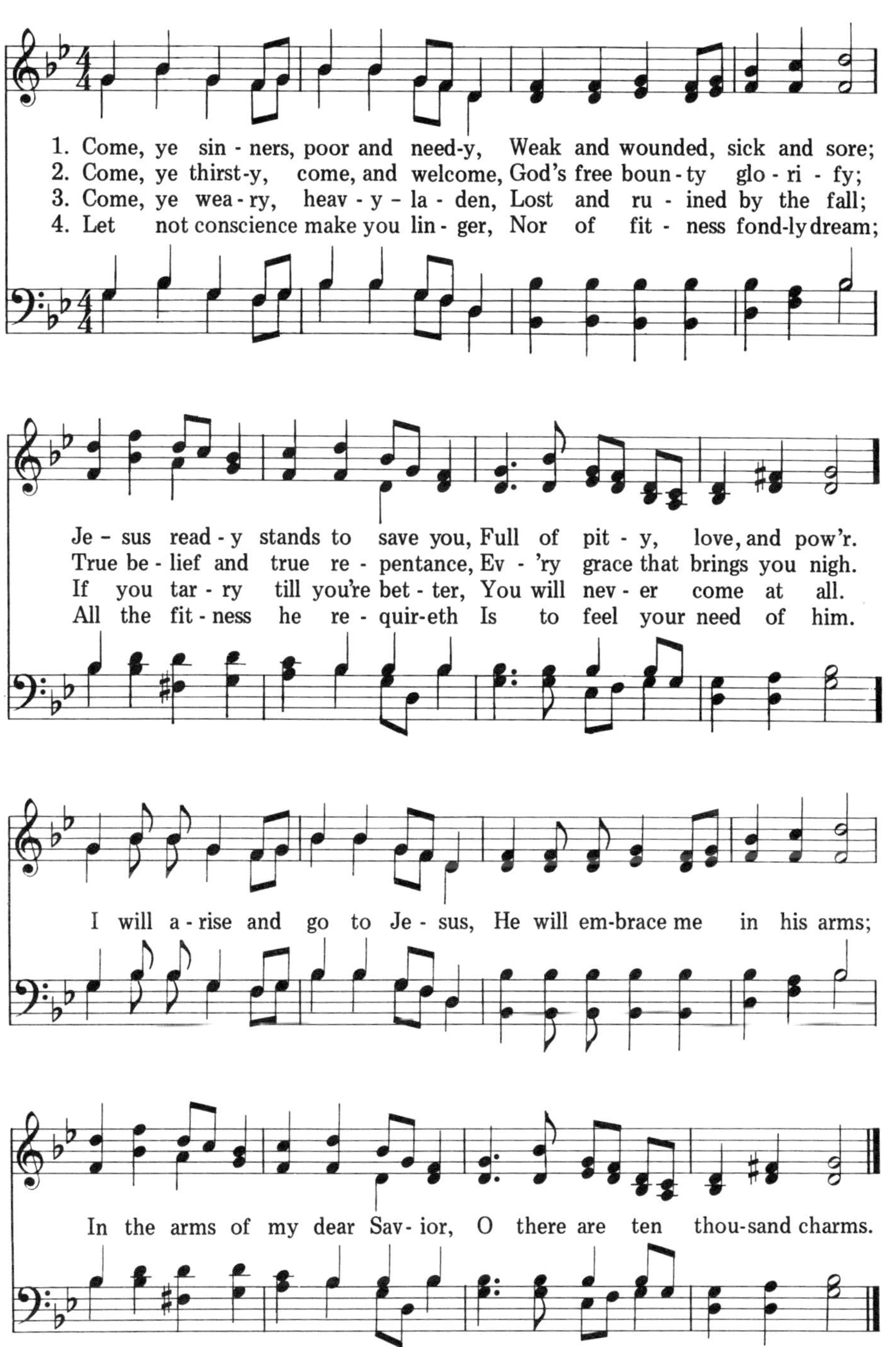

1. Come, ye sin - ners, poor and need-y, Weak and wounded, sick and sore;
2. Come, ye thirst-y, come, and welcome, God's free boun - ty glo - ri - fy;
3. Come, ye wea-ry, heav - y – la - den, Lost and ru - ined by the fall;
4. Let not conscience make you lin - ger, Nor of fit - ness fond-ly dream;
Je – sus read - y stands to save you, Full of pit - y, love, and pow'r.
True be - lief and true re - pentance, Ev - 'ry grace that brings you nigh.
If you tar - ry till you're bet - ter, You will nev - er come at all.
All the fit - ness he re - quir-eth Is to feel your need of him.
I will a - rise and go to Je - sus, He will em-brace me in his arms;
In the arms of my dear Sav - ior, O there are ten thou-sand charms.

Words, Joseph Hart, 1759; Refrain, Anonymous. Tune ARISE, Walker's *Southern Harmony*, 1835.

198 Turn Your Eyes upon Jesus

1. O soul, are you wea-ry and trou-bled? No light in the
2. Thro' death in-to life ev-er-last-ing He passed, and we
3. His word shall not fail you—he prom-ised; Be-lieve him, and
dark-ness you see? There's light for a look at the Sav-ior, And
fol-low him there; O-ver us sin no more hath do-min-ion—For
all will be well: Then go to a world that is dy-ing, His
life more a-bun-dant and free!
more than con-q'rors we are! Turn your eyes up-on Je-sus,
per-fect sal-va-tion to tell!
Look full in his won-der-ful face, And the things of
earth will grow strange-ly dim In the light of his glo-ry and grace.

1. Je - sus waits to wel-come you, Will you come? Will you come?
2. Je - sus stands at mer-cy's door, Will you come? Will you come?
3. Peace and joy you will pos - sess, Will you come? Will you come?
4. Man - sions great a - wait his own, Will you come? Will you come?

Arms of love outstretched to you, Will you come? Will you come?
Par - don free the Sav - ior gives, Will you come? Will you come?
Life e - ter - nal will be yours, Will you come? Will you come?
Loved ones dear you'll meet a - gain, Will you come? Will you come?

Will you come? Will you come? O the Sav - ior bids you come;

He will wel-come you with words of love, Will you come? Will you come?

Words and tune IRONDALE, Isham E. Reynolds, c. 1920.

200 Without Him

1. With - out him I could do noth - ing, With - out him
2. With - out him I could be dy - ing, With - out him
I'd sure - ly fail; With - out him I would be drift - ing
I'd be en - slaved; With - out him life would be hope - less,
Like a ship with - out a sail.
But with Je - sus, thank God, I'm saved.
Je - sus, O Je - sus,
Do you know him to - day? You can't turn him a - way. O
Je - sus, O Je - sus, With - out him, how lost I would be.

# Our Hope Is in the Living God 201

1. Our hope is in the liv - ing God With - in whose love
2. Trou - bled are we but not dis - tressed Who by his hands
3. He holds the fate of ev - 'ry land Deep in the hol -

our fa - thers trod, And who, thro' - out his vast do - main,
are dai - ly blessed; Doubt does not lead us to de - spair
low of his hand, And grants to all his warm em - brace,

Doth still in love for - ev - er reign. Face we the fu - ture
For he is with us ev - 'ry - where. Face we the fu - ture
Whole - ness and health and heal - ing grace. O may we grow with -

un - a - fraid, On the foun - da - tion he has laid.
with - out fear, Know - ing our help is al - ways near.
in his love, Wor - thy to reign with him a - bove. A - MEN.

202 Guide Me, O Thou Great Jehovah

1. Guide me, O thou great Je - ho - vah, Pil - grim through this
2. O - pen now the crys - tal foun - tain, Whence the heal - ing
3. When I tread the verge of Jor - dan, Bid my anx - ious

bar - ren land; I am weak, but thou art might-y; Hold me with thy
stream doth flow; Let the *fire and cloud-y pil - lar Lead me all my
fears sub - side; Bear me thro' the swell-ing cur -rent, Land me safe on

pow'r - ful hand; Bread of heav - en, Bread of heav - en,
jour - ney through; Strong De - liv - erer, strong De - liv - erer,
Ca - naan's side; Songs of prais - es, songs of prais - es

Feed me till I want no more, Feed me till I want no more.
Be thou still my strength and shield, Be thou still my strength and shield.
I will ev - er give to thee, I will ev - er give to thee. A - MEN.

Words, William Williams, 1745; translated, st. 1, Peter Williams, 1771; st. 2, 3, William Williams, 1772. Tune CWM RHONDDA, John Hughes, 1907. Music copyright used by permission of Mrs. Dilys S. Webb, Glamorganshire.
*Exodus 13:21.

If You Will Only Let God Guide You 203

1. If you will on - ly let God guide you, And hope in
2. On - ly be still, and wait his lei - sure In cheer - ful
3. Sing, pray, and swerve not from his ways, But do your

him thro' all your ways, What - ev - er comes, he'll stand be - side you,
hope, with heart con - tent To take what - e'er the Fa - ther's plea - sure
part in con - science true; Trust his rich prom - is - es of grace,

To bear you thro' the e - vil days; Who trusts in God's un -
And all dis - cern - ing love have sent; Nor doubt our in - most
So shall they be ful - filled in you; God hears the call of

chang - ing love Builds on the rock that can - not move.
wants are known To him who chose us for his own.
those in need, The souls that trust in him in - deed.

Psalm 55:22. Words, Georg Neumark, 1657; translated, Catherine Winkworth, 1855, 1863, alt. Tune NEUMARK, Georg Neumark, 1657.

204 In Heavenly Love Abiding

1. In heav'n-ly love a-bid-ing, No change my heart shall fear;
2. Wher-ev-er he may guide me, No want shall turn me back;
3. Green pas-tures are be-fore me, Which yet I have not seen;

And safe is such con-fid-ing, For noth-ing chang-es here:
My Shep-herd is be-side me, And noth-ing can I lack:
Bright skies will soon be o'er me, Where the dark clouds have been:

The storm may roar with-out me, My heart may low be laid;
His wis-dom ev-er wak-eth, His sight is nev-er dim;
My life I can-not meas-ure, The path of life is free;

But God is round a-bout me, And can I be dis-mayed?
He knows the way he tak-eth, And I will walk with him.
My Sav-ior has my trea-sure, And he will walk with me.

Words, Anna L. Waring, 1850. Tune NYLAND, Finnish Hymn Melody; arranged, David Evans, 1927. From *The Revised Church Hymnary*, by permission Oxford University Press.

There Is a Balm in Gilead 205

There is a balm in Gil - e - ad to make the wound-ed whole;
There is a balm in Gil - e - ad to heal the sin - sick soul.
1. Some-times I feel dis - cour - aged, And think my work's in vain,
2. If you can't preach like Pet - er, If you can't pray like Paul,
But then the Ho - ly Spir - it Re - vives my soul a - gain.
Just tell the love of Je - sus, And say he died for all.
Fine
D.C. al Fine

Jeremiah 8:22. Words and tune BALM IN GILEAD, Traditional Negro Spiritual.

206 Our Father God, Thy Name We Praise

1. Our Fa - ther God, thy name we praise, To thee our hymns ad - dress - ing, And joy - ful - ly our voic - es raise Thy faith - ful - ness con - fess - ing; As - sem - bled by thy grace, O Lord, We seek fresh guid - ance from thy Word;
2. Touch, Lord, the lips that speak for thee; Set words of truth be - fore us, That we may grow in con - stan - cy, The light of wis - dom o'er us. Give us this day our dai - ly bread; May hun - gry souls a - gain be fed;
3. As with our breth - ren here we meet, Thy grace a - lone can feed us. As here we gath - er at thy feet We pray that thou wilt heed us. The pow'r is thine, O Lord di - vine, The king - dom and the rule are thine.

Matthew 6:9-13. Words, from the Anabaptist *Ausbund*, 16th Century; translated, Ernest A. Payne, 1960. Used by permission of Ernest A. Payne. Tune MIT FREUDEN ZART, Bohemian Brethren *Kirchengesänge*, 1566.

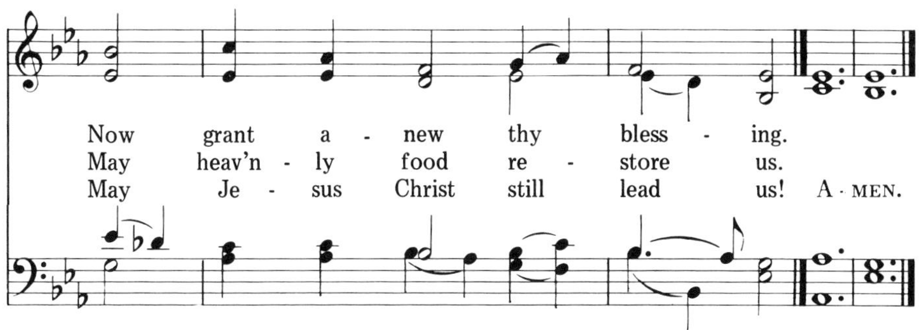

Now grant a - new thy bless - ing.
May heav'n - ly food re - store us.
May Je - sus Christ still lead us! A - MEN.

Children of the Heavenly Father 207

1. Chil - dren of the heav'n - ly Fa - ther Safe - ly
2. God his own doth tend and nour - ish; In his
3. Nei - ther life nor death shall ev - er From the
4. Tho he giv - eth or he tak - eth, God his

in his bos - om gath - er; Nest - ling bird nor star in
ho - ly courts they flour - ish. From all e - vil things he
Lord his chil - dren sev - er; Un - to them his grace he
chil - dren ne'er for - sak - eth; His the lov - ing pur - pose

heav - en Such a ref - uge ne'er was giv - en.
spares them; In his might - y arms he bears them.
show - eth, And their sor - rows all he know - eth.
sole - ly To pre - serve them pure and ho - ly. A - MEN.

Words, Caroline V. Sandell-Berg, 1858; translated, Ernst W. Olson, 1925. Tune TRYGGARE KAN INGEN VARA, Traditional Swedish Melody.

208 Like a River Glorious

1. Like a riv-er glo-rious Is God's per-fect peace, O-ver
2. Hid-den in the hol-low Of his bless-ed hand, Nev-er
3. Ev-'ry joy or tri-al Fall-eth from a-bove, Trac'd up-

all vic-to-rious In its bright in-crease; Per-fect, yet it
foe can fol-low, Nev-er trai-tor stand; Not a surge of
on our di-al By the Sun of Love; We may trust him

flow-eth Ful-ler ev-'ry day; Per-fect, yet it grow-eth
wor-ry, Not a shade of care, Not a blast of hur-ry
ful-ly All for us to do; They who trust him whol-ly

Deep-er all the way.
Touch the spir-it there. Stayed up-on Je-ho-vah, Hearts are
Find him whol-ly true.

ful-ly blest; Find-ing, as he prom-ised, Per-fect peace and rest.

Words, Frances R. Havergal, 1874. Tune WYE VALLEY, James Mountain, 1876.

My Lord Is Near Me All the Time 209

1. In the light-ning flash a-cross the sky his might-y pow'r I
2. When the thun-der shakes the might-y hills and trem-bles ev-'ry
3. When re-fresh-ing show-ers cool the earth and sweep a-cross the
see, And I know if he can reign on high, his light can shine on me.
tree, Then I know a God so great and strong can sure-ly har-bor me.
sea, Then his rain-bow shines within my heart, his near-ness comforts me.
I've seen it in the light-ning, heard it in the thun-der, and
felt it in the rain; My Lord is near me all the
time, My Lord is near me all the time.

210 Come, Come, Ye Saints

1. Come, come, ye saints, no toil nor la-bor fear; But with joy
2. The world of care is with us ev-'ry day; Let it not
3. We'll find the rest which God for us pre-pared, When at last
wend your way. Tho hard to you the jour-ney may ap-pear,
this ob-scure: Here we can serve the Mas-ter on the way,
he will call; Where none will come to hurt or make a-fraid,
Grace shall be as your day. We have a liv-ing
And in him be se-cure. Gird up your loins; fresh
He will reign o-ver all. We will make the air with
Lord to guide, And we can trust him to pro-vide; Do
cour-age take; Our God will nev-er us for-sake; And
mu-sic ring, Shout prais-es to our God and King; O

Words, William Clayton, 1846; altered, Joseph F. Green, 1960. © Copyright 1960 Broadman Press. All rights reserved. Tune ALL IS WELL, adapted from J. T. White, *The Sacred Harp*, 1844.

this, and joy your hearts will swell: All is well! All is well!
so our song no fear can quell: All is well! All is well!
how we'll make the cho - rus swell: All is well! All is well!

Come, Ye Disconsolate 211

1. Come, ye dis - con - so - late, wher - e'er ye lan - guish, Come to the
2. Joy of the des - o - late, light of the stray - ing, Hope of the
3. Here see the Bread of Life; see wa - ters flow - ing Forth from the

*mer - cy seat, fer - vent - ly kneel; Here bring your wound - ed hearts,
pen - i - tent, fade - less and pure! Here speaks the Com - fort - er,
throne of God, pure from a - bove: Come to the feast of love;

here tell your an - guish: Earth has no sor-row that heav'n can-not heal.
ten - der - ly say - ing, "Earth has no sor-row that heav'n can-not cure."
come, ev - er know - ing Earth has no sor-row but heav'n can re - move.

Words, Thomas Moore, 1816; altered, Thomas Hastings, 1831. Tune CONSOLATOR,
Samuel Webbe, 1792. *Exodus 25:17-22.

212 Be Thou My Vision

Unison
1. Be thou my vi - sion, O Lord of my heart;
2. Be thou my wis - dom, and thou my true word;
3. Rich - es I heed not, or man's emp - ty praise,
4. High King of heav - en, my vic - to - ry won,
Naught be all else to me, save that thou art:
I ev - er with thee and thou with me, Lord:
Thou mine in - her - it - ance, now and al - ways:
May I reach heav - en's joys, O bright heav'n's Sun!
Thou my best thought, by day or by night,
Thou my great Fa - ther, I thy true son,
Thou and thou on - ly, first in my heart,
Heart of my own heart, what - ev - er be - fall,
Wak - ing or sleep - ing, thy pres - ence my light.
Thou in me dwell - ing, and I with thee one.
High King of heav - en, my trea - sure thou art.
Still be my vi - sion, O Rul - er of all. A-MEN.

Words, Ancient Irish; translated, Mary Byrne, 1905; versified, Eleanor Hull, 1912. Words used by permission Chatto & Windus, Ltd. Tune SLANE, Traditional Irish Melody; harmonized, David Evans, 1927. Music from the *Revised Church Hymnary* by permission of Oxford University Press.

Savior, Like a Shepherd Lead Us   213

1. Sav - ior, like a shep-herd lead us, Much we need thy ten-der care;
2. We are thine; do thou be - friend us, Be the guard-ian of our way;
3. Thou hast prom-ised to re - ceive us, Poor and sin - ful though we be;
4. Ear - ly let us seek thy fa - vor; Ear - ly let us do thy will;

In thy pleas-ant pas-tures feed us, For our use thy folds pre - pare:
Keep thy flock, from sin de - fend us, Seek us when we go a - stray:
Thou hast mer - cy to re - lieve us, Grace to cleanse, and pow'r to free:
Bless -ed Lord and on - ly Sav - ior, With thy love our bos -oms fill:

Bless - ed Je - sus, bless - ed Je - sus, Thou hast bought us, thine we are;
Bless - ed Je - sus, bless - ed Je - sus, Hear, O hear us when we pray;
Bless - ed Je - sus, bless - ed Je - sus, Ear - ly let us turn to thee;
Bless - ed Je - sus, bless - ed Je - sus, Thou hast loved us, love us still;

Bless - ed Je - sus, bless - ed Je - sus, Thou hast bought us, thine we are.
Bless - ed Je - sus, bless - ed Je - sus, Hear, O hear us when we pray.
Bless - ed Je - sus, bless - ed Je - sus, Ear - ly let us turn to thee.
Bless - ed Je - sus, bless - ed Je - sus, Thou hast loved us, love us still.

Words, Dorothy Thrupp's *Hymns for the Young*, 1836. Tune BRADBURY, William B. Bradbury, 1859.

214 All the Way My Savior Leads Me

1. All the way my Sav-ior leads me; What have I to ask be-side?
2. All the way my Sav-ior leads me; Cheers each wind-ing path I tread,
3. All the way my Sav-ior leads me; Oh, the full-ness of his love!
Can I doubt his ten-der mer-cy, Who thro' life has been my guide?
Gives me grace for ev-'ry tri-al, Feeds me with the liv-ing bread:
Per-fect rest to me is prom-is'd In my Fa-ther's house a-bove:
Heav'n-ly peace, di-vin-est com-fort, Here by faith in him to dwell!
Tho' my wea-ry steps may fal-ter, And my soul a-thirst may be,
When my spir-it, cloth'd im-mor-tal, Wings its flight to realms of day,
For I know what-e'er be-fall me, Je-sus do-eth all things well;
Gush-ing from the Rock be-fore me, Lo! a spring of joy I see;
This my song thro' end-less a-ges: Je-sus led me all the way;

Words, Fanny J. Crosby, 1875. Tune ALL THE WAY, Robert Lowry, 1875.

For I know what-e'er be-fall me, Je-sus do-eth all things well.
Gush-ing from the Rock be-fore me, Lo! a spring of joy I see.
This my song thro' end-less a-ges: Je-sus led me all the way.

The King of Love My Shepherd Is 215

1. The King of love my Shep-herd is, Whose
2. Where streams of liv-ing wa-ter flow, My
3. Per-verse and fool-ish, oft I strayed, But
4. In death's dark vale I fear no ill With
5. And so through all the length of days Thy

good-ness fail-eth nev-er; I noth-ing lack if
ran-somed soul he lead-eth, And, where the ver-dant
yet in love he sought me, And on his shoul-der
thee, dear Lord, be-side me; Thy rod and staff my
good-ness fail-eth nev-er: Good Shep-herd, may I

I am his And he is mine for-ev-er.
pas-tures grow, With food ce-les-tial feed-eth.
gen-tly laid, And home, re-joic-ing, brought me.
com-fort still, Thy cross be-fore to guide me.
sing thy praise With-in thy house for-ev-er.   A-MEN.

Psalm 23. Words, Henry W. Baker, 1868. Tune DOMINUS REGIT ME, John B. Dykes, 1868.

 Great Is Thy Faithfulness

1. Great is thy faith-ful-ness, O God my Fa-ther, There is no
2. Sum-mer and win-ter, and spring-time and har-vest, Sun, moon, and
3. Par-don for sin and a peace that en-dur-eth, Thine own dear

shad-ow of turn-ing with thee; Thou chang-est not, thy com-
stars in their cours-es a-bove Join with all na-ture in
pres-ence to cheer and to guide; Strength for to-day and bright

pas-sions, they fail not; As thou hast been thou for-ev-er wilt be.
man-i-fold wit-ness To thy great faith-ful-ness, mer-cy, and love.
hope for to-mor-row, Bless-ings all mine, with ten thou-sand be-side!

Great is thy faith-ful-ness! Great is thy faith-ful-ness!

Morn-ing by morn-ing new mer-cies I see; All I have need-ed thy

hand hath pro - vid - ed; Great is thy faith - ful - ness, Lord, un - to me!

Abide with Me 217

1. A - bide with me: fast falls the e - ven - tide; The dark - ness deep - ens;
2. Swift to its close ebbs out life's lit - tle day; Earth's joys grow dim, its
3. I need thy pres - ence ev - 'ry pass - ing hour; What but thy grace can
4. Hold thou thy cross be - fore my clos - ing eyes; Shine thro' the gloom, and

Lord, with me a - bide: When oth - er help - ers fail, and com - forts
glo - ries pass a - way; Change and de - cay in all a - round I
foil the tempt - er's pow'r? Who like thy - self my guide and stay can
point me to the skies: Heav'n's morning breaks and earth's vain shad - ows

flee, Help of the help - less, O a - bide with me!
see: O thou who chang - est not, a - bide with me!
be? Thro' cloud and sun - shine, O a - bide with me!
flee: In life, in death, O Lord, a - bide with me! A - MEN.

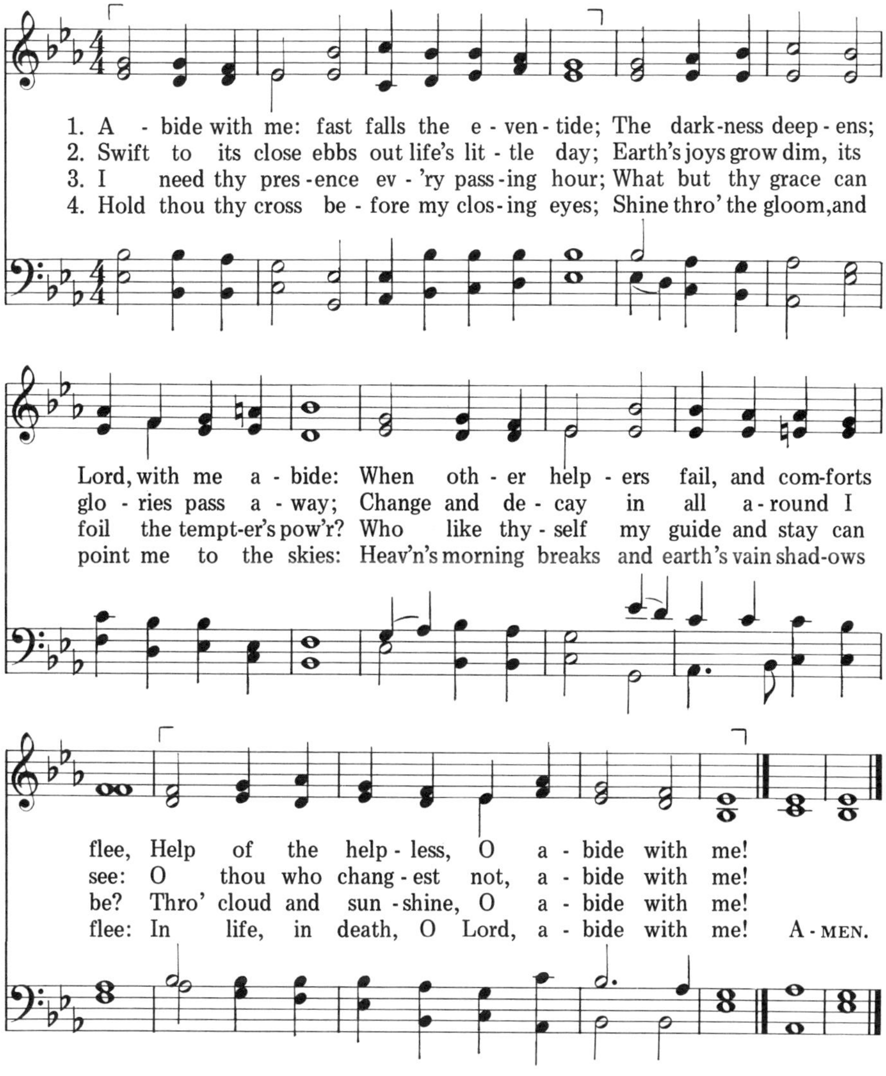

Words, Henry F. Lyte, 1847. Tune EVENTIDE, William H. Monk, 1861.

218 He Leadeth Me! O Blessed Thought

1. He lead-eth me! O bless-ed tho't! O words with heav'n-ly comfort fraught!
2. Sometimes 'mid scenes of deep-est gloom, Sometimes where E-den's bow-ers bloom,
3. Lord, I would clasp thy hand in mine, Nor ev-er mur-mur nor re-pine,
4. And when my task on earth is done, When, by thy grace, the vic-t'ry's won,
What-e'er I do, wher-e'er I be, Still 'tis God's hand that lead-eth me!
By wa-ters still, o'er trou-bled sea, Still 'tis his hand that lead-eth me!
Con-tent, what-ev-er lot I see, Since 'tis thy hand that lead-eth me!
E'en death's cold wave I will not flee, Since God thro' Jor-dan lead-eth me!
He lead-eth me, he lead-eth me, By his own hand he lead-eth me:
His faith-ful fol-l'wer I would be, For by his hand he lead-eth me.

Psalm 23. Words, Joseph H. Gilmore, 1862. Tune HE LEADETH ME, William B. Bradbury, 1864.

God Will Take Care of You 219

1. Be not dis-may'd what-e'er be-tide, God will take care of you;
2. Thro' days of toil when heart doth fail, God will take care of you;
3. No mat-ter what may be the test, God will take care of you;

Be-neath his wings of love a-bide, God will take care of you.
When dan-gers fierce your path as-sail, God will take care of you.
Lean, wea-ry one, up-on his breast, God will take care of you.

God will take care of you, Thro' ev-'ry day, o'er all the way;

He will take care of you, God will take care of you.

Words, Civilla D. Martin, 1905. Tune GOD CARES, W. Stillman Martin, 1905.

220 Just When I Need Him Most

1. Just when I need him, Je-sus is near, Just when I fal-ter,
2. Just when I need him, Je-sus is true, Nev-er for-sak-ing
3. Just when I need him, Je-sus is strong, Bear-ing my bur-dens
4. Just when I need him, he is my all, An-swer-ing when up-
just when I fear; Read-y to help me, read-y to cheer,
all the way thro'; Giv-ing for bur-dens pleas-ures a-new,
all the day long; For all my sor-row giv-ing a song,
on him I call; Ten-der-ly watch-ing lest I should fall,
Just when I need him most. Just when I need him most,
Just when I need him most; Je-sus is near to
com-fort and cheer, Just when I need him most.

Words, William C. Poole, 1907. Tune GABRIEL, Charles H. Gabriel, 1907. Copyright 1908 by Charles H. Gabriel. © Copyright Renewed 1936 (extended). The Rodeheaver Co., Owner. Used by permission.

Sometimes a Light Surprises 221

1. Some-times a light sur - pris - es The Chris - tian while he sings;
2. In ho - ly con - tem - pla - tion We sweet - ly then pur - sue
3. It can bring with it noth - ing But he will bear us thro';
4. Tho vine nor fig tree nei - ther Their wont - ed fruit should bear,

It is the Lord who ris - es With heal - ing in his wings.
The theme of God's sal - va - tion, And find it ev - er new;
Who gives the lil - ies cloth - ing Will clothe his peo - ple, too;
Tho all the field should with - er, Nor flocks nor herds be there;

When com - forts are de - clin - ing, He grants the soul a - gain
Set free from pres - ent sor - row, We cheer - ful - ly can say,
Be - neath the spread-ing heav-ens, No crea - ture but is fed;
Yet God the same a - bid - ing, His praise shall tune my voice,

A sea - son of clear shin - ing, To cheer it af - ter rain.
Let the un - known to - mor - row Bring with it what it may.
And he who feeds the ra - vens Will give his chil - dren bread.
For while in him con - fid - ing, I can - not but re - joice.

Matthew 6:25-34, Habakkuk 3:17, 18. Words, William Cowper, 1779. Tune LLANFYLLIN, Traditional
Welsh Melody, 1865, 1938.
This tune in a higher key, No. 264. Alternate tune AURELIA, No. 236.

222 Day by Day

1. Day by day and with each pass - ing mo - ment, Strength I
2. Ev - 'ry day the Lord him - self is near me With a
3. Help me then in ev - 'ry trib - u - la - tion So to

find to meet my tri - als here; Trust - ing in my Fa - ther's
spe - cial mer - cy for each hour; All my cares he fain would
trust thy prom - is - es, O Lord, That I lose not faith's sweet

wise be - stow - ment, I've no cause for wor - ry or for fear.
bear, and cheer me, He whose name is Coun - sel - lor and Pow'r.
con - so - la - tion Of - fered me with - in thy ho - ly Word.

He whose heart is kind be - yond all mea - sure Gives un -
The pro - tec - tion of his child and trea - sure Is a
Help me, Lord, when toil and trou - ble meet - ing, E'er to

Words, Caroline V. Sandell-Berg, 1865; translated, A. L. Skoog. Tune BLOTT EN DAG, Oscar Ahnfelt.

to each day what he deems best — Lov-ing-ly, its part of
charge that on him-self he laid; "As thy days, thy strength shall
take, as from a fa-ther's hand, One by one, the days, the

pain and plea-sure, Min-gling toil with peace and rest.
be in mea-sure," This the pledge to me he made.
mo-ments fleet-ing, Till I reach the prom-ised land. A-MEN.

O God, Our Help in Ages Past 223

1. O God, our help in a-ges past, Our hope for years to come,
2. Un-der the shad-ow of thy throne Thy saints have dwelt se-cure;
3. Be-fore the hills in or-der stood, Or earth re-ceived her frame,
4. A thou-sand a-ges in thy sight Are like an eve-ning gone;
5. Time, like an ev-er-roll-ing stream, Bears all its sons a-way;
6. O God, our help in a-ges past, Our hope for years to come,

Our shel-ter from the storm-y blast, And our e-ter-nal home!
Suf-fi-cient is thine arm a-lone, And our de-fense is sure.
From ev-er-last-ing thou art God, To end-less years the same.
Short as the watch that ends the night Be-fore the ris-ing sun.
They fly, for-got-ten, as a dream Dies at the op-'ning day.
Be thou our guard while life shall last, And our e-ter-nal home. A-MEN.

Psalm 90:1-5. Words, Isaac Watts, 1719. Tune ST. ANNE, William Croft, 1708.

224 Give to the Winds Your Fears

Unison
1. Give to the winds your fears; In hope be un - dis-mayed:
2. O put your trust in God; In du- ty's path go on.
God hears your sighs and counts your tears, God shall lift up your
Walk in his strength with faith and hope, So shall your work be
head. To him com-mit your griefs; Your ways put in his hands —
done. Leave to his sov-'reign sway To choose and to com-mand;
To his sure truth and ten - der care Who earth and heav'n com -
So you shall, faith - ful, seek his way — How wise, how strong his

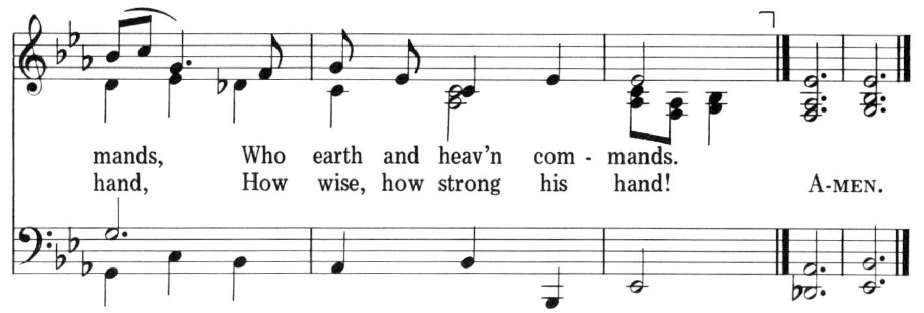

mands, Who earth and heav'n com - mands.
hand, How wise, how strong his hand! A-MEN.

Have No Fear, Little Flock 225

Unison

1. Have no fear, lit - tle flock, have no fear, lit - tle
2. Have good cheer, lit - tle flock, have good cheer, lit - tle
3. Praise the Lord high a - bove, praise the Lord high a -
4. Thank - ful hearts raise to God, thank - ful hearts raise to

flock, for the Fa - ther has cho - sen to
flock, for the Fa - ther will keep you in
bove, for he stoops down to heal you, up -
God, for he stays close be - side you, in

give you the King - dom, Have no fear, lit - tle flock!
his love for - ev - er, Have good cheer, lit - tle flock!
lift and re - store you, Praise the Lord high a - bove!
all things works with you, Thank - ful hearts raise to God!

Words, st. 1, Luke 12:32; st. 2-4, Marjorie Jillson, 1972. Tune LITTLE FLOCK 1971,
Heinz Werner Zimmermann, 1971. From *Five Hymns* by Heinz Werner Zimmermann, copyright 1973
by Concordia Publishing House. Used by permission.

226 Follow On

1. Down in the val-ley with my Sav-ior I would go,
2. Down in the val-ley with my Sav-ior I would go,
3. Down in the val-ley or up-on the moun-tain steep,
Where the flow'rs are bloom-ing and the sweet wa-ters flow;
Where the storms are sweep-ing and the dark wa-ters flow;
Close be-side my Sav-ior would my soul ev-er keep;
Ev-'ry-where he leads me I would fol-low, fol-low on,
With his hand to lead me I will nev-er, nev-er fear,
He will lead me safe-ly in the path that he has trod,
Walk-ing in his foot-steps till the crown be won.
Dan-ger can-not fright me if my Lord is near.
Up to where they gath-er on the hills of God.

Words, W. O. Cushing, 1880. Tune FOLLOW ON, Robert Lowry, 1880.

Fol-low! Fol-low! I would fol-low Je - sus! An - y - where, ev - 'ry - where,
I would fol-low on! Ev - 'ry-where he leads me I would fol - low on!

Show, O Lord, Thy Blessed Face 227

1. Show, O Lord, thy bless - ed face, Com - fort give and lov - ing grace.
2. To the vi - sions of the night, Grant the day of clear in-sight.
3. Speak thro' chan-nels of thy choice, And grant us to know thy voice,

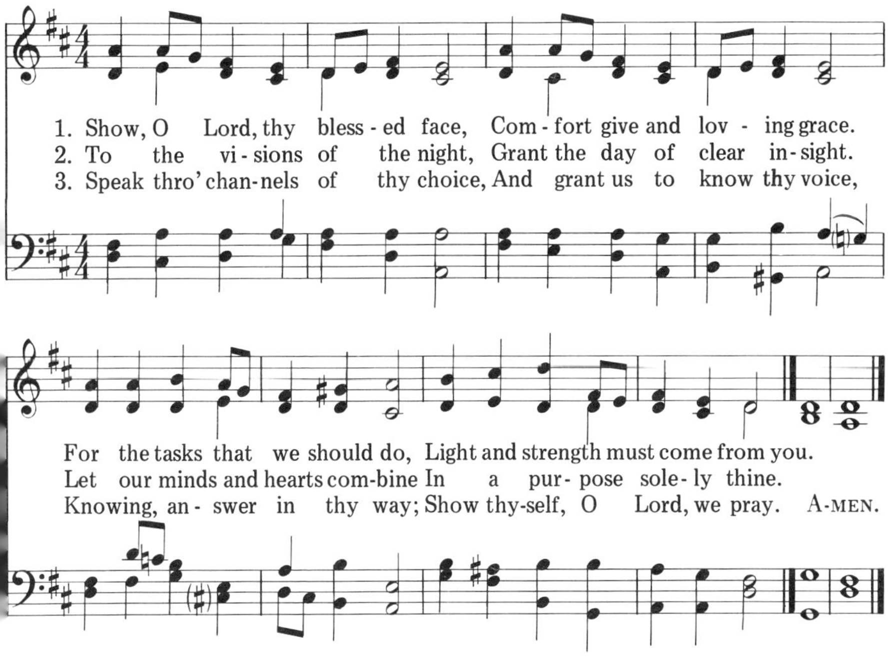

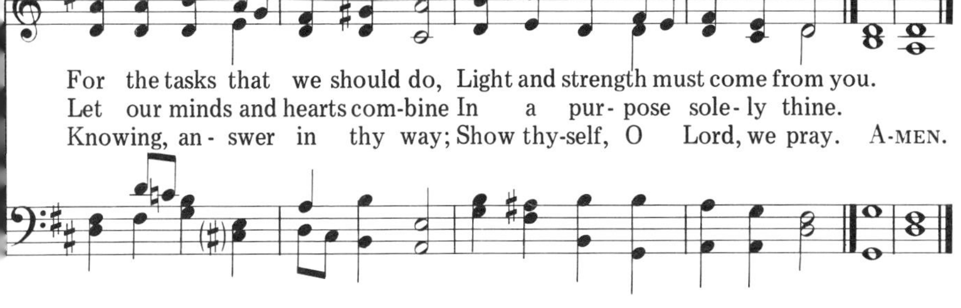
For the tasks that we should do, Light and strength must come from you.
Let our minds and hearts com-bine In a pur - pose sole-ly thine.
Knowing, an - swer in thy way; Show thy-self, O Lord, we pray. A-MEN.

228 Surely Goodness and Mercy

1. A pil-grim was I, and a-wan-d'ring, In the
2. He re-stor-eth my soul when I'm wea-ry, He
3. When I walk thro' the dark, lone-some val-ley, My

cold night of sin I did roam, When Je-sus the
giv-eth me strength day by day; He leads me be-
Sav-ior will walk with me there; And safe-ly his

kind Shep-herd found me, And now I am on my way home.
side the still wa-ters, He guards me each step of the way.
great hand will lead me To the man-sions he's gone to pre-pare.

Sure-ly good-ness and mer-cy shall fol-low me All the days,

all the days of my life; Sure-ly good-ness and

Words and tune GOODNESS, John W. Peterson and Alfred B. Smith, 1958. © Copyright 1958
Singspiration, Inc. All rights reserved. Used by permission.

mer - cy shall fol - low me All the days, all the days of my life.

(may be omitted until final refrain)

And I shall dwell in the house of the Lord for - ev - er,

And I shall feast at the ta - ble spread for me;

Sure - ly good - ness and mer - cy shall fol - low me All the days,

all the days of my life, All the days, all the days of my life.

229 We Gather Together

1. We gath - er to - geth - er to ask the Lord's bless - ing,
2. Be - side us to guide us, our God with us join - ing,
3. We all do ex - tol thee, thou lead - er in bat - tle,

He chas - tens and has - tens his will to make known;
Or - dain - ing, main - tain - ing his king - dom di - vine;
And pray that thou still our de - fend - er wilt be.

The wick - ed op - press - ing now cease from dis - tress - ing,
So from the be - gin - ning the fight we were win - ning,
Let thy con - gre - ga - tion es - cape trib - u - la - tion;

Sing prais - es to his name, he for - gets not his own.
Thou, Lord, wast at our side: the glo - ry be thine!
Thy name be ev - er praised: O Lord, make us free! A-MEN.

Words, Anonymous Dutch Hymn, 16th Century; translated, Theodore Baker, 1894. Tune KREMSER, Dutch Folk Song; harmonized, Edward Kremser, 1877.

How Gracious Are Thy Mercies, Lord 230

1. How gra-cious are thy mer-cies, Lord, They hal-low all my days;
2. How love-ly are thy mer-cies, Lord, The earth, the sky, the sea,
3. How ten-der are thy mer-cies, Lord, Thy grace when days are long,

Thy gifts of ten-der-ness and love In-spire my heart to praise.
For all things good and beau-ti-ful I of-fer praise to thee.
And in the lone-ly mid-night hour Thy pre-cious gift of song.

The grow-ing mir-a-cle of faith As-sures me I am thine;
For clouds by day and stars by night, For blos-soms frail and fair,
When I ap-proach the gates of death And life is at an end,

Oh, praise thy name that I can share This fel-low-ship di-vine!
For all thy glo-rious hand-i-work My heart is moved to prayer.
Thy pres-ence will sus-tain me still, My Sav-ior and my Friend!

231 Count Your Blessings

1. When up-on life's bil-lows you are tem-pest tossed, When you are dis-
2. Are you ev-er burdened with a load of care? Does the cross seem
3. When you look at oth-ers with their lands and gold, Think that Christ has
4. So, a-mid the con-flict, wheth-er great or small, Do not be dis-

cour-aged, think-ing all is lost, Count your man-y bless-ings, name them
heav-y you are called to bear? Count your man-y bless-ings, ev-'ry
prom-ised you his wealth un-told; Count your man-y bless-ings, mon-ey
cour-aged, God is o-ver all; Count your man-y bless-ings, an-gels

one by one, And it will sur-prise you what the Lord hath done.
doubt will fly, And you will be sing-ing as the days go by.
can-not buy Your re-ward in heav-en, nor your home on high.
will at-tend, Help and com-fort give you to your jour-ney's end.

Count your bless-ings, name them one by one: Count your
Count your many bless-ings, name them one by one; Count your many

Words, Johnson Oatman, Jr., 1897. Tune BLESSINGS, Edwin O. Excell, 1897.

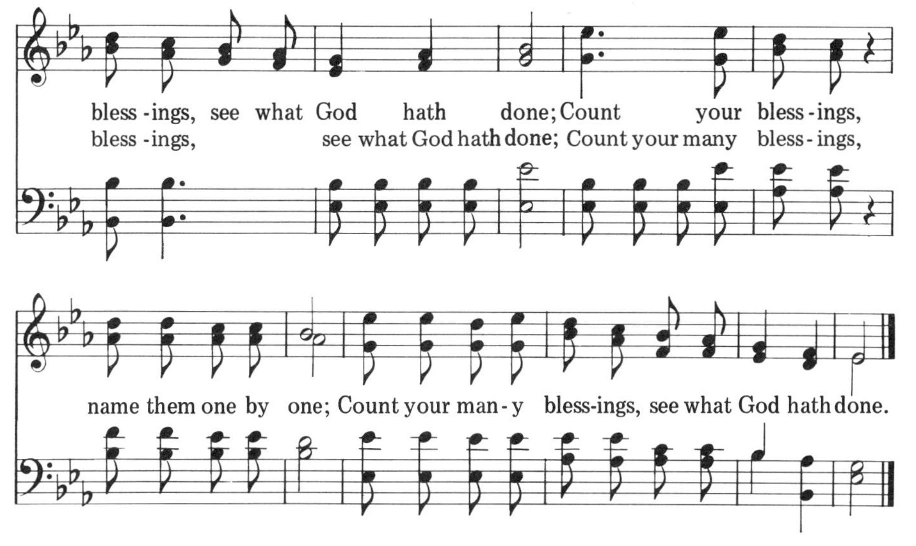

bless-ings, see what God hath done; Count your bless-ings,
bless-ings, see what God hath done; Count your many bless-ings,
name them one by one; Count your man-y bless-ings, see what God hath done.

Sing to the Lord of Harvest 232

Unison
1. Sing to the Lord of har-vest, Sing songs of love and praise;
2. By him the roll-ing sea-sons In fruit-ful or-der move;
3. Bring to his sa-cred al-tar The gifts his good-ness gave,
4. Your hearts lay down be-fore him When at his feet you fall;

With joy-ful hearts and voic-es Your al - le-lu-ias raise.
O sing to the Lord of har-vest, A song of hap-py love.
The gold-en sheaves of har-vest, The souls he died to save.
And with your lives a-dore him Who gave his life for all.

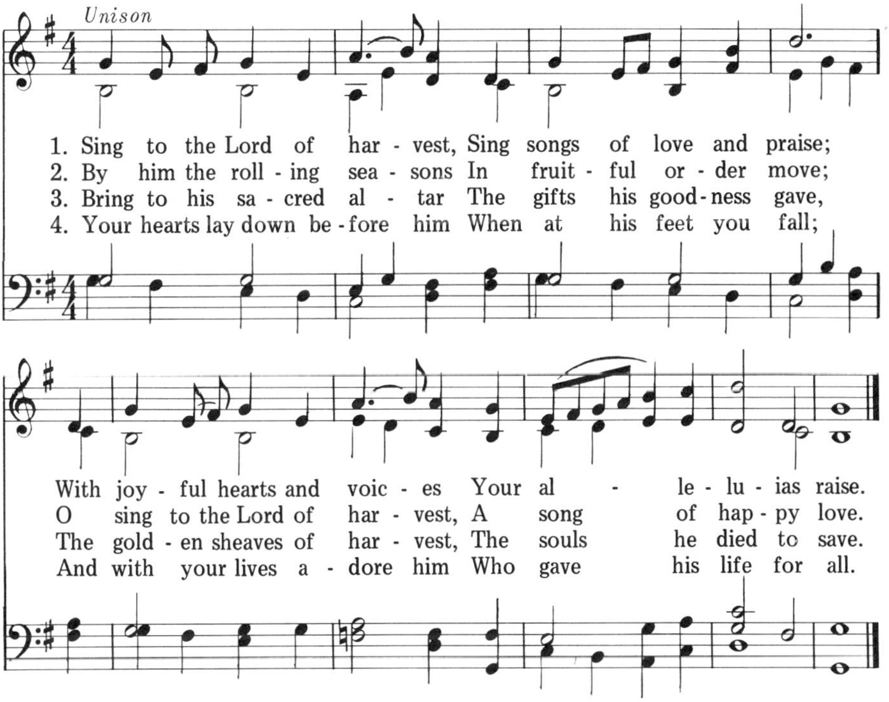

233 Come, Ye Thankful People, Come

1. Come, ye thank-ful peo-ple, come, Raise the song of har-vest home!
2. We our-selves are God's own field, Fruit un-to his praise to yield;
3. For the Lord our God shall come, And shall take his har-vest home;
4. E-ven so, Lord, quick-ly come, Bring thy fi-nal har-vest home;
All is safe-ly gath-ered in, Ere the win-ter storms be-gin;
Wheat and tares to-geth-er sown Un-to joy or sor-row grown;
From his field shall purge a-way All that doth of-fend that day;
Gath-er thou thy peo-ple in, Free from sor-row, free from sin;
God, our Mak-er, doth pro-vide For our wants to be sup-plied:
First the blade, and then the ear, Then the full corn shall ap-pear;
Give his an-gels charge at last In the fire the tares to cast;
There, for-ev-er pu-ri-fied, In thy pres-ence to a-bide;
Come to God's own tem-ple, come, Raise the song of har-vest home.
Lord of har-vest! grant that we Wholesome grain and pure may be.
But the fruit-ful ears to store In his gar-ner ev-er-more.
Come, with all thine an-gels, come, Raise the glo-rious har-vest home.

Words, Henry Alford, 1844. Tune ST. GEORGE'S WINDSOR, George J. Elvey, 1858.

Now Thank We All Our God 234

1. Now thank we all our God With heart and hands and voic - es,
2. O may this boun- teous God Thro' all our life be near us,
3. All praise and thanks to God The Fa - ther now be giv - en,

Who won-drous things hath done, In whom his world re - joic - es;
With ev - er joy - ful hearts And bless - ed peace to cheer us;
The Son, and him who reigns With them in high - est heav - en,

Who, from our moth - er's arms, Hath blest us on our way
And keep us in his grace, And guide us when per - plexed,
The one e - ter - nal God, Whom earth and heav'n a - dore;

With count-less gifts of love, And still is ours to - day.
And free us from all ills In this world and the next.
For thus it was, is now, And shall be ev - er - more. A - MEN.

Words, Martin Rinkart, 1636; translated, Catherine Winkworth, 1858. Tune NUN DANKET, Johann Crüger, 1647; harmonized, Felix Mendelssohn, 1840.

235 Built on the Rock the Church Doth Stand

1. Built on the Rock the church doth stand, E - ven when stee-ples are
2. Not in our tem - ples made with hands God, the al - might - y, is
3. We are God's house of liv - ing stones, Built for his own hab - i -

fall - ing; Crum-bled have spires in ev - 'ry land, Bells still are
dwell - ing; High in the heav'ns his tem - ple stands, All earth-ly
ta - tion; He fills our hearts, his hum - ble thrones, Grant-ing us

chim-ing and call - ing; Call-ing the young and old to rest, Call-ing the
tem-ples ex - cell - ing; Yet he who dwells in heav'n a - bove Deigns to a -
life and sal - va - tion; Were two or three to seek his face, He in their

souls of men dis-tressed, Long-ing for life ev - er - last - ing.
bide with us in love, Mak - ing our bod-ies his tem - ple.
midst would show his grace, Bless-ings up - on them be-stow - ing. — MEN.

Matthew 16:18. Words, Nicolai F. S. Grundtvig, 1837; translated, Carl Doving, 1913; revised,
Fred C. M. Hansen, 1958. From *The Service Book and Hymnal* by permission of the Commission on the
Liturgy and Hymnal. Tune KIRKEN, Ludwig M. Lindeman, 1840.

The Church's One Foundation 236

1. The church-'s one foun - da - tion Is Je - sus Christ her Lord;
2. E - lect from ev - 'ry na - tion, Yet one o'er all the earth,
3. 'Mid toil and trib - u - la - tion, And tu - mult of her war,

She is his new cre - a - tion, By Spir - it and the Word:
Her char - ter of sal - va - tion, One Lord, one faith, one birth;
She waits the con - sum - ma - tion Of peace for - ev - er - more;

From heav'n he came and sought her To be his ho - ly bride,
One ho - ly name she bless - es, Par - takes one ho - ly food,
Till with the vi - sion glo - rious, Her long - ing eyes are blest,

With his own blood he bought her, And for her life he died.
And to one hope she press - es, With ev - 'ry grace en - dued.
And the great church vic - to - rious Shall be the church at rest.

Words, Samuel J. Stone, 1866. Tune AURELIA, Samuel S. Wesley, 1864.

237 O Church of God, Triumphant

1. O Church of God, tri - um-phant A - bove the world's dark fears,
2. On Christ-mas eve her car - ols Have set our hearts a - glow,
3. Her task on earth un - fin-ished Till threats of war shall cease,
4. O Church of God, tri - um-phant, We of - fer now in prayer

Where - in our souls find ref - uge Thro' all these earth - ly years!
Her bells on Eas - ter morn - ing With faith still o - ver - flow;
Her voice must raise a pro - test Where greed still robs men's peace;
Our youth, our full - er man - hood, For Christ's great cause to dare,

Christ's stead - fast, ho - ly pur - pose, Il - lu - mined by the cross,
Be - fore her hal - lowed al - tars We pledge our love in youth,
One broth - er - hood Christ called for, Of ev - 'ry class and race:
That his re - deem - ing pur - pose May prove be - yond de - feat,

Guards her from e - vil's pow - er, Re - veal - ing it but dross.
While in her sa - cred por - tals Our minds have found God's truth.
The church must live the vi - sion That shone in Je - sus' face.
Till in the life im - mor - tal With joy his chil - dren meet.

To Worship, Work, and Witness 238

1. To wor - ship, work, and wit - ness, The Good News spread a - broad,
2. Be thine thy Mas - ter's pur - pose To seek and save the lost,
3. Be thou to Christ his bod - y, Hold fast to Christ thy Head;
4. Head of the Church, in - spire us To have in us thy mind,

We mag - ni - fy thy mis - sion, Church of the liv - ing God;
To ran - som those in bond - age, To dare nor count the cost;
Be thou Christ's o - pen let - ter By all men to be read;
To hum - bly wait thy guid - ance, Thy joy in serv - ing find.

The Fa - ther's new cre - a - tion Thro' Je - sus Christ his Son,
To love and lift the low - ly, To heed the pris - 'ner's groan,
Be thou Christ's ho - ly tem - ple, Him - self the cor - ner - stone;
Be - stow the Spir - it's grace - gifts To serve the com - mon good,

The Spir - it has em - pow - ered To do as Christ has done.
To take up oth - ers' bur - dens And bear them as thine own.
Be thou Christ's liv - ing al - tar Where - on his love is shown.
While help - ing each the oth - er To love thy broth - er - hood. A-MEN.

Words, Henry Lyle Lambdin, 1969. Copyright 1969 by The Hymn Society of America. Used by permission.
Tune WEBB, George J. Webb, 1837.
This tune in a lower key, No. 391.

239 Lord, Who Dost Give to Thy Church

Unison

1. Lord, who dost give to thy church for its heal - ing
2. Clear be the voic - es of preach - ers and proph - ets
3. Ten - der and wise be the hearts of the pas - tors,
4. May those who teach grow in knowl - edge and pa - tience,
5. Lord, ev - er give to us gifts in due mea - sure,

Gifts, and the grace to sus - tain and re - new,
Fear - less - ly speak - ing the word of the Lord,
Guid - ing and guard - ing the souls in their care,
Guid - ing to wis - dom the young and the old,
Each need - ing oth - er, and all hav - ing worth;

Hear as we pray that to - day and each mor - row
Word of re - demp - tion thro' God's Son in - car - nate,
Firm with the way - ward, a strength to the doubt - ing,
Train - ing for wor - ship and wit - ness and ser - vice,
So to the Fa - ther, the Son, and the Spir - it,

We to thy pur - pose may show our - selves true.
Bless - ing for curs - ing, and peace for the sword.
Help - ing the need - y their bur - dens to bear.
Foes to all false - hood, in truth - ful - ness bold.
Glo - ry be shown by the church here on earth. A - MEN.

I Love Thy Kingdom, Lord 240

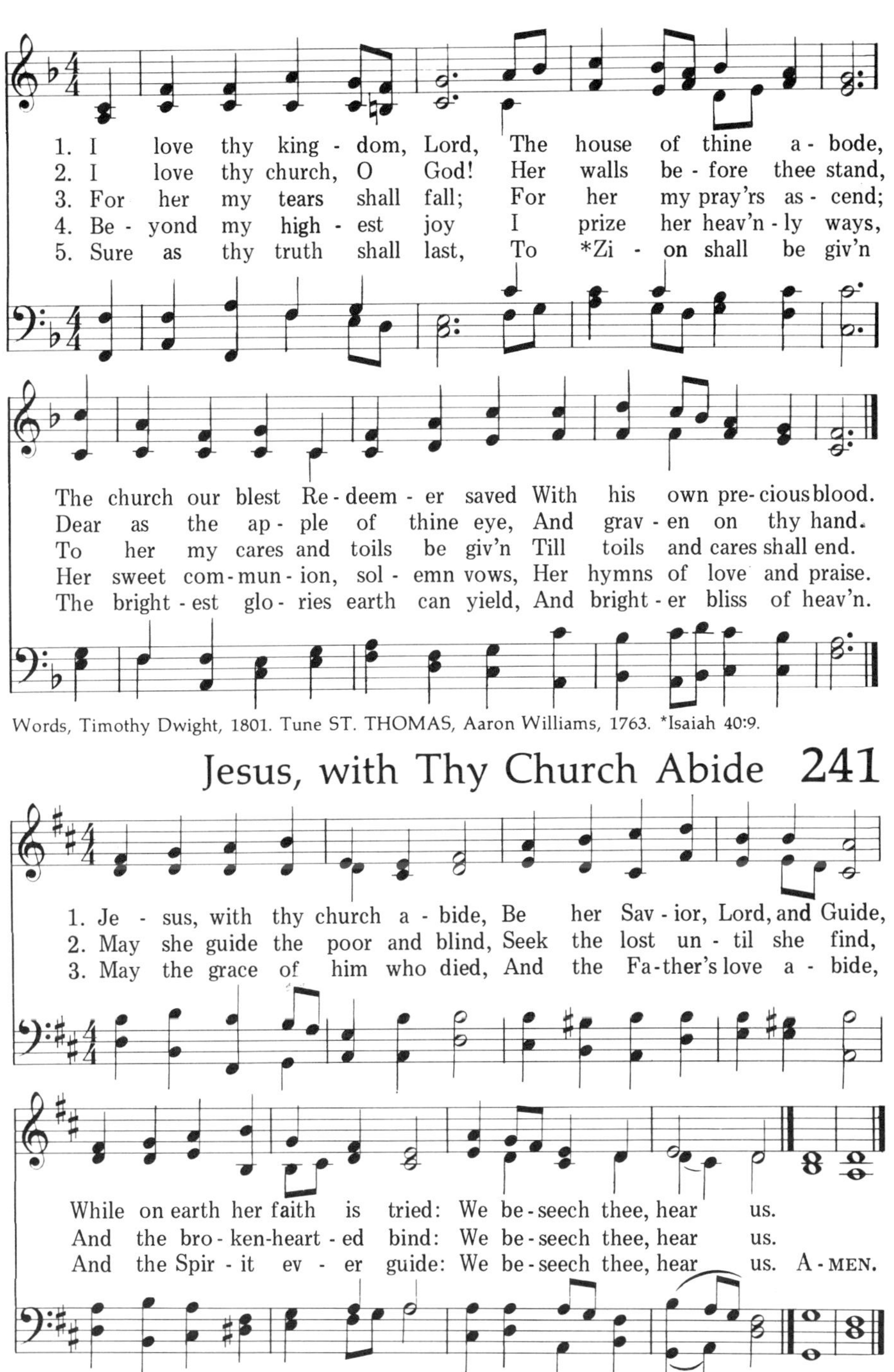

1. I love thy king-dom, Lord, The house of thine a-bode,
2. I love thy church, O God! Her walls be-fore thee stand,
3. For her my tears shall fall; For her my pray'rs as-cend;
4. Be-yond my high-est joy I prize her heav'n-ly ways,
5. Sure as thy truth shall last, To *Zi-on shall be giv'n

The church our blest Re-deem-er saved With his own pre-cious blood.
Dear as the ap-ple of thine eye, And grav-en on thy hand.
To her my cares and toils be giv'n Till toils and cares shall end.
Her sweet com-mun-ion, sol-emn vows, Her hymns of love and praise.
The bright-est glo-ries earth can yield, And bright-er bliss of heav'n.

Words, Timothy Dwight, 1801. Tune ST. THOMAS, Aaron Williams, 1763. *Isaiah 40:9.

Jesus, with Thy Church Abide 241

1. Je-sus, with thy church a-bide, Be her Sav-ior, Lord, and Guide,
2. May she guide the poor and blind, Seek the lost un-til she find,
3. May the grace of him who died, And the Fa-ther's love a-bide,

While on earth her faith is tried: We be-seech thee, hear us.
And the bro-ken-heart-ed bind: We be-seech thee, hear us.
And the Spir-it ev-er guide: We be-seech thee, hear us. A-MEN.

Words, Thomas B. Pollock, 1871. Tune SONG 13, Orlando Gibbons, 1623.

242 Come, Holy Spirit, Dove Divine

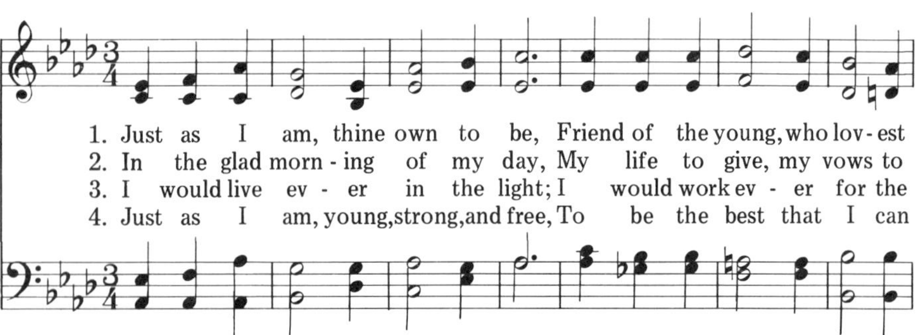

1. Come, Ho - ly Spir - it, Dove di - vine, On these bap-
2. We love thy name, we love thy laws, And joy - ful-
3. We sink be - neath the wa - ter's face; And thank thee
4. And as we rise with thee to live, O let the

tis - mal wa - ters shine, And teach our hearts, in
ly em - brace thy cause; We love thy cross, the
for thy sav - ing grace; We die to sin, and
Ho - ly Spir - it give The seal - ing unc - tion

high - est strain, To praise the Lamb for sin - ners slain.
shame, the pain, O Lamb of God, for sin - ners slain.
seek a grave With thee, be - neath the yield - ing wave.
from a - bove, The joy of life, the fire of love. A - MEN.

Words, Adoniram Judson, c. 1829. Tune MARYTON, H. Percy Smith, 1874.

243 Just As I Am, Thine Own to Be

1. Just as I am, thine own to be, Friend of the young, who lov - est
2. In the glad morn - ing of my day, My life to give, my vows to
3. I would live ev - er in the light; I would work ev - er for the
4. Just as I am, young, strong, and free, To be the best that I can

Words, Marianne Hearn, 1887. Tune JUST AS I AM, Joseph Barnby, 1892.

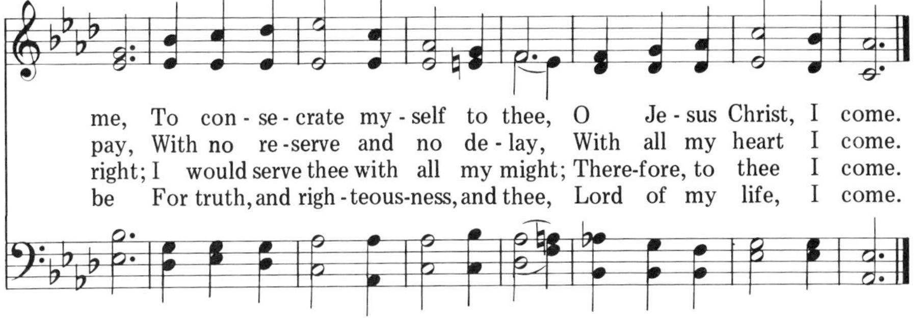

me, To con-se-crate my-self to thee, O Je-sus Christ, I come.
pay, With no re-serve and no de-lay, With all my heart I come.
right; I would serve thee with all my might; There-fore, to thee I come.
be For truth, and righ-teous-ness, and thee, Lord of my life, I come.

We Bless the Name of Christ the Lord 244

Unison

1. We bless the name of Christ the Lord, We bless him
2. We fol-low him with pure de-light To sanc-ti-
3. Bap-tized in God the Fa-ther, Son, And Ho-ly
4. By grace we "Ab-ba, Fa-ther," cry; By grace the

for his ho-ly Word, Who loved to do his
fy his sa-cred rite, And thus our faith with
Spir-it, Three in One, With con-science free we
Com-fort-er comes nigh; And for thy grace our

Fa-ther's will, And all his righ-teous-ness ful - fill.
wa-ter seal To prove o-be-dience that we feel.
rest in God, In love and peace, thro' Je-sus' blood.
love shall be For-ev-er, on-ly, Lord, for thee.

Romans 6:4. Words, Samuel F. Coffman. Tune RETREAT, Thomas Hastings, 1840.

245 Where Can We Find Thee, Lord, So Near

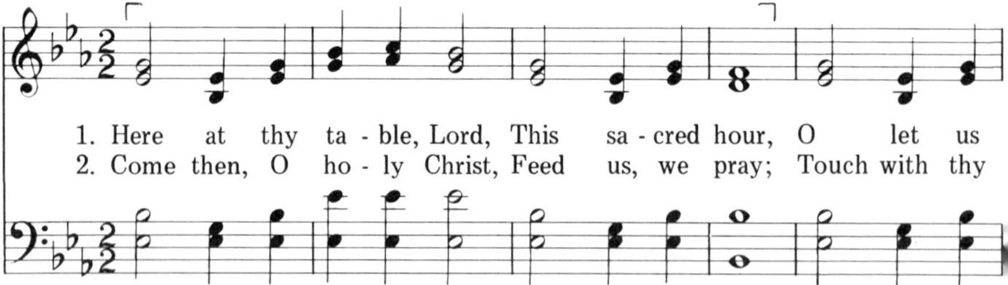

Unison

1. Where can we find thee, Lord, so near, So real, so
2. Where may we thy sal - va - tion know In full - est,
3. Where may we know the lib - er - ty Of those whom
4. Thus to thy ta - ble would we come, Re - mem-b'ring

gra - cious, so di - vine, As at the ta - ble
glad - dest cer - tain - ty, As with the em - blems
thou thro' faith hast freed, As, gath - ered in thy
thee with bread and wine, Re - joic - ing most of

set with love By those who know them-selves as thine?
of thy grace Spread out for sin - ful man to see?
bless - ed name, We own thee Host and Friend in - deed?
all to know That here we nour - ish life di - vine.

Words, Thomas B. McDormand, 1974. Used by permission of the author. Tune FEDERAL STREET, Henry K. Oliver, 1832.

246 Here at Thy Table, Lord

1. Here at thy ta - ble, Lord, This sa - cred hour, O let us
2. Come then, O ho - ly Christ, Feed us, we pray; Touch with thy

Words, May P. Hoyt. Tune BREAD OF LIFE, William F. Sherwin, 1877.

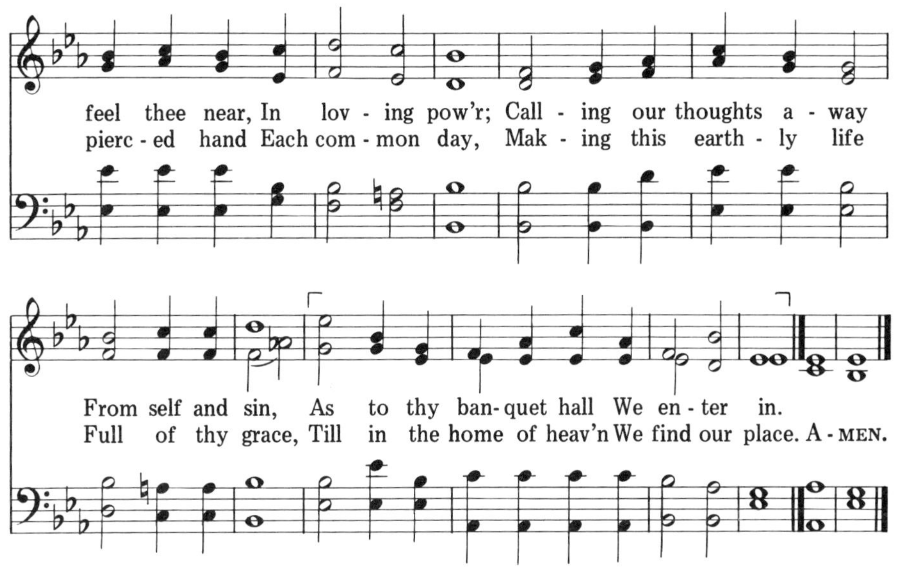

feel thee near, In lov - ing pow'r; Call - ing our thoughts a - way
pierc - ed hand Each com - mon day, Mak - ing this earth - ly life
From self and sin, As to thy ban-quet hall We en - ter in.
Full of thy grace, Till in the home of heav'n We find our place. A - MEN.

From Every Race, from Every Clime   247

Unison
1. From ev - 'ry race, from ev - 'ry clime Thy peo - ple gath - ered 'round,
2. Par - tak - ing of the bread, we know Our strength from thee de - rives,
3. Thro'-out the world thy ta - ble's set, Dear Lord, our Sav - ior, Guide,
4. From north to south, from east to west Men gath - er to re - call

The em - blems of thy grace sub - lime With grat - i - tude a - bound.
And as we take the cup, we go To wit - ness with our lives.
In hope we know that men shall yet In broth - er - hood a - bide.
In rev - 'rent mem - o - ry thy blest Re - demp - tive love for all.

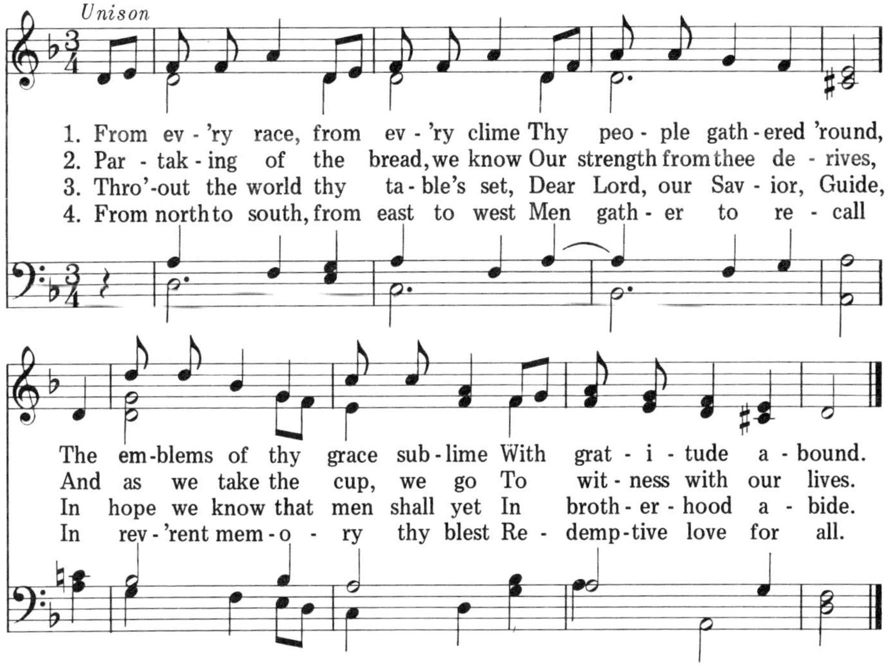

Words, Thomas B. McDormand. Used by permission of the author. Tune DAUGAVA, Latvian Folk Melody.

248 Thy Supper, Lord, Before Us Spread

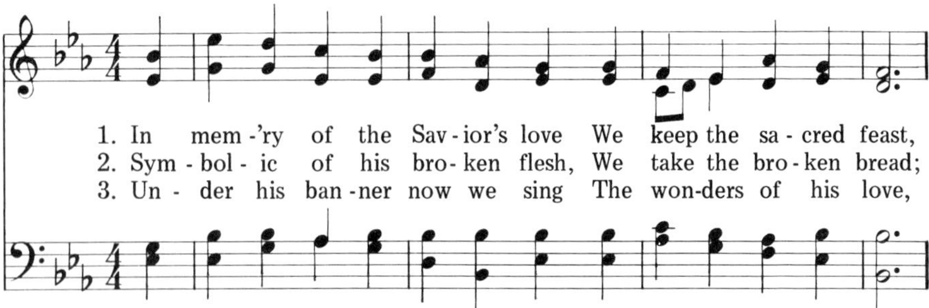

Unison

1. Thy sup - per, Lord, be - fore us spread, The cup be -
2. Thy sac - ri - fice was for our gain; To save us
3. In fel - low - ship with thee we feel That thou art
4. Now may the wor - ship we know here Re - mind us

side the bro - ken bread, Re - minds us of thy life laid
thou didst bear the pain. Thy love is clear for all to
here, thy pres - ence real; For thou hast ris - en and dost
al - ways thou art near; Help us to live our lives each

down — The shame - ful cross, the thorn - y crown.
see; We bow in thank - ful prayer to thee.
live With - in our hearts, new life to give.
day In love and faith, O Lord, we pray.

Words, Joseph F. Green, 1961. Tune REYNOLDS, Irving Wolfe, 1961. ©Copyright 1961, 1964 Broadman Press. All rights reserved.

249 In Memory of the Savior's Love

1. In mem -'ry of the Sav - ior's love We keep the sa - cred feast,
2. Sym - bol - ic of his bro - ken flesh, We take the bro - ken bread;
3. Un - der his ban - ner now we sing The won - ders of his love,

Words, Thomas Cotterill, 1805. Tune ST. PETER, Alexander R. Reinagle, 1836.
This tune in a lower key, No. 464.

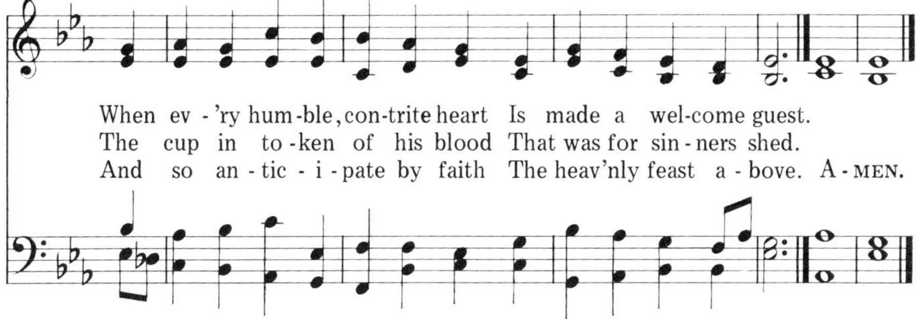

When ev-'ry hum-ble, con-trite heart Is made a wel-come guest.
The cup in to-ken of his blood That was for sin-ners shed.
And so an-tic-i-pate by faith The heav'nly feast a-bove. A-MEN.

The Bread of Life for All Men Broken 250

Unison

1. The bread of life for all men bro-ken! He drank the
2. With god-ly fear we seek thy pres-ence; Our hearts are
3. O Lord, we pray, come thou a-mong us, Light-en our

cup on Gol-go-tha. His grace we trust, and spread with
sad, peo-ple dis-tressed. Thy ho-ly face is stained with
eyes, bright-ly ap-pear! Im-man-u-el, heav'n's joy un-

rev-er-ence This ho-ly feast, and thus re-mem - ber.
bit-ter tears, Our hu-man pain still bear-est thou with us.
end - ing, Our life with thine for-ev-er blend - ing.

Words, Timothy T'ing-fang Lew, 1936; translated, Walter R. O. Taylor, 1943. Tune SHENG EN, Su Yin-lan, 1934.

251 As We Gather Around the Table

Unison

1. As we gath - er a - round the ta - ble of our Lord,
2. As we gath - er a - round the ta - ble of our Lord,
3. As we gath - er a - round the ta - ble of our Lord,

We re - call his hum - ble birth in Beth - le - hem,
We re - call his ag - o - ny up - on the cross.
We re - call the emp - ty tomb where he was laid.

As the an - gels sang, As the shep-herds came, Let us a-
There our Sav - ior died; A - lone was cru - ci - fied; Let us a-
He is liv - ing still; Our long - ing hearts to fill; Let us a-

dore and wor - ship the Lord, Let us re - mem - ber him.
dore and wor - ship the Lord, Let us re - mem - ber him.
dore and wor - ship the Lord, Let us re - mem - ber him.

Let Us Break Bread Together   252

Unison
1. Let us break bread to-geth-er on our knees,
2. Let us drink the cup to-geth-er on our knees,
3. Let us praise God to-geth-er on our knees,
Let us break bread to-geth-er on our knees;
Let us drink the cup to-geth-er on our knees;
Let us praise God to-geth-er on our knees;
When I fall on my knees, With my face to the ris-ing
sun, O Lord, have mer-cy on me.

Words and tune BREAK BREAD, Traditional Negro Spiritual.

253 Christian Hearts, in Love United

1. Chris-tian hearts, in love u-nit-ed, Seek a-lone in Je-sus rest;
2. Come, then, come, O flock of Je-sus, Cov-e-nant with him a-new;
3. Grant, Lord, that with thy di-rec-tion, "Love each oth-er," we com-ply,
4. O that such may be our u-nion, As thine with the Fa-ther is,

Has he not your love ex-cit-ed? Then let love in-spire each breast;
Un-to him who con-quered for us, Pledge we love and ser-vice true;
Aim-ing with un-feigned af-fec-tion Thy love to ex-em-pli-fy;
And not one of our com-mun-ion E'er for-sake the path of bliss;

Mem-bers on our Head de-pend-ing Lights re-flect-ing him, our Sun,
And should our love's u-nion ho-ly Firm-ly linked no more re-main,
Let our mu-tual love be glow-ing, Thus will all men plain-ly see,
May our light 'fore men with brightness, From thy light re-flect-ed, shine;

Brethren his com-mands at-tend-ing, We in him, our Lord, are one.
Wait ye at his foot-stool low-ly, Till he draw it close a-gain.
That we, as on one stem grow-ing, Liv-ing branch-es are in thee.
Thus the world will bear us wit-ness, That we, Lord, are tru-ly thine. A-MEN.

Words, Nicolaus L. von Zinzendorf, 1725; translated, Frederick W. Foster, 1789, alt. Tune CASSELL, Traditional German Melody.

Leaning on the Everlasting Arms 254

1. What a fel-low-ship, what a joy di-vine, Lean-ing on the ev-er-
2. Oh, how sweet to walk in this pil-grim way, Lean-ing on the ev-er-
3. What have I to dread, what have I to fear, Lean-ing on the ev-er-
last-ing arms; What a bless-ed-ness, what a peace is mine,
last-ing arms; Oh, how bright the path grows from day to day,
last-ing arms? I have bless-ed peace with my Lord so near,
Lean-ing on the ev-er-last-ing arms.
Lean-ing on the ev-er-last-ing arms. Lean - ing,
Lean-ing on the ev-er-last-ing arms. Lean-ing on Je-sus,
lean - ing, Safe and se-cure from all a-larms; Lean -
lean-ing on Je-sus, Lean-ing on
ing, lean - ing, Lean-ing on the ev-er-last-ing arms.
Je-sus, lean-ing on Je-sus,

Words, Elisha A. Hoffman, 1887. Tune SHOWALTER, Anthony J. Showalter, 1887.

255 Sweet, Sweet Spirit

1. There's a sweet, sweet spir-it in this place, And I
sweet ex - pres-sions on each face, And I
2. There are bless-ings you can-not re - ceive Till you
one to prof-it when you say, "I am
know that it's the spir-it of the Lord.______ There are
know that it's the pres-ence of the
know him in his full - ness, and be - lieve. ______ You're the
going to walk with Je - sus all the
Lord.______
way."______
Sweet Ho-ly Spir-it, Sweet Heav'n-ly Dove,
Stay right here with us Fill-ing us with your love. And for these

bless-ings We lift our hearts in praise; With-out a doubt we'll know
that we have been re-vived, When we shall leave this place.

Blest Be the Tie 256

1. Blest be the tie that binds Our hearts in Chris-tian love;
2. Be - fore our Fa - ther's throne We pour our ar - dent pray'rs;
3. We share our mu - tual woes, Our mu - tual bur - dens bear;
4. When we a - sun - der part, It gives us in - ward pain;

The fel - low - ship of kin-dred minds Is like to that a - bove.
Our fears, our hopes, our aims are one, Our comforts and our cares.
And of - ten for each oth - er flows The sym-pa - thiz-ing tear.
But we shall still be joined in heart, And hope to meet a - gain. A-MEN.

Words, John Fawcett, 1782. Tune DENNIS, Johann G. Nägeli; arranged, Lowell Mason, 1845.

257 Where Charity and Love Prevail

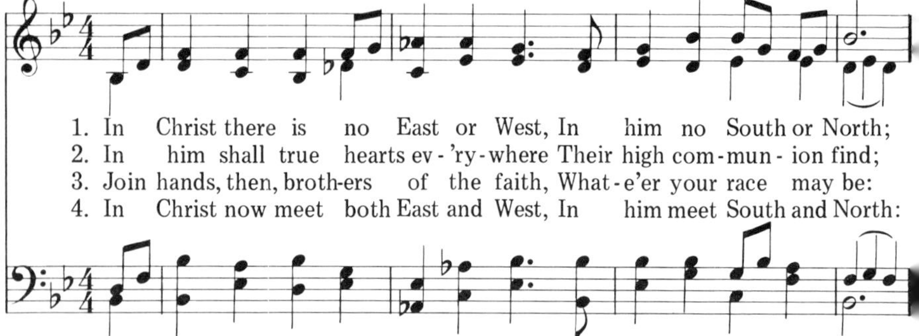

Unison

1. Where char - i - ty and love pre - vail There God is ev - er found;
2. With grate - ful joy and ho - ly fear His char - i - ty we learn;
3. For - give we now each oth - er's faults As we our faults con - fess,
4. Let strife a - mong us be un - known, Let all con - ten - tion cease;
5. Let us re - call that in our midst Dwells God's be - got - ten Son;

Brought here to - geth - er by Christ's love, By love are we thus bound.
Let us with heart and mind and soul Now love him in re - turn.
And let us love each oth - er well In Chris - tian ho - li - ness.
Be his the glo - ry that we seek, Be ours his ho - ly peace.
As mem - bers of his bod - y joined, We are in him made one.

Words, Latin Hymn, 9th Century; paraphrased, Omer Westendorf, 1961. Tune CHRISTIAN LOVE, Paul Benoit, 1961. Reprinted by permission of World Library Publications, Inc., Cincinnati, Ohio.

258 In Christ There Is No East or West

1. In Christ there is no East or West, In him no South or North;
2. In him shall true hearts ev - 'ry-where Their high com-mun - ion find;
3. Join hands, then, broth-ers of the faith, What-e'er your race may be:
4. In Christ now meet both East and West, In him meet South and North:

Words, John Oxenham, 1908. Used by permission of Miss Theo Oxenham, Worthing, Sussex. Tune MCKEE, adapted from a Negro Spiritual by Harry T. Burleigh, 1939. Alternate tune ST. PETER, No. 464.

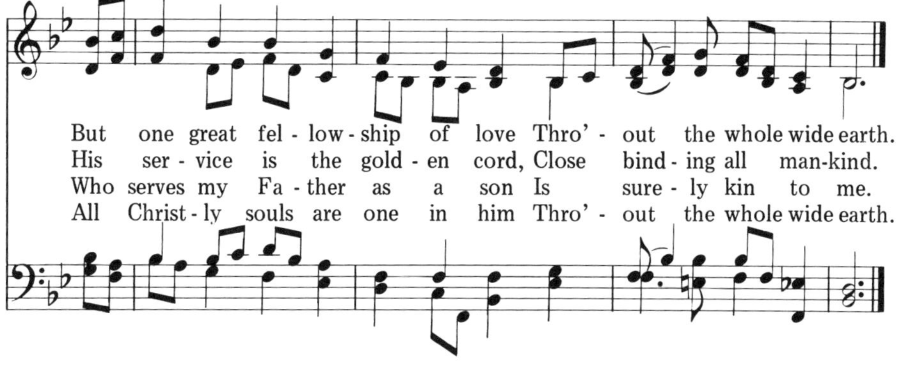

But one great fel - low - ship of love Thro' - out the whole wide earth.
His ser - vice is the gold - en cord, Close bind - ing all man-kind.
Who serves my Fa - ther as a son Is sure - ly kin to me.
All Christ - ly souls are one in him Thro' - out the whole wide earth.

The Bond of Love 259

1. We are one in the bond of love; We are one in the
2. Let us sing now, ev - 'ry - one; Let us feel his

bond of love. We have joined our spir - it with the
love be - gun. Let us join our hands that the

Spir - it of God; We are one in the bond of love.
world will know We are one in the bond of love.

260 Brethren, We Have Met to Worship

1. Breth - ren, we have met to wor - ship And a -
2. Breth - ren, see poor sin - ners round you Slum - b'ring
3. Sis - ters, will you join and help us? Mo - ses'
4. Let us love our God su - preme - ly, Let us

dore the Lord our God; Will you pray with all your pow - er,
on the brink of woe; Death is com - ing, hell is mov - ing,
sis - ter aid - ed him; Will you help the trem - bling mourners
love each oth - er, too; Let us love and pray for sin - ners,

While we try to preach the Word? All is vain un - less the
Can you bear to let them go? See our fa - thers and our
Who are strug - gling hard with sin? Tell them all a - bout the
Till our God makes all things new. Then he'll call us home to

Spir - it Of the Ho - ly One comes down; Breth - ren, pray,
moth - ers, And our chil - dren sink - ing down; Breth - ren, pray,
Sav - ior, Tell them that he will be found; Sis - ters, pray,
heav - en, At his ta - ble we'll sit down; Christ will gird

Words, George Atkins. Tune HOLY MANNA, William Moore, 1825.
This tune in a lower key, No. 419.

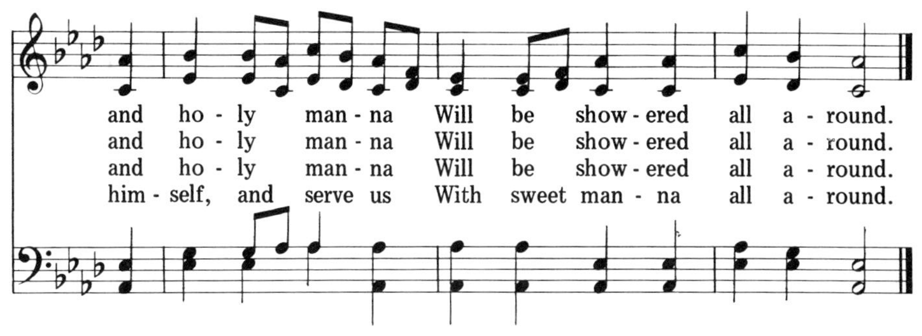

and ho - ly man - na Will be show - ered all a - round.
and ho - ly man - na Will be show - ered all a - round.
and ho - ly man - na Will be show - ered all a - round.
him - self, and serve us With sweet man - na all a - round.

God Be with You 261

1. God be with you till we meet a - gain! By his
2. God be with you till we meet a - gain! 'Neath his

coun - sels guide, up - hold you, With his sheep se - cure - ly fold you;
wings se - cure - ly hide you, Dai - ly man - na still pro - vide you;

God be with you till we meet a - gain!
God be with you till we meet a - gain! A - MEN.

Words, Jeremiah E. Rankin, 1880. Tune GOD BE WITH YOU, William G. Tomer, 1880.

262 Make Me a Channel of Blessing

1. Is your life a chan-nel of bless-ing? Is the love of God
2. Is your life a chan-nel of bless-ing? Are you bur-dened for
3. Is your life a chan-nel of bless-ing? Is it dai - ly
flow - ing thro' you? Are you tell - ing the lost of the Sav - ior?
those who are lost? Have you urged up - on those who are stray - ing
tell - ing for him? Have you spo-ken the word of sal - va - tion
Are you read - y his ser - vice to do?
The Sav - ior who died on the cross? Make me a chan-nel of
To those who are dy - ing in sin?
bless-ing to-day, Make me a chan-nel of bless-ing, I pray; My life pos-
sess - ing, my ser - vice bless-ing, Make me a chan-nel of bless-ing to - day.

Words and tune EUCLID, Harper G. Smyth, 1903.

Revive Us Again 263

1. We praise thee, O God! for the Son of thy love,
2. We praise thee, O God! for thy Spir-it of light,
3. All glo-ry and praise to the Lamb that was slain,
4. Re-vive us a-gain; fill each heart with thy love;

For Je-sus who died, and is now gone a-bove.
Who hath shown us our Sav-ior, and scat-ter'd our night.
Who hath borne all our sins, and hath cleans'd ev-'ry stain.
May each soul be re-kin-dled with fire from a-bove.

Hal-le-lu-jah! thine the glo-ry, Hal-le-lu-jah! a-men;

Hal-le-lu-jah! thine the glo-ry, Re-vive us a-gain.

Habakkuk 3:2. Words, William P. Mackay, 1863. Tune REVIVE US AGAIN, John J. Husband, c. 1820.

264 O Spirit of the Living God

Unison
1. O Spir - it of the liv - ing God, Thou light and fire di - vine,
2. Blow, wind of God! With wis - dom blow Un - til our minds are free
3. Teach us to ut - ter liv - ing words Of truth which all may hear,
4. So shall we know the pow'r of him Who came man - kind to save.

De - scend up - on thy Church once more, And make it tru - ly thine!
From mists of er - ror, clouds of doubt, Which blind our eyes to thee!
The lan - guage all men un - der - stand When love speaks loud and clear;
So shall we rise with him to life Which soars be - yond the grave;

Fill it with love and joy and pow'r, With righ - teous - ness and peace,
Burn, wing - ed fire! In - spire our lips With flam - ing love and zeal,
Till ev - 'ry age and race and clime Shall blend their creeds in one,
And earth shall win true ho - li - ness, Which makes thy chil - dren whole,

Till Christ shall dwell in hu - man hearts, And sin and sor - row cease.
To preach to all thy great good news, God's glo - rious common - weal!
And earth shall form one broth - er - hood By whom thy will is done.
Till, per - fect - ed by thee, we reach Cre - a - tion's glo - rious goal! A - MEN.

Acts 2. Words, Henry H. Tweedy, 1935. Tune LLANFYLLIN, Traditional Welsh Melody, 1865, 1938.
This tune in a lower key, No. 221.

God of Grace and God of Glory 265

1. God of grace and God of glo - ry, On thy peo - ple
2. Lo! the hosts of e - vil round us Scorn thy Christ, as -
3. Set our feet on loft - y plac - es; Gird our lives that
pour thy pow'r; Crown thine an - cient church - 's sto - ry, Bring her
sail his ways! Fears and doubts too long have bound us, Free our
they may be Ar - mored with all Christ - like grac - es In the
bud to glo - rious flow'r. Grant us wis - dom, Grant us cour - age,
hearts to work and praise. Grant us wis - dom, Grant us cour - age,
fight to set men free. Grant us wis - dom, Grant us cour - age,
For the fac - ing of this hour, For the fac - ing of this hour.
For the liv - ing of these days, For the liv - ing of these days.
That we fail not man nor thee! That we fail not man nor thee! A - MEN.

Words, Harry Emerson Fosdick, 1930. Used by permission of Elinor F. Downs. Tune CWM RHONDDA,
John Hughes, 1907. Music copyright used by permission of Mrs. Dilys S. Webb, Glamorganshire.

266 Search Me, O God

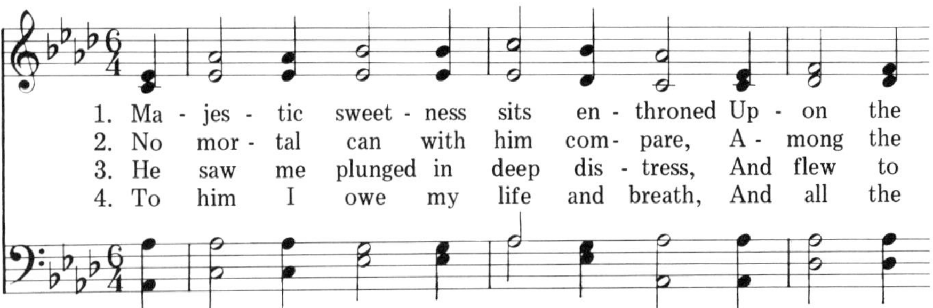

1. Search me, O God, and know my heart to-day; Try me, O
2. I praise thee, Lord, for cleans-ing me from sin; Ful - fill thy
3. Lord, take my life and make it whol-ly thine; Fill my poor
4. O Ho - ly Spir - it, re - viv - al comes from thee; Send a re-

Sav - ior, know my thoughts, I pray. See if there be some wick - ed
Word and make me pure with - in. Fill me with fire where once I
heart with thy great love di - vine. Take all my will, my pas - sion,
viv - al, start the work in me. Thy Word de - clares thou wilt sup-

way in me; Cleanse me from ev - 'ry sin and set me free.
burned with shame; Grant my de - sire to mag - ni - fy thy name.
self, and pride; I now sur - ren - der; Lord, in me a - bide.
ply our need; For bless - ings now, O Lord, I hum - bly plead. A - MEN.

Psalm 139:23, 24. Words, J. Edwin Orr, 1936. Words copyright by J. Edwin Orr, International copyright secured, Renewed copyright 1964. Tune ELLERS, Edward J. Hopkins, 1869.
This tune in a higher key, No. 65.

267 Majestic Sweetness Sits Enthroned

1. Ma - jes - tic sweet - ness sits en - throned Up - on the
2. No mor - tal can with him com - pare, A - mong the
3. He saw me plunged in deep dis - tress, And flew to
4. To him I owe my life and breath, And all the

Words, Samuel Stennett, 1787. Tune ORTONVILLE, Thomas Hastings, 1837.

Sav - ior's brow; His head with ra - diant glo - ries crowned,
sons of men; Fair - er is he than all the fair
my re - lief; For me he bore the shame - ful cross,
joys I have; He makes me tri - umph o - ver death,

His lips with grace o'er - flow, His lips with grace o'er - flow.
Who fill the heav'n - ly train, Who fill the heav'n - ly train.
And car - ried all my grief, And car - ried all my grief.
And saves me from the grave, And saves me from the grave.

Rise Up, O Men of God 268

1. Rise up, O men of God! Have done with less - er things;
2. Rise up, O men of God! His king - dom tar - ries long;
3. Rise up, O men of God! The church for you doth wait,
4. Lift high the cross of Christ! Tread where his feet have trod;

Give heart and mind and soul and strength To serve the King of kings.
Bring in the day of broth - er - hood And end the night of wrong.
Her strength un - e - qual to her task; Rise up, and make her great!
As broth - ers of the Son of man, Rise up, O men of God!

Words, William P. Merrill, 1911. Words used by permission *The Presbyterian Outlook*, Richmond, Va.
Tune ST. THOMAS, Aaron Williams, 1763. Alternate tune FESTAL SONG, No. 476.

269 Stir Thy Church, O God, Our Father

Unison
1. Stir thy church, O God, our Fa - ther, Move through-out its
2. Make thy church a liv - ing wit - ness To the pow - er
3. Give to us a so - cial con-science Which en - a - bles
4. Chal - lenge us, O God, our Fa - ther, To the tasks which

life to - day; Cul - ti - vate a sense of mis - sion In our
of her Lord; Send us to the world a - round us With thy
us to see That all men are thy cre - a - tion And that
must be done For thy church to find ful - fill - ment In the

hearts and minds, we pray. Help us to re - new com - mit - ment
spir - it and thy Word: To the in - ner - cit - y tur - moil,
help - ing them serves thee. Let us feel, with real com - pas - sion,
way taught by thy Son. With a - ware - ness of our pur - pose,

To a way of life in thee Which in - ter - prets
To the sub - urbs where men flee, To all men who
Needs of bod - y, mind, and soul; For these needs may
With com - mit - ment to thy call, May we help pre -

for our cul - ture How thy truth can make men free.
need thy mes - sage; Help us, Lord, to live for thee.
we pro - vide men Min - is - try which makes them whole.
pare the time when Christ will reign as Lord of all.

Dear Lord and Father of Mankind 270

1. Dear Lord and Fa - ther of man - kind, For - give our
2. Drop thy still dews of qui - et - ness, Till all our
3. Breathe thro' the heats of our de - sire Thy cool - ness
4. In sim - ple trust like theirs who heard, Be - side the

fool - ish ways; Re - clothe us in our right - ful mind; In pur - er
striv - ings cease; Take from our souls the strain and stress, And let our
and thy balm; Let sense be dumb, let flesh re - tire; Speak thro' the
Syr - ian sea, The gra - cious call - ing of the Lord, Let us, like

lives thy ser - vice find, In deep - er rev - 'rence, praise.
or - dered lives con - fess The beau - ty of thy peace.
earth - quake, wind, and fire, O still small voice of calm!
them, with - out a word, Rise up and fol - low thee. A - MEN.

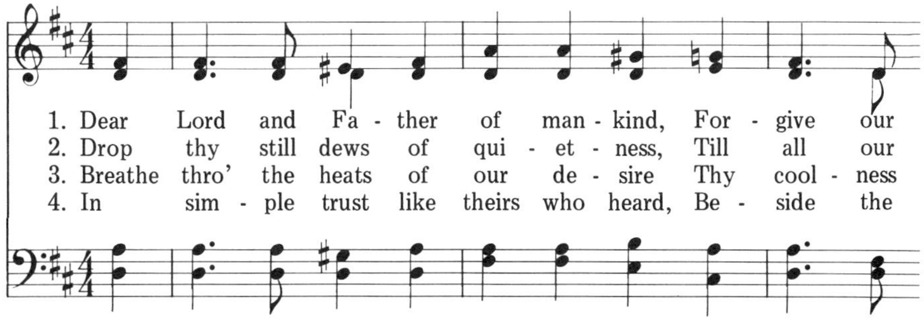

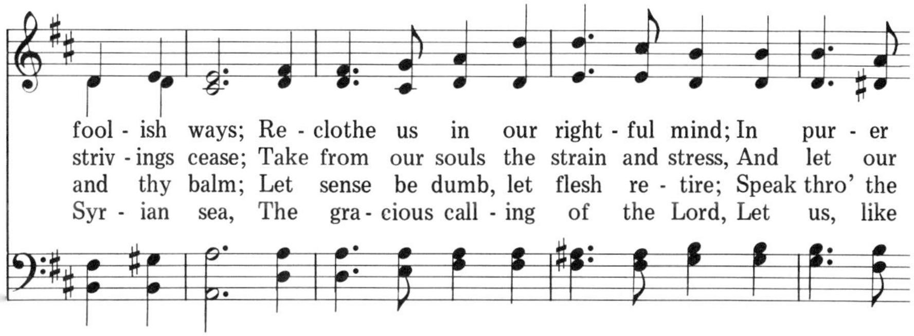

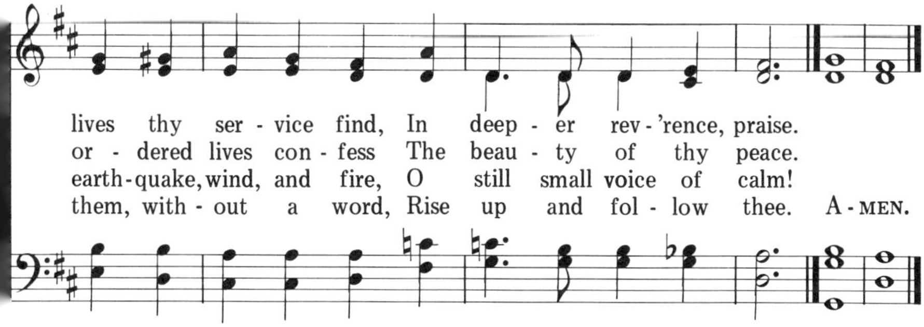

Words, John Greenleaf Whittier, 1872. Tune REST (ELTON), Frederick C. Maker. Music used by permission Psalms and Hymns Trust.

271 Send a Great Revival

1. Com-ing now to thee, O Christ my Lord, Trust-ing on - ly in thy
2. Send the Ho - ly Spir - it now with - in, Burn - ing out the dross and
3. Send a great re - viv - al, Lord, in me, Help me that I may re -
4. Help me go for thee, dear Lord, to - day, To some lone - ly soul that's
pre - cious word, Let my hum - ble pray'r to thee be heard, And send a
guilt of sin; Let thy might - y works of grace be - gin, Oh, send a
joice in thee; Give me strength to win the vic - to - ry, And send a
gone a - stray; Help me lead them in the home-ward way, Oh, send a
great re - viv - al in my soul. Send a great re - viv - al in my
soul, Send a great re - viv - al in my soul; Let the Ho - ly
in my soul, in my soul;
Spir - it come and take con - trol, And send a great re - viv - al in my soul.

Lord, Send a Revival 272

1. Send a re-viv-al, O Christ, my Lord, Let it go o-ver the land and sea,
2. Send a re-viv-al a-mong thine own, Help us to turn from our sins a-way,
3. Send a re-viv-al to those in sin, Help them, O Je-sus, to turn to thee,
4. Send a re-viv-al in ev-'ry heart, Draw the world nearer, O Lord, to thee,

Send it ac-cord-ing to thy dear Word, And let it be-gin in me.
Let us get near-er the Fa-ther's throne, Re-vive us a-gain, we pray.
Let them the new life in thee be-gin, Oh, give them the vic-to-ry.
Let thy sal-va-tion true joy im-part, And let it be-gin in me.

Lord, send a re-viv-al, Lord, send a re-viv-al,

Lord, send a re-viv-al, And let it be-gin in me.

273 There Shall Be Showers of Blessing

1. There shall be show-ers of bless-ing: This is the prom-ise of love;
2. There shall be show-ers of bless-ing, Pre-cious re-viv-ing a-gain;
3. There shall be show-ers of bless-ing: Send them up-on us, O Lord;
4. There shall be show-ers of bless-ing: Oh, that to-day they might fall,
There shall be sea-sons re-fresh-ing, Sent from the Sav-ior a-bove.
O-ver the hills and the val-leys, Sound of a-bun-dance of rain.
Grant to us now a re-fresh-ing, Come, and now hon-or thy Word.
Now as to God we're con-fess-ing, Now as on Je-sus we call!
Show - ers of bless-ing, Show-ers of bless-ing we need:
Show-ers, show-ers of bless-ing,
Mer-cy-drops round us are fall-ing, But for the show-ers we plead.

Ezekiel 34:26. Words, Daniel W. Whittle, 1883. Tune SHOWERS OF BLESSING, James McGranahan, 1883.

Christ Is the World's True Light 274

1. Christ is the world's true light, Its cap-tain of sal-va-tion,
2. In Christ all rac-es meet, Their an-cient feuds for-get-ting,
3. One Lord, in one great name U-nite us all who own thee,

The day-star clear and bright Of ev-'ry man and na-tion;
The whole round world com-plete, From sun-rise to its set-ting:
Cast out our pride and shame That hin-der to en-throne thee;

New life, new hope a-wakes Wher-e'er men own his sway:
When Christ is throned as Lord, Men shall for-sake their fear,
The world has wait-ed long, Has tra-vailed long in pain,

Free-dom her bond-age breaks, And night is turned to day.
To plow-share beat the sword, To prun-ing-hook the spear.
To heal its an-cient wrong, Come, Prince of Peace, and reign.

Words, George W. Briggs, 1931. Words from *Enlarged Songs of Praise* by permission of Oxford University Press. Tune DARMSTADT, Ahasuerus Fritsch, 1679; harmonized, J. S. Bach, *c.* 1765.

275 Tell It Out with Gladness

1. Tell it! Tell it out with glad - ness, God's good news to
2. Lord, we thank thee for the trea - sure Hid with - in the
3. "Go and teach," thus spoke the Mas - ter, Ris - en vic - tor

ev - 'ry man, Sin for - giv - en, lives trans - fig - ured, All in
sa - cred page. We would be thy faith - ful her - alds To our
from the grave. Still he gives this great com - mis - sion To his

God's great lov - ing plan. In the Book is found the wit - ness
deep - ly trou - bled age; We would pub - lish thy sal - va - tion,
faith - ful ones, and brave. Let men know the gos - pel sto - ry

To his might - y acts of yore: Lis - ten, heed, o -
Ev - er on thy side to stand, Liv - ing, serv - ing,
Of what man thro' Christ can be. Send it! Send it

Words, Georgia Harkness, 1966. Copyright 1966 by The Hymn Society of America. Used by permission.
Tune HYMN TO JOY, Ludwig van Beethoven, 1824; adapted, Edward Hodges, 1864.
This tune in a higher key, No. 31.

bey, and serve him, Kneel be - fore him and a - dore.
giv - ing, send - ing Life to quick - en ev - 'ry land.
to the na - tions That God's love may set men free.

Lord, Speak to Me, that I May Speak 276

1. Lord, speak to me, that I may speak In liv - ing
2. O teach me, Lord, that I may teach The pre - cious
3. O fill me with thy full - ness, Lord, Un - til my
4. O use me, Lord, use e - ven me, Just as thou

ech - oes of thy tone; As thou hast sought, so
things thou dost im - part; And wing my words, that
ver - y heart o'er - flow In kin - dling tho't and
wilt, and when, and where; Un - til thy bless - ed

let me seek Thy err - ing chil - dren lost and lone.
they may reach The hid - den depths of many a heart.
glow - ing word, Thy love to tell, thy praise to show.
face I see, Thy rest, thy joy, thy glo - ry share. A-MEN.

Romans 14:7. Words, Frances R. Havergal, 1872. Tune CANONBURY, Robert Schumann, 1839.

277 We Have Heard the Joyful Sound

1. We have heard the joy-ful sound: Je-sus saves! Je-sus saves!
2. Waft it on the roll-ing tide: Je-sus saves! Je-sus saves!
3. Sing a-bove the bat-tle strife: Je-sus saves! Je-sus saves!
4. Give the winds a might-y voice: Je-sus saves! Je-sus saves!

Spread the ti-dings all a-round: Je-sus saves! Je-sus saves!
Tell to sin-ners far and wide: Je-sus saves! Je-sus saves!
By his death and end-less life, Je-sus saves! Je-sus saves!
Let the na-tions now re-joice, Je-sus saves! Je-sus saves!

Bear the news to ev-'ry land, Climb the steeps and cross the waves;
Sing, ye is-lands of the sea; Ech-o back, ye o-cean caves;
Sing it soft-ly thro' the gloom, When the heart for mer-cy craves;
Shout sal-va-tion full and free; High-est hills and deep-est caves;

On-ward! 'tis our Lord's com-mand; Je-sus saves! Je-sus saves!
Earth shall keep her ju-bi-lee: Je-sus saves! Je-sus saves!
Sing in tri-umph o'er the tomb, Je-sus saves! Je-sus saves!
This our song of vic-to-ry: Je-sus saves! Je-sus saves!

Words, Priscilla Owens, c. 1882. Tune JESUS SAVES, William J. Kirkpatrick, 1882.

We Have Heard the Joyful Sound 278

1. We have heard the joy - ful sound: Je - sus saves!
2. Sing a - bove the bat - tle strife: Je - sus saves!
3. Give the winds a might - y voice: Je - sus saves!
Spread the ti - dings all a - round: Je - sus saves! Bear the news to
By his death and end - less life, Je - sus saves! Sing it soft - ly
Let the na - tions now re - joice: Je - sus saves! Shout sal - va - tion
ev - 'ry land, Climb the steeps and cross the waves;
thro' the gloom, When the heart for mer - cy craves;
full and free; High - est hills and deep - est caves;
On - ward! 'tis our Lord's com - mand; Je - sus saves!
Sing in tri - umph o'er the tomb: Je - sus saves!
This our song of vic - to - ry: Je - sus saves!

Words, Priscilla Owens, c. 1882. Tune LIMPSFIELD, Josiah Booth, 1898.

279 Walk Ye in Him

Unison
1. Walk ye in him, all earth-ly paths for-sak-ing,
2. Walk ye in him, his foot-steps ev-er fol-low
3. Walk ye in him, your path will lead to oth-ers,
4. Walk ye in him, ye who would tell the sto-ry,
He lights the way to par-don from all sin;
Wher-e'er they lead, o'er moun-tain, sea, or sand;
No hands but yours can do his work to-day;
Un-lock your heart, re-ceive his prom-ise true;
He is the way, his prom-is-es sus-tain-ing,
Serve him to-day, he knows what waits the mor-row,
Go near and far to make all men your broth-ers,
Then tell the world of Je-sus and his glo-ry,
Walk ye in him, and feel his pow'r with-in.
Walk ye in him, ful-fill his great com-mand.
Walk ye in him, a-long the nar-row way.
Walk ye in him, and he will walk with you.

1. So send I you, by grace made strong to tri-umph O'er hosts of
2. So send I you, to take to souls in bond-age The word of
3. So send I you, my strength to know in weak-ness, My joy in
4. So send I you, to bear my cross with pa-tience, And then one

hell, o'er dark-ness, death and sin, My name to bear, and in that
truth that sets the cap-tive free, To break the bonds of sin, to
grief, my per-fect peace in pain, To prove my pow'r, my grace, my
day with joy to lay it down, To hear my voice, "Well done, my

St. 1,2,3
name to con-quer, So send I you, my vic-to-ry to win.
loose death's fet-ters, So send I you, to bring the lost to me.
prom-ised pres-ence, So send I you, e-ter-nal fruit to gain.
faith-ful ser-vant, Come, share my throne, my king-dom and my

St. 4
crown!" "As the Fa-ther hath sent me, So send I you."

John 20:21. Words, E. Margaret Clarkson, 1963. Tune TORONTO, John W. Peterson, 1954. Copyright 1954, 1963 by Singspiration, Inc. All rights reserved. Used by permission.

281 We've a Story to Tell

Unison
1. We've a sto - ry to tell to the na - tions, That shall
2. We've a song to be sung to the na - tions, That shall
3. We've a mes - sage to give to the na - tions, That the
4. We've a Sav - ior to show to the na - tions, Who the
turn their hearts to the right, A sto - ry of truth and mer - cy,
lift their hearts to the Lord, A song that shall con - quer e - vil,
Lord who reign - eth a - bove Hath sent us his Son to save us,
path of sor - row hath trod, That all of the world's great peo - ples
A sto - ry of peace and light, A sto - ry of peace and light.
And shat - ter the spear and sword, And shat - ter the spear and sword.
And show us that God is love, And show us that God is love.
May come to the truth of God, May come to the truth of God!
For the dark-ness shall turn to dawn-ing, And the dawning to noon-day bright,

Words and tune MESSAGE, H. Ernest Nichol, 1896.

And Christ's great king-dom shall come on earth, The king-dom of love and light.

Jesus Shall Reign Where'er the Sun 282

1. Je - sus shall reign wher - e'er the sun Does his suc -
2. From north to south the princ - es meet To pay their
3. To him shall end - less pray'r be made, And end - less
4. Peo - ple and realms of ev - 'ry tongue Dwell on his

ces - sive jour - neys run; His king - dom spread from
hom - age at his feet; While west - ern em - pires
prais - es crown his head; His name like sweet per -
love with sweet - est song, And in - fant voic - es

shore to shore, Till moons shall wax and wane no more.
own their Lord, And sav - age tribes at - tend his word.
fume shall rise With ev - 'ry morn - ing sac - ri - fice.
shall pro - claim Their ear - ly bless - ings on his name. A - MEN.

Psalm 72. Words, Isaac Watts, 1719. Tune DUKE STREET, John Hatton, 1793.

283 Rescue the Perishing

1. Res - cue the per - ish - ing, Care for the dy - ing,
2. Tho they are slight - ing him, Still he is wait - ing,
3. Down in the hu - man heart, Crush'd by the tempt - er,
4. Res - cue the per - ish - ing, Du - ty de - mands it;

Snatch them in pit - y from sin and the grave;
Wait - ing the pen - i - tent child to re - ceive;
Feel - ings lie bur - ied that grace can re - store;
Strength for thy la - bor the Lord will pro - vide;

Weep o'er the err - ing one, Lift up the fall - en,
Plead with them ear - nest - ly, Plead with them gent - ly,
Touch'd by a lov - ing heart, Wak - en'd by kind - ness,
Back to the nar - row way Pa - tient - ly win them;

Tell them of Je - sus the might - y to save.
He will for - give if they on - ly be - lieve.
Chords that are bro - ken will vi - brate once more. Res-cue the
Tell the poor wan - d'rer a Sav - ior has died.

Words, Fanny J. Crosby, 1869. Tune RESCUE, William H. Doane, 1869.

per-ish-ing, Care for the dy-ing; Je-sus is mer-ci-ful, Je-sus will save.

Spread, O Spread the Mighty Word 284

1. Spread, O spread the might-y word, Spread the king-dom
2. Word of how the Fa-ther's will Made the world, and
3. Word of how the Sav-ior's love Earth's sore bur-den
4. Might-y word God's Spir-it gave, Man for heav'n-ly
5. Word of life, most pure and strong, Word for which the

of the Lord, That to earth's re-mot-est bound
keeps it, still; How his on-ly Son he gave,
does re-move; How for-ev-er, in its need,
life to save; Word thro' whose all-ho-ly might
na-tions long, Spread a-broad, un-til from night

Men may heed the joy-ful sound.
Man from sin and death to save.
Thro' his death the world is freed.
Man can will and do the right.
All the world a-wakes to light. A - MEN.

Words, Jonathan Friedrich Bahnmaier, 1827; translated, Arthur W. Farlander and C. Winfred Douglas, 1938. Used by permission The Church Pension Fund. Tune GOTT SEI DANK, Freylinghausen's *Gesangbuch*, 1704.

285 Share His Love

Unison
1. The love of God is broad-er than earth's vast ex-panse,
2. All those who have trust-ed in God's on-ly Son,
3. We show the love of God each day we live,
'Tis deep-er and wid-er than the sea.
And hold this pre-cious trea-sure in their hearts,
Re-veal Christ's pres-ence in our lives;
Love reach-es out to all to bring a-bun-dant life,
Seek ways to make it known to all who need to know
And how the Ho-ly Spir-it guides us day by day,
For God so loved the world his on-ly Son he gave.
That God so loved the world his on-ly Son he gave.
For God so loved the world his on-ly Son he gave.
Share his love by tell-ing what the Lord has done for you,

Share his love by shar-ing of your faith, And show the world that
Je-sus Christ is real to you ev-'ry mo-ment, ev-'ry day.

I Bless the Christ of God 286

1. I bless the Christ of God; I rest on love di-vine; And
2. I praise the God of grace; I trust his truth and might; He
3. 'Tis he who sav-eth me, And free-ly par-don gives; I
4. My life with him is hid, My death has passed a-way, My

with un-fal-t'ring tongue and heart, I call the Sav-ior mine.
calls me his, I call him mine, My God, my joy, my light.
love be-cause he lov-eth me, I live be-cause he lives.
clouds have melt-ed in-to light, My mid-night in-to day.

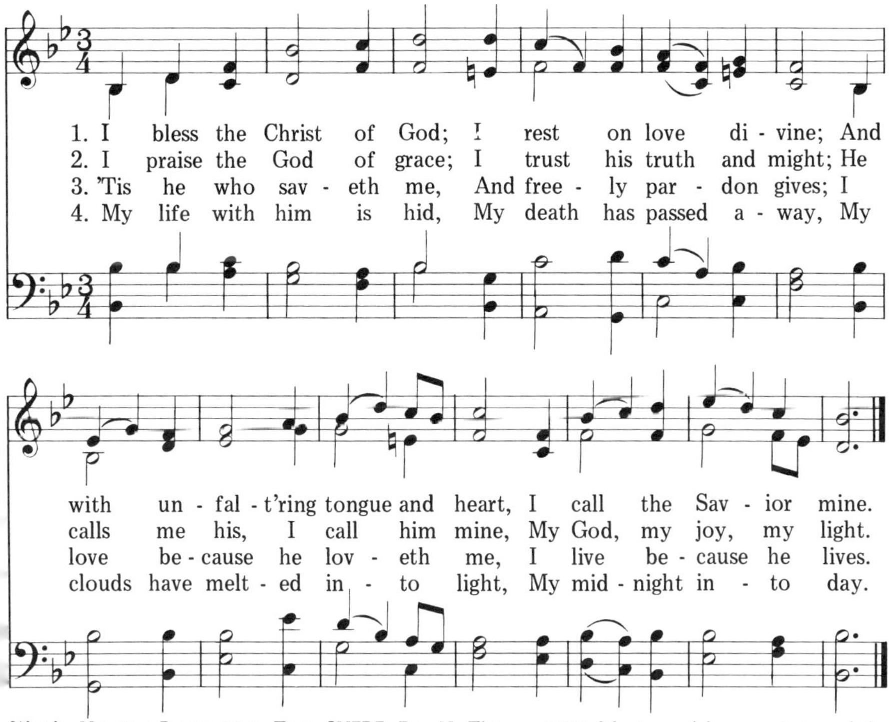

Words, Horatius Bonar, 1861. Tune SHERE, Eric H. Thiman, 1930. Music used by permission of the composer. Alternate tune ST. THOMAS, No. 240.

287 Pass It On

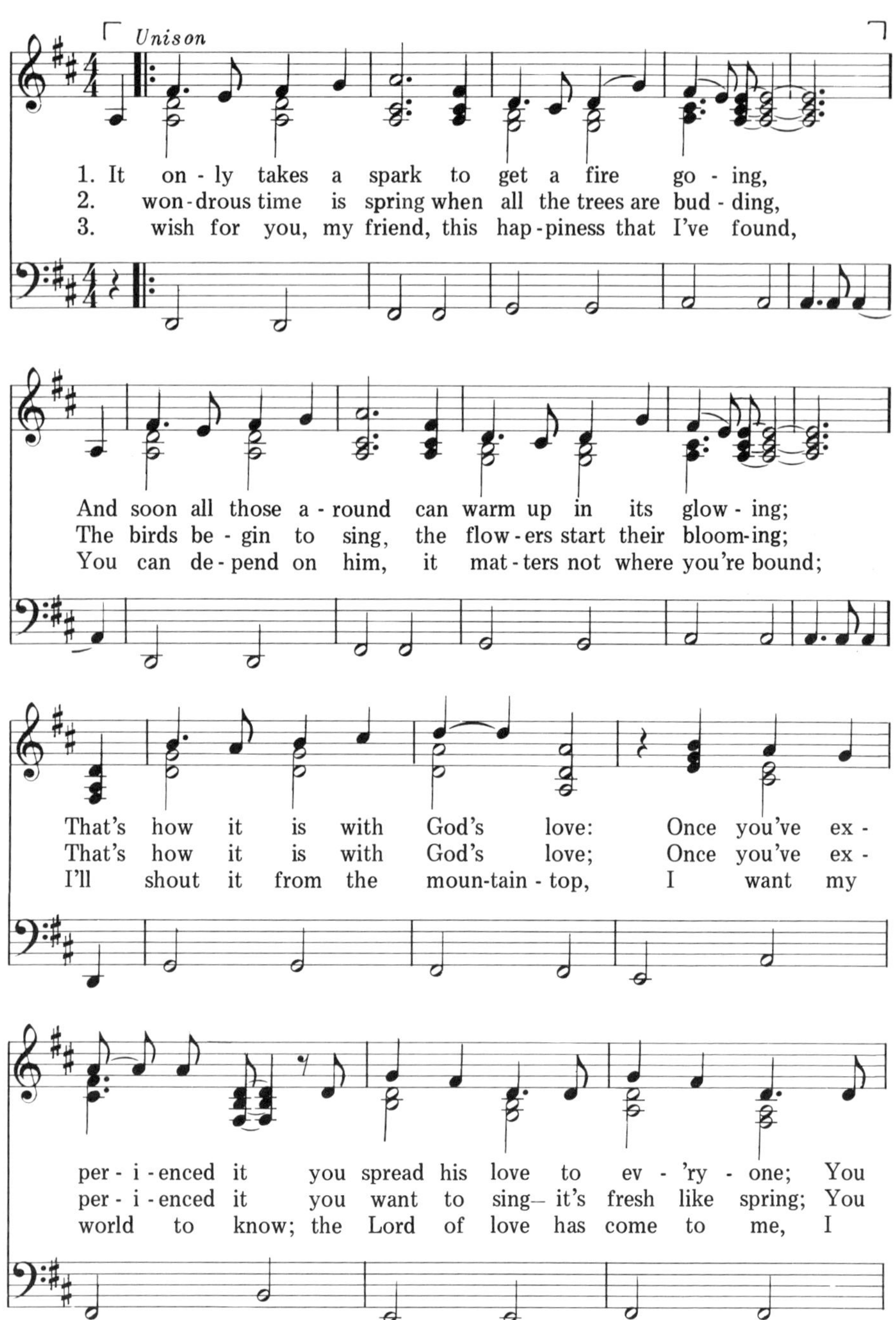

Unison
1. It on-ly takes a spark to get a fire go-ing,
2. won-drous time is spring when all the trees are bud-ding,
3. wish for you, my friend, this hap-piness that I've found,
And soon all those a-round can warm up in its glow-ing;
The birds be-gin to sing, the flow-ers start their bloom-ing;
You can de-pend on him, it mat-ters not where you're bound;
That's how it is with God's love: Once you've ex-
That's how it is with God's love; Once you've ex-
I'll shout it from the moun-tain-top, I want my
per-i-enced it you spread his love to ev-'ry-one; You
per-i-enced it you want to sing— it's fresh like spring; You
world to know; the Lord of love has come to me, I

want to pass it on.
want to pass it on.
want to pass it on.
2. What a
3. I
I'll shout it from the moun-tain-top, I want my
world to know, The Lord of love has
come to me, I want to pass it on.

288 Tell the Good News

1. Christ was born in a dis-tant land,
2. Christ be-came a man on earth,
3. Christ a-rose and to heav-en went,
4. Christ still lives in the world to-day,
Tell the good news,
tell the good news; Lived on earth for the good of man,
tell the good news; Gave his life for man's re-birth,
tell the good news; All may fol-low who re-pent,
tell the good news; Giv-ing strength to all souls who pray,
Tell the good news, tell the good news.
Tell the good news, tell the good news.
Tell the good news, tell the good news.
Tell the good news, tell the good news.
Tell the good news,
tell the good news, Tell the good news that Christ has come; Tell the good news,

tell the good news, Tell the good news to ev-'ry-one.

Ye Christian Heralds! 289

1. Ye Chris-tian her-alds! go, pro-claim Sal-va-tion
2. He'll shield you with a wall of fire, With flam-ing
3. And when our la-bors all are o'er, Then shall we

thro' Im-man-uel's name; To dis-tant climes the ti-dings bear,
zeal your hearts in-spire, Bid rag-ing winds their fu-ry cease,
meet to part no more, Meet with the blood-bo't throng to fall,

And plant the * Rose of Shar-on there.
And hush the tem-pest in-to peace.
And crown our Je-sus Lord of all. A-MEN.

Words, Bourne Hall Draper, c. 1803. Tune DUKE STREET, John Hatton, 1793. *Song of Solomon 2:1.

290 Make Me a Blessing

1. Out in the high-ways and by-ways of life, Man-y are
2. Tell the sweet sto-ry of Christ and his love, Tell of his
3. Give as 'twas giv-en to you in your need, Love as the

wea-ry and sad; Car-ry the sun-shine where
are wea-ry and sad;
pow'r to for-give; Oth-ers will trust him if
his pow'r to for-give;
Mas-ter loved you; Be to the help-less a
the Mas-ter loved you;

dark-ness is rife, Mak-ing the sor-row-ing glad.
on-ly you prove True, ev-'ry mo-ment you live.
help-er in-deed, Un-to your mis-sion be true.

Make me a bless-ing, Make me a bless-ing, Out of my

Words, Ira B. Wilson, *c.* 1909. Tune SCHULER, George S. Schuler, 1924. Copyright 1924 by Geo. S. Schuler. © Copyright Renewed 1952. The Rodeheaver Co., Owner. Used by permission.

life.   May Je - sus shine; Make me a bless - ing, O Sav - ior,
out of my life

I pray,   Make me a bless - ing to some - one to - day.
I pray thee, my Sav - ior,

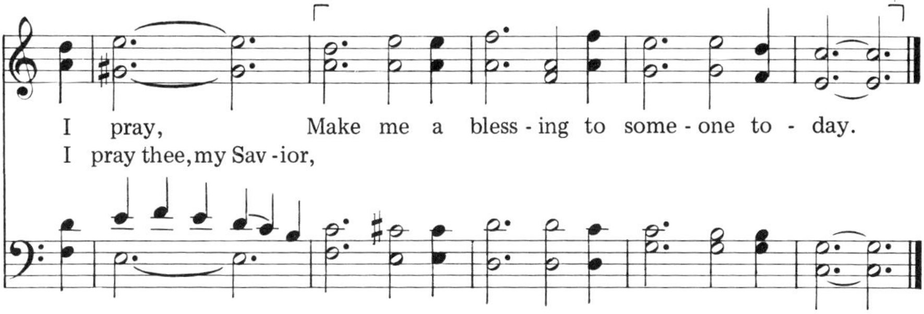

Savior, Teach Me Day by Day 291

1. Sav - ior, teach me day by day Love's sweet les - son to o - bey;
2. With a child's glad heart of love At thy bid - ding may I move,
3. Teach me thus thy steps to trace, Strong to fol - low in thy grace,
4. Thus may I re - joice to show That I feel the love I owe;

Sweet - er les - son can - not be, Lov - ing him who first loved me.
Prompt to serve and fol - low thee, Lov - ing him who first loved me.
Learn - ing how to love from thee, Lov - ing him who first loved me.
Sing - ing, till thy face I see, Of his love who first loved me. A - MEN.

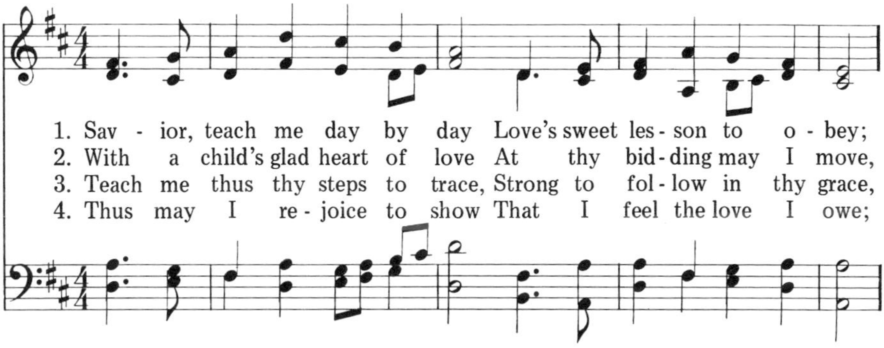

Words, Jane E. Leeson, 1842. Tune INNOCENTS, *Parish Choir*, 1850.

292 Ye Servants of God

1. Ye ser - vants of God, your Mas - ter pro - claim,
2. God rul - eth on high, al - might - y to save;
3. Sal - va - tion to God who sits on the throne,
4. Then let us a - dore and give him his right,

And pub - lish a - broad his won - der - ful name;
And still he is nigh, his pres - ence we have;
Let all cry a - loud and hon - or the Son:
All glo - ry and pow'r, all wis - dom and might;

The name all - vic - to - rious of Je - sus ex - tol;
The great con - gre - ga - tion his tri - umph shall sing,
The prais - es of Je - sus the an - gels pro - claim,
All hon - or and bless - ing, with an - gels a - bove,

His king - dom is glo - rious and rules o - ver all.
As - crib - ing sal - va - tion to Je - sus our King.
Fall down on their fac - es and wor - ship the Lamb.
And thanks nev - er - ceas - ing, and in - fi - nite love. A-MEN.

Words, Charles Wesley, 1744. Tune HANOVER, William Croft, 1708. Alternate tune LYONS, No. 30.

Send Me, O Lord, Send Me 293

1. O God of might, O Son of light, O Ho - ly Spir - it sweet,
2. With ho - ly fire my heart in - spire Thy Spir - it's sword to wield;
3. O that in me my Lord may see A bear - er of the name;
Thy church ex - pand till all shall stand At Je - sus' pierc - ed feet.
With bor - rowed might I'll take thy light, Till dark - ness' doom be sealed.
That men may see his love so free From age to age the same.
Let all who once thy Son disowned Re - joice to see him now enthroned;
If oth - ers stop to count the cost, For fear of earth - ly trea-sures lost,
Be this my ev - er - last - ing song, He took up - on him - self my wrong,
Yet while one stray - ing soul there be, Send me, O Lord, send me.
I'll count it gain to die for thee; Send me, O Lord, send me.
And cried while fac - ing Cal - va - ry, "Send me, O Lord, send me."

294 Let Others See Jesus in You

1. While pass-ing thro' this world of sin, And oth-ers your
2. Your life's a book be-fore their eyes, They're read-ing it
3. What joy 'twill be at set of sun, In man-sions be-
4. Then live for Christ both day and night, Be faith-ful, be

life shall view, Be clean and pure with-out, with-in,
thro' and thro'; Say, does it point them to the skies,
yond the blue, To find some souls that you have won;
brave, and true, And lead the lost to life and light;

Let oth-ers see Je-sus in you.
Do oth-ers see Je-sus in you?
Let oth-ers see Je-sus in you.
Let oth-ers see Je-sus in you.

Let oth-ers see Je-sus in

you, Let oth-ers see Je-sus in you; Keep tell-ing the
in you, in you;

sto-ry, be faith-ful and true, Let oth-ers see Je-sus in you.

1. O *Zi - on, haste, thy mis - sion, high ful - fill - ing, To tell to
2. Be - hold how man - y thou - sands still are ly - ing, Bound in the
3. Pro - claim to ev - 'ry peo - ple, tongue, and na - tion That God, in
4. Give of thy sons to bear the mes - sage glo - rious; Give of thy

all the world that God is Light; That he who made all na - tions
dark - some pris - on house of sin, With none to tell them of the
whom they live and move, is Love: Tell how he stoop'd to save his
wealth to speed them on their way; Pour out thy soul for them in

is not will - ing One soul should per - ish, lost in shades of night.
Sav - ior's dy - ing, Or of the life he died for them to win.
lost cre - a - tion, And died on earth that man might live a - bove.
pray'r vic - to - rious; And all thou spend - est Je - sus will re - pay.

Pub - lish glad ti - dings, ti - dings of peace,

Ti - dings of Je - sus, re - demp - tion and re - lease.

Words, Mary Ann Thomson, 1868. Tune TIDINGS, James Walch, 1875. *Joel 2:1. By extension the word refers to the people of God.

296 One World, One Lord, One Witness

Unison
1. One world, bound to-geth-er by God's love, One Lord,
2. One world, joined in Chris - tian broth-er - hood, One Lord,
3. One world, found in com - mon fel - low-ship, One Lord,
our Sav - ior, Christ the King, One wit-ness to our faith in him,
our ris - en Lord of lords, One wit-ness to re-deem-ing grace,
our reign-ing King of kings, One wit-ness to his won-drous love,
This is the song to all we sing. One world, one
Lord, one wit - ness, One world, one Lord, one wit-ness,
Christ is Lord of all, Crown him Lord of all,

One world, one Lord, one wit-ness. Lord, one wit-ness.

God of Mercy, God of Grace 297

1. God of mer-cy, God of grace, Show the bright-ness of thy face;
2. Let the peo-ple praise thee, Lord; Be by all that live a-dored;
3. Let the peo-ple praise thee, Lord; Earth shall then her fruits af-ford,

Shine up-on us, Sav-ior, shine, Fill thy church with light di-vine,
Let the na-tions shout and sing Glo-ry to their Sav-ior King,
God to man his bless-ings give, Man to God de-vot-ed live,

And thy sav-ing health ex-tend Un-to earth's re-mot-est end.
At thy feet their tri-bute pay, And thy ho-ly will o-bey.
All be-low and all a-bove, One in joy and light and love. A-MEN.

Psalm 67. Words, Henry F. Lyte, 1834. Tune DIX, Conrad Kocher, 1838; adapted, William H. Monk, 1861.

298 Lord, Lay Some Soul upon My Heart

1. Lord, lay some soul up - on my heart, And love that soul thro' me;
2. Lord, lead me to some soul in sin, And grant that I may be
3. To win that soul for thee a - lone Will be my con-stant prayer;

And may I brave - ly do my part To win that soul for thee.
En - dued with pow'r and love to win That soul, dear Lord, for thee.
That when I've reached the great white throne I'll meet that dear one there.

Some soul for thee, some soul for thee, This is my ear - nest plea;

Help me each day, on life's high-way, To win some soul for thee.

New Life for You 299

1. The Son of God, our Sav - ior, Has pow'r to cleanse from sin,
2. Re - demp-tion is com - plet - ed Thro' faith in Christ a - lone;
3. His love so great, un - bound - ed, Is of - fered free to all
4. Sal - va - tion calls for ser - vice, A walk with Christ each day;
To make men pure and ho - ly, Re - newed with - out, with - in.
He is the Word in - car - nate In whom our God is known.
Who come to him con - fess - ing And yield - ing to his call.
The Mas - ter speaks to oth - ers As we his life por - tray.
New life in Je - sus, New life in him; To
crown him Sav - ior, Lord and King, Brings new life for you.

300 Ring the Bells of Heaven

1. Ring the bells of heav-en! There is joy to-day, For a soul, re-
2. Ring the bells of heav-en! There is joy to-day, For the wan-d'rer
3. Ring the bells of heav-en! Spread the feast to-day! An-gels, swell the
turn - ing from the wild! See, the Fa - ther meets him
now is rec - on - ciled; Yes, a soul is res - cued
glad tri - um - phant strain! Tell the joy - ful ti - dings,
D.S. 'Tis the ran - somed ar - my,
out up - on the way, Wel - com-ing his wea - ry, wan-d'ring child.
from his sin - ful way, And is born a - new a ran-somed child.
bear it far a - way! For a pre - cious soul is born a - gain.
like a might - y sea, Peal -ing forth the an-them of the free.
Glo - ry! Glo - ry! How the an- gels sing; Glo-ry! Glo-ry! How the loud harps ring!

Luke 15:10. Words, William O. Cushing, 1875. Tune RING THE BELLS, George F. Root, 1875.

We Have a Gospel to Proclaim 301

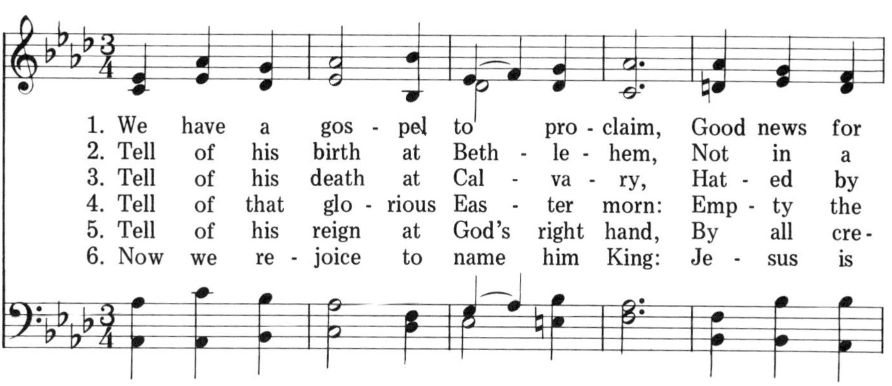

1. We have a gos - pel to pro - claim, Good news for
2. Tell of his birth at Beth - le - hem, Not in a
3. Tell of his death at Cal - va - ry, Hat - ed by
4. Tell of that glo - rious Eas - ter morn: Emp - ty the
5. Tell of his reign at God's right hand, By all cre -
6. Now we re - joice to name him King: Je - sus is

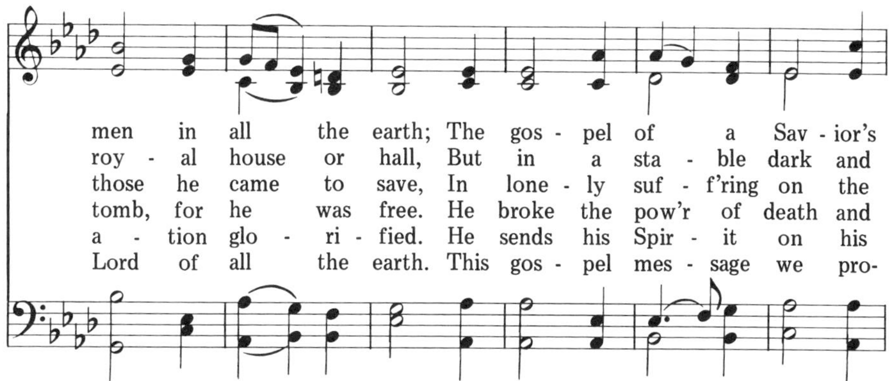

men in all the earth; The gos - pel of a Sav - ior's
roy - al house or hall, But in a sta - ble dark and
those he came to save, In lone - ly suf - f'ring on the
tomb, for he was free. He broke the pow'r of death and
a - tion glo - ri - fied. He sends his Spir - it on his
Lord of all the earth. This gos - pel mes - sage we pro -

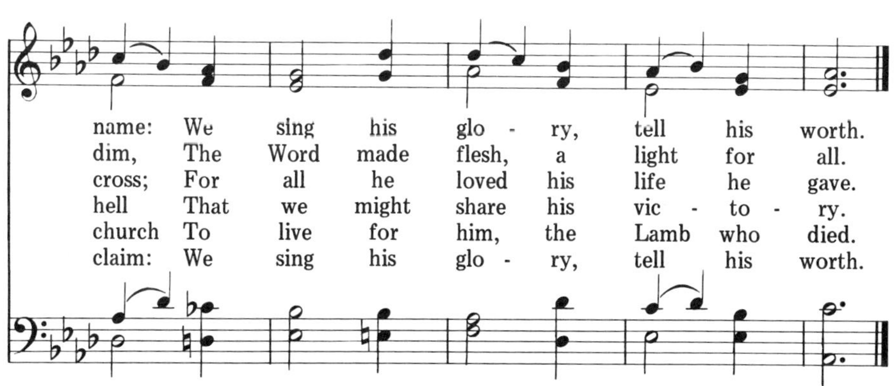

name: We sing his glo - ry, tell his worth.
dim, The Word made flesh, a light for all.
cross; For all he loved his life he gave.
hell That we might share his vic - to - ry.
church To live for him, the Lamb who died.
claim: We sing his glo - ry, tell his worth.

Words, Edward J. Burns. Used by permission of the author. Tune GERMANY, William Gardiner's *Sacred Melodies*, 1815.
This tune in a higher key, No. 311.

302 Set My Soul Afire

1. Set my soul a-fire, Lord, for thy ho-ly Word, Burn it deep with-
2. Set my soul a-fire, Lord, for the lost in sin, Give to me a
3. Set my soul a-fire, Lord, in my dai-ly life, Far too long I've
in me, let thy voice be heard; Mil-lions grope in dark-ness
pas-sion as I seek to win; Help me not to fal-ter,
wan-dered in this day of strife; Noth-ing else will mat-ter
in this day and hour, I will be a wit-ness, fill me with thy pow'r.
nev-er let me fail, Fill me with thy Spir-it, let thy will pre-vail.
but to live for thee, I will be a wit-ness, for Christ lives in me.
Set my soul a-fire, Lord, set my soul a-fire, Make my life a
wit-ness of thy sav-ing pow'r. Mil-lions grope in dark-ness,

wait-ing for thy Word, Set my soul a-fire, Lord, Set my soul a-fire.

Thou, Whose Almighty Word 303

1. Thou, whose al-might-y word Cha-os and dark-ness heard,
2. Thou who didst come to bring On thy re-deem-ing wing,
3. Spir-it of truth and love, Life-giv-ing, ho-ly dove,
4. Ho-ly and bless-ed Three, Glo-ri-ous Trin-i-ty,

And took their flight; Hear us, we hum-bly pray, And where the
Heal-ing and sight, Health to the sick in mind, Sight to the
Speed forth thy flight; Move o'er the wa-ters' face Bear-ing the
Wis-dom, love, might; Bound-less as o-cean's tide Roll-ing in

gos-pel day Sheds not its glo-rious ray, Let there be light!
in-ly blind; O now, to all man-kind, Let there be light!
lamp of grace; And in earth's dark-est place, Let there be light!
full-est pride, Thro' the world far and wide, Let there be light! A-MEN.

Words, John Marriott, 1813. Tune SERUG, Lowell Mason's *Modern Psalmist,* 1839. Alternate tune ITALIAN HYMN, No. 2.

304 Send the Light

1. There's a call comes ring-ing o'er the rest-less wave, "Send the light!
2. We have heard the *Mac - e - do-nian call to-day, "Send the light!
3. Let us pray that grace may ev-'ry-where abound, "Send the light!
4. Let us not grow wea-ry in the work of love, "Send the light!
Send the light!

Send the light!" There are souls to res-cue, there are souls to save,
Send the light!" And a gold-en of-f'ring at the cross we lay,
Send the light!" And a Christ-like spir-it ev-'ry-where be found,
Send the light!" Let us gath-er jew-els for a crown a-bove,
Send the light!

Send the light! Send the light! Send the light, the
Send the light! Send the light! Send the light,

bless-ed gos - pel light; Let it shine from shore to
the bless-ed gos-pel light; Let it shine

Words and tune MCCABE, Charles H. Gabriel, 1890. *Acts 16:9.

shore!   shine   for - ev - er - more!
from shore to shore!   Let it shine   for - ev - er - more!

O God, We Pray for All Mankind 305

1. O   God,   we   pray   for   all   man - kind,   The   na - tions
2. Thou know - est, Lord, man's sin - ful state,   The   source   of
3. With   hum - ble   plea   on   thee   we   call   For   na - tions
4. Help   all   the   na - tions, near and   far,   A - wake,   thy

far a - stray;   We   plead that   all   thy   grace may   find,
hu - man woe,   His   e - vil heart, his greed and hate,
in dis - tress;   Of   one   hast thou not made us   all?
glo - ry   see;   Be - hold the Bright and Morn - ing Star,

In   this thy gra - cious day,   In   this thy gra - cious day.
But whith - er can he   go?   But whith - er can he   go?
O   God, our kin - dred bless, O   God, our kin - dred bless!
The Christ of Cal - va - ry,   The Christ of Cal - va - ry!   A-MEN.

Words, Howard J. Conover. Tune ORTONVILLE, Thomas Hastings, 1837.

306 Let the Song Go Round the Earth

Unison
1. Let the song go round the earth, Je - sus Christ is
2. Let the song go round the earth, Where the sum - mer
3. Let the song go round the earth, Je - sus Christ is
Lord! Sound his praise, tell his worth, Be
smiles; Let the notes of ho - ly mirth Break
King! With the sto - ry of his worth Let
his name a - dored; Ev - 'ry clime and ev - 'ry
from dis - tant isles; In - land for - ests, dark and
the whole earth ring; Him cre - a - tion all a-
tongue Join the grand, the glo - ri - ous song!
dim, Ice - bound coasts give back the hymn.
dore Ev - er - more and ev - er - more.

Let the song go round the earth, Je - sus
Let the song go round the earth, Where the
Let the song go round the earth, Je - sus

1,2
Christ is Lord!
sum - mer smiles.
3
Christ is King!

Draw Thou My Soul, O Christ 307

1. Draw thou my soul, O Christ, Clos - er to thine; Breathe in - to
2. Lead forth my soul, O Christ, One with thine own, Joy - ful to
3. Not for my - self a - lone May my prayer be; Lift thou thy

ev - 'ry wish Thy will di - vine! Raise my low self a - bove, Won
fol - low thee Thro' paths un - known! In thee my strength re - new; Give
world, O Christ, Clos - er to thee! Cleanse it from guilt and wrong; Teach

by thy death-less love; Ev - er, O Christ, thro' mine Let thy life shine.
me my work to do! Thro' me thy truth be shown, Thy love made known.
it sal - va - tion's song, Till earth, as heav'n, ful - fill God's ho - ly will.

Words, Lucy Larcom, 1892. Tune ST. EDMUND, Arthur S. Sullivan, 1872.

308 People to People

Unison
1. How do you share the love of Je - sus with a
2. How do you tell a dy - ing man a - bout e -
3. How do you tell a love - less world that God him -
lone - ly man?
ter - nal life?
self is love?
How do you tell a hun - gry
How do you tell an or - phan
How do you help a man who's
man a - bout the Bread of Life?
child a - bout the Fa - ther's love?
down to lift his eyes a - bove?
How do you tell a thirst - y man a - bout the
How do you tell a man who's poor a - bout the
How do you tell a bleed - ing man a - bout the

Liv - ing Wa - ter of the Lord?
won - drous rich - es of the Lord?
heal - ing pow - er of the Lord?
How do you tell him of his Word?
Peo - ple who know go to peo - ple who need to know
Je - sus;
Peo - ple who love go to
peo - ple a - lone with - out Je - sus;
For there are

peo - ple who need to see, peo - ple who need to love,
peo - ple who need to know God's re - deem - ing love.
Peo - ple who see go to those who are blind with - out
Je - sus, And this is peo - ple to peo - ple, yes,
peo - ple to peo - ple, All shar - ing to - geth - er God's love.

O Lord, Who Came to Earth to Show 309

1. O Lord, who came to earth to show Thy way of truth and love,
2. En - a - ble us to hear the cries Of those who, in de - spair,
3. With su - per - fi - cial ges - tures, we Have tried to com - fort men
4. "Thy king - dom come on earth," we pray With hearts which are re-solved,

Who min - is - tered to var - ied needs With grace sent from a - bove,
Call out for some - one who will hear, For some - one who will care.
Who long to find ful - fill - ment for The hol - low - ness with - in.
And yet, in man-kind's prob - lems still We fail to be in - volved;

E - quip us now to like - wise go, And thus ful - fill thy word
Then, hear - ing, let us ac - tive - ly Pur - sue with one ac - cord
In - vest us in a high - er cause Which, shown by Christ our Lord,
The min - is - tries of com - fort, peace, And hope may we af - ford

Com - pel - ling us to min - is - ter: Give us thy love, O Lord.
A min - is - try which meets their needs: Give us thy love, O Lord.
Makes us to seek men's deep - est needs: Give us thy love, O Lord.
To all who strug - gle in their needs: Give us thy love, O Lord. A - MEN.

310 Peace in Our Time, O Lord

Unison
1. Peace in our time, O Lord; for this we pray:
heart, O Lord; for this I pray:
May ev - 'ry na - tion know peace as the way;
May I know calm - ness now in ev - 'ry way;
May no more sons be killed in bat - tle's fray,
Help me to trust in you each ur - gent day,
May each one know the truth of peace your
That I may be as - sured of peace your

1.
2.
way.   2. Peace   in   my
way.

Where Cross the Crowded Ways of Life 311

1. Where cross the crowd-ed ways of life, Where sound the
2. In haunts of wretch-ed-ness and need, On shad-ow'd
3. From ten-der child-hood's help-less-ness, From wom-an's
4. O Mas-ter, from the moun-tain-side, Make haste to
5. Till sons of men shall learn thy love And fol-low

cries of race and clan, A-bove the noise of
thresh-olds dark with fears, From paths where hide the
grief, man's bur-den'd toil, From fam-ish'd souls, from
heal the hearts of pain; A-mong these rest-less
where thy feet have trod; Till glo-rious from thy

self-ish strife, We hear thy voice, O Son of man!
lures of greed, We catch the vi-sion of thy tears.
sor-row's stress, Thy heart has nev-er known re-coil.
throngs a-bide; O tread the cit-y's streets a-gain,
heav'n a-bove Shall come the cit-y of our God.   A-MEN.

Matthew 22:9. Words, Frank Mason North, 1903. Tune GERMANY, William Gardiner's *Sacred Melodies*, 1815.
This tune in a lower key, No. 301.

312 Teach Me, O Lord, to Care

Unison
1. I see the poor, I see the lame, I hear the
2. I see the hun - gry, sick, and ill; I see them
3. I see the lost and dy - ing world, I watch as
4. Teach me, O Lord, teach me to care, And then thy
sobs, the cries of pain; Yet with this
as I sit and fill A bod - y
Sa - tan's darts are hurled; I know the
mes - sage may I bear; May I a
hurt I sel - dom share,
clothed with clothes so fair,
an - swer, yet don't share,
wit - ness al - ways share,
Teach me, O

Words, Broadman Ware, 1970. Tune HUNTER'S GLEN, James D. Cram, 1970. ©Copyright 1970 Broadman Press. All rights reserved.

Lord, teach me to care, to care.

Thou, Whose Purpose Is to Kindle 313

Unison

1. Thou, whose pur-pose is to kin - dle: Now ig-nite us with thy fire;
2. O - ver - come our sin - ful calm - ness, Rouse us with re -demp-tive shame;
3. Thou who, in thy ho - ly gos - pel, Wills that man should tru - ly live,
4. Teach us cour-age as we strug - gle In all lib - er - at - ing strife;
5. Thou, who still a sword de - liv - ers Rath - er than a plac - id peace,
6. Save us now from sat - is - fac - tion, When we pri - vate - ly are free,

While the earth a - waits thy burn - ing, With thy pas - sion us in - spire.
Bap - tize with thy fi - ery Spir - it, Crown our lives with tongues of flame.
Make us sense our share of fail - ure, Our tran - quil - li - ty for - give.
Lift the small-ness of our vi - sion By thine own a - bun - dant life.
With thy sharp-ened word dis-turb us, From com-pla - cen - cy re - lease!
Yet are un - dis-turbed in spir - it By our broth-er's mis - er - y.

Luke 12:49. Words, David Elton Trueblood, 1967. "Baptism by Fire" from *The Incendiary Fellowship*. Copyright © 1967 by David Elton Trueblood. Reprinted by permission of Harper & Row, Publishers, Inc. Tune LIBERTY, American Folk Tune; arranged, Don Riddle, 1974. © Copyright 1975 Broadman Press. All rights reserved. Alternate tune STUTTGART, No. 34.

314 Reach Out and Touch

Unison
1. Reach out and touch a soul that is hun-gry; Reach out and touch
2. Reach out and touch a friend who is wea-ry; Reach out and touch
a spir-it in de-spair; Reach out and touch a life torn and
a seek-er un-a-ware; Reach out and touch, tho touch-ing means
dirt-y, A man who is lone-ly— If you care! Reach out and
los-ing A part of your own self— If you dare! Reach out and
touch that neigh-bor who hates you; Reach out and touch that stran-ger who
give your love to the love-less; Reach out and make a home for the
meets you; Reach out and touch the broth-er who needs you; Reach out and
home-less; Reach out and shed God's light in the dark-ness; Reach out and

Words and tune REACH OUT, Charles F. Brown, 1971. ©Copyright 1971 by Word, Inc. Arr. © 1975
by Word Music, Inc. All rights reserved. Used by permission.

let the smile of God touch thro' you. you.

Soldiers of Christ, in Truth Arrayed 315

1. Sol - diers of Christ, in truth ar - rayed, A world in ru - ins needs your aid: A world by sin de - stroyed and dead; A world for which the Sav - ior died.

2. His gos - pel to the lost pro - claim, Good news for all in Je - sus' name; Let light up - on the dark - ness break That sin - ners from their death may wake.

3. Morn - ing and eve - ning sow the seed, God's grace the ef - fort shall suc - ceed. Seed - times of tears have oft been found With sheaves of joy and plen - ty crowned.

4. We meet to part, but part to meet, When earth - ly la - bors are com - plete, To join in yet more blest em - ploy, In an e - ter - nal world of joy. A-MEN.

Words, Basil Manly, Jr., 1860. Tune MENDON, German Melody.

316 Do You Really Care?

Unison

1. I look a-round in the place that I live;
2. I see peo-ple just long-ing to know

I see peo-ple with so much to give; Yet there are
What they can live for and where they can go; We have the

those who are dy-ing to know Just that some-bod-y cares.
hope and the pur-pose to share, But, do we real-ly care?

Do you real-ly care? Do you know how to share
Will you take the dare? Spread Good News ev-'ry-where?

With peo-ple ev-'ry-where? Do you real-ly care?
The cross of Christ to bear? Do you real-ly care?

Peo-ple grope in dark-ness, Search-ing for a way,
D.S. al fine
Don't you know of some-one You can help to-day?

Breathe on Me, Breath of God 317

1. Breathe on me, Breath of God, Fill me with life a-new, That I
2. Breathe on me, Breath of God, Un-til my heart is pure, Un-til
3. Breathe on me, Breath of God, Till I am whol-ly thine, Till all
4. Breathe on me, Breath of God, So shall I nev-er die, But live

may love what thou dost love, And do what thou wouldst do.
with thee I will thy will, To do and to en-dure.
this earth-ly part of me Glows with thy fire di-vine.
with thee the per-fect life Of thine e-ter-ni-ty. A-MEN.

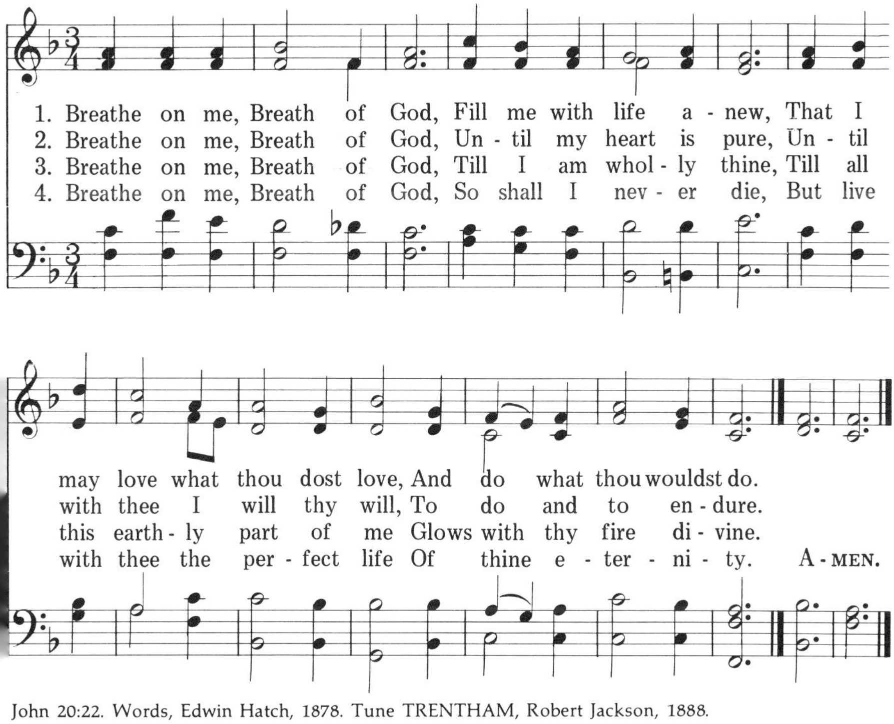

John 20:22. Words, Edwin Hatch, 1878. Tune TRENTHAM, Robert Jackson, 1888.

318 His Gentle Look

Unison
1. His look, his gen - tle look, Can carve a
2. His touch, his kind - ly touch, Can rus - tle
3. His voice, his ten - der voice, Can reach the
moun - tain, Bend a rain - bow, Ease the suf - f'ring on all the
tree - tops, Scat - ter rain - drops, Ease the suf - f'ring on all the
heav - ens, Whis - per par - don, Ease the suf - f'ring on all the
earth.
earth.
O use me,
Use me, Lord, As your eyes to see the need, Your
hands the poor to feed, Your voice the truth to sing.

When the Church of Jesus 319

Unison
1. When the church of Je - sus Shuts its out - er door,
2. If our hearts are lift - ed Where de - vo - tion soars
3. Lest the gifts we of - fer, Mon - ey, tal - ents, time,
Lest the roar of traf - fic Drown the voice of prayer:
High a - bove this hun - gry Suf - f'ring world of ours:
Serve to salve our con - science To our se - cret shame:
May our prayers, Lord, make us Ten times more a - ware
Lest our hymns should drug us To for - get its needs,
Lord, re - prove, in - spire us By the way you give;
That the world we ban - ish Is our Chris - tian care.
Forge our Chris - tian wor - ship In - to Chris - tian deeds.
Teach us, dy - ing Sav - ior, How true Chris - tians live.

Words, F. Pratt Green, 1960. Words copyright, used by permission Oxford University Press. Tune KING'S WESTON, Ralph Vaughan Williams, 1925. Music from *Enlarged Songs of Praise* used by permission Oxford University Press.

320 O God of Every Time and Place

Unison

1. O God of ev-'ry time and place, Pre-vail a-mong us too;
2. O thou whose will we can re-sist, But can-not o-ver-come,
3. Our fa-thers stayed their minds on thee In vil-lage, farm, and plain;
4. Grant us, O God, who la-bor here With-in this throb-bing maze,

With-in the cit-y that we love, Its prom-ise to re-new.
For-give our harsh and stri-dent ways, The harm that we have done.
Help us, their crowd-ed, har-ried kin, No less thy peace to claim.
A for-ward-look-ing, sav-ing hope To gal-va-nize our days.

Our peo-ple move with down-cast eyes, Tight, sul-len and a-fraid;
Like Ba-bel's build-ers long a-go We raise our loft-y tow'rs,
Give us to know that thou dost love Each soul that thou hast made;
Let Christ, who loved Je-ru-sa-lem, And wept its sins to mourn,

Sur-prise us with thy joy di-vine, For we would be re-made.
And like them, too, our words di-vide, And pride lays waste our pow'rs.
That size does not di-min-ish grace, Nor con-crete hide thy gaze.
Make just our laws and pure our hearts; So shall we be re-born.

Make Room Within My Heart, O God 321

Unison
1. Make room with-in my heart, O God, That you may form in me
2. Di - rect my will, O King of kings, Sub - ject it to your own,
The im - age you have shown in Christ, My ver - y life to be.
That ev - 'ry im - pulse, ac - tion, word, May make your king - dom known.
In - spire my thought, O loft - y One, To reach the high - est plane,
Ef - fect my prayer, great Trin - i - ty, E - ter - nal Three in One;
That I may know the mind of Christ, And him as great - est gain.
Com - bine each part of me to praise The Fa - ther, Spir - it, Son. A - MEN.

322 Lord, I Want to Be a Christian

Words and tune I WANT TO BE A CHRISTIAN, Traditional Negro Spiritual; adapted, John W. Work, Jr., and Frederick J. Work, 1907.

Purer in Heart, O God 323

1. Pur - er in heart, O God, Help me to be;
2. Pur - er in heart, O God, Help me to be;
3. Pur - er in heart, O God, Help me to be;
May I de - vote my life Whol - ly to thee:
Teach me to do thy will Most lov - ing - ly:
Un - til thy ho - ly face One day I see:
Watch thou my way - ward feet, Guide me with coun - sel sweet;
Be thou my friend and guide, Let me with thee a - bide;
Keep me from se - cret sin, Reign thou my soul with - in;
Pur - er in heart Help me to be.
Pur - er in heart Help me to be.
Pur - er in heart Help me to be. A - MEN.

Matthew 5:8. Words, Fannie Estelle Davison, 1877. Tune PURER IN HEART, James H. Fillmore, 1877.

324 Higher Ground

1. I'm press-ing on the up-ward way, New heights I'm
2. My heart has no de - sire to stay Where doubts a -
3. I want to live a - bove the world, Tho Sa - tan's
4. I want to scale the ut - most height And catch a

gain - ing ev - 'ry day; Still pray-ing as I on - ward bound,
rise and fears dis - may; Tho some may dwell where these a - bound,
darts at me are hurled; For faith has caught the joy - ful sound,
gleam of glo - ry bright; But still I'll pray till heav'n I've found,

"Lord, plant my feet on high - er ground."
My prayer, my aim is high - er ground.
The song of saints on high - er ground.
"Lord, lead me on to high - er ground."

Lord, lift me

up and let me stand, By faith, on heav - en's ta - ble - land, A high - er

plane than I have found; Lord, plant my feet on high - er ground.

Words, Johnson Oatman, Jr., 1892. Tune HIGHER GROUND, Charles H. Gabriel, 1902.

1. Sweet-ly, Lord, have we heard thee call-ing,"Come, fol-low me!"
2. Tho they lead o'er the cold, dark moun-tains, Seek-ing his sheep,
3. If they lead thro' the tem-ple ho-ly, Preach-ing the Word,
4. Then at last, when on high he sees us, Our jour-ney done,
And we see where thy foot-prints fall-ing, Lead us to thee.
Or a-long by *Si-lo-am's foun-tains, Help-ing the weak.
Or in homes of the poor and low-ly, Serv-ing the Lord.
We will rest where the steps of Je-sus End at his throne.
Foot-prints of Je-sus that make the path-way glow;
We will fol-low the steps of Je-sus wher-e'er they go.

Words, Mary B. C. Slade, 1871. Tune FOOTSTEPS, Asa B. Everett, 1871. *John 9:1-11.

326 Jesus, Thy Boundless Love to Me

1. Je - sus, thy bound-less love to me No tho't can reach, no
2. O grant that noth - ing in my soul May dwell but thy pure
3. O Love, how gra - cious is thy way! All fear be - fore thy

tongue de - clare; O knit my thank - ful heart to thee,
love a - lone; O may thy love pos - sess me whole,
pres - ence flies; Care, an - guish, sor - row melt a - way,

And reign with - out a ri - val there: Thine whol - ly, thine a -
My joy, my trea - sure, and my crown: All cold - ness from my
Wher - e'er thy heal - ing beams a - rise: O Je - sus, noth - ing

lone, I am; Be thou a - lone my con - stant flame.
heart re - move; May ev - 'ry act, word, tho't, be love.
may I see, Noth - ing de - sire, or seek, but thee. A-MEN.

Words, Paul Gerhardt, 1653; translated, John Wesley, 1739. Tune ST. CATHERINE,
Henri F. Hemy, 1864; Refrain, James G. Walton, 1874.
This tune in a higher key, No. 143.

More About Jesus 327

1. More a-bout Je-sus would I know, More of his grace to oth-ers show;
2. More a-bout Je-sus let me learn, More of his ho-ly will dis-cern;
3. More a-bout Je-sus in his Word, Hold-ing communion with my Lord;
4. More a-bout Je-sus on his throne, Rich-es in glo-ry all his own;

More of his sav-ing full-ness see, More of his love who died for me.
Spir-it of God, my teach-er be, Show-ing the things of Christ to me.
Hear-ing his voice in ev-'ry line, Mak-ing each faith-ful say-ing mine.
More of his kingdom's sure increase; More of his com-ing, Prince of peace.

More, more a-bout Je-sus, More, more a-bout Je-sus; More of his

sav-ing full-ness see, More of his love who died for me.

Words, Eliza E. Hewitt, 1887. Tune SWENEY, John R. Sweney, 1887.

328 May the Mind of Christ My Savior

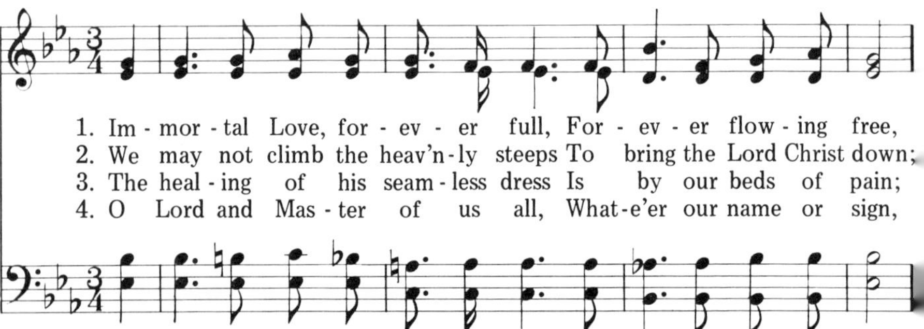

1. May the mind of Christ my Sav-ior, Live in me from day to
2. May the word of God dwell rich-ly In my heart from hour to
3. May the peace of God, my Fa-ther, Rule my life in ev-'ry-
4. May the love of Je-sus fill me, As the wa-ters fill the
5. May I run the race be-fore me, Strong and brave to face the
6. May his beau-ty rest up-on me As I seek the lost to

day, By his love and pow'r con-trol-ling All I do and say.
hour, So that all may see I tri-umph On-ly thro' his pow'r.
thing, That I may be calm to com-fort Sick and sor-row-ing.
sea; Him ex-alt-ing, self a-bas-ing—This is vic-to-ry.
foe, Look-ing on-ly un-to Je-sus As I on-ward go.
win, And may they for-get the chan-nel, See-ing on-ly him.

Words, Kate B. Wilkinson, 1925. Words copyright used by permission of Gordon Hitchcock, Surrey.
Tune ST. LEONARDS, A. Cyril Barham-Gould, 1925.

329 Immortal Love, Forever Full

1. Im-mor-tal Love, for-ev-er full, For-ev-er flow-ing free,
2. We may not climb the heav'n-ly steeps To bring the Lord Christ down;
3. The heal-ing of his seam-less dress Is by our beds of pain;
4. O Lord and Mas-ter of us all, What-e'er our name or sign,

Words, John Greenleaf Whittier, 1866. Tune SERENITY, William V. Wallace, 1856.

For - ev - er shared, for - ev - er whole, A nev - er - ebb - ing sea!
In vain we search the low-est deeps, For him no depths can drown.
We touch him in life's throng and press, And we are whole a - gain.
We own thy sway, we hear thy call, We test our lives by thine. A - MEN.

Teach Me Thy Way, O Lord 330

1. Teach me thy way, O Lord, Teach me thy way! Thy guid - ing grace
2. When I am sad at heart, Teach me thy way! When earth - ly joys
3. When doubts and fears a - rise, Teach me thy way! When storms o'erspread
4. Long as my life shall last, Teach me thy way! Wher- e'er my lot

af - ford, Teach me thy way! Help me to walk a - right, More by faith,
de - part, Teach me thy way! In hours of lone - li - ness, In times of
the skies, Teach me thy way! Shine thro' the cloud and rain, Thro' sor - row,
be cast, Teach me thy way! Un - til the race is run, Un - til the

less by sight; Lead me with heav'n-ly light, Teach me thy way!
dire dis -tress, In fail - ure or suc - cess, Teach me thy way!
toil and pain; Make thou my path-way plain, Teach me thy way!
jour -ney's done, Un - til the crown is won, Teach me thy way! A - MEN.

Psalm 27:11. Words, and tune CAMACHA, B. Mansell Ramsey. Copyright used by permission of Geo. Taylor. The Cross Printing Works, Stainland, Halifax, Yorkshire.

331 Free to Be Me

Unison

1. Free to be me, God, I real-ly am free; Free to be-
2. Free-dom, pos-ses-sion that makes me like you, Fright-ens me,
3. Free to live ful-ly, to fol-low your way, Give my-self

come what you want me to be; Free to de-cide wheth-er
God, when its mean-ing seeps through; Bless-ing or curse, Lord, con-
whol-ly, to die ev-'ry day; Free to be real, God, to

I should be lord, Or be your slave and o-bey your word.
demned to be free? Free, but re-spon-si-ble, free to be me.
strip off my mask, Be your cre-a-tion, it's all that I ask.

Words, Kate Wilkins Woolley, 1970. Tune CHISLEHURST, William L. Hooper, 1970. © Copyright 1970 Broadman Press. All rights reserved.

332 My Heart Looks in Faith

Unison

1. My heart looks in faith To the Lamb di-vine;
2. My heart looks in hope To the Son of God;
3. My heart looks in love To Je-sus my friend;
4. Faith and hope and love, All to Christ I give;

Words, T. C. Chao, 1931; translated, Frank W. Price. Tune SONG OF THE YANGTZE BOATMAN, Chinese Folk Melody.

His pre-cious blood flows down For these sins of mine.
He saves me, he leads me On the road he trod.
He does my soul strength-en And my life de-fend.
His sol-dier I will be So long as I live.

Nearer, My God, to Thee 333

1. Near-er, my God, to thee, Near-er to thee! E'en tho it
2. *There let the way ap-pear, Steps un-to heav'n; All that thou
3. Then with my wak-ing tho'ts Bright with thy praise, Out of my

be a cross That rais-eth me; Still all my song shall be,
send-est me, In mer-cy giv'n; An-gels to beck-on me
ston-y griefs**Beth-el I'll raise; So by my woes to be

Near-er, my God, to thee! Near-er, my God, to thee, Near-er to thee!
Near-er, my God, to thee! Near-er, my God, to thee, Near-er to thee!
Near-er, my God, to thee! Near-er, my God, to thee, Near-er to thee! A-MEN.

Words, Sarah F. Adams, 1840. Tune BETHANY, Lowell Mason, 1856. *Genesis 28:12. **Genesis 35:15.

334 Blessed Assurance, Jesus Is Mine

1. Bless - ed as - sur - ance, Je - sus is mine! Oh, what a fore-taste of
2. Per - fect sub - mis - sion, per - fect de - light, Vi - sions of rap - ture now
3. Per - fect sub - mis - sion, all is at rest, I in my Sav - ior am

glo - ry di - vine! Heir of sal - va - tion, pur-chase of God,
burst on my sight: An - gels de - scend - ing bring from a - bove
hap - py and blest: Watch-ing and wait - ing, look - ing a - bove,

Born of his Spir - it, wash'd in his blood.
Ech - oes of mer - cy, whis-pers of love. This is my sto - ry, this is my
Fill'd with his good-ness, lost in his love.

song, Prais-ing my Sav - ior all the day long; This is my sto - ry,

this is my song, Prais - ing my Sav - ior all the day long.

Words, Fanny J. Crosby, 1873. Tune ASSURANCE, Phoebe P. Knapp, 1873.

Standing on the Promises 335

1. Stand-ing on the prom-is-es of Christ my King, Thro' e - ter - nal a - ges
2. Stand-ing on the prom-is-es that can - not fail, When the howl-ing storms of
3. Stand-ing on the prom-is-es of Christ the Lord, Bound to him e - ter - nal-
4. Stand-ing on the prom-is-es I can - not fall, Lis - t'ning ev - 'ry mo-ment

let his prais- es ring; Glo - ry in the high-est, I will shout and sing,
doubt and fear as - sail, By the liv-ing word of God I shall pre - vail,
ly by love's strong cord, O - ver-com-ing dai - ly with the Spir- it's Sword,
to the Spir - it's call, Rest-ing in my Sav -ior as my all in all,

Standing on the promises of God. Stand - ing, stand - ing,
Standing on the promises, standing on the promises,

Standing on the prom-is-es of God my Sav-ior; Stand - ing,
Stand-ing on the prom-is - es,

stand - ing, I'm stand-ing on the prom- is -es of God.
stand-ing on the prom- is- es,

Words and tune PROMISES, R. Kelso Carter, 1886.

336 Jesus Loves Me

1. Je - sus loves me! this I know, For the Bi - ble tells me so;
2. Je - sus loves me! he who died Heav - en's gates to o - pen wide!
3. Je - sus loves me! loves me still, Tho I'm ver - y weak and ill;
4. Je - sus loves me! he will stay Close be - side me all the way;
Lit - tle ones to him be - long; They are weak, but he is strong.
He will wash a - way my sin, Let his lit - tle child come in.
From his shin - ing throne on high, Comes to watch me where I lie.
If I love him, when I die He will take me home on high.
Yes, Je - sus loves me, Yes, Je - sus loves me,
Yes, Je - sus loves me, The Bi - ble tells me so.

Words, Anna B. Warner, 1860. Tune CHINA, William B. Bradbury, 1862.

1. My hope is built on noth-ing less Than Je-sus' blood and righ-teous-ness;
2. When dark-ness seems to hide his face, I rest on his un-chang-ing grace;
3. His oath, his cov-e-nant, his blood Sup-port me in the whelm-ing flood;
4. When he shall come with trumpet sound, Oh, may I then in him be found;

I dare not trust the sweet-est frame, But whol-ly lean on Je-sus' name.
In ev-'ry high and storm-y gale, My an-chor holds with-in the veil.
When all a-round my soul gives way, He then is all my hope and stay.
Dressed in his righ-teous-ness a-lone, Faultless to stand be-fore the throne.

On Christ, the sol-id Rock, I stand; All oth-er ground is

sink-ing sand, All oth-er ground is sink-ing sand.

Words, Edward Mote, 1832. Tune SOLID ROCK, William B. Bradbury, 1863.

338 My Soul in Sad Exile

1. My soul in sad ex - ile was out on life's sea, So burdened with
2. I yield - ed my - self to his ten - der em - brace, And faith tak - ing
3. The song of my soul, since the Lord made me whole, Has been the old
4. Oh, come to the Sav - ior, he pa - tient - ly waits To save by his
sin, and dis-tressed, Till I heard a sweet voice say-ing, "Make me your
hold of the word, My fet - ters fell off, and I an - chored my
sto - ry so blessed, Of Je - sus who'll save who-so - ev - er will
pow - er di - vine; Come, an - chor your soul in the ha - ven of
choice," And I en - tered the ha - ven of rest.
soul: The ha - ven of rest is my Lord.
have A home in the ha - ven of rest.
rest, And say, "My Be - lov - ed is mine."
I've an-chored my soul
in the ha - ven of rest, I'll sail the wide seas no more; The
tempest may sweep o'er the wild stormy deep, In Je-sus I'm safe ev-er-more.

Words, Henry L. Gilmour, 1890. Tune HAVEN OF REST, George D. Moore, 1890.

It Is Well with My Soul 339

1. When peace, like a riv - er, at - tend -eth my way, When sor - rows like
2. Though Sa - tan should buf -fet, tho tri - als should come, Let this blest as -
3. My sin —oh, the bliss of this glo - ri - ous tho't:My sin not in
4. And, Lord, haste the day when the faith shall be sight, The clouds be roll'd

sea bil-lows roll; What-ev - er my lot, thou hast taught me to say,
sur - ance con -trol, That Christ has re - gard - ed my help -less es - tate,
part, but the whole Is nail'd to the cross and I bear it no more,
back as a scroll,The trump shall re-sound and the Lord shall de - scend,

It is well, it is well with my soul.
And hath shed his own blood for my soul.
Praise the Lord,praise the Lord,O my soul!
"E - ven so," it is well with my soul.

It is well with my

It is well

soul, It is well, it is well with my soul.
with my soul,

Words, Horatio G. Spafford, 1873. Tune VILLE DU HAVRE, Philip P. Bliss, 1876.

340 O the Deep, Deep Love of Jesus

1. O the deep, deep love of Je - sus, Vast, un - mea - sured,
2. O the deep, deep love of Je - sus, Spread his praise from
3. O the deep, deep love of Je - sus, Love of ev - 'ry
bound - less, free! Roll - ing as a might - y o - cean In its
shore to shore! How he lov - eth, ev - er lov - eth, Chang - eth
love the best! 'Tis an o - cean vast of bless - ing, 'Tis a
full - ness o - ver me. Un - der - neath me,
nev - er, nev - er - more. How he watch - es
ha - ven sweet of rest. O the deep, deep
all a - round me, Is the cur - rent of thy love; Lead - ing
o'er his loved ones, Died to call them all his own; How for
love of Je - sus, 'Tis a heav'n of heav'ns to me; And it

on - ward, lead - ing home - ward, To my glo - rious rest a - bove.
them he in - ter - ced - eth, Watch - eth o'er them from the throne!
lifts me up to glo - ry, For it lifts me up to thee.

The Lord's My Shepherd 341

1. The Lord's my Shep - herd, I'll not want; He makes me
2. My soul he doth re - store a - gain, And me to
3. Yea, though I walk in death's dark vale, Yet will I
4. My ta - ble thou hast fur - nish - ed In pres - ence
5. Good - ness and mer - cy all my life Shall sure - ly

down to lie In pas - tures green; he
walk doth make With - in the paths of
fear no ill; For thou art with me,
of my foes: My head thou dost with
fol - low me, And in God's house for -

lead - eth me The qui - et wa - ters by.
righ - teous - ness, E'en for his own name's sake.
and thy rod And staff me com - fort still.
oil a - noint, And my cup o - ver - flows.
ev - er - more My dwell - ing place shall be. A - MEN.

Psalm 23. Metrical version from the *Scottish Psalter*, 1650. Tune CRIMOND, Jessie Seymour Irvine, 1872.

342 I Am His, and He Is Mine

1. Loved with ev - er - last - ing love, Led by grace that love to know;
2. Heav'n a - bove is soft - er blue, Earth a - round is sweet - er green!
3. Things that once were wild a - larms Can - not now dis - turb my rest;
4. His for - ev - er, on - ly his; Who the Lord and me shall part?

Gra - cious Spir - it from a - bove, Thou hast taught me it is so!
Some-thing lives in ev - 'ry hue Christ-less eyes have nev - er seen:
Closed in ev - er - last - ing arms, Pil - lowed on the lov - ing breast.
Ah, with what a rest of bliss Christ can fill the lov - ing heart!

O this full and per - fect peace! O this trans - port all di - vine!
Birds with glad - der songs o'er - flow, Flow'rs with deep - er beau - ties shine,
O to lie for - ev - er here, Doubt and care and self re - sign,
Heav'n and earth may fade and flee, First - born light in gloom de - cline;

In a love which can-not cease, I am his, and he is mine. mine.
Since I know, as now I know, I am his, and he is mine. mine.
While he whis-pers in my ear, I am his, and he is mine. mine.
But while God and I shall be, I am his, and he is mine. mine.

Words, George W. Robinson, 1890. Tune EVERLASTING LOVE, James Mountain, c. 1890. Copyright used by permission of Marshall, Morgan and Scott.

God Is My Strong Salvation 343

Unison
1. God is my strong sal - va - tion: What foe have I to fear?
2. Place on the Lord re - li - ance; My soul, with cour - age wait;

In dark - ness and temp - ta - tion, My light, my help is near.
His truth be thine af - fi - ance, When faint and des - o - late.

Tho hosts en - camp a - round me, Firm in the fight I stand;
His might thy heart shall strength - en, His love thy joy in - crease;

What ter - ror can con-found me, With God at my right hand?
Mer - cy thy days shall length - en; The Lord will give thee peace. A-MEN.

Psalm 27:1-3. Words, James Montgomery, 1822. Tune WEDLOCK, American Folk Hymn; harmonized, Donald P. Hustad, 1973.

344 I Know Whom I Have Believed

1. I know not why God's wondrous grace To me he hath made known,
2. I know not how this sav - ing faith To me he did im - part,
3. I know not how the Spir - it moves, Con-vinc - ing men of sin,
4. I know not when my Lord may come, At night or noon-day fair,

Nor why, un -wor -thy, Christ in love Re-deemed me for his own.
Nor how be - liev - ing in his Word Wrought peace within my heart.
Re - veal - ing Je - sus thro' the Word, Cre - at - ing faith in him.
Nor if I'll walk the vale with him, Or meet him in the air.

But "I know whom I have be - liev - ed, And am per -suad -ed that he is

a -ble To keep that which I've com-mit-ted Un-to him a-gainst that day."

2 Timothy 1:12. Words, Daniel W. Whittle, 1883. Tune EL NATHAN, James McGranahan, 1883.

Satisfied 345

1. All my life long I had pant - ed For a draught from
2. Feed - ing on the husks a - round me, Till my strength was
3. Poor I was, and sought for rich - es, Some-thing that would
4. Well of wa - ter, ev - er spring - ing, Bread of life so

some clear spring, That I hoped would quench the burn - ing
al - most gone, Longed my soul for some - thing bet - ter,
sat - is - fy, But the dust I gath - ered round me
rich and free, Un - told wealth that nev - er fail - eth,

Of the thirst I felt with - in.
On - ly still to hun - ger on.
On - ly mocked my soul's sad cry.
My Re - deem - er is to me.

Hal - le - lu - jah! I have

found him Whom my soul so long has craved! Je - sus

sat - is - fies my long - ings, Thro' his blood I now am saved.

Words, Clara T. Williams, 1881. Tune SATISFIED, Ralph E. Hudson, 1881.

346 All to Thee

1. I have heard the voice of Je - sus Call - ing clear - ly "Fol - low me;"
2. Tho un-worth - y of sal - va - tion, Je - sus sought me for his own;
3. On - ly Je - sus is the an - swer For the hap - pi - ness men seek;
No one else could ev - er prom - ise Life e - ter - nal and so free.
On the cross he died to save me, Now I long to make him known.
He a - lone can lift life's bur - den, And give strength un-to the weak.
All to thee, I give my all to thee, All to thee,
thine on - ly will I be; All to thee, O Christ of
Cal - va - ry, My prayer shall ev - er be, my all to thee.

1. All to Je-sus I sur-ren-der, All to him I free-ly give;
2. All to Je-sus I sur-ren-der, Make me, Sav-ior, whol-ly thine;
3. All to Je-sus I sur-ren-der, Lord, I give my-self to thee;
I will ev-er love and trust him, In his pres-ence dai-ly live.
Let me feel thy Ho-ly Spir-it, Tru-ly know that thou art mine.
Fill me with thy love and pow-er, Let thy bless-ing fall on me.
I sur-ren-der all, I sur-ren-der all;
I sur-ren-der all, I sur-ren-der all;
All to thee, my bless-ed Sav-ior, I sur-ren-der all.

Words, Judson W. Van DeVenter, 1896. Tune SURRENDER, Winfield S. Weeden, 1896.

348 Living for Jesus

1. Liv-ing for Je-sus a life that is true, Striv-ing to please him
2. Liv-ing for Je-sus who died in my place, Bear-ing on Cal-v'ry
3. Liv-ing for Je-sus thro' earth's lit-tle while, My dear-est trea-sure,
in all that I do, Yield-ing al-le-giance, glad-heart-ed and free,
my sin and dis-grace, Such love con-strains me to an-swer his call,
the light of his smile, Seek-ing the lost ones he died to re-deem,
This is the path-way of bless-ing for me.
Fol-low his lead-ing and give him my all. O Je-sus, Lord and
Bring-ing the wea-ry to find rest in him.
Sav-ior, I give my-self to thee; For thou, in thine a-tone-ment, Didst
give thy-self for me; I own no oth-er Mas-ter, My heart shall be thy

Words, Thomas O. Chisholm, 1917. Tune LIVING, C. Harold Lowden, 1915. Copyright 1917 by Heidelberg Press. © Copyright Renewed 1945 (extended) by C. Harold Lowden. Assigned to The Rodeheaver Co. Used by permission.

throne; My life I give, hence-forth to live, O Christ, for thee a - lone.

Have Thine Own Way, Lord 349

1. Have thine own way, Lord! Have thine own way! Thou art the
2. Have thine own way, Lord! Have thine own way! Search me and
3. Have thine own way, Lord! Have thine own way! Wound - ed and
4. Have thine own way, Lord! Have thine own way! Hold o'er my

pot - ter, I am the clay! Mold me and make me Af - ter thy
try me, Mas - ter, to - day! Whit - er than snow, Lord, Wash me just
wea - ry, Help me, I pray! Pow - er, all pow - er Sure - ly is
be - ing Ab - so - lute sway! Fill with thy Spir - it Till all shall

will, While I am wait - ing, Yield - ed and still.
now, As in thy pres - ence Hum - bly I bow.
thine! Touch me and heal me, Sav - ior di - vine.
see Christ on - ly, al - ways, Liv - ing in me. A - MEN.

Words, Adelaide A. Pollard, 1907. Tune ADELAIDE, George C. Stebbins, 1907. Copyright 1907. Renewal 1935 extended. Hope Publishing Co., owner. All rights reserved. Used by permission.

350 Lead Me to Calvary

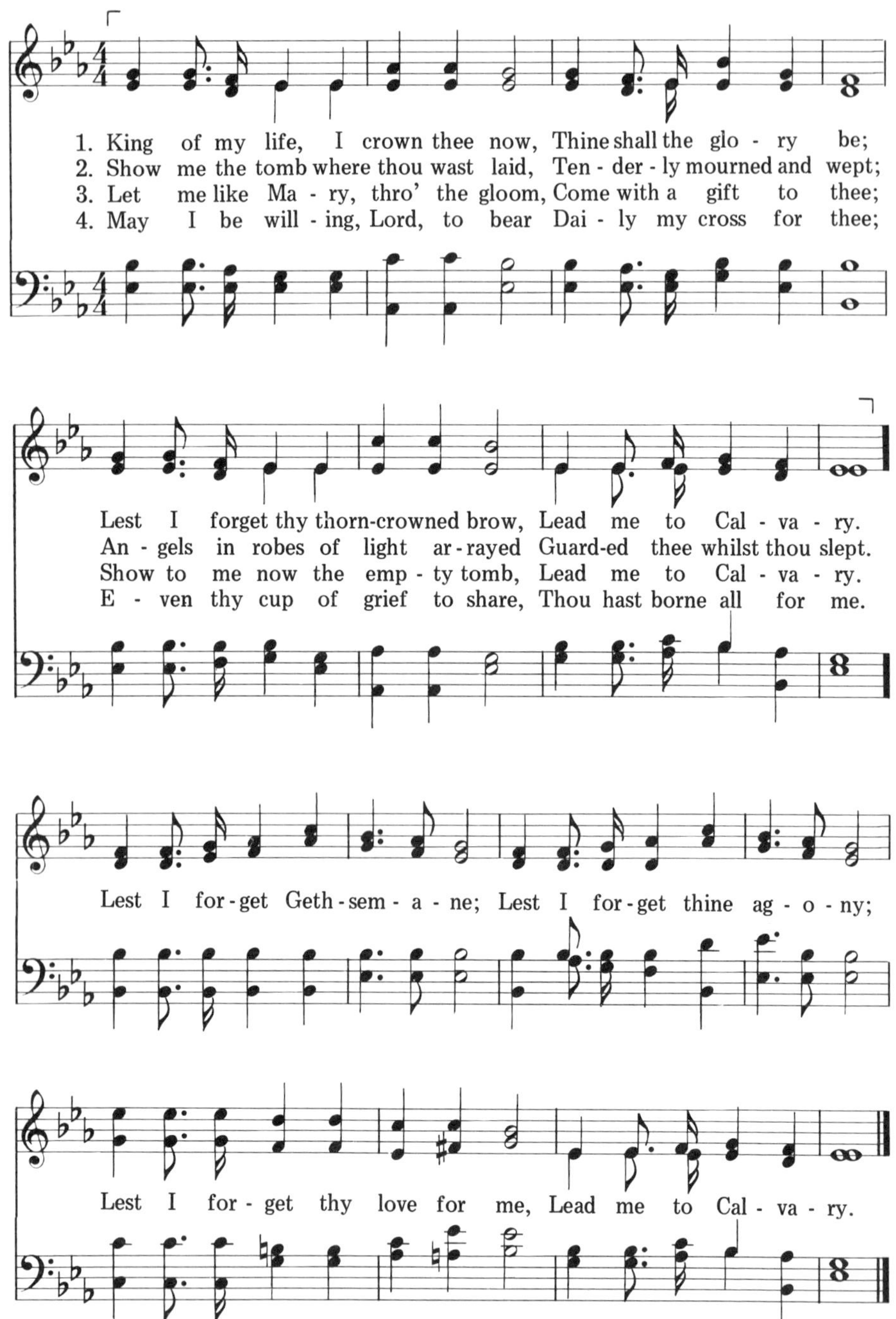

1. King of my life, I crown thee now, Thine shall the glo - ry be;
2. Show me the tomb where thou wast laid, Ten - der - ly mourned and wept;
3. Let me like Ma - ry, thro' the gloom, Come with a gift to thee;
4. May I be will - ing, Lord, to bear Dai - ly my cross for thee;

Lest I forget thy thorn-crowned brow, Lead me to Cal - va - ry.
An - gels in robes of light ar - rayed Guard-ed thee whilst thou slept.
Show to me now the emp - ty tomb, Lead me to Cal - va - ry.
E - ven thy cup of grief to share, Thou hast borne all for me.

Lest I for-get Geth-sem - a - ne; Lest I for-get thine ag - o - ny;

Lest I for-get thy love for me, Lead me to Cal - va - ry.

Jesus, Keep Me Near the Cross 351

1. Je - sus, keep me near the cross, There a pre - cious foun - tain,
2. Near the cross, a trem - bling soul, Love and mer - cy found me;
3. Near the cross! O Lamb of God, Bring its scenes be - fore me;
4. Near the cross! I'll watch and wait, Hop - ing, trust - ing ev - er,

Free to all, a heal - ing stream, Flows from Cal - v'ry's moun - tain.
There the Bright and Morn - ing Star Shed his beams a - round me.
Help me walk from day to day With its shad - ow o'er me.
Till I reach the gold - en strand, Just be - yond the riv - er.

In the cross, in the cross Be my glo - ry ev - er,

Till my ran - somed soul shall find Rest be - yond the riv - er.

Words, Fanny J. Crosby, 1869. Tune NEAR THE CROSS, William H. Doane, 1869.

352 I Am Thine, O Lord

1. I am thine, O Lord, I have heard thy voice, And it told thy
2. Con - se - crate me now to thy serv - ice, Lord, By the pow'r of
3. O the pure de - light of a sin - gle hour That be - fore thy
4. There are depths of love that I can - not know Till I cross the

love to me; But I long to rise in the arms of faith, And be
grace di - vine; Let my soul look up with a stead-fast hope, And my
throne I spend; When I kneel in pray'r, and with thee, my God, I com-
nar - row sea; There are heights of joy that I may not reach Till I

clos - er drawn to thee. Draw me near - er, near - er, bless - ed
will be lost in thine.
mune as friend with friend!
rest in peace with thee. near - er, near-er,

Lord, To the cross where thou hast died; Draw me near - er, near - er,

near - er, bless - ed Lord, To thy pre - cious, bleed - ing side.

Hebrews 10:22. Words, Fanny J. Crosby, 1875. Tune I AM THINE, William H. Doane, 1875.

1. Je - sus is Sav - ior and Lord of my life,
2. Bless - ed Re - deem - er, all glo - ri - ous King,
3. Will you sur - ren - der your all to him now?

My hope, my glo - ry, my all; Won - der - ful Mas - ter in
Wor - thy of rev - 'rence I pay; Trib - ute and prais - es I
Fol - low his will and o - bey, Crown him as Sov - 'reign, be -

joy and in strife, On him you too may call.
joy - ful - ly bring To him, the Life, the Way.
fore his throne bow; Give him your heart to - day.

Je - sus is Lord of all, Je - sus is Lord of all, Lord of my

thoughts and my ser - vice each day, Je - sus is Lord of all.

354 Near to the Heart of God

1. There is a place of qui-et rest, Near to the heart of God,
2. There is a place of com-fort sweet, Near to the heart of God,
3. There is a place of full re-lease, Near to the heart of God,
A place where sin can-not mo-lest, Near to the heart of God.
A place where we our Sav-ior meet, Near to the heart of God.
A place where all is joy and peace, Near to the heart of God.
O Je-sus, blest Re-deem-er, Sent from the heart of God,
Hold us who wait be-fore thee Near to the heart of God.

Words and tune MCAFEE, Cleland B. McAfee, 1901.

Speak to My Heart 355

1. Speak to my heart, Lord Je - sus, Speak that my soul may hear;
2. Speak to my heart, Lord Je - sus, Purge me from ev - 'ry sin;
3. Speak to my heart, Lord Je - sus, It is no long - er mine:

Speak to my heart, Lord Je - sus, Calm ev - 'ry doubt and fear.
Speak to my heart, Lord Je - sus, Help me the lost to win.
Speak to my heart, Lord Je - sus, I would be whol - ly thine.

Speak to my heart, oh, speak to my heart, Speak to my heart, I pray;

Yield - ed and still, seek - ing thy will, Oh, speak to my heart to - day.

356 Here Is My Life

Unison

1. Lord, you placed me in this world of time and space and
2. Lord, you asked for all my life in heal - ing hurts and
3. Lord, I give my life to you, my time, my tal - ents,

mis - siles hurled, With eyes I've seen the ghet - to gloom, With ears I've
end - ing strife, With mind to al - ways seek the truth, With voice to
each day new, With faith to wit - ness to your plan, With hope to

heard the son - ic boom, And man cry out for breath - ing room,
al - ways speak the truth, And live to man - i - fest Christ's worth,
glad - ly take my stand, And love to min - is - ter to man,

I can - not wait, I can - not wait!

Here is my life, I want to live it,

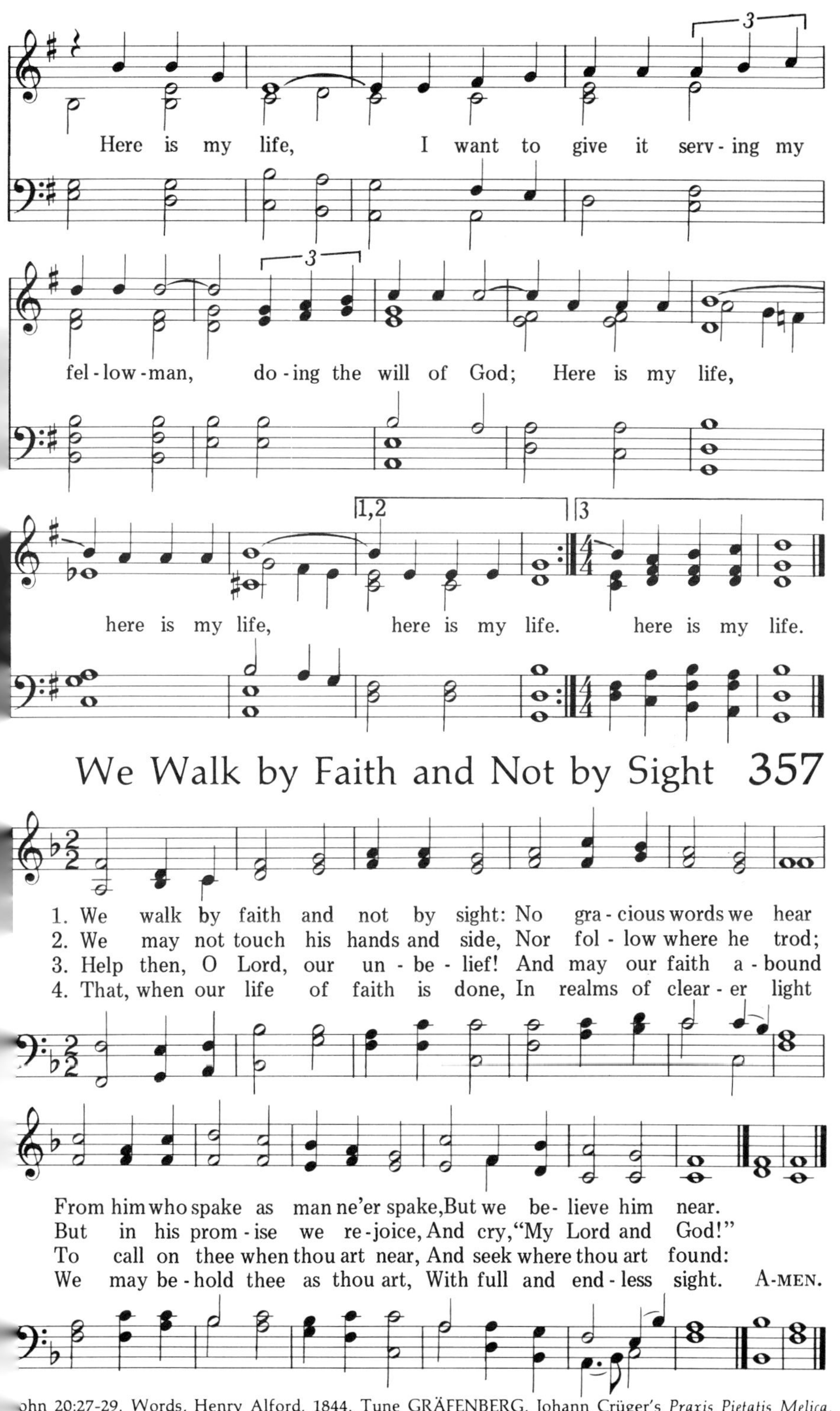

Here is my life, I want to give it serv-ing my
fel-low-man, do-ing the will of God; Here is my life,
here is my life, here is my life. here is my life.

We Walk by Faith and Not by Sight 357

1. We walk by faith and not by sight: No gra-cious words we hear
2. We may not touch his hands and side, Nor fol-low where he trod;
3. Help then, O Lord, our un-be-lief! And may our faith a-bound
4. That, when our life of faith is done, In realms of clear-er light

From him who spake as man ne'er spake, But we be-lieve him near.
But in his prom-ise we re-joice, And cry, "My Lord and God!"
To call on thee when thou art near, And seek where thou art found:
We may be-hold thee as thou art, With full and end-less sight. A-MEN.

John 20:27-29. Words, Henry Alford, 1844. Tune GRÄFENBERG, Johann Crüger's *Praxis Pietatis Melica*, 1647.

358 Open My Eyes that I May See

1. O-pen my eyes that I may see Glimpses of truth thou hast for me;
2. O-pen my ears that I may hear Voic-es of truth thou sendest clear;
3. O-pen my mouth and let me bear Glad-ly the warm truth ev-'ry-where;
Place in my hands the won-der-ful key That shall un-clasp, and
And while the wave-notes fall on my ear, Ev - 'ry-thing false will
O - pen my heart, and let me pre-pare Love with thy chil - dren
set me free: Si-lent-ly now I wait for thee, Ready, my God, thy
dis - ap-pear: Si-lent-ly now I wait for thee, Ready, my God, thy
thus to share: Si-lent-ly now I wait for thee, Ready, my God, thy
will to see; O-pen my eyes, il - lu - mine me, Spir-it di - vine!
will to see; O-pen my ears, il - lu - mine me, Spir-it di - vine!
will to see; O-pen my heart, il - lu - mine me, Spir-it di - vine!

Words and tune SCOTT, Clara H. Scott, 1895.

Unison
1. O God who gives us ev - 'ry-thing, Who gives this life to me,
2. O help me learn to share my faith With all men ev - 'ry-where,
3. O Lord, to - day I give my - self, And now I hum - bly pray
I come a - gain to praise thy name And ask for light to see
And give me strength to go to those Who need thy heal - ing care:
For faith and strength and Chris - tian love To fol - low in thy way,
The life that I must live this day, The per - son I must be;
Re - veal - ing to all men on earth The love that Christ gave me;
And wait - ing not to do thy will, To serve my fel - low - man;
Then help me, Lord, to know my place In God's world to - day.
Then will I find, O Lord, my place In God's world to - day.
Then yield - ing all, I find my place In God's world to - day.

Words, Ed Seabough, 1966. Tune EL DORADO, William J. Reynolds, 1966. © Copyright 1966 Broadman Press. All rights reserved.

360 Beneath the Cross of Jesus

1. Be-neath the cross of Je-sus I fain would take my stand,
2. Up-on that cross of Je-sus Mine eye at times can see
3. I take, O Cross, thy shad-ow For my a-bid-ing place;
The shad-ow of a might-y rock With-in a wea-ry land;
The ver-y dy-ing form of One Who suf-fered there for me;
I ask no oth-er sun-shine than The sun-shine of his face;
A home with-in the wil-der-ness, A rest up-on the way,
And from my smit-ten heart with tears Two won-ders I con-fess,
Con-tent to let the world go by, To know no gain or loss,
From the burn-ing of the noon-tide heat And the burden of the day.
The won-ders of his glo-rious love And my un-wor-thi-ness.
My sin-ful self my on-ly shame, My glo-ry all the cross.

Words, Elizabeth C. Clephane, 1872. Tune ST. CHRISTOPHER, Frederick C. Maker, 1881. Music used by permission the Psalms and Hymns Trust.

Wherever He Leads I'll Go 361

1. "Take up thy cross and fol - low me," I heard my Mas-ter say;
2. He drew me clos - er to his side, I sought his will to know,
3. It may be thro' the shad - ows dim, Or o'er the storm-y sea,
4. My heart, my life, my all I bring To Christ who loves me so;

"I gave my life to ran - som thee, Sur - ren-der your all to - day."
And in that will I now a - bide, Wher - ev - er he leads I'll go.
I take my cross and fol - low him, Wher - ev - er he lead - eth me.
He is my Mas - ter, Lord, and King, Wher - ev - er he leads I'll go.

Wher - ev - er he leads I'll go, Wher - ev - er he leads I'll go,

I'll fol-low my Christ who loves me so, Wher - ev - er he leads I'll go.

362 Come, All Christians, Be Committed

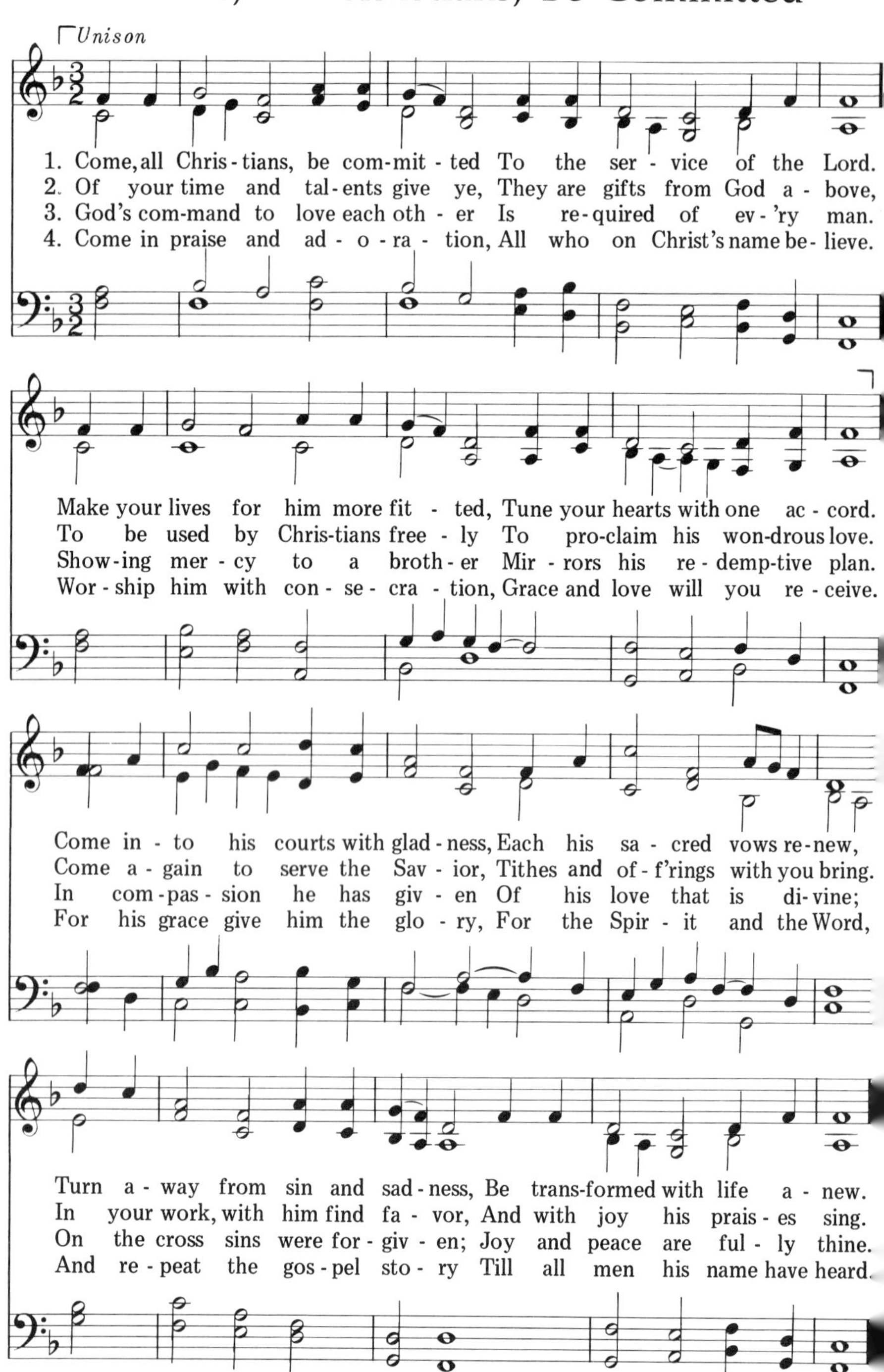

Unison
1. Come, all Chris-tians, be com-mit-ted To the ser-vice of the Lord.
2. Of your time and tal-ents give ye, They are gifts from God a-bove,
3. God's com-mand to love each oth-er Is re-quired of ev-'ry man.
4. Come in praise and ad-o-ra-tion, All who on Christ's name be-lieve.
Make your lives for him more fit-ted, Tune your hearts with one ac-cord.
To be used by Chris-tians free-ly To pro-claim his won-drous love.
Show-ing mer-cy to a broth-er Mir-rors his re-demp-tive plan.
Wor-ship him with con-se-cra-tion, Grace and love will you re-ceive.
Come in-to his courts with glad-ness, Each his sa-cred vows re-new,
Come a-gain to serve the Sav-ior, Tithes and of-f'rings with you bring.
In com-pas-sion he has giv-en Of his love that is di-vine;
For his grace give him the glo-ry, For the Spir-it and the Word,
Turn a-way from sin and sad-ness, Be trans-formed with life a-new.
In your work, with him find fa-vor, And with joy his prais-es sing.
On the cross sins were for-giv-en; Joy and peace are ful-ly thine.
And re-peat the gos-pel sto-ry Till all men his name have heard.

This tune in a higher key, No. 196. Alternate tune HYFRYDOL, No. 11.

Unison

1. At the name of Je - sus Ev - 'ry knee shall bow,
2. Hum - bled for a sea - son, To re - ceive a name
3. In your hearts en - throne him; There let him sub - due
4. Broth - ers, this Lord Je - sus Shall re - turn a - gain,

Ev - 'ry tongue con - fess him King of glo - ry now;
From the lips of sin - ners Un - to whom he came,
All that is not ho - ly, All that is not true:
With his Fa - ther's glo - ry O'er the earth to reign;

'Tis the Fa - ther's plea - sure We should call him Lord,
Faith - ful - ly he bore it Spot - less to the last,
Crown him as your cap - tain In temp - ta - tion's hour;
For all wreaths of em - pire Meet up - on his brow,

Who from the be - gin - ning Was the might - y Word.
Brought it back vic - to - rious When from death he passed.
Let his will en - fold you In its light and pow'r.
And our hearts con - fess him King of glo - ry now.

Philippians 2:5-11. Words, Caroline M. Noel, 1870. Tune KING'S WESTON, Ralph Vaughan Williams, 1925. From *Enlarged Songs of Praise* by permission of Oxford University Press.

364 Hope of the World

1. Hope of the world, thou Christ of great com-pas-sion,
2. Hope of the world, God's gift from high-est heav-en,
3. Hope of the world, who by thy cross didst save us
4. Hope of the world, O Christ, o'er death vic-to-rious,

Speak to our fear-ful hearts by con-flict rent;
Bring-ing to hun-gry souls the bread of life,
From death and dark de-spair, from sin and guilt;
Who by this sign didst con-quer grief and pain,

Save us, thy peo-ple, from con-sum-ing pas-sion,
Still let thy Spir-it un-to us be giv-en
We ren-der back the love thy mer-cy gave us,
We would be faith-ful to thy gos-pel glo-rious:

Who by our own false hopes and aims are spent.
To heal earth's wounds and end her bit-ter strife.
Take thou our lives and use them as thou wilt.
Thou art our Lord! Thou dost for-ev-er reign. A-MEN.

Words, Georgia Harkness, 1954. Copyright 1954 by The Hymn Society of America. Used by permission.
Tune O PERFECT LOVE, Joseph Barnby, 1889.

O Jesus, I Have Promised 365

1. O Je - sus, I have prom - ised To serve thee to the end;
2. O Je - sus, thou hast prom - ised To all who fol - low thee,
3. O let me feel thee near me! The world is ev - er near;
4. O let me hear thee speak - ing In ac - cents clear and still,

Be thou for - ev - er near me, My Mas - ter and my friend;
That where thou art in glo - ry There shall thy ser - vant be;
I see the sights that daz - zle, The tempt - ing sounds I hear;
A - bove the storms of pas - sion, The mur - murs of self - will.

I shall not fear the bat - tle If thou art by my side,
And, Je - sus, I have prom - ised To serve thee to the end;
My foes are ev - er near me, A - round me and with - in;
O speak to re - as - sure me, To has - ten or con - trol!

Nor wan - der from the path - way If thou wilt be my guide.
O give me grace to fol - low My Mas - ter and my friend!
But, Je - sus, draw thou near - er And shield my soul from sin.
O speak, and make me lis - ten, Thou guard - ian of my soul! A - MEN.

Words, John E. Bode, 1868. Tune ANGEL'S STORY, Arthur H. Mann, 1881.

366 Take My Life, Lead Me, Lord

1. Take my life, lead me, Lord, Take my life, lead me, Lord,
2. Take my life, teach me, Lord, Take my life, teach me, Lord,
3. Here am I, send me, Lord, Here am I, send me, Lord,

Make my life use-ful to thee; Take my life, lead me, Lord,
Make my life use-ful to thee; Take my life, teach me, Lord,
Make my life use-ful to thee; Here am I, send me, Lord,

Take my life, lead me, Lord, Make my life use-ful to thee.
Take my life, teach me, Lord, Make my life use-ful to thee.
Here am I, send me, Lord, Make my life use-ful to thee.

367 Jesus Calls Us o'er the Tumult

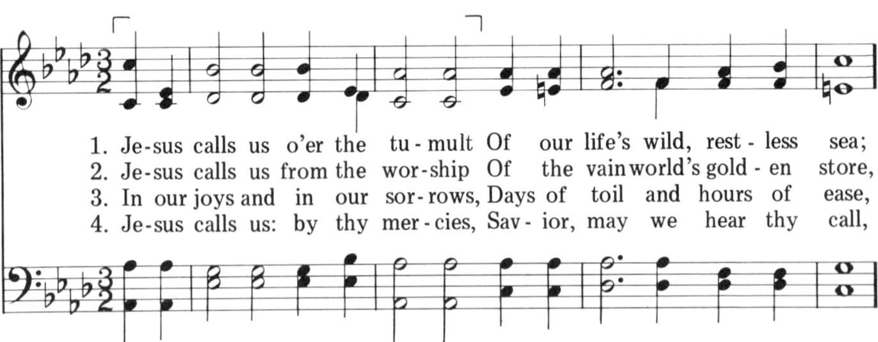
1. Je-sus calls us o'er the tu-mult Of our life's wild, rest-less sea;
2. Je-sus calls us from the wor-ship Of the vain world's gold-en store,
3. In our joys and in our sor-rows, Days of toil and hours of ease,
4. Je-sus calls us: by thy mer-cies, Sav-ior, may we hear thy call,

Matthew 4:18-20. Words, Cecil Frances Alexander, 1852. Tune GALILEE, William H. Jude, 1887.

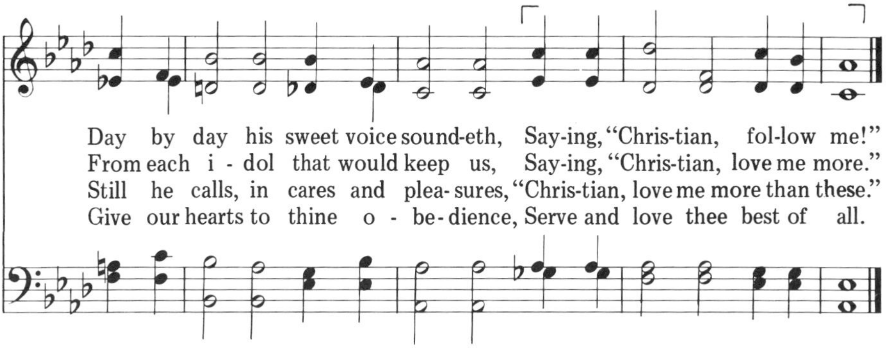

Day by day his sweet voice sound-eth, Say-ing, "Chris-tian, fol-low me!"
From each i - dol that would keep us, Say-ing, "Chris-tian, love me more."
Still he calls, in cares and plea- sures, "Chris-tian, love me more than these."
Give our hearts to thine o - be-dience, Serve and love thee best of all.

O Love That Wilt Not Let Me Go 368

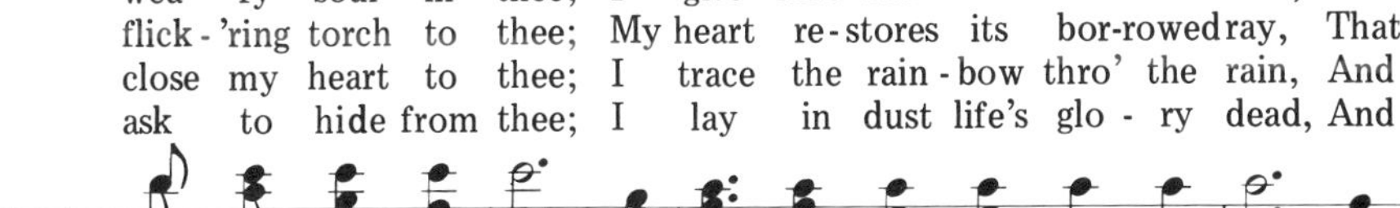

1. O Love that wilt not let me go, I rest my
2. O Light that fol - lowest all my way, I yield my
3. O Joy that seek - est me through pain, I can - not
4. O Cross that lift - est up my head, I dare not

wea - ry soul in thee; I give thee back the life I owe, That
flick - 'ring torch to thee; My heart re-stores its bor-rowed ray, That
close my heart to thee; I trace the rain - bow thro' the rain, And
ask to hide from thee; I lay in dust life's glo - ry dead, And

in thine o - cean depths its flow May rich - er, full - er be.
in thy sun -shine's glow its day May bright - er, fair - er be.
feel the prom - ise is not vain That morn shall tear-less be.
from the ground there blossoms red Life that shall end-less be. A-MEN.

Words, George Matheson, 1882. Tune ST. MARGARET, Albert L. Peace, 1884.

369 O Master, Let Me Walk with Thee

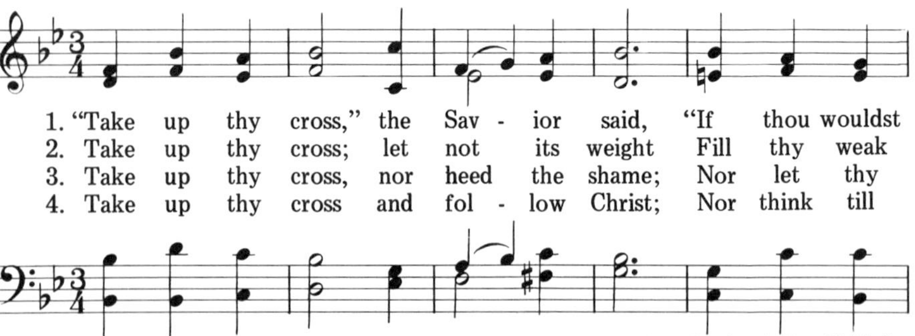

1. O Mas - ter, let me walk with thee In low - ly paths of
2. Help me the slow of heart to move By some clear, win - ning
3. Teach me thy pa - tience; still with thee In clos - er, dear - er
4. In hope that sends a shin - ing ray Far down the fu - ture's

serv - ice free; Tell me thy se - cret, help me bear
word of love; Teach me the way - ward feet to stay,
com - pa - ny, In work that keeps faith sweet and strong,
broad - 'ning way, In peace that on - ly thou canst give,

The strain of toil, the fret of care.
And guide them in the home - ward way.
In trust that tri - umphs o - ver wrong.
With thee, O Mas - ter, let me live. A - MEN.

Words, Washington Gladden, 1879. Tune MARYTON, H. Percy Smith, 1874.

370 Take Up Thy Cross

1. "Take up thy cross," the Sav - ior said, "If thou wouldst
2. Take up thy cross; let not its weight Fill thy weak
3. Take up thy cross, nor heed the shame; Nor let thy
4. Take up thy cross and fol - low Christ; Nor think till

Matthew 16:24, 25. Words, Charles W. Everest, 1833. Tune GERMANY, William Gardiner's *Sacred Melodies*, 1815.
This tune in a lower key, No. 301.

my dis - ci - ple be; De - ny thy - self, the world for -
spir - it with a - larm; His strength shall bear thy spir - it
fool - ish pride re - bel; Thy Lord for thee the cross en -
death to lay it down; For on - ly he who bears the

sake, And hum - bly fol - low af - ter me."
up, And brace thy heart and nerve thine arm.
dured, To save thy soul from death and hell.
cross May hope to wear the glo - rious crown. A - MEN.

Where He Leads Me 371

1. I can hear my Sav - ior call - ing, I can hear my Sav - ior call - ing,
2. I'll go with him thro' the gar - den, I'll go with him thro' the gar - den,
3. I'll go with him thro' the judg-ment, I'll go with him thro' the judg-ment,
4. He will give me grace and glo - ry, He will give me grace and glo - ry,

Where he leads me I will fol - low, Where he leads me I will fol - low,
D.C. for Refrain

I can hear my Sav - ior call - ing, "Take thy cross and fol - low, fol - low me."
I'll go with him thro' the gar - den, I'll go with him, with him all the way.
I'll go with him thro' the judg-ment, I'll go with him, with him all the way.
He will give me grace and glo - ry, And go with me, with me all the way.

Where he leads me I will fol - low, I'll go with him, with him all the way.

Words, E. W. Blandy, c. 1890. Tune NORRIS, J. S. Norris, c. 1890.

372 O Thou, in Whose Presence

1. O thou, in whose pres - ence my soul takes de - light,
2. The ros - es of Sha - ron, the lil - ies that grow
3. His voice as the sound of a dul - ci - mer sweet
4. Dear Shep - herd, I hear and will fol - low thy call;
On whom in af - flic - tion I call, My com - fort by
In vales on the banks of the streams; His cheeks in the
Is heard through the shad - ow of death, The ce - dars of
I know the sweet sound of thy voice; Re - store and de -
day and my song in the night, My hope, my sal - va - tion, my all.
beau - ty of ex - cel - lence blow, His eye all in - vit - ing - ly beams.
Leb - a - non bow at his feet, The air is per - fumed with his breath.
fend me, for thou art my all, In thee I will ev - er re - joice.

Words, Joseph Swain, 1791. Tune DAVIS, Freeman Lewis, 1813.

373 Take My Life, and Let It Be

1. Take my life and let it be Con - se - crat - ed,
2. Take my feet and let them be Swift and beau - ti -
3. Take my sil - ver and my gold, Not a mite would
4. Take my will and make it thine, It shall be no

Words, Frances R. Havergal, 1874. Tune HENDON, Henri A. C. Malan, 1823; harmonized, Lowell Mason, 1841.

Lord, to thee; Take my hands and let them move At the im-pulse
ful for thee; Take my voice and let me sing Al - ways, on - ly,
I with-hold; Take my mo - ments and my days, Let them flow in
long - er mine; Take my heart, it is thine own, It shall be thy

of thy love, At the im - pulse of thy love.
for my King, Al - ways, on - ly, for my King.
cease - less praise, Let them flow in cease - less praise.
roy - al throne, It shall be thy roy - al throne. A - MEN.

Take My Life, and Let It Be 374

1. Take my life, and let it be Con - se - crat - ed, Lord, to thee;
2. Take my feet, and let them be Swift and beau - ti - ful for thee;
3. Take my sil - ver and my gold, Not a mite would I with- hold;
4. Take my will, and make it thine, It shall be no long - er mine;

Lord, I give my life to thee, Thine for - ev - er-more to be;

D. C. for Refrain

Take my hands and let them move At the im-pulse of thy love.
Take my voice and let me sing Al - ways, on - ly, for my King.
Take my mo-ments and my days, Let them flow in cease-less praise.
Take my heart, it is thine own, It shall be thy roy - al throne.

Lord, I give my life to thee, Thine for - ev - er - more to be.

Words, Frances R. Havergal, 1874. Tune YARBROUGH, Anonymous.

375 'Tis So Sweet to Trust in Jesus

1. 'Tis so sweet to trust in Je - sus, Just to take him
2. O how sweet to trust in Je - sus, Just to trust his
3. Yes, 'tis sweet to trust in Je - sus, Just from sin and
4. I'm so glad I learned to trust him, Pre - cious Je - sus,
at his word; Just to rest up - on his prom - ise,
cleans - ing blood; Just in sim - ple faith to plunge me
self to cease; Just from Je - sus sim - ply tak - ing
Sav - ior, friend; And I know that he is with me,
Just to know, "Thus saith the Lord."
'Neath the heal - ing, cleans - ing flood! Je - sus, Je - sus,
Life and rest, and joy and peace.
Will be with me to the end.
how I trust him! How I've proved him o'er and o'er!
Je - sus, Je - sus, pre - cious Je - sus! O for grace to trust him more!

Words, Louisa M. R. Stead, c. 1882. Tune TRUST IN JESUS, William J. Kirkpatrick, 1882.

Have Faith in God 376

1. Have faith in God when your path-way is lone-ly, He sees and
2. Have faith in God when your pray'rs are un-an-swered, Your ear-nest
3. Have faith in God in your pain and your sor-row, His heart is
4. Have faith in God tho all else fail a-bout you; Have faith in

knows all the way you have trod; Nev-er a-lone are the
plea he will nev-er for-get; Wait on the Lord, trust his
touched with your grief and de-spair; Cast all your cares and your
God, he pro-vides for his own; He can-not fail tho all

least of his chil-dren; Have faith in God, have faith in God.
Word and be pa-tient, Have faith in God, he'll an-swer yet.
bur-dens up-on him, And leave them there, oh, leave them there.
king-doms shall per-ish, He rules, he reigns up-on his throne.

Have faith in God, he's on his throne; Have faith in God, he watches o'er his own;

He can-not fail, he must pre-vail; Have faith in God, have faith in God.

377 Faith Is the Victory

1. En-camped a - long the hills of light, Ye Chris-tian sol-diers, rise,
2. His ban - ner o - ver us is love, Our sword the Word of God;
3. To him who o - ver-comes the foe White rai - ment shall be giv'n;
And press the bat - tle ere the night Shall veil the glow - ing skies.
We tread the road the saints a - bove With shouts of tri-umph trod.
Be - fore the an - gels he shall know His name con-fessed in heav'n.
A - gainst the foe in vales be - low, Let all our strength be hurled;
By faith they, like a whirl-wind's breath, Swept on o'er ev - 'ry field;
Then on - ward from the hills of light, Our hearts with love a - flame;
Faith is the vic - to - ry, we know, That o - ver-comes the world.
The faith by which they conquered death Is still our shin - ing shield.
We'll van-quish all the hosts of night In Je - sus' con-q'ring name.

Words, John H. Yates, 1891. Tune SANKEY, Ira D. Sankey, 1891.

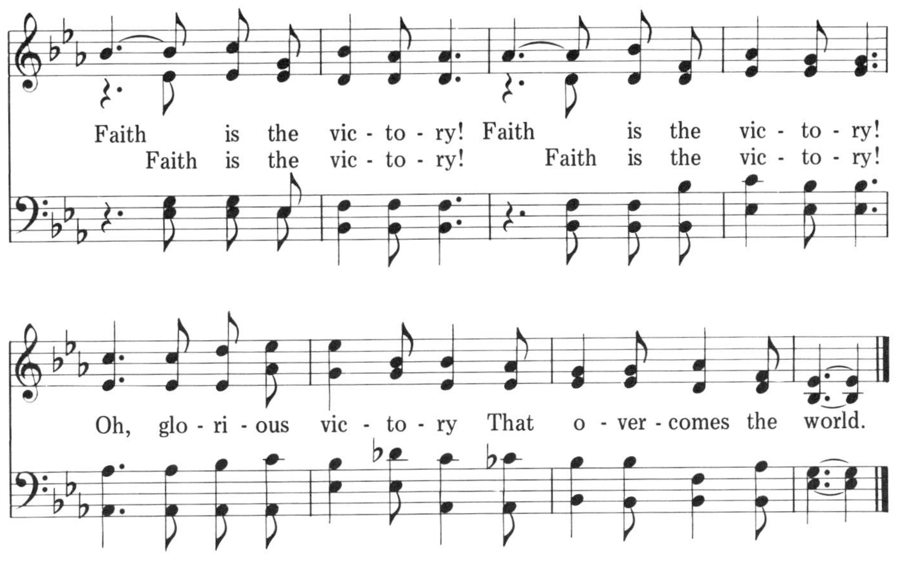

Faith is the vic-to-ry! Faith is the vic-to-ry!
Faith is the vic-to-ry! Faith is the vic-to-ry!
Oh, glo-ri-ous vic-to-ry That o-ver-comes the world.

Lord, You Bid Us Ever 378

Unison

1. Lord, you bid us ev - er Fol - low you with pa - tient hope;
2. Lord, you are our true hope, And in you we do be - lieve;
3. Lord, you bid us ev - er Tru - ly love in word and deed;
4. Lord, you bid us ev - er Fol - low you with pa - tient hope;

And the fu - ture stands be - fore us For our trust is in you.
For our con - fi - dence is ev - er In your tri - umph, O Christ.
Help us prac - tice your love dai - ly, By this love to be known.
Life e - ter - nal free - ly giv - en Those whose trust is in you.

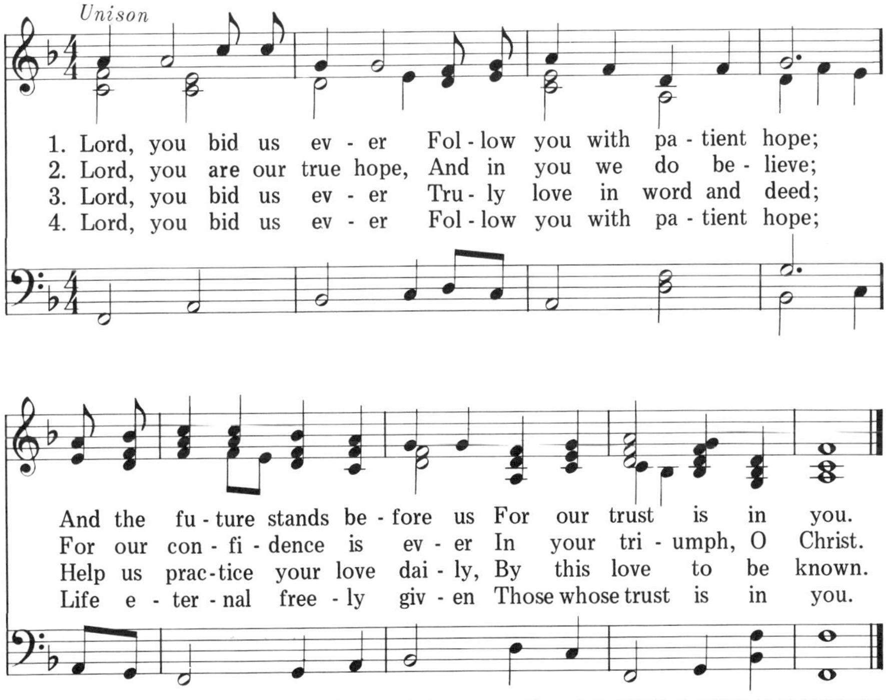

Words, Otmar Schulz, 1967; translated, Harry Eskew, 1974. Tune DU, HERR, HEISST UNS HOFFEN, Otmar Schulz, 1967. Words and music used by permission Verlag Singende Gemeinde, Wuppertal, F.R.G.

379 I Need Thee Every Hour

1. I need thee ev-'ry hour, Most gra-cious Lord;
2. I need thee ev-'ry hour, Stay thou near by;
3. I need thee ev-'ry hour, In joy or pain;
4. I need thee ev-'ry hour, Teach me thy will;
5. I need thee ev-'ry hour, Most Ho-ly One;

No ten-der voice like thine Can peace af-ford.
Temp-ta-tions lose their pow'r When thou art nigh.
Come quick-ly and a-bide, Or life is vain.
Thy prom-is-es so rich In me ful-fill.
O make me thine in-deed, Thou bless-ed Son.

I need thee, O I need thee; Ev-'ry hour I need thee!

O bless me now, my Sav-ior, I come to thee. A - MEN.

Words, Annie S. Hawks, 1872. Tune NEED, Robert Lowry, 1872.

My Faith Has Found a Resting Place 380

1. My faith has found a rest-ing place, Not in de-vice nor creed;
2. E - nough for me that Je - sus saves, This ends my fear and doubt;
3. My heart is lean-ing on the Word, The writ-ten Word of God,
4. My great Phy - si -cian heals the sick, The lost he came to save;

I trust the Ev - er - liv - ing One, His wounds for me shall plead.
A sin - ful soul I come to him, He'll nev - er cast me out.
Sal - va - tion by my Sav - ior's name, Sal - va - tion thro' his blood.
For me his pre-cious blood he shed, For me his life he gave.

I need no oth - er ar - gu - ment, I need no oth - er plea,

It is e - nough that Je - sus died, And that he died for me.

Words, Lidie H. Edmunds, 19th Century. Tune LANDÅS, Norwegian Folk Melody; arranged, William J. Kirkpatrick.

381 Moment by Moment

1. Dy-ing with Je-sus, by death reck-oned mine; Liv-ing with
2. Nev-er a tri-al that he is not there, Nev-er a
3. Nev-er a weak-ness that he doth not feel, Nev-er a

Je-sus, a new life di-vine; Look-ing to Je-sus till
bur-den that he doth not bear, Nev-er a sor-row that
sick-ness that he can-not heal; Mo-ment by mo-ment, in

glo-ry doth shine, Mo-ment by mo-ment, O Lord, I am thine.
he doth not share, Mo-ment by mo-ment, I'm un-der his care.
woe or in weal, Je-sus my Sav-ior a-bides with me still.

Mo-ment by mo-ment I'm kept in his love; Mo-ment by

mo-ment I've life from a-bove; Look-ing to Je-sus till

Words, Daniel W. Whittle, 1893. Tune WHITTLE, May Whittle Moody, 1893.

glo - ry doth shine; Mo - ment by mo - ment, O Lord, I am thine.

My Faith Looks Up to Thee 382

1. My faith looks up to thee, Thou Lamb of Cal - va - ry,
2. May thy rich grace im - part Strength to my faint - ing heart,
3. While life's dark maze I tread, And griefs a - round me spread,
4. When ends life's tran - sient dream, When death's cold, sul - len stream

Sav - ior di - vine! Now hear me while I pray, Take all my
My zeal in - spire; As thou hast died for me, O may my
Be thou my guide; Bid dark - ness turn to day, Wipe sor - row's
Shall o'er me roll, Blest Sav - ior, then, in love, Fear and dis -

guilt a - way, O let me from this day Be whol-ly thine!
love to thee Pure, warm, and change-less be A liv - ing fire!
tears a - way, Nor let me ev - er stray From thee a - side.
trust re-move; O bear me safe a - bove, A ran-somed soul! A-MEN.

Words, Ray Palmer, 1830. Tune OLIVET, Lowell Mason, 1832.

383 How Firm a Foundation

1. How firm a foun - da - tion, ye saints of the Lord,
2. "Fear not, I am with thee; O be not dis - mayed,
3. "When thro' fier - y tri - als thy path - way shall lie,
4. "The soul that on Je - sus hath leaned for re - pose

Is laid for your faith in his ex - cel - lent Word!
For I am thy God, and will still give thee aid;
My grace, all - suf - fi - cient, shall be thy sup - ply;
I will not, I will not de - sert to his foes;

What more can he say than to you he hath said,
I'll strength - en thee, help thee, and cause thee to stand,
The flame shall not hurt thee; I on - ly de - sign
That soul, though all hell should en - deav - or to shake,

To you who for ref - uge to Je - sus have fled?
Up - held by my righ - teous, om - nip - o - tent hand.
Thy dross to con - sume, and thy gold to re - fine.
I'll nev - er, no, nev - er, no, nev - er for - sake!" A - MEN.

Words, John Rippon's *Selection of Hymns*, 1787. Tune FOUNDATION, Joseph Funk's *Genuine Church Music*, 1832.

He Who Would Valiant Be 384

1. He who would val - iant be 'Gainst all di - sas - ter,
2. Who so be - set him round With dis - mal sto - ries;
3. Since, Lord, thou dost de - fend Us with thy Spir - it,
Let him in con - stan - cy Fol - low the Mas - ter.
Do but them - selves con - found; His strength the more is.
We know we at the end Shall life in - her - it.
There's no dis - cour - age - ment Shall make him once re - lent
No foes shall stay his might, Tho he with gi - ants fight;
Then, fan - cies, flee a - way! I'll fear not what men say;
His first a - vowed in - tent To be a pil - grim.
He will make good his right To be a pil - grim.
I'll la - bor night and day To be a pil - grim. A - MEN.

Words, John Bunyan, 1684; adapted, Percy Dearmer, 1906. Words from *The English Hymnal.* Used by permission of Oxford University Press. Tune ST. DUNSTAN'S, C. Winfred Douglas, 1917. Music used by permission of The Church Pension Fund.

385 Once to Every Man and Nation

1. Once to ev-'ry man and na-tion Comes the mo-ment
2. Then to side with truth is no-ble, When we share her
3. By the light of burn-ing mar-tyrs, Christ, thy bleed-ing
4. Tho the cause of e-vil pros-per, Yet the truth a-

to de-cide, In the strife of truth with false-hood, For the
wretch-ed crust, Ere her cause bring fame and prof-it, And 'tis
feet we track, Toil-ing up new Cal-v'ries ev-er With the
lone is strong; Tho her por-tion be the scaf-fold, And up-

good or e-vil side; Some great cause, some
pros-perous to be just; Then it is the
cross that turns not back; New oc-ca-sions
on the throne be wrong: Yet that scaf-fold

great de-ci-sion, Of-f'ring each the bloom or blight, And the
brave man choos-es While the cow-ard stands a-side, Till the
teach new du-ties, Time makes an-cient good un-couth; They must
sways the fu-ture, And, be-hind the dim un-known, Stand-eth

Words, James Russell Lowell, 1845. Tune EBENEZER, Thomas J. Williams, 1890. Music copyright by Gwenlyn Evans, Ltd., Caernarvon. Used by permission.

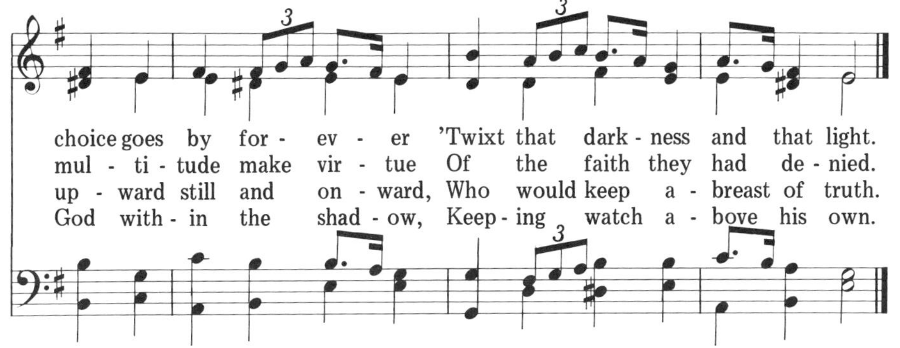

choice goes by for - ev - er 'Twixt that dark - ness and that light.
mul - ti - tude make vir - tue Of the faith they had de - nied.
up - ward still and on - ward, Who would keep a - breast of truth.
God with - in the shad - ow, Keep - ing watch a - bove his own.

Jesus Makes My Heart Rejoice 386

1. Je - sus makes my heart re - joice, I'm his sheep, and know his voice;
2. Trust - ing his mild staff al - ways, I go in and out in peace;
3. Should not I for glad - ness leap, Led by Je - sus as his sheep?

He's a Shep - herd, kind and gra - cious, And his pas - tures are de - li - cious;
He will feed me with the trea - sure Of his grace in rich - est mea - sure;
For when these blest days are o - ver, To the arms of my dear Sav - ior

Con - stant love to me he shows, Yea, my ver - y name he knows.
When a - thirst to him I cry, Liv - ing wa - ter he'll sup - ply.
I shall be con - veyed to rest: A - men, yea, my lot is blest.

Words, Henriette Luise von Hayn, 1778; translated, Frederick W. Foster, 1789. Tune HAYN, *Herrnhuter Choralbuch*, 1735.

387 The Banner of the Cross

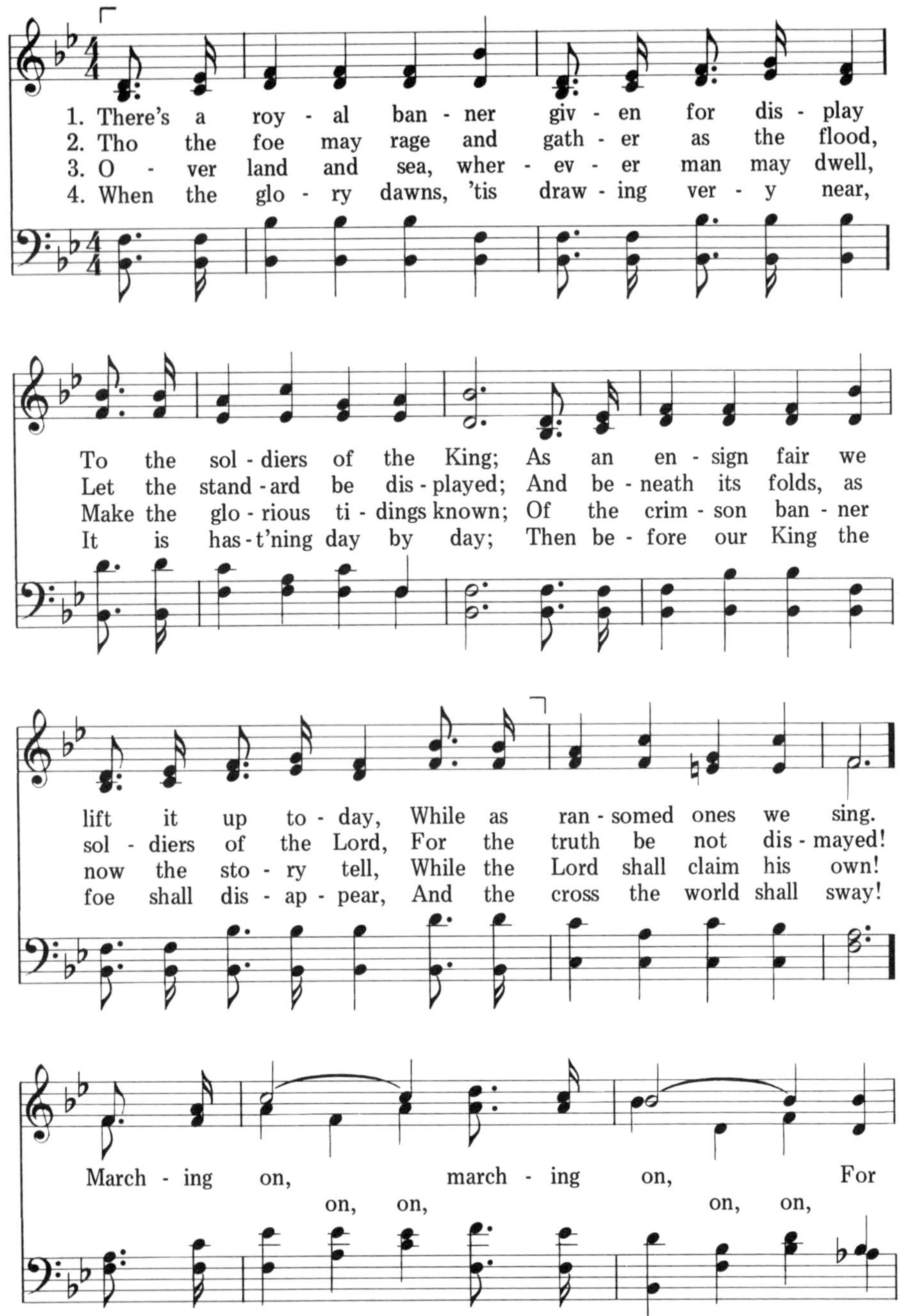

1. There's a roy - al ban - ner giv - en for dis - play
2. Tho the foe may rage and gath - er as the flood,
3. O - ver land and sea, wher - ev - er man may dwell,
4. When the glo - ry dawns, 'tis draw - ing ver - y near,

To the sol - diers of the King; As an en - sign fair we
Let the stand - ard be dis - played; And be - neath its folds, as
Make the glo - rious ti - dings known; Of the crim - son ban - ner
It is has - t'ning day by day; Then be - fore our King the

lift it up to - day, While as ran - somed ones we sing.
sol - diers of the Lord, For the truth be not dis - mayed!
now the sto - ry tell, While the Lord shall claim his own!
foe shall dis - ap - pear, And the cross the world shall sway!

March - ing on, march - ing on, For
on, on, on, on,

Psalm 60:4. Words, Daniel W. Whittle, 1887. Tune ROYAL BANNER, James McGranahan, 1887.

Christ count ev - 'ry - thing but loss! And to
ev - 'ry - thing, ev - 'ry - thing but loss!
crown him King, toil and sing 'Neath the ban - ner of the cross!
we'll Be - neath

Am I a Soldier of the Cross 388

1. Am I a sol - dier of the cross, A fol - l'wer of the Lamb?
2. Must I be car - ried to the skies On flow - 'ry beds of ease,
3. Are there no foes for me to face? Must I not stem the flood?
4. Sure I must fight if I would reign; In - crease my cour - age, Lord!

And shall I fear to own his cause, Or blush to speak his name?
While oth - ers fought to win the prize, And sailed thro' blood - y seas?
Is this vile world a friend to grace, To help me on to God?
I'll bear the toil, en - dure the pain, Sup - port - ed by thy Word.

1 Corinthians 16:13. Words, Isaac Watts, c. 1724. Tune ARLINGTON, Thomas A. Arne, 1762; adapted, Ralph Harrison, 1784.

389 Stand Up, Stand Up for Jesus

Unison

1. Stand up, stand up for Je - sus, Ye sol - diers of the cross;
2. Stand up, stand up for Je - sus, The trum - pet call o - bey;
3. Stand up, stand up for Je - sus, Stand in his strength a - lone;
4. Stand up, stand up for Je - sus, The strife will not be long;

Lift high his roy - al ban - ner, It must not suf - fer loss:
Forth to the might - y con - flict, In this his glo - rious day:
The arm of flesh will fail you, Ye dare not trust your own:
This day the noise of bat - tle, The next, the vic - tor's song:

From vic - t'ry un - to vic - t'ry His ar - my shall he lead,
Ye who are men, now serve him A - gainst un - num - bered foes;
Put on the gos - pel ar - mor, Each piece put on with prayer;
To him who o - ver - com - eth A crown of life shall be;

Till ev - 'ry foe is van - quished, And Christ is Lord in - deed.
Let cour - age rise with dan - ger, And strength to strength op - pose.
Where du - ty calls, or dan - ger, Be nev - er want - ing there.
He, with the King of glo - ry, Shall reign e - ter - nal - ly.

Ephesians 6:10-20. Words, George Duffield, Jr., 1858. Tune GEIBEL, Adam Geibel, 1901.

Harmony
Stand up for Je - sus, Ye sol - diers of the cross; Lift
stand up
high his roy - al ban - ner, It must not, it must not suf - fer loss.

O for a Faith That Will Not Shrink 390

1. O for a faith that will not shrink, Tho pressed by ev - 'ry foe,
2. That will not mur - mur or com - plain Be - neath the chas - t'ning rod,
3. A faith that shines more bright and clear When tem - pests rage with - out;
4. Lord, give me such a faith as this; And then, what - e'er may come,

That will not trem - ble on the brink Of an - y earth - ly woe!
But, in the hour of grief or pain, Will lean up - on its God.
That when in dan - ger knows no fear, In dark - ness feels no doubt.
I'll know while here the hal - lowed bliss Of my e - ter - nal home. A - MEN.

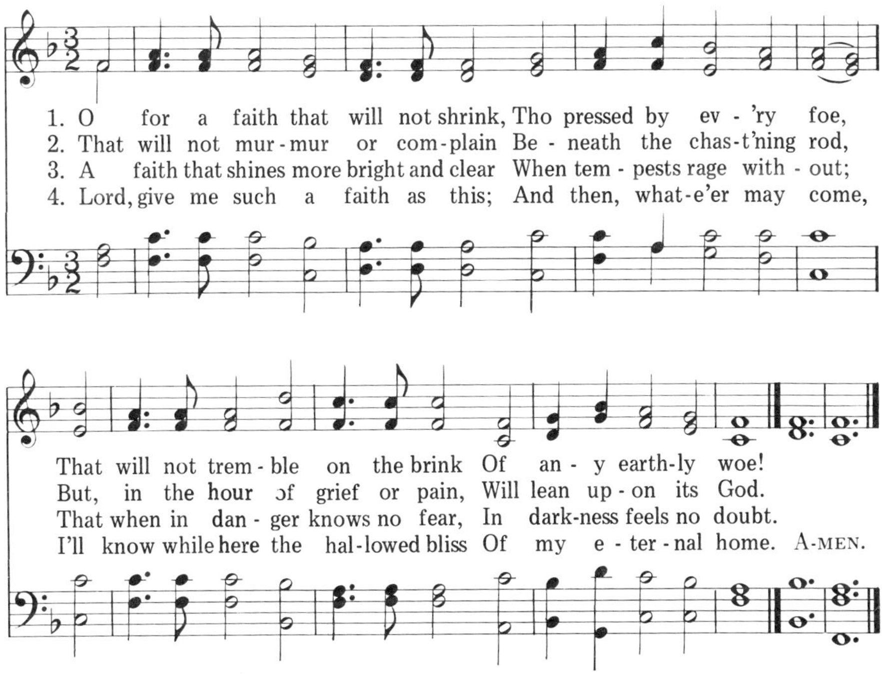

Words, William H. Bathurst, 1831. Tune ARLINGTON, Thomas A. Arne, 1762.

391 Stand Up, Stand Up for Jesus

1. Stand up, stand up for Je - sus, Ye sol - diers of the cross;
2. Stand up, stand up for Je - sus, The trum- pet call o - bey;
3. Stand up, stand up for Je - sus, Stand in his strength a - lone;
4. Stand up, stand up for Je - sus, The strife will not be long;

Lift high his roy - al ban - ner, It must not suf - fer loss:
Forth to the might - y con - flict, In this his glo - rious day:
The arm of flesh will fail you, Ye dare not trust your own:
This day the noise of bat - tle, The next the vic - tor's song:

From vic - t'ry un - to vic - t'ry His ar - my shall he lead,
Ye who are men, now serve him A - gainst un - num - bered foes;
Put on the gos - pel ar - mor, Each piece put on with pray'r;
To him who o - ver - com - eth A crown of life shall be;

Till ev - 'ry foe is van-quished, And Christ is Lord in - deed.
Let cour - age rise with dan - ger, And strength to strength op - pose.
Where du - ty calls, or dan - ger, Be nev - er want - ing there.
He, with the King of glo - ry, Shall reign e - ter - nal - ly.

Ephesians 6:10-20. Words, George Duffield, Jr., 1858. Tune WEBB, George J. Webb, 1830.
This tune in a higher key, No. 238.

When Stephen, Full of Power and Grace 392

Unison

1. When Ste-phen, full of pow'r and grace, Went forth thro'-out the land,
2. When Ste-phen, young and doomed to die, Fell crushed be - neath the stones,
3. Let me, O Lord, thy cause de - fend, A knight with- out a sword;

He bore no shield be - fore his face, No weap-on in his hand;
He had no curse nor venge-ful cry For those who broke his bones;
No shield I ask, no faith-ful friend, No ven-geance, no re - ward;

But on - ly in his heart a flame And on his lips a sword
But on - ly in his heart a flame And on his lips a prayer
But on - ly in my heart a flame And in my soul a dream,

Where-with he smote and o - ver - came The foe-men of the Lord.
That God, in sweet for - give-ness' name, Should un- der - stand and spare.
So that the stones of earth-ly shame A jew - eled crown may seem.

Acts 6,7. Words, Jan Struther, 1931. From *Songs of Praise*, Enlarged Edition; used by permission of Oxford University Press. Tune SALVATION, *Kentucky Harmony*, c. 1815.

393 Onward, Christian Soldiers

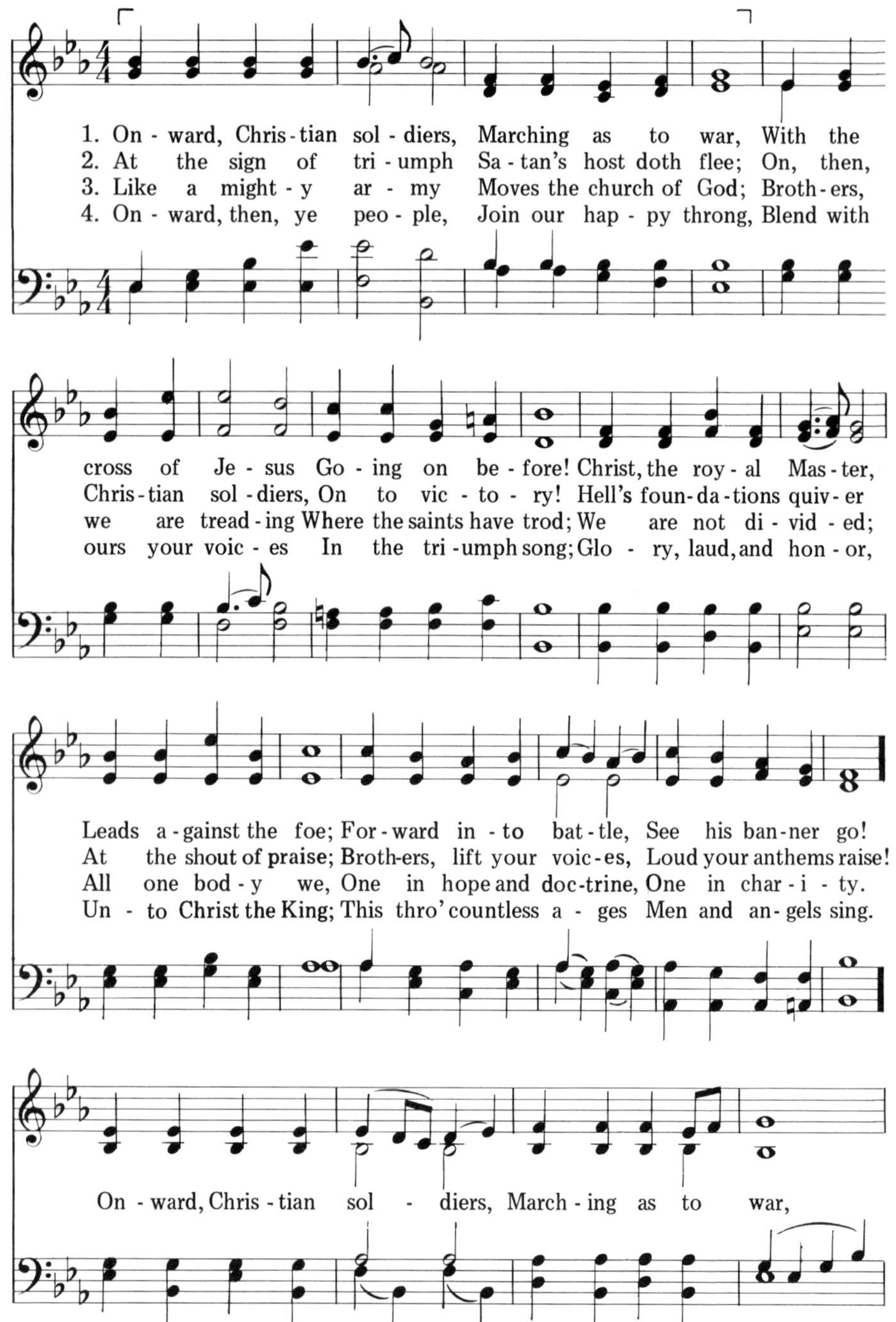

1. On - ward, Chris - tian sol - diers, Marching as to war, With the
2. At the sign of tri - umph Sa - tan's host doth flee; On, then,
3. Like a might - y ar - my Moves the church of God; Broth - ers,
4. On - ward, then, ye peo - ple, Join our hap - py throng, Blend with

cross of Je - sus Go - ing on be - fore! Christ, the roy - al Mas - ter,
Chris - tian sol - diers, On to vic - to - ry! Hell's foun - da - tions quiv - er
we are tread - ing Where the saints have trod; We are not di - vid - ed;
ours your voic - es In the tri - umph song; Glo - ry, laud, and hon - or,

Leads a - gainst the foe; For - ward in - to bat - tle, See his ban - ner go!
At the shout of praise; Broth - ers, lift your voic - es, Loud your anthems raise!
All one bod - y we, One in hope and doc - trine, One in char - i - ty.
Un - to Christ the King; This thro' countless a - ges Men and an - gels sing.

On - ward, Chris - tian sol - diers, March - ing as to war,

Words, Sabine Baring-Gould, 1864. Tune ST. GERTRUDE, Arthur S. Sullivan, 1871.

With the cross of Je - sus Go - ing on be - fore!

Fight the Good Fight 394

1. Fight the good fight with all thy might! Christ is thy
2. Run thou the race thro' God's good grace, Lift up thine
3. Cast care a - side, lean on thy guide, Thy ev - 'ry
4. Faint not nor fear, his arms are near, He chang - eth

strength, and Christ thy right; Lay hold on life, and
eyes, and seek his face; Life with its way be -
need he will pro - vide; Trust - ing in him will
not and thou art dear; On - ly be - lieve, and

it shall be Thy joy and crown e - ter - nal - ly.
fore us lies, Christ is the path, and Christ the prize.
ev - er prove Christ is thy life, thy hope, thy love.
thou shalt see That Christ is all in all to thee.

1 Timothy 6:12. Words, John S. B. Monsell, 1863. Tune PENTECOST, William Boyd, 1864.

395 O Perfect Love

1. O per-fect Love, all hu-man thought tran-scend-ing,
2. O per-fect Life, be thou their full as-sur-ance
3. Grant them the joy which bright-ens earth-ly sor-row;

Low-ly we kneel in prayer be-fore thy throne,
Of ten-der char-i-ty and stead-fast faith,
Grant them the peace which calms all earth-ly strife,

That theirs may be the love which knows no end-ing,
Of pa-tient hope and qui-et brave en-dur-ance,
And to life's day the glo-rious un-known mor-row

Whom thou for-ev-er-more dost join in one.
With child-like trust that fears no pain nor death.
That dawns up-on e-ter-nal love and life. A-MEN.

Words, Dorothy B. Gurney, 1883. Tune O PERFECT LOVE, Joseph Barnby, 1889; adapted, John Stainer, 1898.

O God in Heaven, Whose Loving Plan 396

1. O God in heav'n, whose lov - ing plan Or - dained for us our
2. May young and old to - geth - er find In Christ the Lord of
3. The sins that mar our homes for - give; From all self - seek - ing
4. O Fa - ther, in our homes pre - side; Their du - ties shared as
par - ents' care, And, from the time our life be - gan, The
ev - 'ry day, That fel - low - ship our homes may bind In
set us free; As parents and chil - dren, may we live In
in thy sight; In kind - ly ways be thou our guide, On
shel - ter of a home to share; Our Fa - ther, on the
joy and sor - row, work and play. Our Fa - ther, on the
glad o - be - di - ence to thee. Our Fa - ther, on the
mirth and trou - ble shed thy light. Our Fa - ther, bless the
homes we love, Send down thy bless - ing from a - bove.
homes we love, Send down thy bless - ing from a - bove.
homes we love, Send down thy bless - ing from a - bove.
homes we love, And make them like thy home a - bove.

Words, Hugh Martin. Used by permission. Tune ST. PETERSBURG, Dmitri S. Bortniansky, 1825.

397 God, Give Us Christian Homes

1. God, give us Chris-tian homes! Homes where the Bi-ble is
2. God, give us Chris-tian homes! Homes where the fa-ther is
3. God, give us Chris-tian homes! Homes where the moth-er, in
4. God, give us Chris-tian homes! Homes where the chil-dren are

loved and taught, Homes where the Mas-ter's will is sought,
true and strong, Homes that are free from the blight of wrong,
queen-ly quest, Strives to show oth-ers thy way is best,
led to know Christ in his beau-ty who loves them so,

Homes crowned with beau-ty thy love hath wrought; God, give us
Homes that are joy-ous with love and song; God, give us
Homes where the Lord is an hon-ored guest; God, give us
Homes where the al-tar fires burn and glow; God, give us

Chris-tian homes; God, give us Chris-tian homes!
Chris-tian homes; God, give us Chris-tian homes!
Chris-tian homes; God, give us Chris-tian homes!
Chris-tian homes; God, give us Chris-tian homes! A - MEN.

O God, Who to a Loyal Home 398

Unison

1. O God, who to a loy-al home Didst trust thy Son di-vine,
2. De-liv-er us from sins which harm Our homes, and mar their peace,
3. Thou art our Fa-ther, and from thee All faith-ful fam-'lies spring,
4. We pray that child-hood's la-tent pow'rs May grow to bless man-kind,

Where faith-ful love and pa-tient work Made dai-ly life be-nign;
May self-less and de-vot-ed love Make strife and dis-cord cease.
To homes where love and hon-or dwell Thou dost thy bless-ing bring.
That we may guide a-right young lives, For un-guessed good de-signed.

With con-trite shame thy grace we claim, And lift to thee our pray'r;
With anx-ious zeal, for man-kind's weal And world-wide peace we pray;
O God of life, send from a-bove Thy suc-cor, swift and strong,
O Fa-ther God, whose Son has trod Such low-ly paths as we,

Re-deem our oft un-wor-thy homes Till all is Christ-like there.
But all in vain, if wayward homes Cause childhood's steps to stray.
That from such homes stout souls may come To tri-umph o-ver wrong.
Help us to build on earth true homes, Till we come home to thee.

399 Teach Me to Pray

1. Teach me to pray, Lord, teach me to pray; This is my heart-cry
2. Pow-er in pray'r, Lord, pow-er in pray'r! Here mid earth's sin and
3. My weak-ened will, Lord, thou canst re-new; My sin-ful na-ture
4. Teach me to pray, Lord, teach me to pray; Thou art my pat-tern

day un-to day; I long to know thy will and thy way;
sor-row and care, Men lost and dy-ing, souls in de-spair;
thou canst sub-due; Fill me just now with pow-er a-new;
day un-to day; Thou art my sure-ty, now and for aye;

Teach me to pray, Lord, teach me to pray.
O give me pow-er, pow-er in pray'r!
Pow-er to pray and pow-er to do! Liv-ing in thee, Lord,
Teach me to pray, Lord, teach me to pray.

and thou in me, Con-stant a-bid-ing, this is my plea; Grant me thy pow - er, boundless and free, Pow-er with men and pow-er with thee.

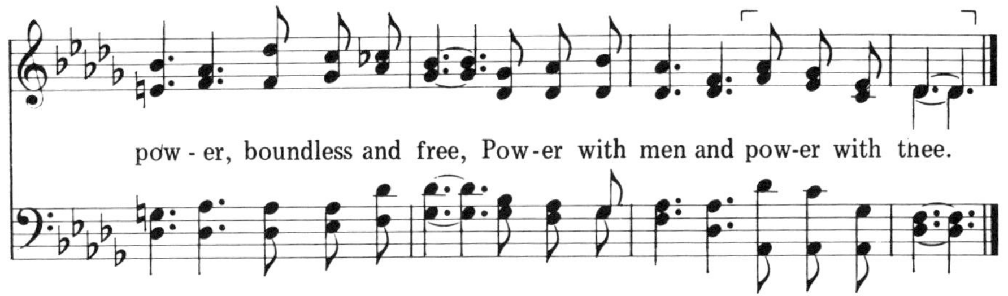

Prayer Is the Soul's Sincere Desire   400

Unison

1. Prayer is the soul's sin - cere de - sire, Un - ut - tered or ex - pressed, The
2. Prayer is the bur - den of a sigh, The fall - ing of a tear, The
3. Prayer is the sim - plest form of speech That in - fant lips can try; —
4. Prayer is the Chris-tian's vi - tal breath, The Chris-tian's na - tive air, His
5. O thou by whom we come to God, The Life, the Truth, the Way, The

mo - tion of a hid - den fire That trem - bles in the breast.
up - ward glanc - ing of an eye When none but God is near.
Prayer the sub - lim - est strains that reach The Maj - es - ty on high.
watch - word at the gates of death: He en - ters heav'n with prayer.
path of prayer thy - self hast trod: Lord, teach us how to pray. A - MEN.

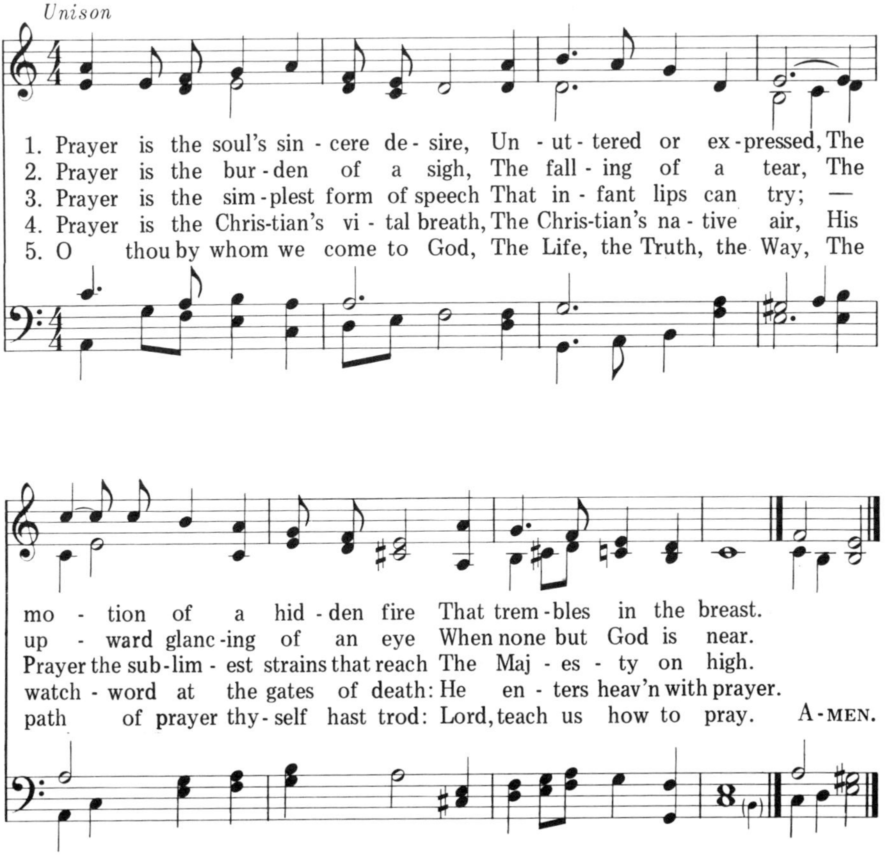

Words, James Montgomery, 1818. Tune OREMUS, Donald P. Hustad, 1974. © Copyright 1975 Broadman Press. All rights reserved.

401 Sweet Hour of Prayer

1. Sweet hour of prayer, sweet hour of prayer, That calls me from a
2. Sweet hour of prayer, sweet hour of prayer, Thy wings shall my pe-
3. Sweet hour of prayer, sweet hour of prayer, May I thy conso-

world of care And bids me at my Fa-ther's throne Make all my
ti - tion bear To him whose truth and faith-ful-ness En - gage the
la - tion share, Till, from*Mount Pisgah's loft - y height, I view my

wants and wish - es known! In sea-sons of dis - tress and grief,
wait - ing soul to bless: And since he bids me seek his face,
home and take my flight: This robe of flesh I'll drop and rise

My soul has oft - en found re - lief, And oft es - caped the
Be - lieve his word and trust his grace, I'll cast on him my
To seize the ev - er - last - ing prize; And shout, while pass - ing

Words, William Walford, c. 1840. Tune SWEET HOUR, William B. Bradbury, c. 1861.
*Deuteronomy 3:27.

tempt - er's snare By thy re - turn, sweet hour of prayer.
ev - 'ry care, And wait for thee, sweet hour of prayer.
thro' the air, "Fare - well, fare - well, sweet hour of prayer!"

I Waited for the Lord My God 402

1. I wait - ed for the Lord my God, And pa - tient - ly did bear;
2. He took me from a fear - ful pit, And from the mi - ry clay,
3. He put a new song in my mouth, Our God to mag - ni - fy:
4. O bless - ed is the man whose trust Up - on the Lord re - lies;
5. O Lord, my God, full man - y are The won - ders thou hast done;

At length to me he did in - cline My voice and cry to hear.
And on a rock he set my feet, Es - tab - lish - ing my way.
Man - y shall see it, and shall fear, And on the Lord re - ly.
Re - spect - ing not the proud, nor such As turn a - side to lies.
Thy gra - cious thoughts to us-ward far A - bove all thoughts are gone. A-MEN.

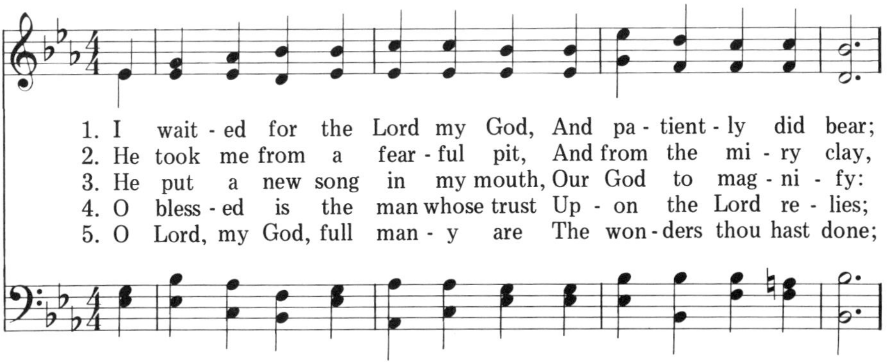

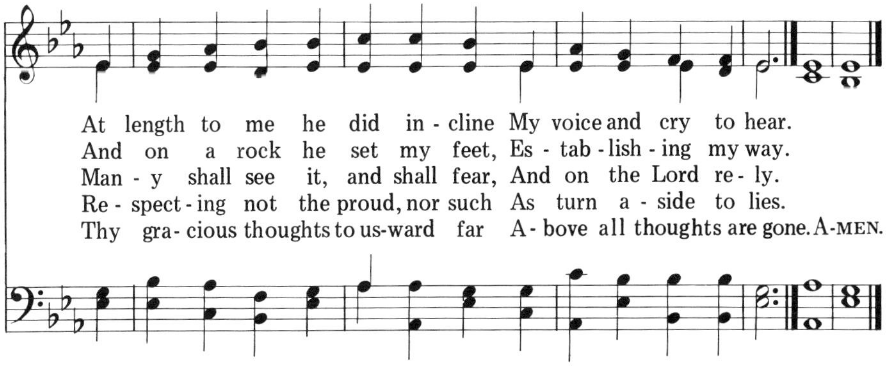

Psalm 40:1-5. Words, *Scottish Psalter*, 1650. Tune TALLIS' ORDINAL, Thomas Tallis, *c.* 1561.

403 What a Friend We Have in Jesus

1. What a friend we have in Je - sus, All our sins and griefs to bear!
2. Have we tri - als and temp - ta - tions? Is there trou - ble an - y - where?
3. Are we weak and heav - y lad - en, Cum - bered with a load of care?
What a priv - i - lege to car - ry Ev - 'ry-thing to God in prayer!
We should nev - er be dis - cour - aged, Take it to the Lord in prayer:
Pre - cious Sav - ior, still our ref - uge; Take it to the Lord in prayer:
Oh, what peace we of - ten for - feit, Oh, what need-less pain we bear,
Can we find a friend so faith - ful Who will all our sor - rows share?
Do thy friends de -spise, for - sake thee? Take it to the Lord in prayer;
All be - cause we do not car - ry Ev - 'ry-thing to God in prayer!
Je - sus knows our ev - 'ry weak-ness, Take it to the Lord in prayer.
In his arms he'll take and shield thee; Thou wilt find a sol - ace there.

Words, Joseph Scriven, 1855. Tune CONVERSE, Charles C. Converse, 1868.

1. Are you wea-ry, are you heav-y-heart-ed? Tell it to Je-sus,
2. Do the tears flow down your cheeks un-bid-den? Tell it to Je-sus,
3. Do you fear the gath-'ring clouds of sor-row? Tell it to Je-sus,
4. Are you trou-bled at the thought of dy-ing? Tell it to Je-sus,
Tell it to Je-sus; Are you griev-ing o-ver joys de-part-ed?
Tell it to Je-sus; Have you sins that to men's eyes are hid-den?
Tell it to Je-sus; Are you anx-ious what shall be to-mor-row?
Tell it to Je-sus; For Christ's com-ing king-dom are you sigh-ing?
Tell it to Je-sus a-lone. Tell it to Je-sus, tell it to
Je-sus, He is a friend that's well-known; You've no oth-er
such a friend or broth-er, Tell it to Je-sus a-lone.

Words, Edmund S. Lorenz, 1876; translated, Jeremiah E. Rankin, 1877. Tune DAYTON, Edmund S. Lorenz, 1876.

405 We Are Called to Be God's People

1. We are called to be God's peo-ple, Show-ing by our lives his grace,
2. We are called to be God's ser-vants, Work-ing in his world to-day;
3. We are called to be God's proph-ets, Spokesmen for the truth and right;

One in heart and one in spir-it, Sign of hope for all the race.
Tak-ing his own task up-on us, All his sa-cred words o-bey.
Stand-ing firm for god-ly jus-tice, Bring-ing e-vil in-to light.

Let us show how he has changed us, And re-made us as his own,
Let us rise, then, to his sum-mons, Ded-i-cate to him our all,
Let us seek the cour-age need-ed, Our high call-ing to ful-fill,

Let us share our life to-geth-er As we shall a-round his throne.
That we may be faith-ful ser-vants, Quick to an-swer now his call.
That man-kind may know the bless-ing Of the do-ing of God's will.

Teach Me, O Lord, I Pray 406

1. Teach me, O Lord, I pray, Thy pre-cious truth di-vine;
2. Train me, O Lord, I pray, In knowl-edge and in skill;
3. Use me, O Lord, I pray, To shed thy light sub-lime

Lead me to un-der-stand thy Word And make its pre-cepts mine.
O dai-ly let me walk with thee And do thy per-fect will.
To rich and poor, to high and low Of ev-'ry race and clime.

Im-part thy wis-dom, Lord, Shed light up-on my way,
Train thou my heart and mind To serve thee un-a-shamed,
O may thy flam-ing zeal Burn con-stant-ly in me,

That I may know thy bound-less love; Teach me, O Lord, I pray.
At home, a-broad, wher-e'er the Christ Has yet to be proclaimed.
Till souls in dark-ness ev-'ry-where Fall down and wor-ship thee.

Words, G. Kearnie Keegan, 1959. © Copyright 1959 Broadman Press. All rights reserved. Tune
DIADEMATA, George J. Elvey, 1868.
This tune in a higher key, No. 52.

407 A Charge to Keep I Have

1. A charge to keep I have, A God to glo-ri-fy,
2. Help me to watch and pray, And on thy-self re-ly,
Who gave his Son my soul to save, And fit it for the sky.
As-sured, if I my trust be-tray, I shall my Lord de-ny.
To serve the pres-ent age, My call-ing to ful-fill,
Arm me with jeal-ous care, As in thy sight to live;
O may it all my pow'rs en-gage To do my Mas-ter's will!
And O thy ser-vant, Lord, pre-pare A strict ac-count to give.

Leviticus 8:35. Words, Charles Wesley, 1762. Tune KEEGAN, William J. Reynolds, 1956.

1. Read-y to suffer grief or pain, Read-y to stand the test;
2. Read-y to go, read-y to bear, Read-y to watch and pray;
3. Read-y to speak, read-y to think, Read-y with heart and brain;
4. Read-y to speak, read-y to warn, Read-y o'er souls to yearn;

Read-y to stay at home and send Oth-ers, if he sees best.
Read-y to stand a - side and give, Till he shall clear the way.
Read-y to stand where he sees fit, Read-y to stand the strain.
Read-y in life, read-y in death, Read-y for his re - turn.

Read-y to go, read-y to stay, Read-y my place to fill;

Read-y for ser - vice, low-ly or great, Read-y to do his will.

Words, A. C. Palmer. Tune TILLMAN, Charles D. Tillman, 1903.

409 When We Walk with the Lord

1. When we walk with the Lord In the light of his Word
2. Not a bur-den we bear, Not a sor-row we share,
3. But we nev-er can prove The de-lights of his love
4. Then in fel-low-ship sweet We will sit at his feet

What a glo-ry he sheds on our way! Let us do his good will;
But our toil he doth rich-ly re-pay; Not a grief or a loss,
Un-til all on the al-tar we lay; For the fa-vor he shows
Or we'll walk by his side in the way; What he says we will do,

He a-bides with us still, And with all who will trust and o-bey.
Not a frown or a cross, But is blest if we trust and o-bey.
And the joy he be-stows Are for them who will trust and o-bey.
Where he sends we will go; Nev-er fear, on-ly trust and o-bey.

Trust and o-bey, for there's no oth-er way To be

hap-py in Je-sus, But to trust and o-bey.

Words, John H. Sammis, 1887. Tune TRUST AND OBEY, Daniel B. Towner, 1887.

We Thank Thee That Thy Mandate 410

1. We thank thee that thy man-date Is ev-'ry age the same:
2. We thank thee for thy preach-ers, Thy her-alds who pro-claim
3. En-light-en all thy teach-ers With wis-dom from on high,
4. We thank thee for the heal-ing Of bod-y, mind, and soul,
5. As we o-bey thy man-date To preach and teach and heal,

To preach and teach the gos-pel, And heal men in thy name;
The good news of sal-va-tion With hearts and tongues a-flame!
And grant them un-der-stand-ing, Men's minds to ed-i-fy;
God's won-drous love re-veal-ing That makes the wound-ed whole;
May ev-'ry gen-er-a-tion Be-come God's com-mon-weal;

May ev-'ry new en-deav-or To match this to our day
Bless thou the words they ut-ter; May all who hear be blest;
May all who teach the gos-pel, And all who hear be fed,
May those by faith who touch thee And those thy touch doth bless
And may this three-fold ef-fort Re-flect thy ho-ly love,

Lead men to own thy Lord-ship, And walk thy ho-ly way.
E-quipped for earth-ly liv-ing, Pre-pared for heav'n-ly rest.
As ev-'ry soul is nour-ished On Christ, the liv-ing Bread.
Be cured of their dis-eas-es, And walk in ho-li-ness.
Un-til our earth-ly king-doms Are one with thine a-bove.

Words, Ernest K. Emurian, 1968. Words Copyright 1968 by Ernest K. Emurian. Used by permission.
Tune LANCASHIRE, Henry T. Smart, 1835.
This tune in a higher key, No. 237.

411 Serve the Lord with Gladness

1. "Serve the Lord with gladness" In our works and ways, Come be-fore his
2. "Serve the Lord with gladness," Thankful all the while For his ten - der
3. "Serve the Lord with gladness," This shall be our theme, As we walk to

pres-ence With our songs of praise; Un - to him our Mak - er We would
mer-cies, For his lov - ing smile: Bless - ed truth en - dur - ing, Al - ways
geth - er In his love su - preme: Lis - t'ning, ev - er lis - t'ning For the

pledge a - new Life's su - preme de - vo - tion To serv - ice true.
    (a-new)
just the same, We will serve with glad - ness And praise his name.
    (the same),
still, small voice, His sweet will so pre - cious Will be our choice.
    (his voice),

"Serve him with glad-ness," En - ter his courts with song; To our Cre -
    (with song);

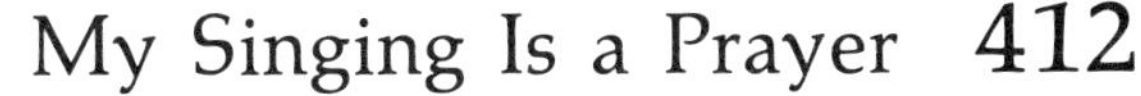

a - tor True prais-es be - long: Great is his mer - cy, Won-der-ful
(be- long):
is his name, We glad - ly serve him, His great love pro-claim.
(his name), (pro-claim).

My Singing Is a Prayer 412

1. My sing - ing is a prayer, O Lord, A prayer of thanks and praise;
2. I give my tal-ents, Lord, to thee, My mind and heart and voice,
3. Ac-cept the wor -ship of my heart, Ac - cept my mu - sic, too:
4. O bless me, Lord, and help me sing Thy love so full and free;

In mu - sic, Lord, I wor-ship thee; Thy beau - ty fills my days.
For thou a - lone art wor -thy, Lord; In thee I do re - joice.
Help me to live al -ways for thee, Lord, keep me strong and true.
And bless all those who lis - ten, Lord, Help them to wor - ship thee.

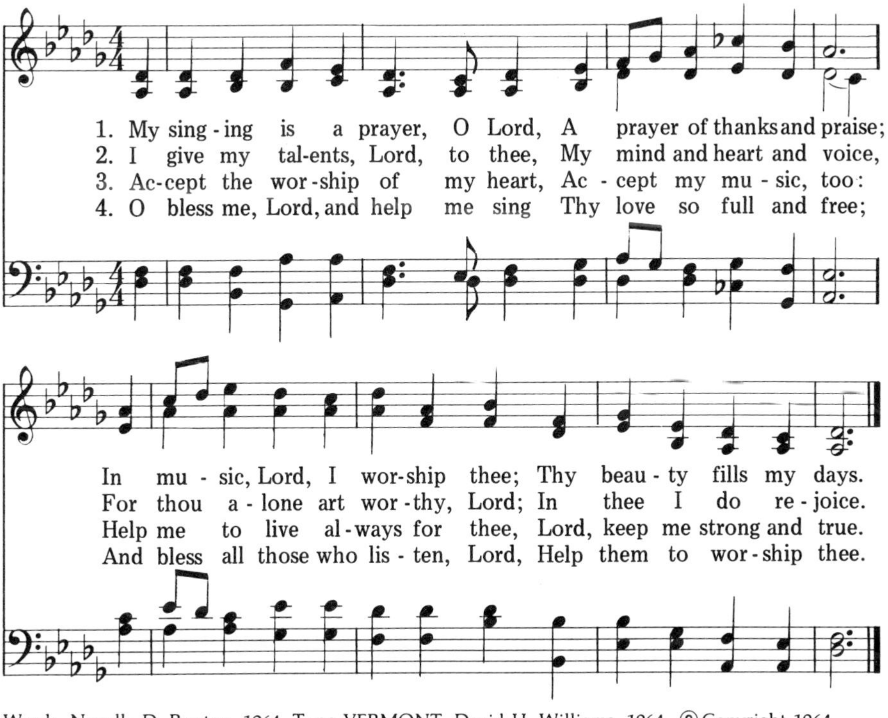

413 Awake, Awake to Love and Work
Unison
1. A - wake, a - wake to love and work, The lark is in the
2. Come, let thy voice be one with theirs, Shout with their shout of
3. To give and give, and give a - gain, What God hath giv - en

sky, The fields are wet with dia - mond dew, The
praise; See how the gi - ant sun soars up, Great
thee; To spend thy - self nor count the cost, To

worlds a - wake to cry Their bless - ings on the
Lord of years and days! So let the love of
serve right glo - rious - ly The God who gave all

Lord of life, As he goes meek - ly by.
Je - sus come And set thy soul a - blaze:
worlds that are, And all that are to be.

1, 2   3

Words, G. A. Studdert-Kennedy, 1921. Tune MORNING SONG, Wyeth's *Repository of Sacred Music, Part Second,* 1813; harmonized, Carlton R. Young, 1964.

Because I Have Been Given Much 414

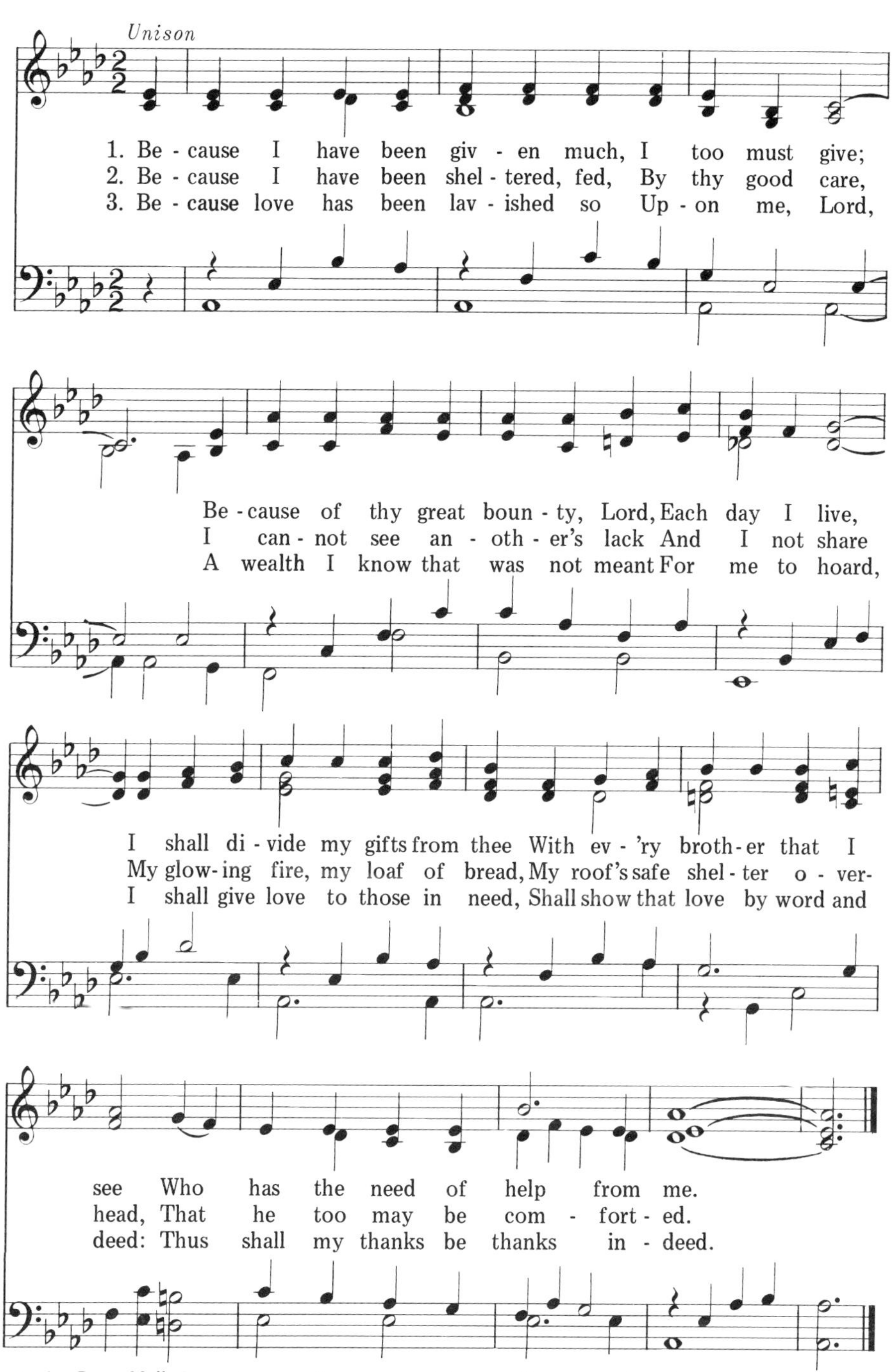

Unison

1. Be - cause I have been giv - en much, I too must give;
2. Be - cause I have been shel - tered, fed, By thy good care,
3. Be - cause love has been lav - ished so Up - on me, Lord,

Be - cause of thy great boun - ty, Lord, Each day I live,
I can - not see an - oth - er's lack And I not share
A wealth I know that was not meant For me to hoard,

I shall di - vide my gifts from thee With ev - 'ry broth - er that I
My glow - ing fire, my loaf of bread, My roof's safe shel - ter o - ver-
I shall give love to those in need, Shall show that love by word and

see Who has the need of help from me.
head, That he too may be com - fort - ed.
deed: Thus shall my thanks be thanks in - deed.

415 Give to the Lord, As He Has Blessed You

1. Give to the Lord, as he has blessed you, E - ven when
2. Give to the Lord, as he has blessed you, Kept you and
3. Give to the Lord, as he has blessed you, Who pours forth

he seems far a - way; Know that his love has e'er pos -
guid - ed from your birth; Look to the day when death will
boun - ties rich and full; Let all your self - ish aims con -

sessed you, Shel - ters and feeds you ev - 'ry day. Heav - en and
wrest you From all your trea - sures here on earth. God has rich
fessed be, Gain not the world and lose your soul! Put all you

earth are God's a - lone: Will you hold back from him his own?
gifts for you a - bove: Give of your sub - stance now in love.
have in God's own hands, In trust o - bey - ing his com - mands.

Words, James Boeringer, 1961, alt. Words from *Ten New Stewardship Hymns,* Copyright 1961 by The Hymn Society of America. Used by permission. Tune KÖNIG, Johann Balthasar König, 1738.

We Lift Our Hearts in Songs of Praise 416

1. We lift our hearts in songs of praise For all thy gifts so rare,
2. To those who live in pov - er - ty, In dire dis - tress and need,
3. We would re - spond with love and care To those in deep - est grief,

For life and love thro' all our days, For fel - low - ship thro' pray'r.
May we show Chris - tian char - i - ty In love and word and deed.
And with them hope and cour - age share To strength - en their be - lief.

We pray that we may ev - er share Thy bless - ings from a - bove,
To men of ev - 'ry race and tongue, The blind, the deaf, the lame,
Good news we'd share with ev - 'ry - one — Thy love at Cal - va - ry,

To show men that we tru - ly care, And teach them of God's love.
To all the lone - ly, old, and young, We serve them in Christ's name.
In giv - ing Christ, thine on - ly Son, That all might come to thee.

417 I Gave My Life for Thee

1. I gave my life for thee, My pre-cious blood I shed,
2. My Fa-ther's house of light, My glo-ry-cir-cled throne,
3. I suf-fer'd much for thee, More than thy tongue can tell,
4. And I have brought to thee, Down from my home a-bove,
That thou might'st ran-somed be, And quick-ened from the dead;
I left for earth-ly night, For wan-d'rings sad and lone;
Of bit-t'rest ag-o-ny, To res-cue thee from hell;
Sal-va-tion full and free, My par-don and my love;
I gave, I gave my life for thee, What hast thou giv'n for me?
I left, I left it all for thee, Hast thou left aught for me?
I've borne, I've borne it all for thee, What hast thou borne for me?
I bring, I bring rich gifts to thee, What hast thou brought to me?
I gave, I gave my life for thee, What hast thou giv'n for me?
I left, I left it all for thee, Hast thou left aught for me?
I've borne, I've borne it all for thee, What hast thou borne for me?
I bring, I bring rich gifts to thee, What hast thou brought to me?

Words, Frances R. Havergal, 1858. Tune KENOSIS, Philip P. Bliss, 1873.

Something for Thee 418

1. Sav - ior, thy dy - ing love Thou gav - est me,
2. At the blest *mer - cy seat, Plead - ing for me,
3. Give me a faith - ful heart, Like - ness to thee,
4. All that I am and have, Thy gifts so free,

Nor should I aught with - hold, Dear Lord, from thee:
My fee - ble faith looks up, Je - sus, to thee:
That each de - part - ing day Hence - forth may see
In joy, in grief, thro' life, Dear Lord, for thee!

In love my soul would bow, My heart ful - fill its vow,
Help me the cross to bear, Thy won - drous love de - clare,
Some work of love be - gun, Some deed of kind - ness done,
And when thy face I see, My ran - som'd soul shall be,

Some of - f'ring bring thee now, Some - thing for thee.
Some song to raise, or pray'r, Some - thing for thee.
Some wan - d'rer sought and won, Some - thing for thee.
Thro' all e - ter - ni - ty, Some - thing for thee. A - MEN.

Words, Sylvanus D. Phelps, 1864. Tune SOMETHING FOR JESUS, Robert Lowry, 1871. *Exodus 25:17-22.

419 Glorious Is Thy Name, Most Holy

1. Glo - rious is thy name, Most Ho - ly, God and Fa - ther of us all;
2. For our world of need and an - guish We would lift to thee our prayer.
3. In the midst of time we jour- ney, From thy hand comes each new day;

We thy ser- vants bow be - fore thee, Strive to an- swer ev - 'ry call.
Faith - ful stew-ards of thy boun-ty, May we with our broth- ers share.
We would use it in thy ser - vice, Hum - bly, wise-ly, while we may.

Thou with life's great good hast blest us, Cared for us from ear - liest years;
In the name of Christ our Sav -ior, Who re-deems and sets us free,
So to thee, Lord and Cre - a - tor, Praise and hon - or we ac - cord,

Un - to thee our thanks we ren - der; Thy deep love o'er-comes all fears.
Gifts we bring of heart and trea - sure, That our lives may wor -thier be.
Thine the earth and thine the heav- ens, Thro' all the E - ter - nal Word.

Words, Ruth Elliot, 1961. Words from *Ten New Stewardship Hymns*, Copyright 1961 by The Hymn Society of America; used by permission. Tune HOLY MANNA, William Moore, 1825.
This tune in a higher key, No. 260.

Lead On, O King Eternal 420

1. Lead on, O King E - ter - nal, The day of march has come;
2. Lead on, O King E - ter - nal, Till sin's fierce war shall cease,
3. Lead on, O King E - ter - nal, We fol - low, not with fears;

Hence-forth in fields of con - quest Thy tents shall be our home:
And ho - li - ness shall whis - per The sweet a - men of peace;
For glad - ness breaks like morn - ing Wher - e'er thy face ap - pears;

Thro' days of prep - a - ra - tion Thy grace has made us strong,
For not with swords' loud clash-ing, Or roll of stir - ring drums;
Thy cross is lift - ed o'er us; We jour - ney in its light:

And now, O King E - ter - nal, We lift our bat - tle song.
With deeds of love and mer - cy The heav'n - ly king - dom comes.
The crown a - waits the con - quest; Lead on, O God of might.

Words, Ernest W. Shurtleff, 1887. Tune LANCASHIRE, Henry Smart, 1835.
This tune in a higher key, No. 237.

421 As Jacob with Travel

Unison
1. As Ja - cob with trav - el was wea - ry one day,
2. The lad - der is long, it is strong and well - made,
3. And when we ar - rive at the ha - ven of rest,
At night on a stone for a pil - low he lay;
Has stood hun - dreds of years and is not yet de - cayed;
We shall hear the glad words, "Come up hith - er, you blest,
He saw in a vi - sion a lad - der so high,
Man - y mil - lions have climbed it and reached Si - on's hill,
Here are re - gions of light, here are man - sions of bliss."
That its foot was on earth and its top in the sky,
And thou - sands by faith are climb - ing it still:
O who would not climb such a lad - der as this:

Genesis 28:10-22. Words, Anonymous Folk Hymn. Tune JACOB'S VISION, Traditional Folk Hymn.

Al - le - lu - ia to Je - sus who died on the tree,

And has raised up a lad - der of mer - cy for me,

And has raised up a lad - der of mer - cy for me.

Alleluia   422

1. Al - le - lu - ia, al - le - lu - ia, Al - le - lu - ia, al - le - lu - ia,
2. He is God's Son, he is God's Son, He is God's Son, he is God's Son,
3. He's my Sav - ior, he's my Sav - ior, He's my Sav - ior, he's my Sav - ior,
4. I will praise him, I will praise him, I will praise him, I will praise him,

Al - le - lu - ia, al - le - lu - ia, Al - le - lu - ia, al - le - lu - ia.
He is God's Son, he is God's Son, He is God's Son, he is God's Son.
He's my Sav - ior, he's my Sav - ior, He's my Sav - ior, he's my Sav - ior.
I will praise him, I will praise him, I will praise him, I will praise him.

423 I've Found a Friend, O Such a Friend

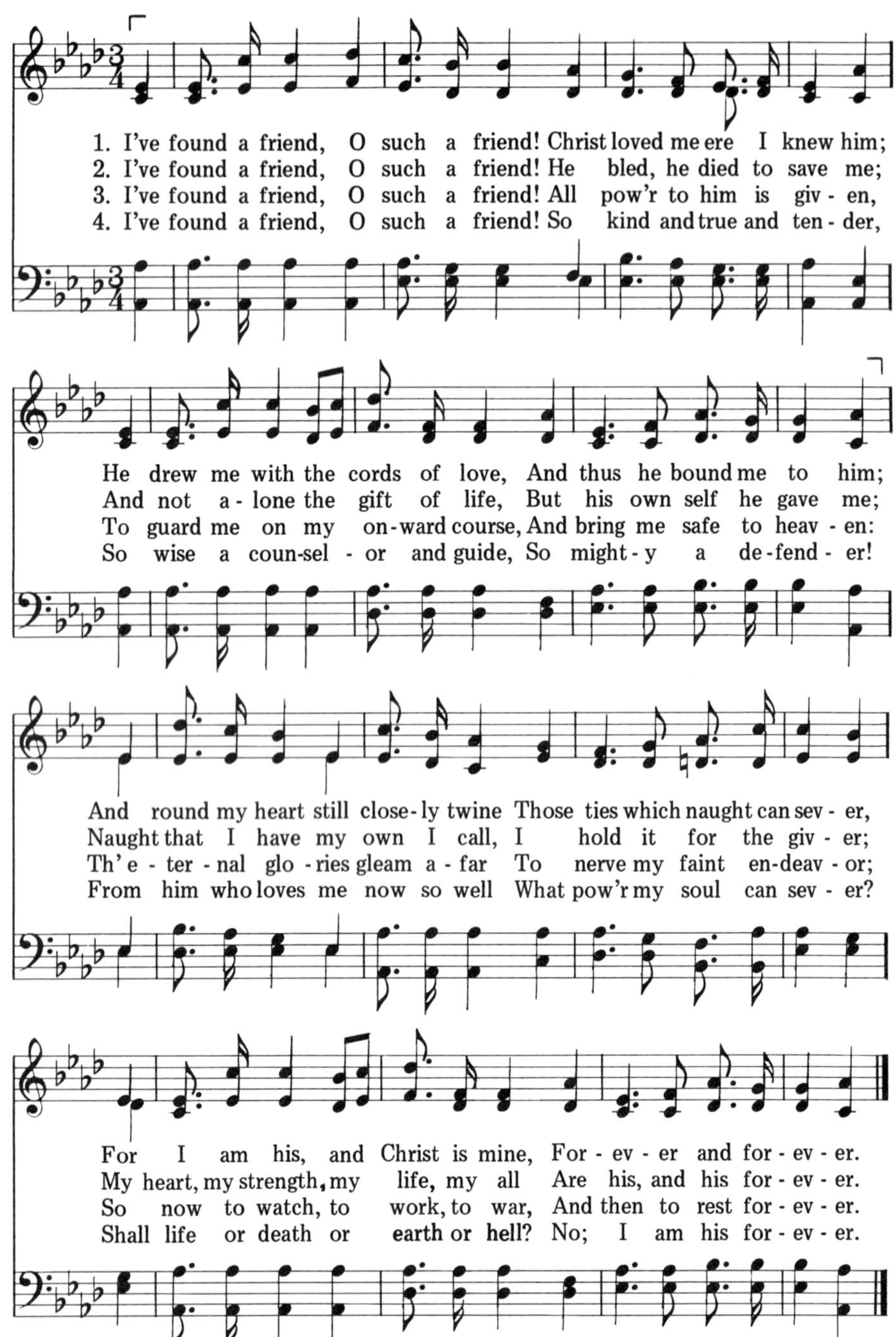

1. I've found a friend, O such a friend! Christ loved me ere I knew him;
2. I've found a friend, O such a friend! He bled, he died to save me;
3. I've found a friend, O such a friend! All pow'r to him is giv-en,
4. I've found a friend, O such a friend! So kind and true and ten-der,

He drew me with the cords of love, And thus he bound me to him;
And not a-lone the gift of life, But his own self he gave me;
To guard me on my on-ward course, And bring me safe to heav-en:
So wise a coun-sel-or and guide, So might-y a de-fend-er!

And round my heart still close-ly twine Those ties which naught can sev-er,
Naught that I have my own I call, I hold it for the giv-er;
Th'e-ter-nal glo-ries gleam a-far To nerve my faint en-deav-or;
From him who loves me now so well What pow'r my soul can sev-er?

For I am his, and Christ is mine, For-ev-er and for-ev-er.
My heart, my strength, my life, my all Are his, and his for-ev-er.
So now to watch, to work, to war, And then to rest for-ev-er.
Shall life or death or earth or hell? No; I am his for-ev-er.

Words, James G. Small, 1863. Tune FRIEND, George C. Stebbins, 1878.

Jesus Is All the World to Me 424

1. Je - sus is all the world to me, My life, my joy, my all;
2. Je - sus is all the world to me, My friend in tri - als sore;
3. Je - sus is all the world to me, And true to him I'll be;
4. Je - sus is all the world to me, I want no bet - ter friend;

He is my strength from day to day, With - out him I would fall:
I go to him for bless - ings, and He gives them o'er and o'er:
Oh, how could I this friend de - ny, When he's so true to me?
I trust him now, I'll trust him when Life's fleet - ing days shall end:

When I am sad, to him I go, No oth - er one can
He sends the sun - shine and the rain, He sends the har - vest's
Fol - low - ing him I know I'm right, He watch - es o'er me
Beau - ti - ful life with such a friend, Beau - ti - ful life that

cheer me so; When I am sad he makes me glad, He's my friend.
gold - en grain; Sun - shine and rain, har - vest of grain, He's my friend.
day and night; Fol - low - ing him by day and night, He's my friend.
has no end; E - ter - nal life, e - ter - nal joy, He's my friend.

Words and tune ELIZABETH, Will L. Thompson, 1904.

425 Heaven Came Down

1. O what a won-der-ful, won-der-ful day— Day I will
2. Born of the Spir-it with life from a-bove In - to God's
3. Now I've a hope that will sure-ly en-dure Af - ter the

nev - er for - get; Af - ter I'd wan-dered in dark-ness a - way,
fam - 'ly di - vine, Jus - ti - fied ful - ly thro' Cal - va - ry's love,
pass - ing of time; I have a fu-ture in heav - en for sure,

Je - sus my Sav - ior I met. O what a ten - der, com-
O what a stand-ing is mine! And the trans-ac - tion so
There in those man - sions sub - lime. And it's be - cause of that

pas - sion - ate friend-He met the need of my heart; Shad-ows dis-pel-ling,
quick - ly was made When as a sin - ner I came, Took of the of - fer
won - der - ful day When at the cross I be - lieved; Rich - es e - ter - nal

With joy I am tell-ing, He made all the dark-ness de-part!
Of grace he did prof-fer—He saved me, O praise his dear name!
And bless-ings su-per-nal From his pre-cious hand I re-ceived.

Heav-en came down and glo-ry filled my soul,

filled my soul,

When at the cross the Sav-ior made me whole;

made me whole;

My

sins were washed a-way — And my night was turned to day —

Heav-en came down and glo-ry filled my soul!

filled my soul!

426 In Loving-Kindness Jesus Came

1. In lov-ing-kind-ness Je-sus came My soul in mer-cy
2. He called me long be-fore I heard, Be-fore my sin-ful
3. His brow was pierced with man-ya thorn, His hands by cru-el
4. Now on a high-er plane I dwell, And with my soul I

to re-claim, And from the depths of sin and shame
heart was stirred, But when I took him at his word,
nails were torn, When from my guilt and grief, for-lorn,
know 'tis well; Yet how or why I can-not tell

Thro' grace he lift-ed me.
For-giv'n, he lift-ed me.
In love he lift-ed me.
He should have lift-ed me.

From sink-ing sand he

he lift-ed me.

lift-ed me, With ten-der hand he lift-ed me, From

Words and tune HE LIFTED ME, Charles H. Gabriel, 1905.

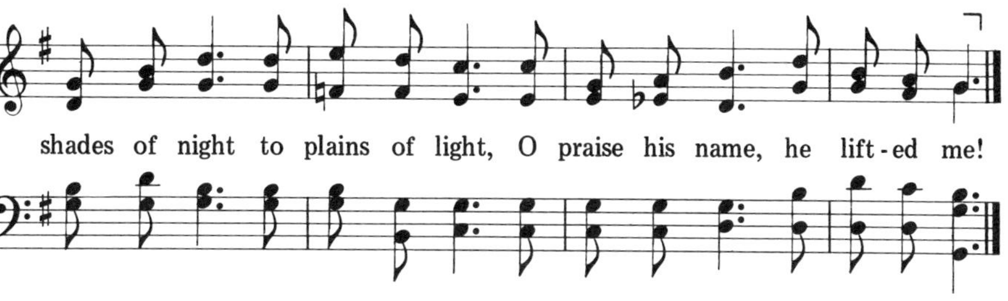

shades of night to plains of light, O praise his name, he lift-ed me!

Blessed Savior, Thee I Love 427

1. Bless - ed Sav - ior, thee I love, All my oth - er joys a - bove;
2. Once a - gain be - side the cross, All my gain I count but loss;
3. Bless - ed Sav - ior, thine am I, Thine to live and thine to die;

All my hopes in thee a - bide, Thou my hope, and naught be - side:
Earth - ly plea - sures fade a - way, Clouds they are that hide my day:
Height or depth or crea - ture pow'r Ne'er shall hide my Sav - ior more:

Ev - er let my glo - ry be On - ly, on - ly, on - ly thee.
Hence, vain shad - ows, let me see Je - sus cru - ci - fied for me.
Ev - er shall my glo - ry be On - ly, on - ly, on - ly thee.

Words, George Duffield, Jr., 1851. Tune SPANISH HYMN, Anonymous; arranged, Benjamin Carr, 1825.

428 In the Garden

1. I come to the gar-den a-lone, While the dew is
2. He speaks, and the sound of his voice Is so sweet the
3. I'd stay in the gar-den with him Tho the night a-

still on the ros-es; And the voice I hear, fall-ing on my ear,
birds hush their sing-ing; And the mel-o-dy that he gave to me
round me be fall-ing; But he bids me go; thro' the voice of woe,

The Son of God dis-clos-es.
With-in my heart is ring-ing. And he walks with me, and he
His voice to me is call-ing.

talks with me, And he tells me I am his own, And the joy we

share as we tar-ry there, None oth-er has ev-er known.

Words and tune GARDEN, C. Austin Miles, 1912. Copyright 1912 by Hall-Mack Co. © Copyright renewal
1940 (extended), The Rodeheaver Co., owner. All rights reserved. Used by permission.

Why Do I Sing About Jesus? 429

1. Deep in my heart there's a glad - ness; Je - sus has saved me from
2. On - ly a glimpse of his good - ness; That was suf - fi - cient for
3. He is the fair - est of fair ones; He is the Lil - y, the

sin! Praise to his name, what a Sav - ior! Cleans - ing with-
me. On - ly one look at the Sav - ior; Then was my
Rose. Riv - ers of mer - cy sur - round him; Grace, love, and

out and with - in!
spir - it set free. Why do I sing a - bout Je - sus?
pit - y he shows.

Why is he pre - cious to me? He is my Lord and my

Sav - ior; Dy - ing, he set me free!
set me free!

430 The Old Rugged Cross

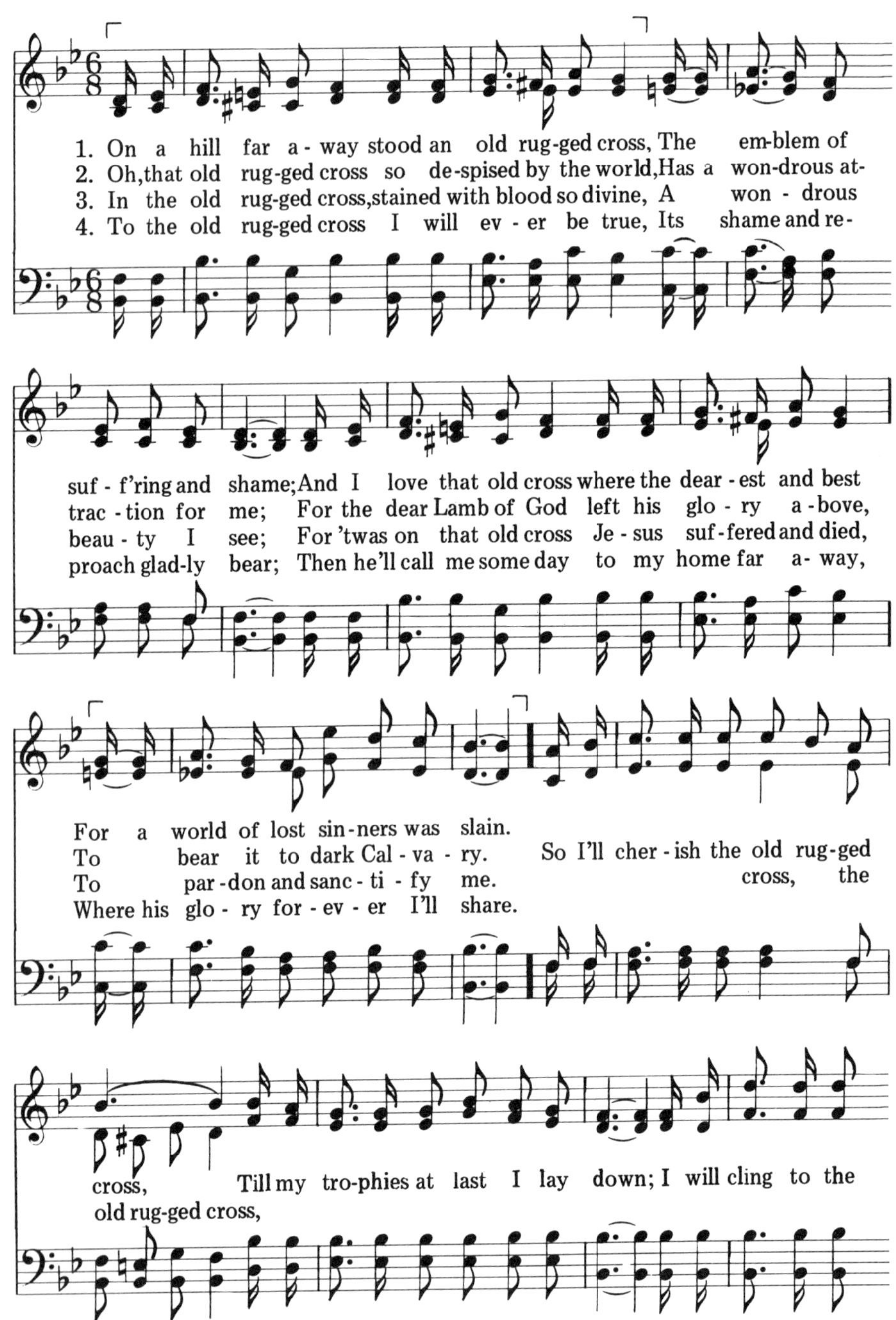

1. On a hill far a-way stood an old rug-ged cross, The emblem of
2. Oh, that old rug-ged cross so de-spised by the world, Has a won-drous at-
3. In the old rug-ged cross, stained with blood so divine, A won - drous
4. To the old rug-ged cross I will ev - er be true, Its shame and re-
suf - f'ring and shame; And I love that old cross where the dear - est and best
trac - tion for me; For the dear Lamb of God left his glo - ry a - bove,
beau - ty I see; For 'twas on that old cross Je - sus suf-fered and died,
proach glad-ly bear; Then he'll call me some day to my home far a- way,
For a world of lost sin -ners was slain.
To bear it to dark Cal - va - ry.
To par -don and sanc - ti - fy me.
Where his glo - ry for - ev - er I'll share.
So I'll cher -ish the old rug-ged
cross, the
cross, Till my tro-phies at last I lay down; I will cling to the
old rug-ged cross,

old rug-ged cross, And ex-change it some day for a crown.
cross, the old rug-ged cross,

My Blessed Savior, Is Thy Love 431

1. My bless - ed Sav - ior, is thy love So great, so
2. I love thee for the glo - rious worth In thy great
3. No man of great - er love can boast Than for his
4. O Lord, I'll cher - ish in my soul The mem - 'ry

full, so free? Be - hold, I give my love, my heart, My
self I see: I love thee for that shame-ful cross Thou
friend to die: But for thy en - e - mies thou wast slain: What
of thy love: And thy dear name shall still to me A

life, my all to thee, My life, my all to thee.
hast en - dured for me, Thou hast en - dured for me.
love with thine can vie, What love with thine can vie!
price - less trea - sure prove, A price - less trea - sure prove.

Words, Joseph Stennett, 1697. Tune NICOLAUS, Nicolaus Hermann, 1554.

432 Wonderful, Wonderful Jesus

1. There is nev-er a day so drear-y, There is nev-er a night so
2. There is nev-er a cross so heav-y, There is nev-er a weight of
3. There is nev-er a care or bur-den, There is nev-er a grief or
4. There is nev-er a guilt-y sin-ner, There is nev-er a wan-d'ring
long (so long), But the soul that is trust-ing Je-sus Will somewhere
woe (of woe), But that Je-sus will help to car-ry Be-cause he
loss (or loss), But that Je-sus in love will light-en When car-ried
one (not one), But that God can in mer-cy par-don Thro' Je-sus
find a song (a song).
lov-eth so (loves so).
to the cross (the cross). Won-der-ful, won-der-ful Je-sus, In the
Christ, his Son (his Son).
heart he im-plant-eth a song: A song of de-liv-'rance,
he plant-eth a song:

Words, Anna B. Russell, 1921. Tune NEW ORLEANS, Ernest O. Sellers, 1921.

of cour-age, of strength; In the heart he im-plant-eth a song (a song).

I Am Not Skilled to Understand 433

1. I am not skilled to un - der - stand What
2. I take him at his word in - deed, "Christ
3. And was there then no oth - er way For
4. That he should leave his place on high, And
5. Yes, liv - ing, dy - ing, let me bring My

God hath willed, what God hath planned; I on - ly know at
died for sin - ners," this I read; And in my heart I
God to take? I can - not say; I on - ly bless him
come for sin - ful man to die, You count it strange? So
strength, my sol - ace from this spring, That he who lives to

his right hand Stands One who is my Sav - ior.
find a need Of him to be my Sav - ior.
day by day, Who saved me thro' my Sav - ior.
once did I, Be - fore I knew my Sav - ior.
be my King Once died to be my Sav - ior.

Words, Dora Greenwell, 1873. Tune GREENWELL, William J. Kirkpatrick, 1885.

434 All That Thrills My Soul

1. Who can cheer the heart like Je - sus, By his pres-ence all di-vine?
2. Love of Christ so free - ly giv - en, Grace of God be - yond de-gree,
3. What a won-der-ful re-demp-tion! Nev - er can a mor-tal know
4. Ev - 'ry need his hand sup-ply - ing, Ev - 'ry good in him I see;
5. By the crys - tal flow-ing riv - er With the ransomed I will sing,

True and ten - der, pure and precious, O how blest to call him mine!
Mer - cy high - er than the heav - en, Deep - er than the deep - est sea!
How my sin, tho red like crim-son, Can be whit - er than the snow.
On his strength divine re - ly - ing, He is all in all to me.
And for - ev - er and for - ev - er Praise and glo - ri - fy the King.

All that thrills my soul is Je - sus, He is more than life to me;
to me;

And the fair-est of ten thou - sand In my bless-ed Lord I see.

He Keeps Me Singing 435

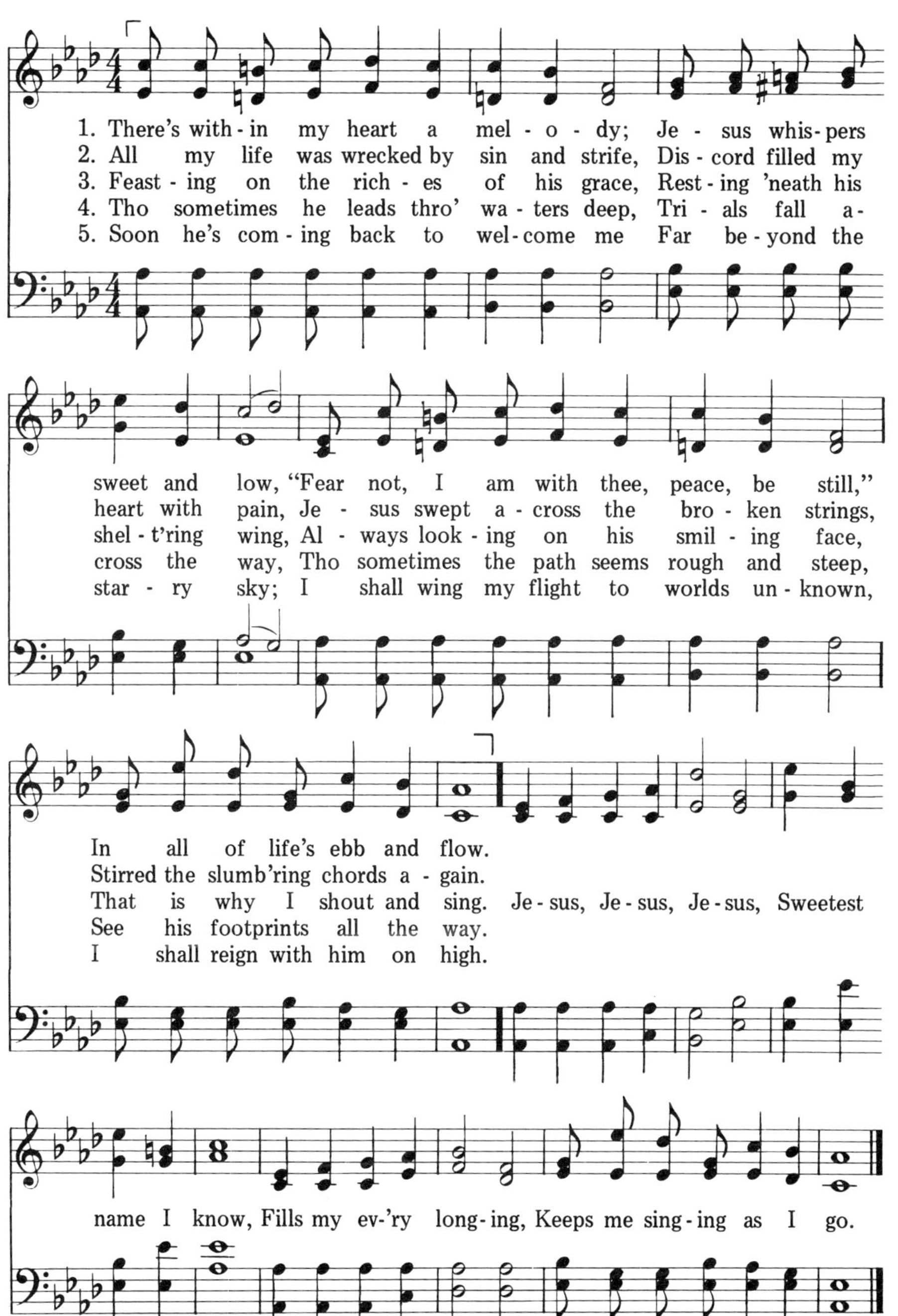

1. There's with-in my heart a mel - o - dy; Je - sus whis-pers
2. All my life was wrecked by sin and strife, Dis - cord filled my
3. Feast - ing on the rich - es of his grace, Rest - ing 'neath his
4. Tho sometimes he leads thro' wa - ters deep, Tri - als fall a -
5. Soon he's com - ing back to wel - come me Far be - yond the
sweet and low, "Fear not, I am with thee, peace, be still,"
heart with pain, Je - sus swept a - cross the bro - ken strings,
shel - t'ring wing, Al - ways look - ing on his smil - ing face,
cross the way, Tho sometimes the path seems rough and steep,
star - ry sky; I shall wing my flight to worlds un - known,
In all of life's ebb and flow.
Stirred the slumb'ring chords a - gain.
That is why I shout and sing. Je - sus, Je - sus, Je - sus, Sweetest
See his footprints all the way.
I shall reign with him on high.
name I know, Fills my ev-'ry long-ing, Keeps me sing-ing as I go.

436 I Know that My Redeemer Lives

Unison

1. I know that my Re-deem-er lives; Glo-ry, hal-le-lu-jah!
2. He lives, he lives, who once was dead, Glo-ry, hal-le-lu-jah!
3. He lives to bless me with his love, Glo-ry, hal-le-lu-jah!
4. He lives, all glo-ry to his name! Glo-ry, hal-le-lu-jah!

What com-fort this sweet sen-tence gives, Glo-ry, hal-le-lu-jah!
He lives, my ev-er-last-ing head, Glo-ry, hal-le-lu-jah!
He lives to plead for me a-bove, Glo-ry, hal-le-lu-jah!
He lives, my Je-sus, still the same, Glo-ry, hal-le-lu-jah!

Shout on, pray on, we're gain-ing ground, Glo-ry, hal-le-lu-jah! The

dead's a-live and the lost is found, Glo-ry, hal-le-lu-jah!

Words, Samuel Medley, 1775; Refrain, Anonymous. Tune SHOUT ON, American Folk Hymn, 19th Century.

Tell Me the Story of Jesus 437

1. Tell me the sto-ry of Je-sus, Write on my heart ev-'ry word;
2. Fast-ing a-lone in the des-ert, Tell of the days that are past,
3. Tell of the cross where they nailed him, Writh-ing in an-guish and pain;
Tell me the sto-ry of Je-sus, Write on my heart ev-'ry word;
Tell me the sto-ry most pre-cious, Sweet-est that ev-er was heard.
How for our sins he was tempt-ed, Yet was tri-um-phant at last.
Tell of the grave where they laid him, Tell how he liv-eth a-gain.
Tell me the sto-ry most pre-cious, Sweet-est that ev-er was heard.
Tell how the an-gels, in cho-rus, Sang as they wel-comed his birth,
Tell of the years of his la-bor, Tell of the sor-row he bore,
Love in that sto-ry so ten-der, Clear-er than ev-er I see:
"Glo-ry to God in the high-est! Peace and good ti-dings to earth."
He was de-spised and af-flict-ed, Home-less, re-ject-ed, and poor.
Stay, let me weep while you whis-per, Love paid the ran-som for me.
Fine
D.C. al Fine

Words, Fanny J. Crosby, 1880. Tune STORY OF JESUS, John R. Sweney, 1880.

438 He Lives

1. I serve a ris - en Sav - ior, he's in the world to - day;
2. In all the world a - round me I see his lov - ing care,
3. Re - joice, re - joice, O Christ - ian, lift up your voice and sing
I know that he is liv - ing, what - ev - er men may say;
And tho my heart grows wea - ry I nev - er will de - spair;
E - ter - nal hal - le - lu - jahs to Je - sus Christ the King!
I see his hand of mer - cy, I hear his voice of cheer,
I know that he is lead - ing thro' all the storm - y blast,
The hope of all who seek him, the help of all who find,
And just the time I need him he's al - ways near.
The day of his ap - pear - ing will come at last.
None oth - er is so lov - ing, so good and kind.
He lives, he lives, Christ Je - sus lives to - day! He walks with me and
He lives, he lives,

talks with me a-long life's nar-row way. He lives, he lives, sal-
He lives, he lives,
va-tion to im-part! You ask me how I know he lives: he lives with-in my heart.

God Moves in a Mysterious Way   439

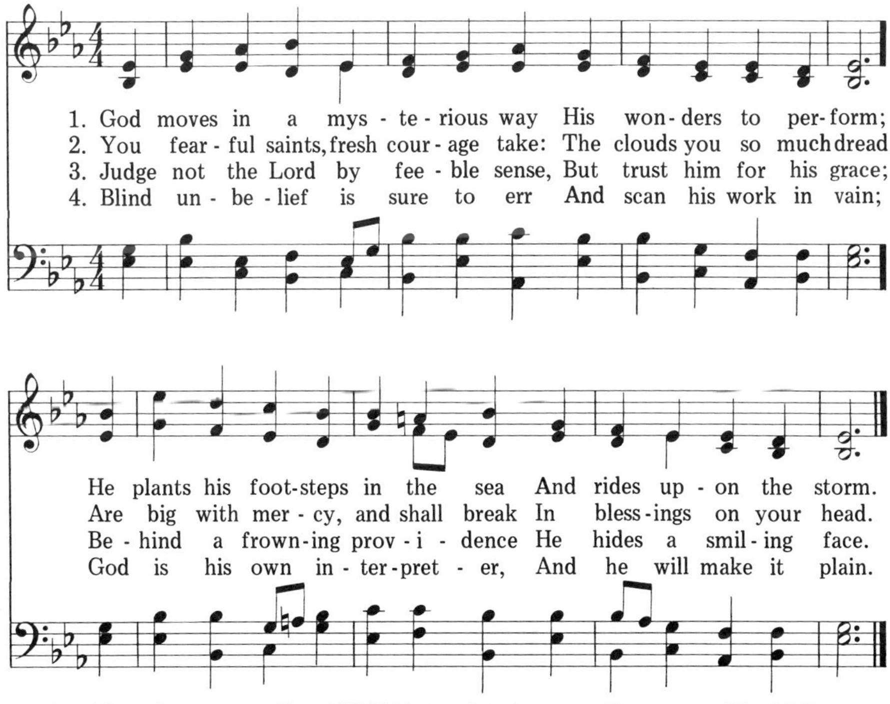

1. God moves in a mys-te-rious way His won-ders to per-form;
2. You fear-ful saints, fresh cour-age take: The clouds you so much dread
3. Judge not the Lord by fee-ble sense, But trust him for his grace;
4. Blind un-be-lief is sure to err And scan his work in vain;

He plants his foot-steps in the sea And rides up-on the storm.
Are big with mer-cy, and shall break In bless-ings on your head.
Be-hind a frown-ing prov-i-dence He hides a smil-ing face.
God is his own in-ter-pret-er, And he will make it plain.

Words, William Cowper, 1774. Tune DUNDEE, *Scottish Psalter*, 1615. Alternate tune ST. ANNE,
No. 223.

440 There Is No Name So Sweet

1. There is no name so sweet on earth, No name so dear in heav-en,
2. 'Twas Ga-briel first that did pro-claim To his most bless-ed moth-er,
3. And when he hung up-on the tree They wrote his name a-bove him,
4. So now up-on his Fa-ther's throne, Al-might-y to re-lieve us

As that be-fore his won-drous birth To Christ the Sav-ior giv-en.
That name which now and ev-er-more We praise a-bove all oth-er.
That all might see the rea-son we For-ev-er-more must love him.
From sin and pain, he ev-er reigns The Prince and Sav-ior, Je-sus.

We love to sing a-round our King, And hail him bless-ed Je-sus;

For there's no word ear ev-er heard, So dear, so sweet as Je-sus.

Words, George W. Bethune, 1861. Tune GOLDEN CHAIN, William B. Bradbury, 1861.

Trusting Jesus 441

1. Sim - ply trust - ing ev - 'ry day, Trust - ing thro' a storm - y way;
2. Bright - ly doth his Spir - it shine In - to this poor heart of mine;
3. Sing - ing if my way is clear, Pray - ing if the path be drear;
4. Trust - ing him while life shall last, Trust - ing him till earth be past;
E - ven when my faith is small, Trust - ing Je - sus, that is all.
While he leads I can - not fall; Trust - ing Je - sus, that is all.
If in dan - ger, for him call; Trust - ing Je - sus, that is all.
Till with - in the *jas - per wall, Trust - ing Je - sus, that is all.
Trust - ing as the mo - ments fly, Trust - ing as the days go by;
Trust - ing him what - e'er be - fall, Trust - ing Je - sus, that is all.

Words, Edgar Page Stites, 1876. Tune TRUSTING JESUS, Ira D. Sankey, 1876. *Revelation 21:18.

442 Since I Have Been Redeemed

1. I have a song I love to sing, Since I have been re - deemed,
2. I have a Christ who sat - is - fies, Since I have been re - deemed,
3. I have a wit - ness bright and clear, Since I have been re - deemed,
4. I have a home pre-pared for me, Since I have been re - deemed,

Of my Re - deem - er, Sav - ior, King, Since I have been re - deemed.
To do his will my high-est prize, Since I have been re - deemed.
Dis - pell - ing ev - 'ry doubt and fear, Since I have been re - deemed.
Where I shall dwell e - ter - nal - ly, Since I have been re - deemed.

Since I have been re-deemed, Since I have been re-
Since I have been re-deemed, Since I have been re-deemed,

deemed, I will glo-ry in his name; Since I have been re-
Since I have been re-deemed, Since

Words and tune OTHELLO, Edwin O. Excell, 1884.

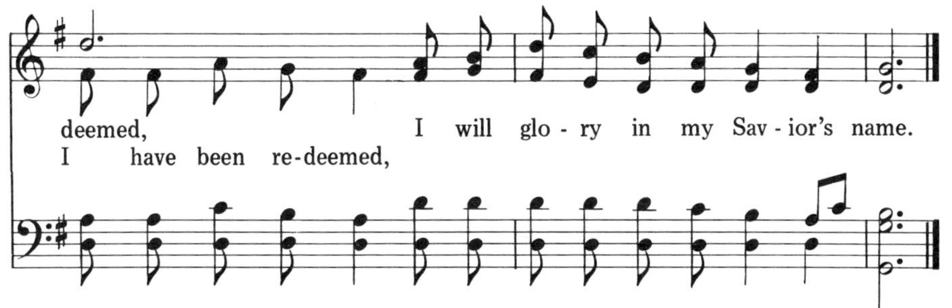

deemed, I will glo-ry in my Sav-ior's name.
I have been re-deemed,

O Teacher, Master of the Skill 443

1. O Teach-er, Mas-ter of the skill That com-passed
2. Make me a chan-nel of thy grace, Make me a
3. Grant me ex-pect-ant faith, O Lord; Grant pa-tient
4. Teach me to strike those chords di-vine That vi-brate

truth and roused the will: A por-tion of thine
mir-ror of thy face, That, tho I teach with
lis-t'ning, hum-ble word; Help me to learn from
hu-man hearts to thine; To wake a tal-ent

art, I pray, Be mine who dare to show thy way.
book and chart, Thro' me God's love may warm each heart.
eag-er youth Thy mes-sage of e-ter-nal truth.
mute too long And gain for all the world a song!

Words, William W. Reid, 1959. From *Fifteen New Christian Education Hymns*, copyright 1959 by The Hymn Society of America. Used by permission. Tune TALLIS' CANON, Thomas Tallis, *c.* 1560.

444 Redeemed

Unison

1. Re-deemed, how I love to pro-claim it! Re-deemed by the
2. Re-deemed, and so hap-py in Je-sus, No lan-guage my
3. I think of my bless-ed Re-deem-er, I think of him

blood of the Lamb; Re-deemed thro' his in-fi-nite mer-cy, His
rap-ture can tell; I know that the light of his pres-ence With
all the day long; I sing, for I can-not be si-lent; His

Harmony

child, and for-ev-er, I am.
me doth con-tin-ual-ly dwell. Re-deemed, re-deemed, Re-
love is the theme of my song.

Unison

deemed by the blood of the Lamb; Re-deemed, how I

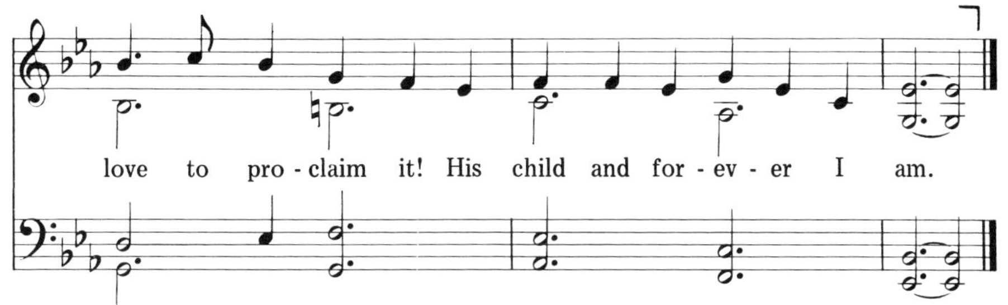

love to pro-claim it! His child and for-ev-er I am.

God Loved the World So That He Gave 445

1. God loved the world so that he gave His on - ly
2. God would not have the sin - ner die, His Son with
3. Christ Je - sus is the ground of faith, Who was made
4. Glo - ry to God, the Fa - ther, Son, And Ho - ly

Son the lost to save, That all who would in
sav - ing grace is nigh; His Spir - it in the
flesh and suf - fered death; All that con - fide in
Spir - it, Three in One! To thee, O bless - ed

him be - lieve Should ev - er - last - ing life re - ceive.
word doth teach How man the bless - ed goal may reach.
him a - lone Are built on this chief cor - ner-stone.
Trin - i - ty, Be praise now and e - ter - nal - ly! A-MEN.

John 3:16-18. Words, Paul Gerhardt, 1661; translated, August Crull, 1941. Tune ST. CRISPIN, George J. Elvey, 1863.

446 Redeemed, How I Love to Proclaim It

1. Re-deemed how I love to pro-claim it! Re-deemed by the
2. Re-deemed, and so hap-py in Je-sus, No lan-guage my
3. I think of my bless-ed Re-deem-er, I think of him
4. I know I shall see in his beau-ty The King in whose
blood of the Lamb; Re-deemed thro' his in-fi-nite mer-cy,
rap-ture can tell; I know that the light of his pres-ence
all the day long; I sing, for I can-not be si-lent;
law I de-light; Who lov-ing-ly guard-eth my foot-steps
His child, and for-ev-er, I am.
With me doth con-tin-ual-ly dwell. Re-deemed, re-
His love is the theme of my song. re-deemed,
And giv-eth me songs in the night.
deemed, Re-deemed by the blood of the Lamb; Re-
re-deemed,
deemed, re-deemed, His child, and for-ev-er, I am.
re-deemed, re-deemed,

Words, Fanny J. Crosby, 1882. Tune REDEEMED, William J. Kirkpatrick, 1882.

Sunshine in My Soul 447

1. There is sunshine in my soul to-day, More glo-ri-ous and bright
2. There is mu-sic in my soul to-day, A car-ol to my King,
3. There is mu-sic in my soul to-day, For when the Lord is near,
4. There is glad-ness in my soul to-day, And hope and praise and love
Than glows in an-y earth-ly sky, For Je-sus is my light.
And Je-sus, lis-ten-ing, can hear The songs I can-not sing.
The dove of peace sings in my heart, The flow'rs of grace ap-pear.
For bless-ings which he gives me now, For joys "laid up" a-bove.
O there's sun - shine, bless-ed sun - shine,
O there's sun-shine in my soul, bless-ed sun-shine in my soul,
When the peace-ful, hap-py mo-ments roll; When
hap-py mo-ments roll;
Je-sus shows his smil-ing face, There is sun-shine in my soul.

Words, Eliza E. Hewitt, 1887. Tune SUNSHINE, John R. Sweney, 1887.

448 Because He Lives

1. God sent his Son, they called him Je - sus;
2. How sweet to hold a new - born ba - by,
3. And then one day I'll cross the riv - er;
He came to love, heal, and for - give;
And feel the pride, and joy he gives;
I'll fight life's fi - nal war with pain;
He lived and died to buy my par - don,
But great - er still the calm as - sur - ance,
And then as death gives way to vic - t'ry,
An emp - ty grave is there to prove my Sav - ior lives.
This child can face un - cer - tain days be - cause he lives.
I'll see the lights of glo - ry and I'll know he lives.

Words, Gloria and William J. Gaither. Tune RESURRECTION, William J. Gaither, 1971.
© Copyright 1971 by William J. Gaither. All rights reserved. Used by permission.

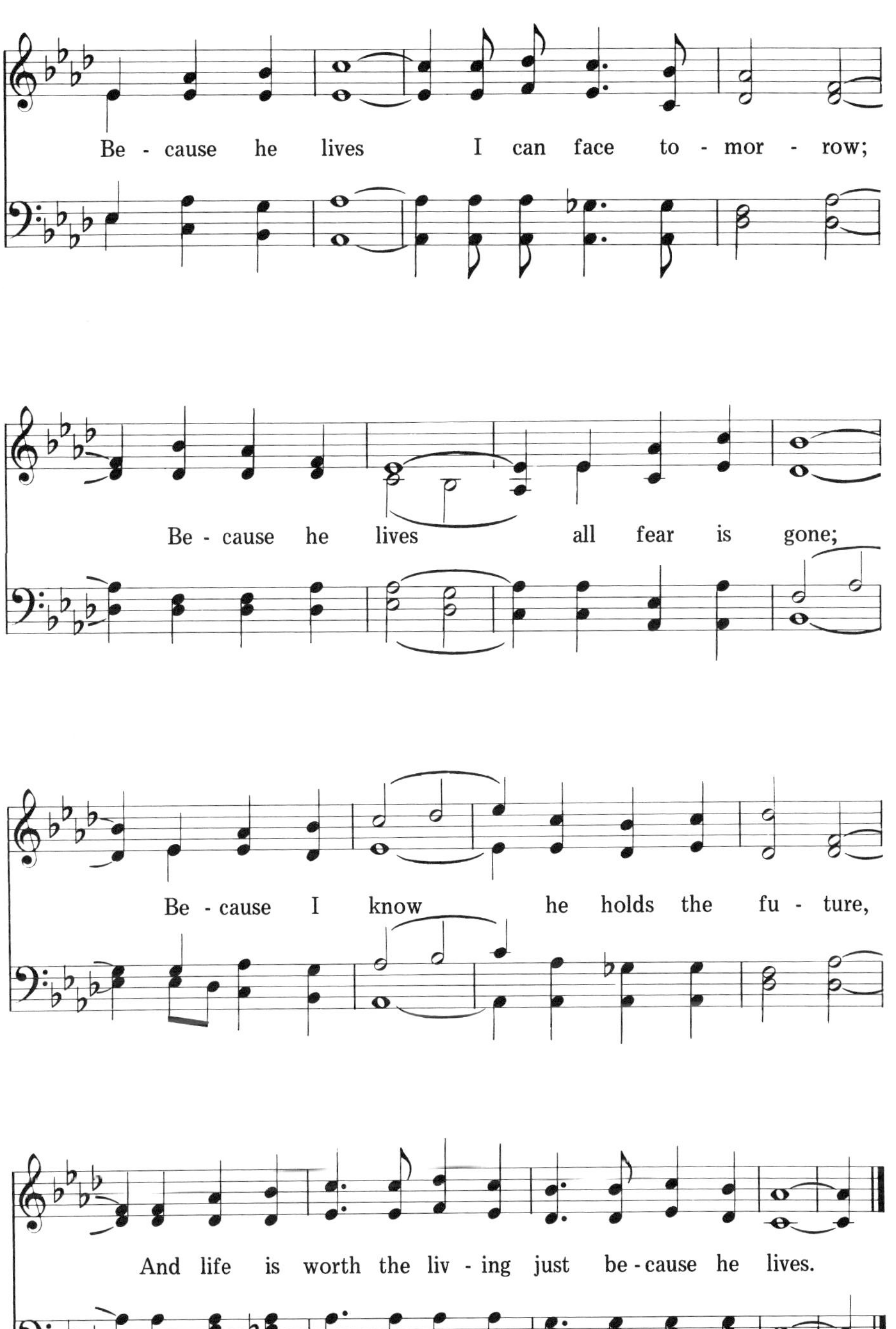

Be - cause he lives I can face to - mor - row;
Be - cause he lives all fear is gone;
Be - cause I know he holds the fu - ture,
And life is worth the liv - ing just be - cause he lives.

449 He Is So Precious to Me

1. So pre - cious is Je - sus, my Sav - ior, my King,
2. He stood at my heart's door in sun - shine and rain,
3. I stand on the moun - tain of bless - ing at last,
4. I praise him be - cause he ap - point - ed a place

His praise all the day long with rap - ture I sing;
And pa - tient - ly wait - ed an en - trance to gain;
No cloud in the heav - ens a shad - ow to cast;
Where, some - day, thro' faith in his won - der - ful grace,

To him in my weak-ness for strength I can cling, For he is so
What shame that so long he en - treat - ed in vain, For he is so
His smile is up - on me, the val - ley is past, For he is so
I know I shall see him, shall look on his face, For he is so

so pre-cious to me,
pre-cious to me. For he is so pre-cious to me,

Words and tune PRECIOUS TO ME, Charles H. Gabriel, 1902.

so pre-cious to me,
For he is so pre-cious to me, 'Tis heav-en be-
low, my Re-deem-er to know, For he is so pre-cious to me.

I'm Not Ashamed to Own My Lord 450

1. I'm not a-shamed to own my Lord, Or to de-fend his cause,
2. Je - sus, my God! I know his name, His name is all my trust;
3. Firm as his throne his prom-ise stands, And he can well se-cure
4. Then will he own my worth-less name Be-fore his Fa-ther's face,

Main-tain the hon-or of his Word, The glo-ry of his cross.
Nor will he put my soul to shame, Nor let my hope be lost.
What I've com-mit-ted to his hands Till the de-ci-sive hour.
And in the New Je-ru-sa-lem Ap-point my soul a place.

1 Timothy 1:12. Words, Isaac Watts, 1707. Tune AZMON, Carl G. Gläser; arranged, Lowell Mason, 1839.
This tune in a higher key, No. 69. Alternate tune SERENITY, No. 329.

451 He Hideth My Soul

1. A won - der - ful Sav - ior is Je - sus my Lord, A
2. A won - der - ful Sav - ior is Je - sus my Lord, He
3. With num - ber - less bless - ings each mo - ment he crowns, And
4. When clothed in his bright-ness, trans - port - ed I rise To
won - der - ful Sav - ior to me; He hid - eth my soul in the
tak - eth my bur - den a - way; He hold - eth me up, and I
filled with his full - ness di - vine, I sing in my rap - ture, oh,
meet him in clouds of the sky, His per - fect sal - va - tion, his
*cleft of the rock, Where riv - ers of plea - sure I see.
shall not be moved, He giv - eth me strength as my day.
glo - ry to God For such a Re - deem - er as mine!
won - der - ful love I'll shout with the mil - lions on high.
He hid - eth my soul in the cleft of the rock That shad - ows a

Words, Fanny J. Crosby, 1890. Tune KIRKPATRICK, William J. Kirkpatrick, 1890. *Exodus 33:22.

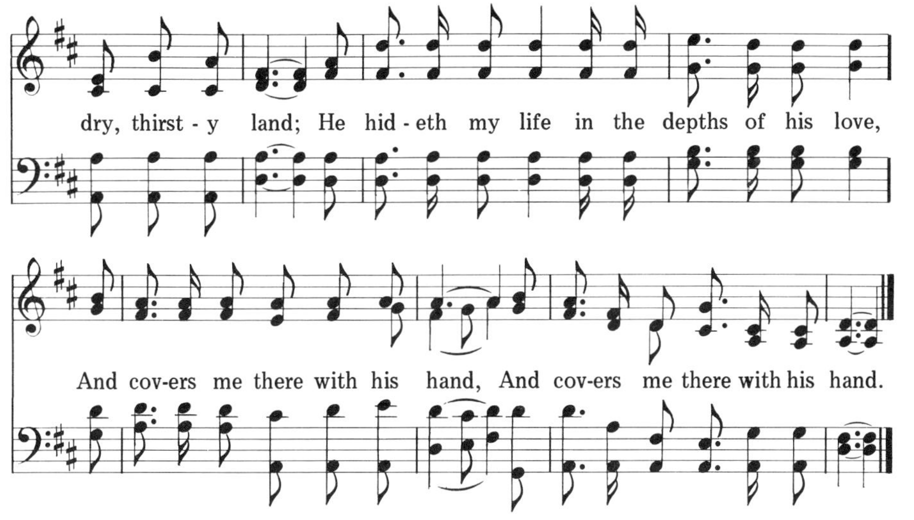

dry, thirst-y land; He hid-eth my life in the depths of his love,
And cov-ers me there with his hand, And cov-ers me there with his hand.

I Will Not Be Afraid 452

1. I will not be a-fraid, fraid; I will look
2. He says he will be with me, with me; He goes be-
3. His arms are un-der-neath me, neath me; His hands up-
4. His Word will stand for-ev-er, ev-er; His truth — it
5. He will give grace and glo-ry, glo-ry; His cross be-
6. So we go sing-ing on-ward, on-ward; We're press-ing

up-ward, And trav-el on-ward, And not be a-fraid.
fore me, And is be-side me, So I'm not a-fraid.
hold me, His love en-folds me, So I'm not a-fraid.
shall be My shield and buck-ler, So I'm not a-fraid.
fore me, His ban-ner o'er me, So I'm not a-fraid.
up-ward, We're march-ing home-ward To him un-a-fraid.

Words, Ellis Govan. Tune UNAFRAID, Anonymous.

453 Love Is the Theme

1. Of the themes that men have known, One su-preme-ly stands a - lone;
2. Let the bells of heav-en ring, Let the saints their trib-ute bring,
3. Since the Lord my soul un-bound, I am tell-ing all a - round,
4. As of old when blind and lame To the bless-ed Mas-ter came,
Thro' the a-ges it has shown, 'Tis his wonder-ful, won-der-ful love.
Let the world true prais-es sing For his wonder-ful, won-der-ful love.
Par-don, peace, and joy are found In his wonder-ful, won-der-ful love.
Sin-ners, call ye on his name, Trust his wonder-ful, won-der-ful love.
Love is the theme, love is su-preme; Sweeter it grows, glo-ry be-stows;
Bright as the sun ev-er it glows! Love is the theme, e-ter-nal theme!

1. Down at the cross where my Sav-ior died, Down where for cleansing from
2. I am so won-drous-ly saved from sin, Je - sus so sweet - ly a -
3. Oh, pre-cious foun-tain that saves from sin, I am so glad I have
4. Come to this foun-tain so rich and sweet, Cast thy poor soul at the

sin I cried, There to my heart was the blood ap- plied; Glo - ry to his name.
bides with - in; There at the cross where he took me in; Glo - ry to his name.
en - tered in; There Je-sus saves me and keeps me clean; Glo - ry to his name
Sav -ior's feet; Plunge in to - day, and be made com-plete; Glo - ry to his name.

Glo - ry to his name, Glo - ry to his name:

There to my heart was the blood ap - plied; Glo - ry to his name.

Words, Elisha A. Hoffman, 1878. Tune GLORY TO HIS NAME, John H. Stockton, 1878.

455 Satisfied with Jesus

1. I am sat-is-fied with Je-sus, He has done so much for me:
2. He is with me in my tri-als, Best of friends of all is he;
3. I can hear the voice of Je-sus, Call-ing out so plead-ing-ly,
4. When my work on earth is end-ed, And I cross the mys-tic sea,

He has suf-fered to re-deem me, He has died to set me free.
I can al-ways count on Je-sus, Can he al-ways count on me?
"Go and win the lost and stray-ing;" Is he sat-is-fied with me?
Oh, that I could hear him say-ing, "I am sat-is-fied with thee."

I am sat-is-fied, I am sat-is-fied, I am sat-is-fied with Je-sus, But the ques-tion comes to me, As I think of Cal-va-ry, Is my Mas-ter sat-is-fied with me?

So Let Our Lips and Lives Express 456

1. So let our lips and lives ex-press The ho-ly
2. Thus shall we best pro-claim a-broad The hon-ors
3. Our flesh and sense must be de-nied, Pas-sion and
4. Re-li-gion bears our spir-its up, While we em-

gos-pel we pro-fess; So let our works and
of our Sav-ior God; When his sal-va-tion
en-vy, lust, and pride; While jus-tice, tem-p'rance,
brace that bless-ed hope, The bright ap-pear-ance

vir-tues shine, To prove the doc-trine all di-vine.
reigns with-in, And grace sub-dues the pow'r of sin.
truth, and love, Our in-ward pi-e-ty ap-prove.
of the Lord; And faith stands lean-ing on his word.

Words, Isaac Watts, 1707. Tune WAREHAM, William Knapp, 1738.

457 O Happy Day That Fixed My Choice

1. O hap-py day that fixed my choice On thee, my
2. 'Tis done – the great trans-ac-tion's done; I am my
3. Now rest, my long - di - vid - ed heart, Fixed on this
4. High heav'n that hears the sol - emn vow, That vow re -

Sav - ior and my God! Well may this glow - ing heart re - joice,
Lord's, and he is mine; He drew me and I fol-lowed on,
bliss - ful cen - ter, rest; Here have I found a no - bler part,
newed shall dai - ly hear; Till in life's lat - est hour I bow,

And tell its rap - tures all a - broad.
Re - joiced to own the call di - vine.
Here heav'n - ly plea - sures fill my breast.
And bless, in death, a bond so dear.

Hap - py day, hap - py day,

When Je - sus washed my sins a - way! He taught me how

to watch and pray, And live re - joic - ing ev - 'ry day;

2 Chronicles 15:15. Words, Philip Doddridge, 1755; Refrain, Anonymous. Tune HAPPY DAY,
William McDonald's *Wesleyan Sacred Harp*, 1854.

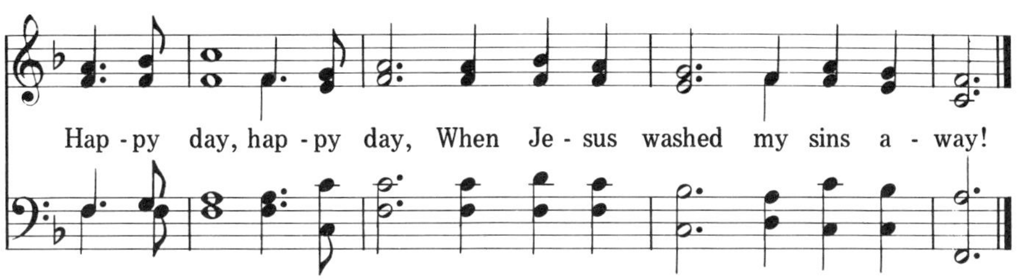

Hap-py day, hap-py day, When Je-sus washed my sins a - way!

I've Got Peace Like a River 458

1. I've got peace like a riv-er, I've got peace like a
2. I've got love like a riv-er, I've got love like a
3. I've got joy like a riv-er, I've got joy like a

riv-er, I've got peace like a riv-er in my
riv-er, I've got love like a riv-er in my
riv-er, I've got joy like a riv-er in my

soul. I've got riv-er in my soul.

Words and tune PEACE LIKE A RIVER, Traditional Spiritual.

459 The Lily of the Valley

1. I have found a friend in Je - sus, he's ev - 'ry - thing to me,
2. He all my grief has tak - en, and all my sor-rows borne;
3. He will nev - er, nev - er leave me, nor yet for - sake me here,
He's the fair - est of ten thou - sand to my soul;
In temp - ta - tion he's my strong and might - y tow'r;
While I live by faith and do his bless - ed will;
The *Lil - y of the Val - ley, in him a - lone I see
I have all for him for - sak - en, and all my i - dols torn
A wall of fire a - bout me, I've noth - ing now to fear,
D. S. —Lil - y of the Val - ley, the**Bright and Morn - ing Star,
Fine
All I need to cleanse and make me ful - ly whole.
From my heart and now he keeps me by his pow'r.
With his man - na he my hun - gry soul shall fill.
He's the fair - est of ten thou - sand to my soul.

Words, Charles W. Fry, 1881. Tune SALVATIONIST, William S. Hays, 1871; adapted, Charles W. Fry, 1881. *Song of Solomon 2:1. **Revelation 22:16.

In sor-row he's my com-fort, in trou-ble he's my stay;
Tho all the world for-sake me, and Sa-tan tempt me sore,
Then sweep-ing up to glo-ry to see his bless-ed face,

D.S. al Fine

He tells me ev-'ry care on him to roll: He's the
Thro' Je-sus I shall safe-ly reach the goal: He's the
Where riv-ers of de-light shall ev-er roll: He's the

Fill Thou My Life, O Lord My God 460

1. Fill thou my life, O Lord my God, In ev-'ry part with praise, That
2. Not for the lip of praise a-lone, Nor for the prais-ing heart; I
3. Praise in the com-mon things of life, Its go-ings out and in; Praise
4. Fill ev-'ry part of me with praise: Let all my be-ing speak Of
5. So shalt thou, Lord, from e-ven me Re-ceive the glo-ry due; And
6. So shall no part of day or night From sa-cred-ness be free; But

my whole be-ing may pro-claim Thy be-ing and thy ways.
ask thee for a life made up Of praise in ev-'ry part.
in each du-ty and each deed, How-ev-er small and mean.
thee and of thy love, O Lord, Poor tho I be, and weak.
so shall I be-gin on earth The song for-ev-er new.
all my life, in ev-'ry step, Be fel-low-ship with thee. A-MEN.

Words, Horatius Bonar, 1866. Tune RICHMOND, Thomas Haweis, 1792.

461 I Love to Tell the Story

1. I love to tell the story Of un-seen things a-bove, Of
2. I love to tell the story; 'Tis pleas-ant to re-peat What
3. I love to tell the story; For those who know it best Seem
Je - sus and his glo-ry, Of Je - sus and his love: I love to
seems each time I tell it, More won-der-ful-ly sweet: I love to
hun-ger-ing and thirst-ing To hear it, like the rest: And when, in
tell the sto-ry Be-cause I know 'tis true; It sat-is-fies my
tell the sto-ry, For some have nev-er heard The mes-sage of sal-
scenes of glo-ry, I sing the new, new song, 'Twill be the old, old
long-ings As noth-ing else can do.
va - tion From God's own ho-ly Word. I love to tell the sto-ry, 'Twill
sto - ry That I have loved so long.
be my theme in glo-ry To tell the old, old sto-ry of Je-sus and his love.

Words, Katherine Hankey, 1866. Tune HANKEY, William G. Fischer, 1869.

1. I was sink-ing deep in sin, Far from the peaceful shore, Ver - y deep-ly
2. All my heart to him I give, Ev - er to him I'll cling, In his bless-ed
3. Souls in dan - ger, look a-bove, Je - sus com-plete-ly saves; He will lift you

stained with-in, Sink-ing to rise no more; But the Mas - ter of the sea
pres - ence live, Ev - er his prais - es sing; Love so might - y and so true
by his love Out of the an - gry waves; He's the Mas - ter of the sea,

Heard my de-spair-ing cry, From the wa-ters lift-ed me, Now safe am I.
Mer - its my soul's best songs; Faith-ful, lov-ing ser-vice, too, To him be-longs.
Bil - lows his will o - bey; He your Sav-ior wants to be, Be saved to-day.

Love lift-ed me! Love lift-ed me! When noth-ing
e - ven me! e - ven me!

else could help, Love lift - ed me. Love lift - ed me.

Words, James Rowe, 1912. Tune SAFETY, Howard E. Smith, 1912. Copyright 1912. Renewal 1940 by Mrs. Howard E. Smith. Assigned to John T. Benson, Jr. All rights reserved. Used by permission.

463 He's Everything to Me

Unison

1. In the stars his hand-i-work I see, On the wind he speaks in
2. I will cel-e-brate na-tiv-i-ty, For it has a place in

maj-es-ty, Tho he rul-eth o-ver land and sea,
his-to-ry, Sure, he came to set his peo-ple free,

1.
What is that to me?

2.
What is that to me?

Till by faith I met him face to face, And I felt the won-der

of his grace, Then I knew that he was more than just a

Words and tune WOODLAND HILLS, Ralph Carmichael, 1964. © Copyright 1964 by Lexicon Music, Inc. All rights reserved. International copyright secured. Used by special permission. Performance rights licensed through ASCAP.

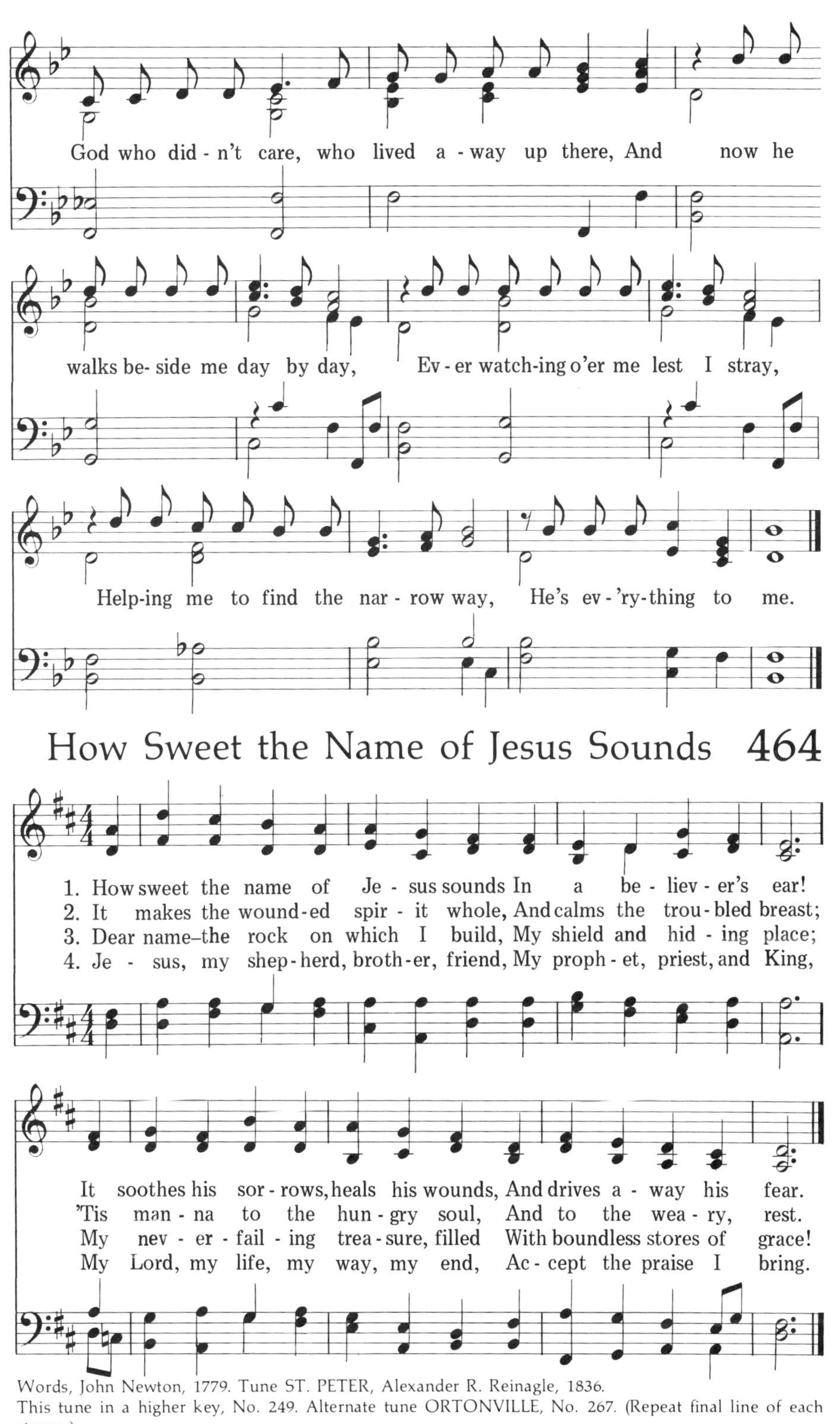

God who did-n't care, who lived a-way up there, And now he

walks be-side me day by day, Ev-er watch-ing o'er me lest I stray,

Help-ing me to find the nar-row way, He's ev-'ry-thing to me.

How Sweet the Name of Jesus Sounds 464

1. How sweet the name of Je - sus sounds In a be - liev - er's ear!
2. It makes the wound-ed spir - it whole, And calms the trou-bled breast;
3. Dear name—the rock on which I build, My shield and hid - ing place;
4. Je - sus, my shep-herd, broth-er, friend, My proph - et, priest, and King,

It soothes his sor - rows, heals his wounds, And drives a - way his fear.
'Tis man - na to the hun - gry soul, And to the wea - ry, rest.
My nev - er - fail - ing trea - sure, filled With boundless stores of grace!
My Lord, my life, my way, my end, Ac - cept the praise I bring.

Words, John Newton, 1779. Tune ST. PETER, Alexander R. Reinagle, 1836.
This tune in a higher key, No. 249. Alternate tune ORTONVILLE, No. 267. (Repeat final line of each stanza.)

465 I Will Sing of My Redeemer

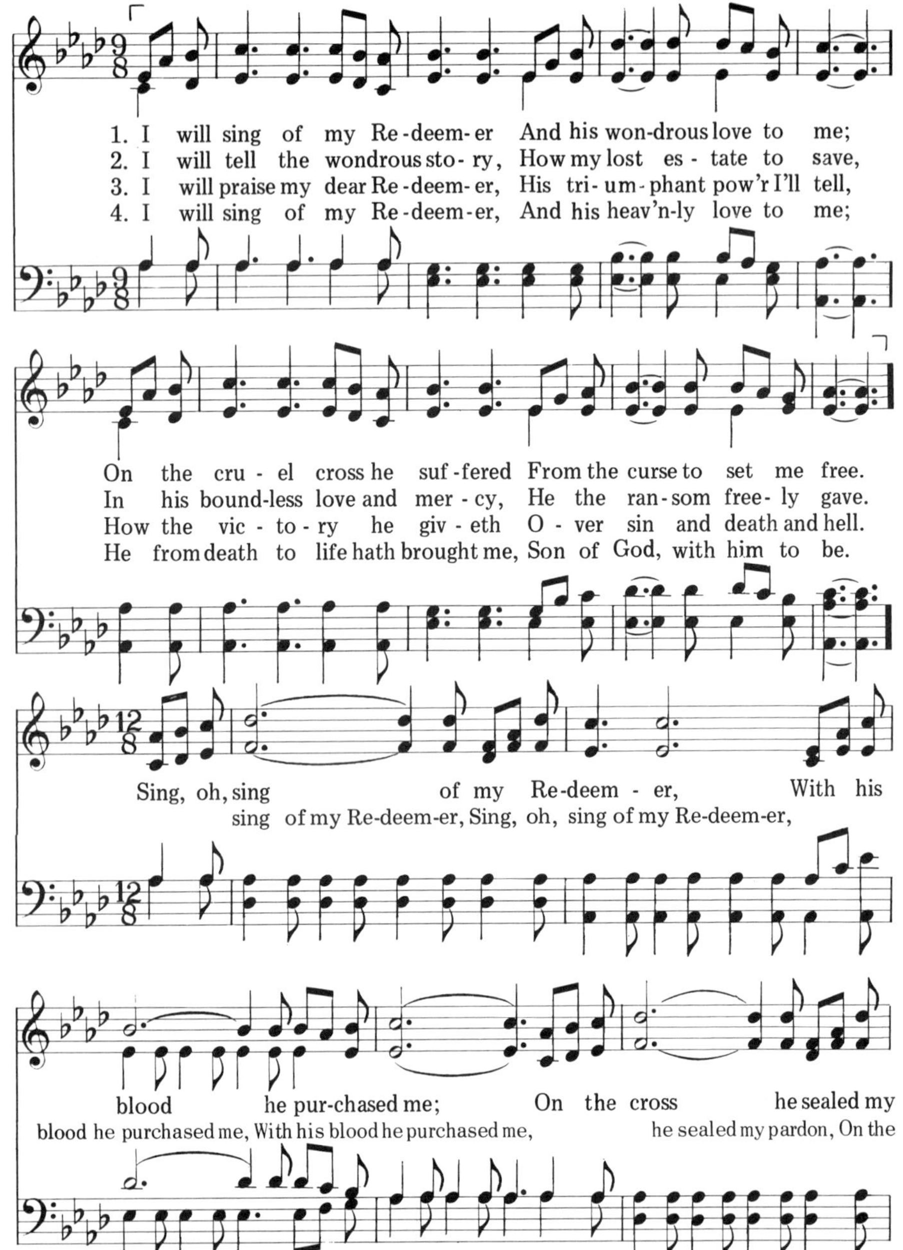

1. I will sing of my Re-deem-er And his won-drous love to me;
2. I will tell the wondrous sto-ry, How my lost es-tate to save,
3. I will praise my dear Re-deem-er, His tri-um-phant pow'r I'll tell,
4. I will sing of my Re-deem-er, And his heav'n-ly love to me;

On the cru-el cross he suf-fered From the curse to set me free.
In his bound-less love and mer-cy, He the ran-som free-ly gave.
How the vic-to-ry he giv-eth O-ver sin and death and hell.
He from death to life hath brought me, Son of God, with him to be.

Sing, oh, sing of my Re-deem-er, With his
sing of my Re-deem-er, Sing, oh, sing of my Re-deem-er,

blood he pur-chased me; On the cross he sealed my
blood he purchased me, With his blood he purchased me, he sealed my pardon, On the

Words, Philip P. Bliss, 1876. Tune MY REDEEMER, James McGranahan, 1877.

par - don, Paid the debt and made me free.
cross he sealed my pardon, and made me free, and made me free.

Thank the Lord with Joyful Heart 466

1. Thank the Lord with joy - ful heart, Who does won-drous things im - part,
2. Un - to him be glo - ry giv'n, Who is Lord of earth and heav'n,
3. Who to us sal - va - tion brings, Coun-sel - lor and King of kings,
4. Who with wis-dom did pre - pare For our use the world so fair,
5. God of heav'n, to thee we raise Cease-less - ly our songs of praise!
For his good-ness rich and pure, Shall for - ev - er - more en - dure.

Words, Matthias Jorissen, 1798; translated, Esther Bergen, 1971. Used by permission. Tune HARTS, Benjamin Milgrove, 1769.

467 It's So Wonderful

To me, (to me,) it's so won-der-ful, (so won-der-ful,) To
me, (to me,) it's so won-der-ful; (so won-der-ful;) To
me, (to me,) it's so won-der-ful (so won-der-ful) To
know that Je-sus is mine. (is mine.)
Fine
1. When I should feel
2. When I am dis-
lone-ly or I should feel sad, I'm so con-tent-ed and
cour-aged or I'm filled with gloom, God sends his an-gels to

my heart is glad. Joy - bells are ring - ing, in my heart I'm
sing in my gloom. I join the sing - ing, for I can't de-

D. C. al Fine

sing - ing; It's won - der - ful to know he is mine. (is mine.)
cline; It's won - der - ful to know he is mine. (is mine.)

When All Thy Mercies, O My God   468

1. When all thy mer - cies, O my God, My ris - ing soul sur - veys, Trans-
2. Un - num-bered com - forts to my soul Thy ten - der care be- stowed, Be-
3. Ten thou-sand thou - sand pre-cious gifts My dai - ly thanks em - ploy; Nor
4. Thro' all e - ter - ni - ty to thee A joy - ful song I'll raise; For

port - ed with the view, I'm lost In won - der, love, and praise.
fore my in - fant heart con-ceived From whom those com-forts flowed.
is the least a cheer - ful heart That tastes those gifts with joy.
O e - ter - ni - ty's too short To ut - ter all thy praise. A-MEN.

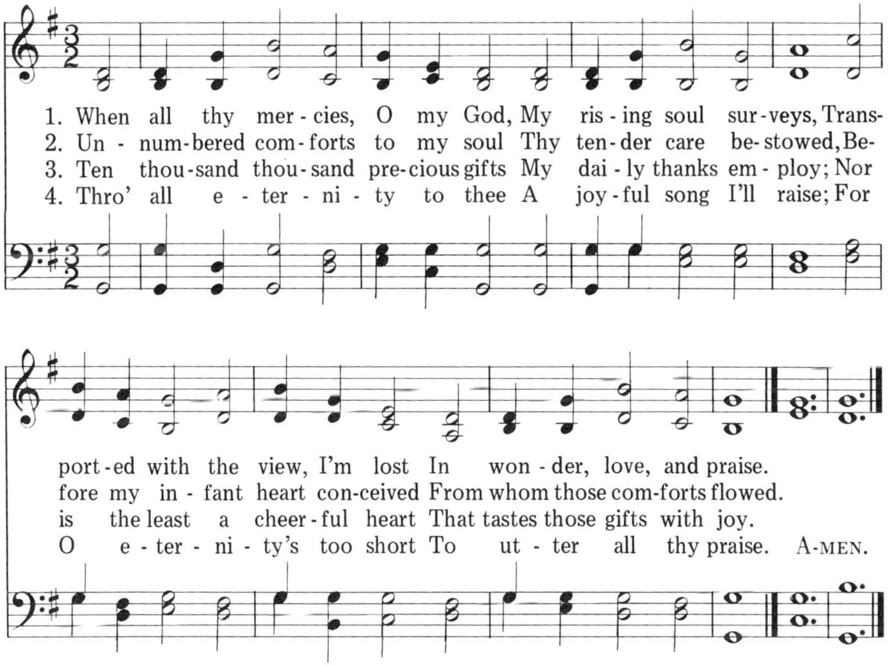

Words, Joseph Addison, 1712. Tune EVAN, William H. Havergal, 1847; adapted, Lowell Mason, 1850.

469 In Times Like These

1. In times like these you need a Sav-ior, In times like these
2. In times like these you need the Bi - ble, In times like these
3. In times like these I have a Sav-ior, In times like these

you need an an - chor; Be ver - y sure, be ver - y sure
O be not i - dle; Be ver - y sure, be ver - y sure
I have an an - chor; I'm ver - y sure, I'm ver - y sure

Your an - chor holds and grips the Sol - id Rock!
Your an - chor holds and grips the Sol - id Rock!
My an - chor holds and grips the Sol - id Rock!

This Rock is Je - sus, Yes, he's the One; This Rock is Je - sus,

The on - ly One! 1,2. Be ver - y sure, be ver - y sure
3. I'm ver - y sure, I'm ver - y sure

Your an - chor holds and grips the Sol - id Rock!
My an - chor holds and grips the Sol - id Rock!

O Thou to Whose All-Searching Sight 470

Unison

1. O thou to whose all - search - ing sight The
2. Wash out its stains, re - fine its dross, Nail
3. If in this dark - some wild I stray, Be
4. Sav - ior, wher - e'er thy steps I see, Daunt -

dark - ness shin - eth as the light, Search, prove my heart; it
my af - fec - tions to the cross; Hal - low each thought; let
thou my light, be thou my way; No foes, no e - vils
less, un - tired, I fol - low thee. O let thy hand sup -

longs for thee; O burst these bonds, and set me free!
all with - in Be clean, as thou, my Lord, art clean.
need I fear, No harm, while thou, my God, art near.
port me still, And lead me to thy ho - ly hill!

Words, Nicolaus L. von Zinzendorf, 1721; translated, John Wesley, 1738. Tune KEDRON (Pilsbury), *United States Sacred Harmony*, 1799. Alternate tunes OLD 100TH, No. 6; DUKE STREET, No. 282.

471 There's a Glad New Song

1. There's a glad new song ring-ing in my heart, Such as an-gels would
2. When my soul was lost in a star-less night Where my feet nev-er
3. When at last I stand with the heav'n-ly choir In the light of the

sing a-bove, And the whole day long it doth joy im-part;
ceased to rove, At a dread-ful cost Je-sus brought me light,
throne a-bove, On the gold-en strand I shall nev-er tire

'Tis the song of re-deem-ing love.
All be-cause of re-deem-ing love. Of his love I shall
Of the song of re-deem-ing love. Of his love

ev-er sing Till a-bove I be-hold the King; Thro' e-
Till a-bove

ter-ni-ty my glad song shall be Of the Sav-ior's re-deem-ing love.

1. Walk-ing in sun-light, all of my jour-ney; O - ver the moun-tains,
2. Shad-ows a - round me, shad-ows a - bove me, Nev - er con - ceal my
3. In the bright sun-light, ev - er re - joic - ing, Press-ing my way to
thro' the deep vale; Je - sus has said "I'll nev - er for - sake thee,"
Sav - ior and Guide; He is the light, in him is no dark - ness;
man - sions a - bove; Sing-ing his prais - es glad - ly I'm walk - ing,
Prom - ise di - vine that nev - er can fail.
Ev - er I'm walk - ing close to his side. Heav - en - ly sun - light,
Walk - ing in sun - light, sun-light of love.
heav - en - ly sun - light, Flood-ing my soul with glo - ry di - vine: Hal - le -
lu - jah, I am re - joic - ing, Sing-ing his prais - es, Je - sus is mine.

Words, H. J. Zelley, 1899. Tune SUNLIGHT, G. H. Cook, 1899.

473 Take the Name of Jesus with You

1. Take the name of Je-sus with you, Child of sor-row and of woe;
2. Take the name of Je-sus ev - er As a shield from ev-'ry snare;
3. O the pre-cious name of Je-sus! How it thrills our souls with joy,
4. At the name of Je-sus bow-ing, Fall-ing pros-trate at his feet,

It will joy and com-fort give you, Take it then wher-e'er you go.
When temp-ta-tions round you gath-er, Breathe that ho-ly name in pray'r.
When his lov-ing arms re-ceive us, And his songs our tongues em-ploy.
King of kings in heav'n we'll crown him, When our jour-ney is com-plete.

Pre-cious name, O how sweet! Hope of
Pre-cious name, O how sweet!

earth and joy of heav'n; Pre-cious name, O how
Pre-cious name, O how

sweet! Hope of earth and joy of heav'n.
sweet, how sweet!

Words, Lydia Baxter, 1870. Tune PRECIOUS NAME, William H. Doane, 1871.

New Born Again 474

1. I found free grace and dy-ing love, I'm new born a-gain,
2. I know my Lord has set me free, I'm new born a-gain,
Been long time a-talk-ing 'bout my tri-als here be-low.
Free grace, free grace, free grace, sin-ner, Free grace, free grace, I'm
new born a-gain. So glad, so glad, I'm new born a-gain,
Been long time a-talk-ing 'bout my tri-als here be-low.

Words and tune NEW BORN AGAIN, Negro Spiritual; arranged, John W. Work, Jr., and Frederick J. Work, 1907.

475 Victory in Jesus

1. I heard an old, old sto-ry, how a Sav-ior came from glo-ry,
2. I heard a-bout his heal-ing, of his cleans-ing pow'r re-veal-ing,
3. I heard a-bout a man-sion he has built for me in glo-ry,
How he gave his life on Cal-va-ry to save a wretch like me:
How he made the lame to walk a-gain and caused the blind to see;
And I heard a-bout the streets of gold be-yond the crys-tal sea;
I heard a-bout his groan-ing, of his pre-cious blood's a-ton-ing,
And then I cried "dear Je-sus, come and heal my bro-ken spir-it,"
A-bout the an-gels sing-ing, and the old re-demp-tion sto-ry,
Then I re-pent-ed of my sins and won the vic-to-ry.
And some-how Je-sus came and bro't to me the vic-to-ry.
And some sweet day I'll sing up there the song of vic-to-ry.
O vic-to-ry in Je-sus, my Sav-ior, for-ev-er, He sought me and

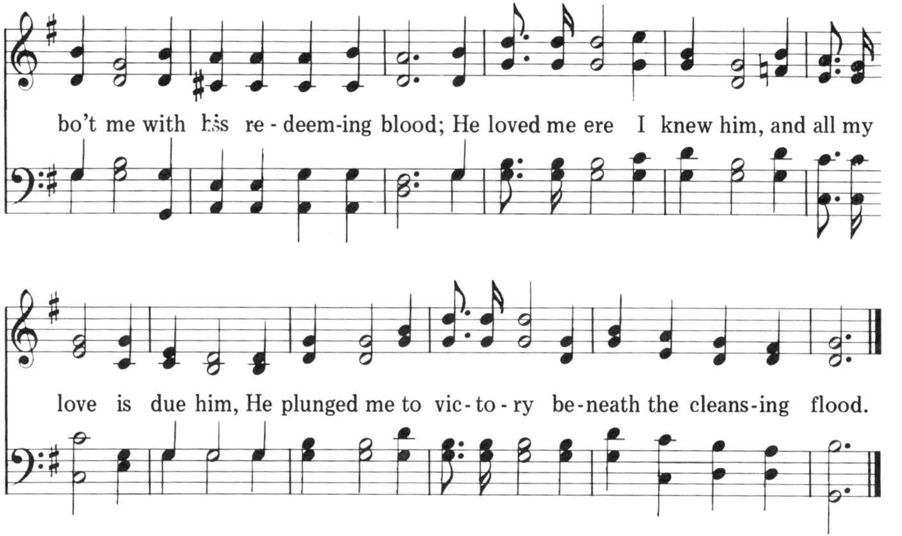

bo't me with his re-deem-ing blood; He loved me ere I knew him, and all my

love is due him, He plunged me to vic-to-ry be-neath the cleans-ing flood.

The Savior's Wondrous Love 476

1. The   Sav - ior's won -drous love Hath made all   na - tions   one,
2. In   this   vast world of   men, A   world so   filled with   pain,
3. In   this   sad world of   war   Can peace be   ev - er   found?
4. The   Mas - ter's new com -mand Was love each oth - er   well.

U - nit - ed   let   us   praise this deed The   Fa - ther's love hath done.
No oth - er theme can   be   our prayer Than this   thy king-dom come.
Un - less the love   of Christ pre - vail, True peace will   not   a - bound.
O broth-ers, let   us   all   u - nite To   do   his   ho - ly will.

477 Now I Belong to Jesus

1. Je - sus, my Lord, will love me for - ev - er, From him no pow'r of
2. Once I was lost in sin's deg - ra - da - tion, Je - sus came down to
3. Joy floods my soul, for Je - sus has saved me, Freed me from sin that
e - vil can sev - er, He gave his life to ran - som my soul,
bring me sal - va - tion, Lift - ed me up from sor - row and shame,
long had en - slaved me, His pre - cious blood he gave to re - deem,
Now I be - long to him; Now I be - long to Je - sus, Je - sus be -
longs to me, Not for the years of time a - lone, But for e - ter - ni - ty.

Words and tune ELLSWORTH, Norman J. Clayton, 1943. Copyright 1943 by Norman J. Clayton.
© Renewed 1966, 1971 by Norman Clayton Publishing Co., owner. Used by permission.

No, Not One 478

1. There's not a friend like the low-ly Je-sus, No, not one! No, not one!
2. No friend like him is so high and ho-ly, No, not one! No, not one!
3. There's not an hour that he is not near us, No, not one! No, not one!
4. Did ev-er saint find this friend for-sake him? No, not one! No, not one!
5. Was e'er a gift like the Sav-ior giv-en? No, not one! No, not one!
None else could heal all our soul's dis-eas-es, No, not one! No, not one!
And yet no friend is so meek and low-ly, No, not one! No, not one!
No night so dark but his love can cheer us, No, not one! No, not one!
Or sin-ner find that he would not take him? No, not one! No, not one!
Will he re-fuse us a home in heav-en? No, not one! No, not one!
Je-sus knows all a-bout our strug-gles, He will guide till the day is done;
There's not a friend like the low-ly Je-sus, No, not one! No, not one!

Words, Johnson Oatman, Jr., 1895. Tune HARPER MEMORIAL, George C. Hugg, 1895.

479 He Is Able to Deliver Thee

1. 'Tis the grand-est theme thro' the a-ges rung; 'Tis the grand-est
2. 'Tis the grand-est theme in the earth or main; 'Tis the grand-est
3. 'Tis the grand-est theme, let the ti-dings roll To the guilt-y
theme for a mor-tal tongue; 'Tis the grand-est theme that the world e'er sung:
theme for a mor-tal strain; 'Tis the grand-est theme, tell the world a-gain:
heart, to the sin-ful soul; Look to God in faith, he will make thee whole:
Our God is a-ble to de-liv-er thee. He is a - ble to de-
a-ble, he is a-ble
liv-er thee, He is a - ble to de-liv-er thee; Tho by
a-ble, he is a-ble
sin op-prest, Go to him for rest; Our God is a-ble to de-liv-er thee.

Daniel 6:16. Words and tune DELIVERANCE, William A. Ogden, 1887.

Somebody's Knocking at Your Door 480

Some - bod - y's knock - ing at your door, Some - bod - y's
knock-ing at your door, O sin - ner, why don't you
an - swer? Some - bod - y's knock - ing at your door.
Fine
Knocks like Je - sus,
Don't you hear him, Some -bod- y's knock - ing at your door;
An - swer Je - sus,
D.S. al Fine
Knocks like Je - sus,
Don't you hear him, Some-bod - y's knock - ing at your door.
An - swer Je - sus,

Revelation 3:20. Words and tune SOMEBODY'S KNOCKING, Negro Spiritual; arranged, Frederick J. Work and John W. Work, Jr., 1907.

481 Just a Closer Walk with Thee

1. I am weak but thou art strong; Je - sus, keep me from all wrong;
2. Thro' this world of toil and snares, If I fal - ter, Lord, who cares?
3. When my fee - ble life is o'er, Time for me will be no more;
Just a clos - er walk with thee, Grant it, Je - sus, is my plea,
D.C. for Refrain
I'll be sat - is - fied as long As I walk, let me walk close to thee.
Who with me my bur - den shares? None but thee, dear Lord, none but thee.
Guide me gent - ly, safe - ly o'er To thy king - dom shore, to thy shore.
Dai - ly walk-ing close to thee, Let it be, dear Lord, let it be.

Words and tune CLOSER WALK, Anonymous.

482 O Love of God Most Full

1. O love of God most full, O love of God most free, Come, warm my
2. Warm as the glow - ing sun, So shines thy love on me; It wraps me
3. The wild - est sea is calm, The tem - pest brings no fear, The dark - est
4. O love of God most full, O love of God most free, Thou warm'st my
heart, come, fill my soul, Come, lead me un - to thee!
'round with kind - ly care, It draws me un - to thee!
night is full of light Be - cause thy love is near.
heart, thou fill'st my soul, With might thou strength'nest me. A - MEN.

Words, Oscar Clute, 1904. Tune TRENTHAM, Robert Jackson, 1888.

1. I saw the cross of Je-sus, When bur-dened with my sin;
2. I love the cross of Je-sus, It tells me what I am—
3. I trust the cross of Je-sus, In ev-'ry try-ing hour,
4. Safe in the cross of Je-sus! There let my wea-ry heart

I sought the cross of Je-sus, To give me peace with-in;
A vile and guilt-y crea-ture, Saved on-ly thro' the Lamb;
My sure and cer-tain ref-uge, My nev-er-fail-ing tow'r;
Still rest in peace un-shak-en, Till with him, ne'er to part;

I brought my soul to Je-sus, He cleansed it in his blood;
No righ-teous-ness nor mer-it, No beau-ty can I plead;
In ev-'ry fear and con-flict, I more than con-queror am;
And then in strains of glo-ry I'll sing his won-drous pow'r,

And in the cross of Je-sus I found my peace with God.
Yet in the cross I glo-ry, My ti-tle there I read.
Liv-ing, I'm safe, or dy-ing, Thro' Christ, the ris-en Lamb.
Where sin can nev-er en-ter, And death is known no more.

Words, Frederick Whitfield, 1861. Tune WHITFIELD, Anonymous.

484 More Love to Thee, O Christ

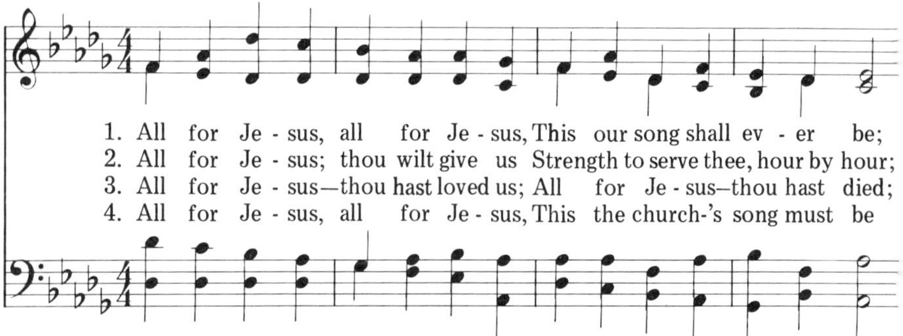

1. More love to thee, O Christ, More love to thee! Hear thou the
2. Once earth-ly joy I craved, Sought peace and rest; Now thee a-
3. Then shall my lat-est breath Whis-per thy praise; This be the

prayer I make On bend-ed knee; This is my ear-nest plea:
lone I seek, Give what is best; This all my prayer shall be:
part-ing cry My heart shall raise; This still its prayer shall be:

More love, O Christ, to thee, More love to thee, More love to thee!

Words, Elizabeth Prentiss, 1856. Tune MORE LOVE TO THEE, William H. Doane, 1870.

485 All for Jesus, All for Jesus

1. All for Je-sus, all for Je-sus, This our song shall ev-er be;
2. All for Je-sus; thou wilt give us Strength to serve thee, hour by hour;
3. All for Je-sus—thou hast loved us; All for Je-sus—thou hast died;
4. All for Je-sus, all for Je-sus, This the church's song must be

Words, William J. Sparrow Simpson, 1887. Tune ALL FOR JESUS, John Stainer, 1887.

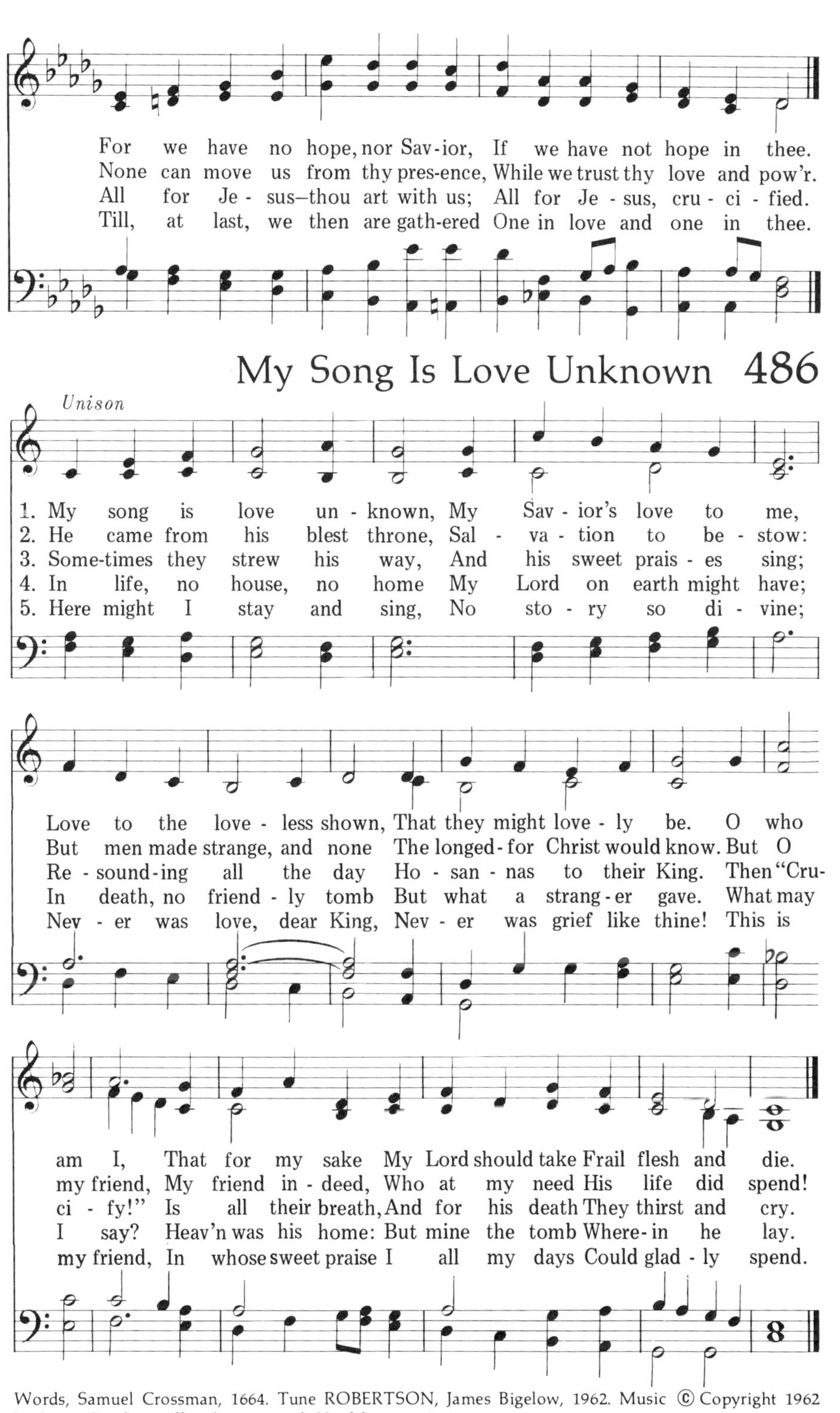
For we have no hope, nor Sav-ior, If we have not hope in thee.
None can move us from thy pres-ence, While we trust thy love and pow'r.
All for Je - sus—thou art with us; All for Je - sus, cru - ci - fied.
Till, at last, we then are gath-ered One in love and one in thee.

My Song Is Love Unknown 486

Unison

1. My song is love un - known, My Sav - ior's love to me,
2. He came from his blest throne, Sal - va - tion to be - stow:
3. Some-times they strew his way, And his sweet prais - es sing;
4. In life, no house, no home My Lord on earth might have;
5. Here might I stay and sing, No sto - ry so di - vine;

Love to the love - less shown, That they might love - ly be. O who
But men made strange, and none The longed - for Christ would know. But O
Re - sound-ing all the day Ho - san - nas to their King. Then "Cru-
In death, no friend - ly tomb But what a strang - er gave. What may
Nev - er was love, dear King, Nev - er was grief like thine! This is

am I, That for my sake My Lord should take Frail flesh and die.
my friend, My friend in - deed, Who at my need His life did spend!
ci - fy!" Is all their breath, And for his death They thirst and cry.
I say? Heav'n was his home: But mine the tomb Where- in he lay.
my friend, In whose sweet praise I all my days Could glad - ly spend.

487 Since Jesus Came into My Heart

1. What a won-der-ful change in my life has been wrought
2. I'm pos-sessed of a hope that is stead-fast and sure,
3. There's a light in the val-ley of death now for me,
4. I shall go there to dwell in that cit-y, I know,

Since Je-sus came in-to my heart! I have light in my soul
Since Je-sus came in-to my heart! And no dark clouds of doubt
Since Je-sus came in-to my heart! And the gates of the cit-
Since Je-sus came in-to my heart! And I'm hap-py, so hap-

for which long I had sought, Since Je-sus came in-to my heart!
now my path-way ob-scure, Since Je-sus came in-to my heart!
y be-yond I can see, Since Je-sus came in-to my heart!
py, as on-ward I go, Since Je-sus came in-to my heart!

Since Je-sus came in-to my heart, Since
Since Je-sus came in, came in-to my heart, Since

Words, Rufus H. McDaniel, 1914. Tune MCDANIEL, Charles H. Gabriel, 1914. Copyright 1914 by Charles H. Gabriel. © Copyright Renewed 1942 (extended), The Rodeheaver Co., Owner. Used by permission.

Je - sus came in - to my heart, Floods of joy o'er my
Je - sus came in, came in - to my heart,
soul like the sea bil - lows roll, Since Je - sus came in - to my heart.

Jerusalem, My Happy Home 488

1.*Je - ru - sa - lem, my hap - py home, When shall I come to thee?
2. Thy saints are crowned with glo - ry great; They see God face to face;
3. There Da - vid stands with harp in hand As mas - ter of the choir;
4. Je - ru - sa - lem, Je - ru - sa - lem, God grant that I may see
When shall my sor - rows have an end? Thy joys, when shall I see?
They tri - umph still, they still re - joice; Most hap - py is their case.
Ten thou - sand times that man were blest That might this mu - sic hear.
Thine end - less joy, and of the same Par - tak - er ev - er be!

Words, F.P.B., 16th Century. Tune LAND OF REST, American Folk Hymn; arranged, Annabel M. Buchanan, 1938. Copyright 1938 by J. Fischer & Bro. Copyright renewed 1966. Used with permission. All rights reserved. *Revelation 21:2.

489 Face to Face with Christ My Savior

1. Face to face with Christ, my Sav - ior, Face to face—what will it be,
2. On - ly faint - ly now I see him, With the dark - ling veil be - tween,
3. What re - joic - ing in his pres - ence, When are ban-ish'd grief and pain;
4. Face to face—oh, bliss-ful mo - ment! Face to face—to see and know;

When with rap-ture I be - hold him, Je - sus Christ who died for me.
But a bless-ed day is com - ing, When his glo - ry shall be seen.
When the crook-ed ways are straighten'd, And the dark things shall be plain.
Face to face with my Re-deem - er, Je - sus Christ who loves me so.

Face to face I shall be - hold him, Far be-yond the star - ry sky;

Face to face in all his glo - ry, I shall see him by and by!

Words, Carrie E. Breck, 1898. Tune FACE TO FACE, Grant Colfax Tullar, 1898.

On Jordan's Stormy Banks 490

1. On Jor-dan's storm-y banks I stand, And cast a wish-ful eye
2. All o'er those wide-ex-tend-ed plains Shines one e-ter-nal day;
3. No chill-ing winds nor pois'nous breath Can reach that healthful shore;
4. When shall I reach that hap-py place, And be for-ev-er blest?

To Ca-naan's fair and hap-py land, Where my pos-ses-sions lie.
There God the Son for-ev-er reigns And scat-ters night a-way.
Sick-ness and sor-row, pain and death Are felt and feared no more.
When shall I see my Fa-ther's face, And in his bos-om rest?

I am bound for the promised land, I am bound for the promised land;

O who will come and go with me? I am bound for the promised land.

Words, Samuel Stennett, 1787. Tune PROMISED LAND, American Folk Hymn; arranged,
Rigdon M. McIntosh, 1895.

491 When We All Get to Heaven

1. Sing the won-drous love of Je-sus, Sing his mer-cy
2. While we walk the pil-grim path-way, Clouds will o-ver-
3. Let us then be true and faith-ful, Trust-ing, serv-ing
4. On-ward to the prize be-fore us! Soon his beau-ty

and his grace: In the man-sions bright and bless-ed,
spread the sky; But when trav-'ling days are o-ver,
ev-'ry day; Just one glimpse of him in glo-ry
we'll be-hold; Soon the pearl-y gates will o-pen;

He'll pre-pare for us a place.
Not a shad-ow, not a sigh.
Will the toils of life re-pay.
We shall tread the streets of gold.
1. for us a place.

When we all get to
When we all

heav-en, What a day of re-joic-ing that will be! When we
What a day of re-joic-ing that will be!

Words, Eliza E. Hewitt, 1898. Tune HEAVEN, Emily D. Wilson, 1898.

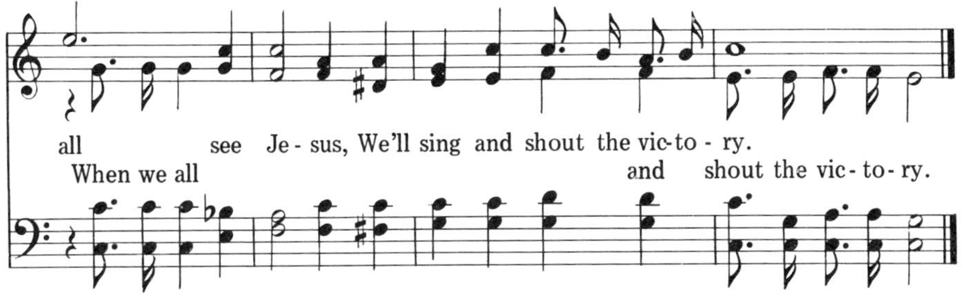

all   see Je-sus, We'll sing and shout the vic-to-ry.
When we all   and   shout the vic-to-ry.

I Know Not What the Future 492

1. I   know not what the fu - ture hath Of   mar - vel or   sur - prise,
2. And if   my heart and flesh are weak To   bear an un - tried pain,
3. And so   be - side the si - lent sea I   wait the muf - fled   oar;
4. I   know not where his is - lands lift Their frond-ed   palms in   air;
5. And thou, O Lord, by whom are seen Thy crea-tures as   they   be,

As - sured a - lone that life   and death His mer - cy un - der - lies.
The bruis - ed reed thou wilt   not break, But strength-en   and sus - stain.
No harm from him can come   to me On o - cean or   on shore.
I   on - ly know I can - not drift Be - yond   his love and care.
For-give   me if   too close   I lean My hu - man heart on thee.

Words, John Greenleaf Whittier, 1867. Tune IRISH, *A Collection of Hymns and Sacred Poems*, Dublin, 1749.

493 Sing We the King

1. Sing we the King who is com-ing to reign, Glo-ry to
2. Souls shall be saved from the bur-den of sin, Doubt shall not
3. King-dom of Christ, for thy com-ing we pray, Has-ten, O

Je-sus, the Lamb that was slain. Life and sal-va-tion his
dark-en his wit-ness with-in. Hell hath no ter-rors, and
Fa-ther, the dawn of the day When this new song thy cre-

em-pire shall bring, Joy to the na-tions when Je-sus is King.
death hath no sting; Love is vic-to-rious when Je-sus is King.
a-tion shall sing, Sa-tan is van-quished and Je-sus is King.

Come let us sing Praise to our King,
Come let us sing Praise to our

Words, Charles Silvester Horne, c. 1910. Tune GLORY SONG, Charles H. Gabriel, 1900.

Must Jesus Bear the Cross Alone 494

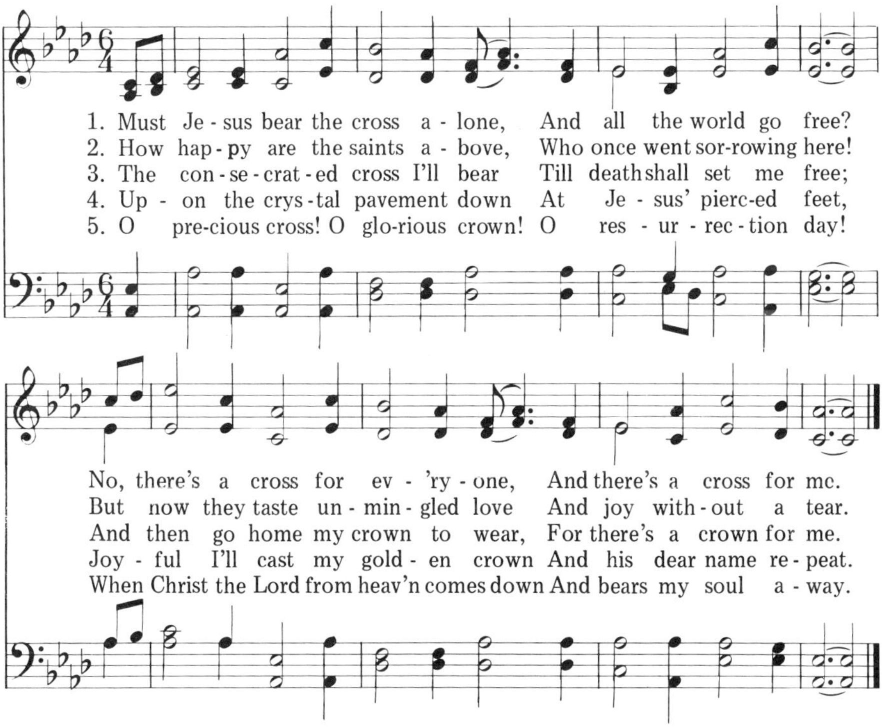

Words, Thomas Shepherd, 1693, and others. Tune MAITLAND, George N. Allen, 1844.

495 There's a Land That Is Fairer than Day

1. There's a land that is fair-er than day, And by faith we can
2. We shall sing on that beau-ti-ful shore The me-lo-di-ous
3. To our boun-ti-ful Fa-ther a-bove, We will of-fer the

see it a-far; For the Fa-ther waits o-ver the way To pre-
songs of the blest, And our spir-its shall sor-row no more, Not a
trib-ute of praise For the glo-ri-ous gift of his love, And the

pare us a dwell-ing place there. In the sweet by and
sigh for the bless-ing of rest.
bless-ings that hal-low our days. In the sweet

by, We shall meet on that beau-ti-ful shore; In the
by and by, by and by;

sweet by and by, We shall meet on that beau-ti-ful shore.
In the sweet by and by,

Words, Sanford F. Bennett, 1868. Tune SWEET BY AND BY, Joseph P. Webster, 1868.

Shall We Gather at the River 496

1. Shall we gath-er at the riv-er, Where bright an-gel feet have trod;
2. On the mar-gin of the riv-er, Wash-ing up its sil-ver spray,
3. Ere we reach the shin-ing riv-er, Lay we ev-'ry bur-den down;
4. Soon we'll reach the shin-ing riv-er, Soon our pil-grim-age will cease;

With its crys-tal tide for-ev-er Flow-ing by the throne of God?
We will walk and wor-ship ev-er, All the hap-py gold-en day.
Grace our spir-its will de-liv-er, And pro-vide a robe and crown.
Soon our hap-py hearts will quiv-er With the mel-o-dy of peace.

Yes, we'll gath-er at the riv-er, The beau-ti-ful, the beau-ti-ful riv-er;

Gath-er with the saints at the riv-er That flows by the throne of God.

Revelation 22:1. Words and tune HANSON PLACE, Robert Lowry, 1864.

497 O That Will Be Glory

1. When all my la - bors and tri - als are o'er, And I am
2. When, by the gift of his in - fi - nite grace, I am ac -
3. Friends will be there I have loved long a - go; Joy like a

safe on that beau - ti - ful shore, Just to be near the dear
cord - ed in heav - en a place, Just to be there and to
riv - er a - round me will flow; Yet just a smile from my

Lord I a - dore, Will thro' the a - ges be glo - ry for me.
look on his face, Will thro' the a - ges be glo - ry for me.
Sav - ior, I know, Will thro' the a - ges be glo - ry for me.

O that will be glo - ry for me, Glo - ry for
O that will be glo - ry for me,

me, glo - ry for me, When by his grace I shall
Glo - ry for me, glo - ry for me,

Words and tune GLORY SONG, Charles H. Gabriel, 1900.

look on his face, That will be glo-ry, be glo-ry for me.

Give Me the Wings of Faith 498

1. Give me the wings of faith to rise With-
2. I asked them whence their vic-t'ry came: They,
3. They marked the foot-steps that he trod, His
4. Our glo-rious lead-er claims our praise, For

in the veil and see The saints a-bove, how
with u-nit-ed breath, As-cribe their con-quest
zeal in-spired their breast; And fol-lowing their in-
his own pat-tern giv'n, While the long cloud of

great their joys, How bright their glo-ries be.
to the Lamb; Their tri-umph to his death.
car-nate God, They gained the prom-ised rest.
wit-ness-es Show the same path to heav'n. A-MEN.

499 When the Morning Comes

1. Tri - als dark on ev - 'ry hand, And we can - not un - der - stand
2. Oft our cher -ished plans have failed, Dis - ap - point-ments have pre-vailed,
3. Temp - ta - tions, hid - den snares Of - ten take us un - a - wares,
All the ways that God would lead us to that bless - ed promised land;
And we've wandered in the dark-ness, heav - y - heart-ed and a - lone;
And our hearts are made to bleed for some tho't-less word or deed,
But he'll guide us with his eye, And we'll fol - low till we die; We will
But we're trust-ing in the Lord, And, ac - cord-ing to his Word, We will
And we won - der why the test When we try to do our best, But we'll
un - der-stand it bet - ter by and by. By and by, when the morn-ing
comes, When the saints of God are gath - ered home, We will tell the sto - ry

Words and tune BY AND BY, Charles A. Tindley, c. 1905; altered and arranged, B. B. McKinney, 1937.

How we've o - ver-come; We will un - der-stand it bet - ter by and by.

Jesus, Still Lead On 500

1. Je - sus, still lead on Till our rest be won; And, al -
2. If the way be drear, If the foe be near, Let not
3. When we seek re - lief From a long - felt grief, When temp -
4. Je - sus, still lead on, Till our rest be won; Heav'n - ly

though the way be cheer -less, We will fol - low, calm and fear - less:
faith - less fears o'er -take us, Let not faith and hope for - sake us:
ta - tions come al - lur - ing, Make us pa - tient and en - dur - ing:
Lead -er, still di - rect us, Still sup - port, con - sole, pro - tect us,

Guide us by thy hand To our fa - ther - land.
For thro' man - y a foe To our home we go.
Show us that bright shore Where we weep no more.
Till we safe - ly stand In our fa - ther - land! A - MEN.

Words, Nicolaus L. von Zinzendorf, 1778; translated, Jane L. Borthwick, 1846. Tune SEELENBRÄUTIGAM, Adam Drese, 1698.

501 We Shall Walk Through the Valley

1. We shall walk thro' the val - ley in peace;
2. There will be no sor - row there;
3. We shall meet our loved ones there;
4. We shall meet our Sav - ior there;
We shall walk thro' the val - ley in peace;
There will be no sor - row there;
We shall meet our loved ones there;
We shall meet our Sav - ior there;
For Je - sus him - self will be our Lead - er.
For Je - sus him - self will be our Lead - er.
For Je - sus him - self will be our Lead - er.
For Je - sus him - self will be our Lead - er.
We shall walk thro' the val - ley in peace.
There will be no sor - row there.
We shall meet our loved ones there.
We shall meet our Sav - ior there.

Words and tune VALLEY, Anonymous.

Day of Judgment! Day of Wonders! 502

1. Day of judg-ment! Day of won - ders! Hark, the trum-pet's
2. See the Judge, our na - ture wear - ing, Clothed in maj - es-
3. At his call the dead a - wak - en, Rise to life from
4. Then to all who have con-fessed him, Loved and served the

aw - ful sound, Loud - er than a thou - sand thun - ders,
ty di - vine; Ye who love the Lord's ap - pear - ing
earth and sea; All the pow'rs of na - ture, shak - en,
Lord be - low, He will say, "Come near, ye bless - ed,

Shakes the vast cre - a - tion round: How the sum - mons,
Then shall say, "This God is mine!" Gra - cious Sav - ior,
At his call pre - pare to flee: Care - less sin - ner,
See the king - dom I be - stow: You for - ev - er,

how the sum - mons Will the sin - ner's heart con - found!
gra - cious Sav - ior, Own me on that day as thine.
care - less sin - ner, What will then be - come of thee?
you for - ev - er Shall my love and glo - ry know."

Words, John Newton, 1774. Tune LAUDA ANIMA (Goss), John Goss, 1869.

503 When the Roll Is Called Up Yonder

1. When the trum-pet of the Lord shall sound, and time shall be no more,
2. On that bright and cloudless morning when the dead in Christ shall rise,
3. Let us la - bor for the Mas - ter from the dawn till set - ting sun,

And the morn - ing breaks, e - ter - nal, bright, and fair; When the
And the glo - ry of his res - ur - rec - tion share; When his
Let us talk of all his won-drous love and care; Then when

saved of earth shall gath - er o - ver on the oth - er shore,
cho - sen ones shall gath - er to their home be - yond the skies,
all of life is o - ver, and our work on earth is done,

And the roll is called up yon - der, I'll be there. When the

roll is called up yon - der, When the
When the roll is called up yon - der, I'll be there,

1 Thessalonians 4:16. Words and tune ROLL CALL, James M. Black, 1893.

roll is called up yon - der, When the roll is
When the roll is called up yon-der, I'll be there, When the roll is
called up yon - der, When the roll is called up yon - der, I'll be there.

There Is a Land of Pure Delight 504

1. There is a land of pure de - light, Where saints im - mor - tal reign,
2. There ev - er - last - ing spring a - bides, And nev - er - with - 'ring flow'rs:
3. O could we make our doubts re - move, Those gloom - y doubts that rise,
4. Could we but climb where Mo - ses stood, And view the land-scape o'er,

In - fin - ite day ex - cludes the night, And plea - sures ban - ish pain.
Death, like a nar - row sea, di - vides This heav'n - ly land from ours.
And see the Ca - naan that we love With un - be - cloud - ed eyes.
Not Jor - dan's stream, nor death's cold flood Should fright us from the shore.

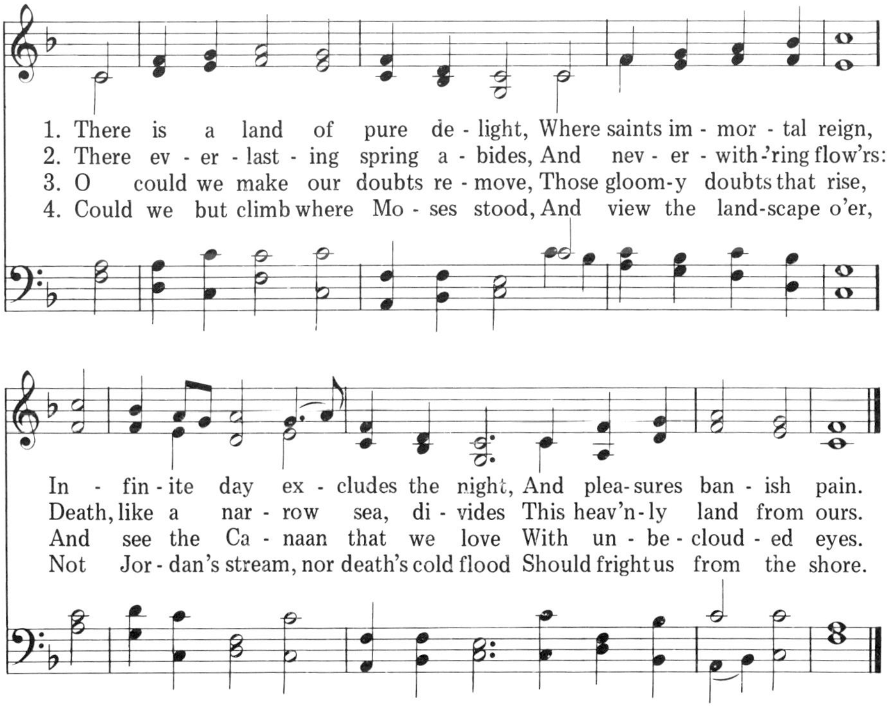

Words, Isaac Watts, 1707. Tune TWENTY-FOURTH, Amzi Chapin, 1813.

505 We're Marching to Zion

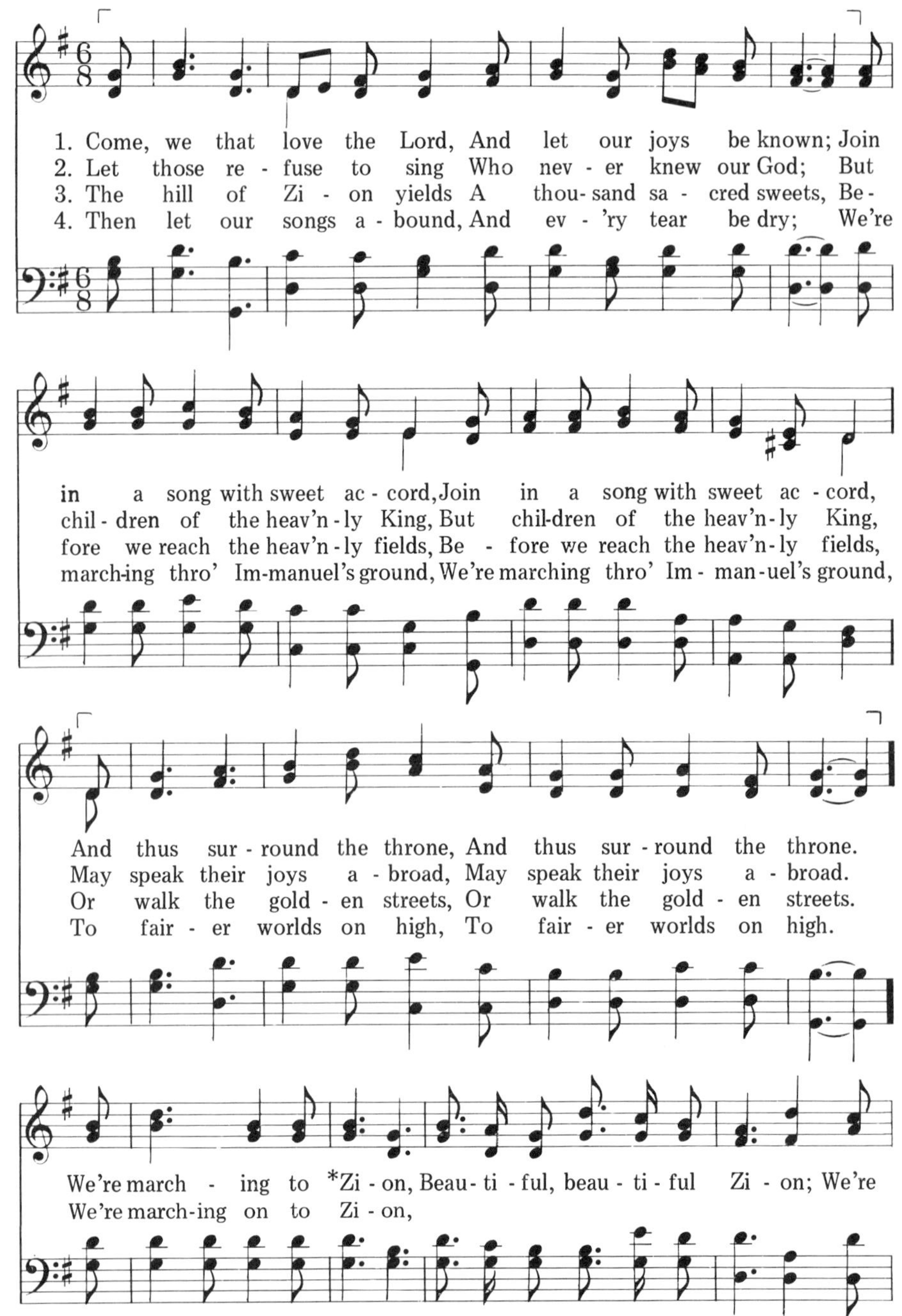

1. Come, we that love the Lord, And let our joys be known; Join
2. Let those re - fuse to sing Who nev - er knew our God; But
3. The hill of Zi - on yields A thou-sand sa - cred sweets, Be -
4. Then let our songs a - bound, And ev - 'ry tear be dry; We're
in a song with sweet ac - cord, Join in a song with sweet ac - cord,
chil - dren of the heav'n - ly King, But chil-dren of the heav'n-ly King,
fore we reach the heav'n - ly fields, Be - fore we reach the heav'n-ly fields,
march-ing thro' Im-manuel's ground, We're marching thro' Im - man-uel's ground,
And thus sur - round the throne, And thus sur - round the throne.
May speak their joys a - broad, May speak their joys a - broad.
Or walk the gold - en streets, Or walk the gold - en streets.
To fair - er worlds on high, To fair - er worlds on high.
We're march - ing to *Zi - on, Beau-ti - ful, beau - ti - ful Zi - on; We're
We're march-ing on to Zi - on,

Words, Isaac Watts, 1707. Tune MARCHING TO ZION and Refrain, Robert Lowry, 1867. *Psalm 2:6. By extension this refers to the new Jerusalem.

march-ing up-ward to Zi - on, The beau-ti-ful cit-y of God.
Zi-on, Zi-on,

By and By 506

O by and by, by and by, I'm going to lay down my

heav-y load. 1. O when I get to heav-en going to
There's no-bod-y there to
2. O Chris-tian, won't you
That Je-sus hath done

sing and shout, I'm going to lay down my heav-y load.
turn me out, I'm going to lay down my heav-y load.
rise and tell, I'm going to lay down my heav-y load.
all things well, I'm going to lay down my heav-y load.

Words and tune HEAVY LOAD, Traditional Negro Spiritual; arranged, John W. Work, Jr., and Frederick J. Work, 1907.

507 O God of Our Fathers

1. O God of our fa - thers, we praise and a - dore thee
2. Help us to be faith - ful to thee and thy king - dom,
3. Our task is no great - er than that which our fa - thers
4. We now re - af - firm our un - dy - ing de - vo - tion;

For all thy great mer - cies through years that are gone;
Thy church, and the work of our Christ in all lands:
As - sumed with fi - del - i - ty, cour - age, and pride:
We pray thou wilt fill us with all strength and grace:

Thy guid - ance and good - ness thro' man - y gen - er - a - tions
May loy - al - ty, sac - ri - fice, cour - age now at - tend us,
We know that all moun - tains will van - ish now be - fore us
Crown all high en - deav - ors with vic - to - ries for - ev - er,

Have brought us now at last to a new day's bright dawn.
And bring to ful - lest tri - umph thy work in our hands.
If thou wilt point the way and re - main at our side.
And may we run with faith - ful - ness life's fate - ful race. A - MEN.

America the Beautiful 508

1. O beau - ti - ful for spa - cious skies, For am - ber waves of grain,
2. O beau - ti - ful for pil - grim feet, Whose stern, im - pas - sioned stress
3. O beau - ti - ful for he - roes proved In lib - er - at - ing strife,
4. O beau - ti - ful for pa - triot dream That sees, be - yond the years,
For pur - ple moun - tain maj - es - ties A - bove the fruit - ed plain!
A thor - ough - fare for free - dom beat A - cross the wil - der - ness!
Who more than self their coun - try loved, And mer - cy more than life!
Thine al - a - bas - ter cit - ies gleam, Un - dimmed by hu - man tears!
A - mer - i - ca! A - mer - i - ca! God shed his grace on thee,
A - mer - i - ca! A - mer - i - ca! God mend thine ev - 'ry flaw,
A - mer - i - ca! A - mer - i - ca! May God thy gold re - fine,
A - mer - i - ca! A - mer - i - ca! God shed his grace on thee,
And crown thy good with broth - er - hood From sea to shin - ing sea.
Con - firm thy soul in self - con - trol, Thy lib - er - ty in law.
Till all suc - cess be no - ble - ness, And ev - 'ry gain di - vine.
And crown thy good with broth - er - hood From sea to shin - ing sea.

Words, Katharine Lee Bates, 1893. Tune MATERNA, Samuel A. Ward, c. 1885.

509 God Is Working His Purpose Out

Unison

1. God is work-ing his pur-pose out As
2. From the east to ut-most west, Wher-
3. March we forth in the strength of God With the
4. All we can do is noth-ing worth Un-

year suc-ceeds to year; God is work-ing his
e'er man's foot hath trod, By the mouth of man-y
ban-ner of Christ un-furled, That the light of the glo-rious
less God bless-es the deed; Vain-ly we hope for the

pur-pose out, And the time is draw-ing near;
mes-sen-gers Goes forth the voice of God;
gos-pel of truth May shine thro'-out the world;
har-vest-tide Till God gives life to the seed; Yet

Octaves to the end

Words, Arthur C. Ainger, 1894. Tune PURPOSE, Martin Shaw, 1931. Music from *Enlarged Songs of Praise* by permission of Oxford University Press.

Near-er and near-er draws the time, The time that shall sure-ly be,
Give ear to me, ye con-ti-nents, Ye isles, give ear to me,
Fight we the fight with sor-row and sin To set their cap-tives free,
near-er and near-er draws the time, The time that shall sure-ly be,

When the earth shall be filled with the glo-ry of God As the
That the earth may be filled with the glo-ry of God As the
That the earth may be filled with the glo-ry of God As the
When the earth shall be filled with the glo-ry of God As the

St.1,2,3
St.4

wa-ters cov-er the sea.
wa-ters cov-er the sea.
wa-ters cov-er the sea.
wa-ters cov-er the sea.

510 Mine Eyes Have Seen the Glory

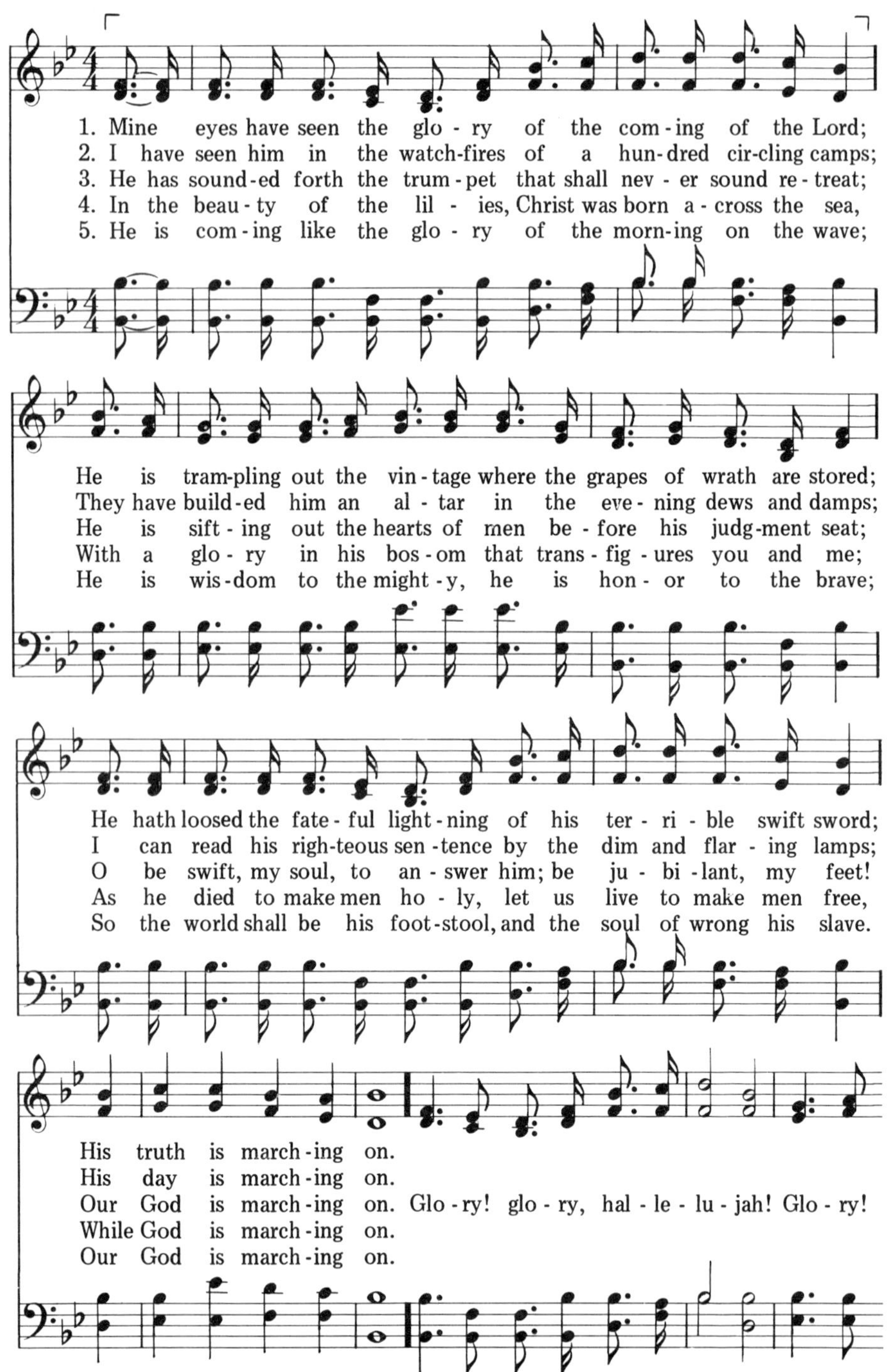
1. Mine eyes have seen the glo-ry of the com-ing of the Lord;
2. I have seen him in the watch-fires of a hun-dred cir-cling camps;
3. He has sound-ed forth the trum-pet that shall nev-er sound re-treat;
4. In the beau-ty of the lil-ies, Christ was born a-cross the sea,
5. He is com-ing like the glo-ry of the morn-ing on the wave;

He is tram-pling out the vin-tage where the grapes of wrath are stored;
They have build-ed him an al-tar in the eve-ning dews and damps;
He is sift-ing out the hearts of men be-fore his judg-ment seat;
With a glo-ry in his bos-om that trans-fig-ures you and me;
He is wis-dom to the might-y, he is hon-or to the brave;

He hath loosed the fate-ful light-ning of his ter-ri-ble swift sword;
I can read his righ-teous sen-tence by the dim and flar-ing lamps;
O be swift, my soul, to an-swer him; be ju-bi-lant, my feet!
As he died to make men ho-ly, let us live to make men free,
So the world shall be his foot-stool, and the soul of wrong his slave.

His truth is march-ing on.
His day is march-ing on.
Our God is march-ing on. Glo-ry! glo-ry, hal-le-lu-jah! Glo-ry!
While God is march-ing on.
Our God is march-ing on.

Words, Julia Ward Howe, 1861. Tune BATTLE HYMN, American Folk Song, 19th Century.

glo-ry, hal-le-lu-jah! Glo-ry! glo-ry, hal-le-lu-jah! Our God is marching on.

My Country, 'Tis of Thee 511

1. My coun-try, 'tis of thee, Sweet land of lib-er-ty,
2. My na-tive coun-try, thee, Land of the no-ble free,
3. Let mu-sic swell the breeze, And ring from all the trees
4. Our fa-thers' God, to thee, Au-thor of lib-er-ty,

Of thee I sing: Land where my fa-thers died, Land of the
Thy name I love: I love thy rocks and rills, Thy woods and
Sweet free-dom's song: Let mor-tal tongues a-wake; Let all that
To thee we sing: Long may our land be bright With free-dom's

pil-grims' pride, From ev-'ry moun-tain-side Let free-dom ring!
tem-pled hills; My heart with rap-ture thrills Like that a-bove.
breathe par-take; Let rocks their si-lence break, The sound pro-long.
ho-ly light; Pro-tect us by thy might, Great God, our King!

Words, Samuel F. Smith, 1831. Tune AMERICA, Anonymous.

512 The Star-Spangled Banner

1. O say, can you see, by the dawn's ear - ly light,
2. O thus be it ev - er when free men shall stand
What so proud - ly we hailed at the twi-light's last gleam - ing,
Be - tween their loved homes and the war's des - o - la - tion;
Whose broad stripes and bright stars, thro' the per - il - ous fight,
Blest with vic - t'ry and peace, may the heav'n - res - cued land
O'er the ram - parts we watched, were so gal - lant - ly stream-ing?
Praise the Pow'r that hath made and pre-served us a na - tion!

Words, Francis Scott Key, 1814. Tune NATIONAL ANTHEM, Origin Unknown, 18th Century.

And the rock - ets' red glare, the bombs burst - ing in air
Then con - quer we must, when our cause it is just;

Gave proof thro' the night that our flag was still there.
And this be our mot-to: "In God is our trust!"

O say, does that Star - span - gled Ban - ner yet
And the Star - span - gled Ban - ner in tri - umph shall

wave O'er the land of the free and the home of the brave?
wave O'er the land of the free and the home of the brave.

Scriptures for Individual, Unison, Responsive, or Antiphonal Reading

The selections of Scripture that follow are designed to be used by the congregation in worship. Four translations of the Bible are represented, the *King James Version* being the major source. Others included are the *Revised Standard Version, Today's English Version,* and the *New American Standard Bible.* In determining the translation to be used, each passage was studied for clarity of thought and for ease of use in group reading. Most of the readings are complete units of Scripture, drawn from single chapters. Where a reading is not a complete passage, the source of each portion of the reading is clearly indicated.

The selections may be read aloud in unison, responsively, or antiphonally by the congregation, the choir, the choir and congregation, or the choir and worship leader. The individual worshiper may wish to read them silently, of course. Those selections designed for unison reading are printed in light face type. In Scriptures designed for responsive or antiphonal reading, light face type and bold face type separated by a slash mark / indicate the alternation of reader. Of course, any of the Scriptures may be read in unison if the worship leader so desires.

Both a Topical Index and a Scriptural Index are provided for the readings. The Topical Index is closely aligned with the Topical Index of the hymns to facilitate a close coordination of hymns and Scripture readings in the worship service.

513

Praise ye the Lord. / **Praise God in his sanctuary:** / praise him in the firmament of his power. / **Praise him for his mighty acts:** / praise him according to his excellent greatness.

Praise him with the sound of the trumpet: / praise him with the psaltery and harp. / **Praise him with the timbrel and dance:** / praise him with stringed instruments and organs. / **Praise him upon the loud cymbals:** / praise him upon the high sounding cymbals.

Let every thing that hath breath praise the Lord. / Praise ye the Lord. / **Praise ye the Lord.**

Psalm 150

514

Lift up your heads, O ye gates; and be ye lift up, ye everlasting doors; / **and the King of glory shall come in.** / Who is this King of glory? / **The Lord strong and mighty, the Lord mighty in battle.**

Lift up your heads, O ye gates; even lift them up, ye everlasting doors; / **and the King of glory shall come in.** / Who is this King of glory? / **The Lord of hosts, he is the King of glory.**

Psalm 24:7–10

515

Bless the Lord, O my soul: and all that is within me, bless his holy name. / **Bless the Lord, O my soul, and forget not all his benefits:** / who forgiveth all thine iniquities; who healeth all thy diseases; / **who re-**deemeth thy life from destruction; **who crowneth thee with lovingkindness and tender mercies.**

The Lord is merciful and gracious, slow to anger, and plenteous in mercy. / **He will not always chide: neither will he keep his anger for ever.**

He hath not dealt with us after our sins; nor rewarded us according to our iniquities. / **For as the heaven is high above the earth, so great is his mercy toward them that fear him.** / As far as the east is from the west, so far hath he removed our transgressions from us. / **Like as a father pitieth his children, so the Lord pitieth them that fear him.**

Bless the Lord, ye his angels, that excel in strength, that do his commandments, hearkening unto the voice of his word. / **Bless ye the Lord, all ye his hosts; ye ministers of his, that do his pleasure.** / Bless the Lord, all his works in all places of his dominion: / **bless the Lord, O my soul.**

Psalm 103:1–4,8–13,20–22

516

The Lord is in his holy temple: let all the earth keep silence before him.

Habakkuk 2:20

517

Blessed is the one who comes in the name of the Lord; We have blessed you from the house of the Lord.

The Lord is God, and He has given us light.

Psalm 118:26–27 (NASB)

518

The heavens declare the glory of God; / **and the firmament showeth his handiwork.** / Day unto day uttereth speech, / **and night unto night showeth knowledge.** / There is no speech nor language, where their voice is not heard.

The law of the Lord is perfect, converting the soul: the testimony of the Lord is sure, making wise the simple. / The statutes of the Lord are right, rejoicing the heart: / **the commandment of the Lord is pure, enlightening the eyes.**

The fear of the Lord is clean, enduring for ever: / **the judgments of the Lord are true and righteous altogether.** / More to be desired are they than gold, yea, than much fine gold: / **sweeter also than honey and the honeycomb.**

Moreover by them is thy servant warned: / **and in keeping of them there is great reward.** / Who can understand his errors? / **cleanse thou me from secret faults.** / Keep back thy servant also from presumptuous sins; let them not have dominion over me: / **then shall I be upright,** / and I shall be innocent from the great transgression.

Let the words of my mouth, and the meditation of my heart, be acceptable in thy sight, O Lord, my strength, and my redeemer.

Psalm 19:1–3, 7–14

519

I was glad when they said unto me, Let us go into the house of the Lord.

Psalm 122:1

520

How amiable are thy tabernacles, O Lord of hosts! / **My soul longeth, yea, even fainteth for the courts of the Lord: my heart and my flesh crieth out for the living God.**

Yea, the sparrow hath found an house, and the swallow a nest for herself, where she may lay her young, even thine altars, O Lord of hosts, my King, and my God. / **Blessed are they that dwell in thy house: they will be still praising thee. For a day in thy courts is better than a thousand [elsewhere].**

I had rather be a doorkeeper in the house of my God, than to dwell in the tents of wickedness. / **For the Lord God is a sun and shield: the Lord will give grace and glory:** / no good thing will he withhold from them that walk uprightly. / **O Lord of hosts, blessed is the man that trusteth in thee.** *Psalm 84:1–4, 10–12*

521

Make a joyful noise unto the Lord, all ye lands. / **Serve the Lord with gladness: come before his presence with singing.**

Know ye that the Lord he is God: it is he that hath made us, and not we ourselves; / **we are his people, and the sheep of his pasture.**

Enter into his gates with thanksgiving, and into his courts with praise: / **be thankful unto him, and bless his name.** / For the Lord is good; his mercy is everlasting; / **and his truth endureth to all generations.**

Psalm 100

522

O come, let us sing unto the Lord: / **let us make a joyful noise to the rock of our salvation.** / Let us come before his presence with thanksgiving, / **and make a joyful noise unto him with psalms.** / For the Lord is a great God, and a great King above all gods.

In his hand are the deep places of the earth: the strength of the hills is his also. The sea is his, and he made it: and his hands formed the dry land.

O come, let us worship and bow down: let us kneel before the Lord our maker. For the Lord is a great God, and a great King above all gods. / **He is our God.**   *Psalm 95:1–6,3,7*

523

O Lord our Lord, how excellent is thy name in all the earth! who hast set thy glory above the heavens.

When I consider thy heavens, the work of thy fingers, the moon and the stars, which thou hast ordained; / what is man, that thou art mindful of him? and the son of man, that thou visitest him? / **For thou hast made him a little lower than the angels, and hast crowned him with glory and honor.**

Thou madest him to have dominion over the works of thy hands: thou hast put all things under his feet: / **all sheep and oxen, yea, and the beasts of the field;** / the fowl of the air, and the fish of the sea, and whatsoever passeth through the paths of the seas.

O Lord our Lord, how excellent is thy name in all the earth!

Psalm 8:1,3–9

524

O sing to the Lord a new song; sing to the Lord, all the earth! / **Sing to the Lord, bless his name; tell of his salvation from day to day.**

Declare his glory among the nations, his marvelous works among all the peoples! / **For great is the Lord, and greatly to be praised; he is to be feared above all gods.** / For all the gods of the peoples are idols; but the Lord made the heavens. / **Honor and majesty are before him; strength and beauty are in his sanctuary.**

Ascribe to the Lord, O families of the peoples, ascribe to the Lord glory and strength! / **Ascribe to the Lord the glory due his name; bring an offering, and come into his courts!**

Worship the Lord in holy array; tremble before him, all the earth! / **Say among the nations, "The Lord reigns!"**

Psalm 96:1–10 (RSV)

525

Every man shall give as he is able, according to the blessing of the Lord thy God which he hath given thee.

Deuteronomy 16:17

526

Praise ye the Lord. Praise God in his sanctuary.

Psalm 150:1

527

Sing a new song to the Lord; he has done wonderful things! By his own power and holy strength, he has won the victory. / **The Lord announced his victory; he made his saving power known to the nations.**

He kept his promise to the people of Israel, with constant love and loyalty for them. All people everywhere have seen the victory of our God!

Sing for joy to the Lord, all the earth; praise him with songs and shouts of joy! / Sing praises to the Lord with harps; play music on the harps! / **With trumpets and horns, shout for joy before the Lord, the king!**
Psalm 98:1–6 (TEV)

528

The earth is the Lord's, and the fulness thereof; the world, and they that dwell therein. For he hath founded it upon the seas, and established it upon the floods.

Who shall ascend into the hill of the Lord? or who shall stand in his holy place? He that hath clean hands, and a pure heart; who hath not lifted up his soul unto vanity, nor sworn deceitfully. He shall receive the blessing from the Lord, and righteousness from the God of his salvation.
Psalm 24:1–5

529

I love the Lord, because he hath heard my voice and my supplications. Because he hath inclined his ear unto me, therefore will I call upon him as long as I live. / **Gracious is the Lord, and righteous; yea, our God is merciful.**

What shall I render unto the Lord for all his benefits toward me? / **I will take the cup of salvation, and call upon the name of the Lord.** / I will offer to thee the sacrifice of thanksgiving, and will call upon the name of the Lord. / **I will pay my vows unto the Lord now in the presence of all his people, in the courts of the Lord's house, in the midst of thee, O Jerusalem.** / Praise ye the Lord. / **Praise ye the Lord.**
Psalm 116:1–2,5,12–13,17–19

530

Surely the Lord is in this place . . . This is none other but the house of God.
Genesis 28:16–17

531

God be merciful unto us, and bless us; / **and cause his face to shine upon us;** / that thy way may be known upon earth, / **thy saving health among all nations.** / Let the people praise thee, O God; / **let all the people praise thee.**

O let the nations be glad and sing for joy: / **for thou shalt judge the people righteously, and govern the nations upon earth.**

Let the people praise thee, O God; / **let all the people praise thee.** / Then shall the earth yield her increase; and God, even our own God, shall bless us. / **God shall bless us; and all the ends of the earth shall fear him.**
Psalm 67

532

O worship the Lord in the beauty of holiness: let the heavens rejoice, and let the earth be glad; let the sea roar, and the fulness thereof.

Let the field be joyful, and all that is therein: then shall all the trees of the wood rejoice before the Lord: for he cometh to judge the earth: he shall judge the world with righteousness, and the people with his truth.

Psalm 96:9,11–13

533

I will extol thee, my God, O king: / **and I will bless thy name for ever and ever.** / Every day will I bless thee; / **and I will praise thy name for ever and ever.** / Great is the Lord, and greatly to be praised; / **and his greatness is unsearchable.**

Psalm 145:1–3

534

Create in me a clean heart, O God; and renew a right spirit within me. Cast me not away from thy presence; and take not thy holy spirit from me. Restore unto me the joy of thy salvation; and uphold me with thy free spirit. Then will I teach transgressors thy ways; and sinners shall be converted unto thee.

Psalm 51:10–13

535

O sing to the Lord a new song. Make a joyful noise to the Lord, all the earth; break forth into joyous song and sing praises!

Psalm 98:1,4 (RSV)

536

There is but one God, the Father, of whom are all things, and we in him; / **and one Lord Jesus Christ, by whom are all things, and we by him.**

1 Corinthians 8:6

Like as a father pitieth his children, so the Lord pitieth them that fear him. / **For he knoweth our frame; he remembereth that we are dust.**

Psalm 103:13–14

O Lord, thou art our father; we are the clay, and thou our potter; / **and we all are the work of thy hand.**

Isaiah 64:8

537

May our Lord Jesus Christ himself, and God our Father, who loved us and in his grace gave us eternal courage and a good hope, fill your hearts with courage and make you strong to do and say all that is good.

2 Thessalonians 2:16–17 (TEV)

538

The people that walked in darkness have seen a great light: / **they that dwell in the land of the shadow of death, upon them hath the light shined.**

For unto us a child is born, unto us a son is given: / **and the government shall be upon his shoulder:** / and his name shall be called Wonderful, / **Counsellor,** / The mighty God, / **The everlasting Father,** / The Prince of Peace. / **Of the increase of his government and peace there shall be no end. . . . The zeal of the Lord of hosts will perform this.**

Isaiah 9:2,6–7

539

Now when Jesus was born in Bethlehem of Judaea in the days of Herod the king, behold, there came wise men from the east to Jerusalem, saying, / **Where is he that is born King of the Jews? for we have seen his star in the east, and are come to worship him.**

When Herod the king had heard these things, he was troubled, and all Jerusalem with him. / **And when he had gathered all the chief priests and scribes of the people together, he demanded of them where Christ should be born.** / And they said unto him, In Bethlehem of Judaea: for thus it is written by the prophet, / **And thou Bethlehem, in the land of Juda, art not the least among the princes of Juda: for out of thee shall come a Governor, that shall rule my people Israel.**

Then Herod, when he had privily called the wise men, inquired of them diligently what time the star appeared. / **And he sent them to Bethlehem, and said, Go and search diligently for the young child; and when you have found him, bring me word again, that I may come and worship him also.**

When they had heard the king, they departed; and, lo, the star, which they saw in the east, went before them, till it came and stood over where the young child was. / **When they saw the star, they rejoiced with exceeding great joy.** / And when they were come into the house, they saw the young child with Mary his mother, and fell down, and worshipped him: and when they had opened their treasures, they presented unto him gifts; gold, and frankincense, and myrrh. / **And being warned of God in a dream that they should not return to Herod, they departed into their own country another way.**   *Matthew 2:1–12*

540

[Jesus Christ] is the image of the invisible God, the firstborn of every creature: / **for by him were all things created, that are in heaven, and that are in earth, visible and invisible, whether they be thrones, or dominions, or principalities, or powers: all things were created by him, and for him:** / and he is before all things, and by him all things consist.

He is the head of the body, the church: who is the beginning, the firstborn from the dead; that in all things he might have the preeminence. / For it pleased the Father that in him should all fulness dwell; / And, having made peace through the blood of his cross, by him to reconcile all things unto himself; by him, I say, whether they be things in earth, or things in heaven.   *Colossians 1:15–20*

541

I beseech you therefore, brethren, by the mercies of God, that ye present your bodies a living sacrifice, holy, acceptable unto God, which is your reasonable service. And be not conformed to this world; but be ye transformed by the renewing of your mind, that you may prove what is that good, and acceptable, and perfect, will of God.   *Romans 12:1–2*

542

In the beginning was the Word, and the Word was with God, and the Word was God. The same was in the beginning with God. All things were made by him; and without him was not any thing made that was made.

In him was life; and the life was the light of men. And the light shineth in darkness; and the darkness comprehended it not.

He was in the world, and the world was made by him, and the world knew him not. He came unto his own, and his own received him not. / **But as many as received him, to them gave he power to become the sons of God, even to them that believe on his name: which were born, not of blood, nor of the will of the flesh, nor of the will of man, but of God. And the Word was made flesh, and dwelt among us, (and we beheld his glory, the glory as of the only begotten of the Father,) full of grace and truth.** *John 1:1–5,10–14*

and wrapped him in swaddling clothes, and laid him in a manger; because there was no room for them in the inn.

And there were in the same country shepherds abiding in the field, keeping watch over their flock by night. / **And, lo, the angel of the Lord came upon them, and the glory of the Lord shone round about them: and they were sore afraid.** / And the angel said unto them, Fear not: for, behold, I bring you good tidings of great joy, which shall be to all people. For unto you is born this day in the city of David a Savior, which is Christ the Lord. And this shall be a sign unto you; Ye shall find the babe wrapped in swaddling clothes, lying in a manger.

And suddenly there was with the angel a multitude of the heavenly host praising God, and saying, Glory to God in the highest, and on earth peace, good will toward men. *Luke 2:1,4–14*

543

And it came to pass in those days that there went out a decree from Caesar Augustus, that all the world should be taxed. / **And Joseph also went up from Galilee, out of the city of Nazareth, into Judaea, unto the city of David, which is called Bethlehem; (because he was of the house and lineage of David:) to be taxed with Mary his espoused wife, being great with child.**

And so it was, that, while they were there, the days were accomplished that she should be delivered. / **And she brought forth her firstborn son,**

544

I will ask the Father, and He will give you another Helper, that He may be with you forever; that is the Spirit of truth whom the world cannot receive, because it does not behold Him or know Him, but you know Him because He abides with you, and will be in you. I will not leave you as orphans; I will come to you.

But the Helper, the Holy Spirit, whom the Father will send in My name, He will teach you all things, and bring to your remembrance all that I said to you. *John 14:16–18,26 (NASB)*

545

And when they came nigh to Jerusalem, unto Bethphage and Bethany, at the mount of Olives, [Jesus] sendeth forth two of his disciples. And he saith unto them / **Go your way into the village over against you: and as soon as ye be entered into it, ye shall find a colt tied, whereon never man sat; loose him, and bring him. And if any man say unto you, Why do ye this? say ye that the Lord hath need of him; and straightway he will send him hither.**

And they went their way, and found the colt tied by the door without in a place where two ways met; and they loose him. And certain of them that stood there said unto them, / **What do ye, loosing the colt?** / And they said unto them even as Jesus had commanded: and they let them go.

And they brought the colt to Jesus, and cast their garments on him; and he sat upon him. / **And many spread their garments in the way: and others cut down branches off the trees, and strawed them in the way.** / And they that went before, and they that followed, cried, saying, / **Hosanna; Blessed is he that cometh in the name of the Lord: Blessed be the kingdom of our father David, that cometh in the name of the Lord: Hosanna in the highest.**

Mark 11:1–10

546

The peace of God, which passeth all understanding, shall keep your hearts and minds through Christ Jesus. *Philippians 4:7*

547

Now unto him that is able to do exceeding abundantly above all that we ask or think, according to the power that worketh in us, unto him be glory in the church by Christ Jesus throughout all ages, world without end. *Ephesians 3:20–21*

548

Then Pilate therefore took Jesus, and scourged him. And the soldiers platted a crown of thorns, and put it on his head, and they put on him a purple robe, and said, / **Hail, King of the Jews!** / and they smote him with their hands. Pilate therefore went forth again, and saith unto them, / **Behold, I bring him forth to you, that ye may know that I find no fault in him.**

Then came Jesus forth, wearing the crown of thorns, and the purple robe. And Pilate saith unto them, / **Behold the man!** / When the chief priests therefore and officers saw him, they cried out, saying, / **Crucify him, crucify him.** / Pilate said unto them, / **Take ye him, and crucify him: for I find no fault in him.**

Then delivered he him therefore unto them to be crucified. And they took Jesus, and led him away. / **And he bearing his cross went forth into a place called the place of a skull, which is called in the Hebrew Golgotha:** / Where they crucified him, and two others with him, on either side one, and Jesus in the midst. / **And Pilate wrote a title, and put it on the cross. And the writing was, JESUS OF NAZARETH THE KING OF THE JEWS.** *John 19:1–6,16–19*

549

Who hath believed our report? and to whom is the arm of the Lord revealed? / **For he shall grow up before him as a tender plant, and as a root out of a dry ground: he hath no form nor comeliness: and when we shall see him, there is no beauty that we should desire him.** / He is despised and rejected of men; a man of sorrows, and acquainted with grief: and we hid as it were our faces from him; he was despised, and we esteemed him not.

Surely he hath borne our griefs, and carried our sorrows: yet we did esteem him stricken, smitten of God, and afflicted. / But he was wounded for our transgressions, he was bruised for our iniquities: the chastisement of our peace was upon him; and with his stripes we are healed. / **All we like sheep have gone astray; we have turned every one to his own way; and the Lord hath laid on him the iniquity of us all.**

Isaiah 53:1–6

550

In the end of the sabbath, as it began to dawn toward the first day of the week, came Mary Magdalene and the other Mary to see the sepulchre. / **And, behold, there was a great earthquake: for the angel of the Lord descended from heaven, and came and rolled back the stone from the door, and sat upon it.**

His countenance was like lightning, and his raiment white as snow: and for fear of him the keepers did shake, and became as dead men. / **And the angel answered and said unto the women, Fear not ye: for I know that ye seek Jesus, which was crucified.** / He is not here: for he is risen. / **He is not here: for he is risen!**

Matthew 28:1–6

551

God be merciful unto us, and bless us; and cause his face to shine upon us; that thy way may be known upon earth, thy saving health among all nations.

Psalm 67:1–2

552

When [the apostles] therefore were come together, they asked of him, saying, / **Lord, wilt thou at this time restore again the kingdom of Israel?** / And he said unto them, / **It is not for you to know the times or the seasons, which the Father hath put in his own power. But ye shall receive power, after that the Holy Ghost is come upon you: and ye shall be witnesses unto me both in Jerusalem, and in all Judaea, and in Samaria, and unto the uttermost part of the earth.**

And when he had spoken these things, while they beheld, he was taken up; and a cloud received him out of their sight. And while they looked steadfastly toward heaven as he went up, behold, two men stood by them in white apparel; which also said, / **Ye men of Galilee, why stand ye gazing up into heaven? this same Jesus, which is taken up from you into heaven, shall so come in like manner as ye have seen him go into heaven.**

Acts 1:6–11

553

Ye men of Galilee, why stand ye gazing up into heaven? this same Jesus, which is taken up from you into heaven, shall so come in like manner as ye have seen him go into heaven.

Acts 1:11

Therefore be ye also ready: for in such an hour as ye think not the Son of man cometh.

Matthew 24:44

For the Lord himself shall descend from heaven with a shout, with the voice of the archangel, and with the trump of God: and the dead in Christ shall rise first: / **then we which are alive and remain shall be caught up together with them in the clouds, to meet the Lord in the air: and so shall we ever be with the Lord.**

1 Thessalonians 4:16–17

Beloved, now are we the sons of God, and it doth not yet appear what we shall be: but we know that, when he shall appear, we shall be like him; for we shall see him as he is.

1 John 3:2

554

I am the good shepherd: the good shepherd giveth his life for the sheep. / **I am the good shepherd, and know my sheep, and am known of mine.** / As the Father knoweth me, even so know I the Father: and I lay down my life for the sheep. / **And other sheep I have, which are not of this fold: them also I must bring, and they shall hear my voice; and there shall be one fold, and one shepherd.**

My sheep hear my voice, and I know them, and they follow me: / **and I**

give unto them eternal life; and they shall never perish, neither shall any man pluck them out of my hand. My Father, which gave them me, is greater than all; and no man is able to pluck them out of my Father's hand.

John 10:11,14–16,27–29

555

I tell you the truth; It is expedient for you that I go away: for if I go not away, the Comforter will not come unto you; but if I depart, I will send him unto you. / **And when [the Holy Spirit] is come, he will reprove the world of sin, and of righteousness, and of judgment:** / of sin, because they believe not on me; / **of righteousness, because I go to my Father, and ye see me no more;** / of judgment, because the prince of this world is judged.

I have yet many things to say unto you, but ye cannot bear them now. / Howbeit when he, the Spirit of truth, is come, he will guide you into all truth: for he shall not speak of himself; but whatsoever he shall hear, that shall he speak: and he will show you things to come. / **He shall glorify me: for he shall receive of mine, and shall show it unto you.**

John 16:7–14

556

May the God of steadfastness and encouragement grant you to live in such harmony with one another, in accord with Christ Jesus, that together you may with one voice glorify the God and Father of our Lord Jesus Christ.

Romans 15:5–6 (RSV)

557

In the beginning God created the heaven and the earth. / **And the earth was without form, and void; and darkness was upon the face of the deep. And the spirit of God moved upon the face of the waters.**

And God said, Let there be light: and there was light. And God saw the light, that it was good: and God divided the light from the darkness. / **And God called the light Day, and the darkness he called Night. And the evening and the morning were the first day.**

Genesis 1:1–5

All things were made by him; and without him was not any thing made that was made. *John 1:3*

O come, let us worship and bow down: let us kneel before the Lord our maker. *Psalm 95:6*

558

And God said, Let us make man in our image, after our likeness: and let them have dominion over the fish of the sea, and over the fowl of the air, and over the cattle, and over all the earth, and over every creeping thing that creepeth upon the earth. / **So God created man in his own image, in the image of God created he him; male and female created he them.**

Genesis 1:26–27

What is man, that thou art mindful of him? and the son of man, that thou visitest him? / **For thou hast made him a little lower than the angels, and hast crowned him with glory and honor.** / Thou madest him to have dominion over the works of thy hands; thou hast put all things under his feet. *Psalm 8:4–6*

O Lord, thou art our father; we are the clay, and thou our potter; and we all are the work of thy hand.

Isaiah 64:8

559

Our Father which art in heaven, Hallowed be thy name. Thy kingdom come. Thy will be done in earth, as it is in heaven. Give us this day our daily bread. And forgive us our debts, as we forgive our debtors. And lead us not into temptation, but deliver us from evil: For thine is the kingdom, and the power, and the glory, for ever. Amen.

Matthew 6:9–13

560

For God so loved the world, that he gave his only begotten Son, / **that whosoever believeth in him should not perish, but have everlasting life.** / For God sent not his Son into the world to condemn the world; / **but that the world through him might be saved.**

He that believeth on him is not condemned: / **but he that believeth not is condemned already because he hath not believed in the name of the only begotten Son of God.**

He that believeth on the Son hath everlasting life: / **and he that believeth not the Son shall not see life; but the wrath of God abideth on him.** *John 3:16–18,36*

561

The Lord bless thee, and keep thee: the Lord make his face shine upon thee, and be gracious unto thee: the Lord lift up his countenance upon thee, and give thee peace.

Numbers 6:24–26

562

All scripture is given by inspiration of God, and is profitable for doctrine, for reproof, for correction, for instruction in righteousness: that the man of God may be perfect, thoroughly furnished unto all good works. *2 Timothy 3:16–17*

The law of the Lord is perfect, converting the soul: the testimony of the Lord is sure, making wise the simple. The statutes of the Lord are right, rejoicing the heart: the commandment of the Lord is pure, enlightening the eyes. *Psalm 19:7–8*

Thy word is a lamp unto my feet, and a light unto my path. The entrance of thy words giveth light; it giveth understanding unto the simple.

Psalm 119:105,130

The word of God is quick, and powerful, and sharper than any two-edged sword, piercing even to the dividing asunder of soul and spirit, and of the joints and marrow, and is a discerner of the thoughts and intents of the heart. *Hebrews 4:12*

563

The grace of the Lord Jesus Christ and the love of God and the fellowship of the Holy Spirit be with you all. *2 Corinthians 13:14 (RSV)*

564

It is good to give thanks to the Lord, to sing praises to thy name, O Most High; / **to declare thy steadfast love in the morning, and thy faithfulness by night, to the music of the lute and the harp, to the melody of the lyre.**

For thou, O Lord, hast made me glad by thy work; at the works of thy hands I sing for joy. How great are thy works, O Lord! / **How great are thy works, O Lord!**

Psalm 92:1–5(RSV)

565

Let not your heart be troubled: ye believe in God, believe also in me. / **In my Father's house are many mansions; if it were not so, I would have told you. I go to prepare a place for you.** / And if I go and prepare a place for you, I will come again, and receive you unto myself; that where I am, there ye may be also. And whither I go ye know, and the way ye know. / **I am the way, the truth, and the life: no man cometh unto the Father, but by me.**

And I will pray the Father, and he shall give you another Comforter, that he may abide with you for ever; / **Even the Spirit of truth; whom the world cannot receive, because it seeth him not, neither knoweth him: but ye know him; for he dwelleth with you, and shall be in you.**

Peace I leave with you, my peace I give unto you: not as the world giveth, give I unto you. Let not your heart be troubled, neither let it be afraid. *John 14:1–4,6,16–17,27*

566

God commendeth his love toward us, in that, while we were yet sinners, Christ died for us. / **Much more then, being now justified by his blood, we shall be saved from wrath through him.** / For if, when we were enemies, we were reconciled to God by the death of his Son, / **much more, being reconciled, we shall be saved by his life.** / And not only so, but we also joy in God through our Lord Jesus Christ, by whom we have now received the atonement.

Romans 5:8–11

For by grace are ye saved through faith; and that not of yourselves: it is the gift of God: not of works, lest any man should boast.

Ephesians 2:8–9

567

If thou shalt confess with thy mouth the Lord Jesus, and shalt believe in thine heart that God hath raised him from the dead, thou shalt be saved. For with the heart man believeth unto righteousness; and with the mouth confession is made unto salvation.

The scripture saith, Whosoever believeth on him shall not be ashamed. For there is no difference between the Jew and the Greek; for the same Lord over all is rich unto all that call upon him. For whosoever shall call upon the name of the Lord shall be saved.

Romans 10:9–13

568

Happy is the man whose sins are forgiven, whose transgressions are pardoned. Happy is the man whom the Lord does not accuse of doing wrong, who is free from all deceit.

Then I confessed my sins to you; I did not conceal my wrongdoings. I decided to confess them to you, and you forgave all my transgressions. You are my hiding place; you will save me from trouble. I sing aloud of your salvation, because you protect me.

All who are righteous, be glad and rejoice, because of what the Lord has done! All who obey him, shout for joy!

Psalm 32:1–2,5,7,11 (TEV)

569

Have mercy upon me, O God, according to thy lovingkindness: according unto the multitude of thy tender mercies blot out my transgressions. / **Wash me thoroughly from mine iniquity, and cleanse me from my sin,** / For I acknowledge my transgressions: and my sin is ever before me.

Purge me with hyssop, and I shall be clean: wash me, and I shall be whiter than snow. / Hide thy face from my sins, and blot out all mine iniquities.

Create in me a clean heart, O God; and renew a right spirit within me. / Cast me not away from thy presence; and take not thy holy spirit from me. / **Restore unto me the joy of thy salvation; and uphold me with thy free spirit. Then will I teach transgressors thy ways; and sinners shall be converted unto thee.**

Psalm 51:1–3,7,9–13

570

God is light, and in him is no darkness at all. / **If we say that we have fellowship with him, and walk in darkness, we lie, and do not the truth:** / But if we walk in the light, as he is in the light, we have fellowship one with another, and the blood of Jesus Christ his Son cleanseth us from all sin.

If we say that we have no sin, we deceive ourselves, and the truth is not in us. / If we confess our sins, he is faithful and just to forgive us our sins, and to cleanse us from all unrighteousness. / **If we say that we have not sinned, we make him a liar, and his word is not in us.**

If any man sin, we have an advocate with the Father, Jesus Christ the righteous: / **And he is the propitiation for our sins: and not for ours only, but also for the sins of the whole world.** *1 John 1:5–10; 2:1–2*

571

For all have sinned, and come short of the glory of God. / **But God commendeth his love toward us, in that, while we were yet sinners, Christ died for us.**

Romans 3:23; 5:8

But as many as received him, to them gave he power to become the sons of God, even to them that believe on his name. *John 1:12*

And this is the record, that God hath given to us eternal life, and this life is in his Son. / He that hath the Son hath life, and he that hath not the Son of God hath not life.

These things have I written unto you that believe on the name of the Son of God; that ye may know that ye have eternal life, and that ye may believe on the name of the Son of God. *1 John 5:11–13*

572

Trust in the Lord, and do good; so shalt thou dwell in the land, and verily thou shalt be fed. Delight thyself also in the Lord; and he shall give thee the desires of thine heart.

Commit thy way unto the Lord; trust also in him; and he shall bring it to pass. And he shall bring forth thy righteousness as the light, and thy judgment as the noonday.

Psalm 37:3–6

573

Seek ye the Lord while he may be found, call ye upon him while he is near: / **Let the wicked forsake his way, and the unrighteous man his thoughts: and let him return unto the Lord, for he will have mercy upon him; and to our God, for he will abundantly pardon.**

Isaiah 55:6–7

Repent ye therefore, and be converted, that your sins may be blotted out, when the times of refreshing shall come from the presence of the Lord. *Acts 3:19*

Come now, and let us reason together, saith the Lord: though your sins be as scarlet, they shall be as white as snow; though they be red like crimson, they shall be as wool. *Isaiah 1:18*

574

Lord, thou hast been our dwelling place in all generations. / **Before the mountains were brought forth, or ever thou hadst formed the earth and the world, even from everlasting to everlasting, thou art God.**

A thousand years in thy sight are but as yesterday when it is past, and as a watch in the night. / **The days of our years are threescore years and ten; and if by reason of strength they be fourscore years, yet is their strength labor and sorrow; for it is soon cut off, and we fly away.** / So teach us to number our days, that we may apply our hearts unto wisdom.

Let thy work appear unto thy servants, and thy glory unto their children. And let the beauty of the Lord our God be upon us.

Psalm 90:1–2,4,10,12,16–17

575

The Lord is my shepherd; I shall not want. He maketh me to lie down in green pastures: he leadeth me beside the still waters. He restoreth my soul: he leadeth me in the paths of righteousness for his name's sake.

Yea, though I walk through the valley of the shadow of death, I will fear no evil: for thou art with me; thy rod and thy staff they comfort me.

Thou preparest a table before me in the presence of mine enemies: thou anointest my head with oil; my cup runneth over. Surely goodness and mercy shall follow me all the days of my life: and I will dwell in the house of the Lord for ever. *Psalm 23*

576

Offer unto God thanksgiving; and pay thy vows unto the most High.

Psalm 50:14

577

O Lord, thou hast searched me, and known me. / **Thou [knowest] my path and my lying down, and art acquainted with all my ways.** / For there is not a word in my tongue, but, lo, O Lord, thou knowest it altogether.

Whither shall I go from thy spirit? or whither shall I flee from thy presence? / If I ascend up into heaven, thou art there: if I make my bed in hell, behold, thou art there. / **If I take the wings of the morning, and dwell in the uttermost parts of the sea;** / even there shall thy hand lead me, and thy right hand shall hold me. / **If I say, Surely the darkness shall cover me; even the night shall be light about me.** / Yea, the darkness hideth not from thee; but the night shineth as the day: the darkness and the light are both alike to thee.

Search me, O God, and know my heart: try me, and know my thoughts: and see if there be any wicked way in me, and lead me in the way everlasting.

Psalm 139:1,3–4,7–12,23–24

578

O give thanks unto the Lord, for he is good: for his mercy endureth for ever. Let the redeemed of the Lord say so. *Psalm 107:1–2*

579

I will praise thee, O Lord, with my whole heart; I will show forth all thy marvellous works.   *Psalm 9:1*

580

I will lift up mine eyes unto the hills, from whence cometh my help. / **My help cometh from the Lord, which made heaven and earth.**

He will not suffer thy foot to be moved: he that keepeth thee will not slumber. / **Behold, he that keepeth Israel shall neither slumber nor sleep.**

The Lord is thy keeper: the Lord is thy shade upon thy right hand. / **The sun shall not smite thee by day, nor the moon by night.**

The Lord shall preserve thee from all evil: he shall preserve thy soul. / **The Lord shall preserve thy going out and thy coming in from this time forth, and even for evermore.**
                    Psalm 121

581

Give to others, and God will give to you: you will receive a full measure, a generous helping, poured into your hands—all that you can hold. The measure you use for others is the one God will use for you.
                    Luke 6:38 (TEV)

582

This is the day which the Lord hath made; we will rejoice and be glad in it.   *Psalm 118:24*

583

Remember the sabbath day, to keep it holy. Six days shalt thou labor, and do all thy work: / **But the seventh day is the sabbath of the Lord thy God: in it thou shalt not do any work.** / For in six days the Lord made heaven and earth, the sea, and all that in them is, and rested the seventh day: / **wherefore the Lord blessed the sabbath day, and hallowed it.**
                    Exodus 20:8–11

And [Jesus] said unto them, The sabbath was made for man, and not man for the sabbath: / **Therefore the Son of man is Lord also of the sabbath.**
                    Mark 2:27–28

584

The Lord is my light and my salvation; whom shall I fear? The Lord is the stronghold of my life; of whom shall I be afraid? / **Though a host encamp against me, my heart shall not fear; though war arise against me, yet I will be confident.**

One thing have I asked of the Lord, that will I seek after; that I may dwell in the house of the Lord all the days of my life, to behold the beauty of the Lord, and to inquire in his temple. / **For he will hide me in his shelter in the day of trouble; he will conceal me under the cover of his tent, he will set me high upon a rock.**

And now my head shall be lifted up above my enemies round about me; and I will offer in his tent sacrifices with shouts of joy; I will sing and make melody to the Lord.
                    Psalm 27:1,3–6 (RSV)

585

When Jesus came into the coasts of Caesarea Philippi, he asked his disciples, saying, Whom do men say that I the Son of man am? / **And they said, Some say that thou art John the Baptist: some, Elias; and others, Jeremias, or one of the prophets.**

He saith unto them, But whom say ye that I am? / **And Simon Peter answered and said, Thou art the Christ, the Son of the living God.**

And Jesus answered and said unto him, Blessed art thou, Simon Barjona: for flesh and blood hath not revealed it unto thee, but my Father which is in heaven. / **And I say also unto thee, That thou art Peter, and upon this rock I will build my church; and the gates of hell shall not prevail against it.** / And I will give unto thee the keys of the kingdom of heaven: and whatsoever thou shalt bind on earth shall be bound in heaven: and whatsoever thou shalt loose on earth shall be loosed in heaven. *Matthew 16:13–19*

586

We were buried therefore with him by baptism into death, / **so that as Christ was raised from the dead by the glory of the Father, we too might walk in newness of life.** / For if we have been united with him in a death like his, we shall certainly be united with him in a resurrection like his.

We know that our old self was crucified with him so that the sinful body might be destroyed, and we might no longer be enslaved to sin. / So you also must consider yourselves dead to sin and alive to God in Christ Jesus. *Romans 6:4–6,11(RSV)*

Go therefore and make disciples of all nations, baptizing them in the name of the Father and of the Son and of the Holy Spirit, teaching them to observe all that I have commanded you; and lo, I am with you always, to the close of the age.
Matthew 28:19–20(RSV)

587

Ye call me Master and Lord: and ye say well; for so I am. If I then, your Lord and Master, have washed your feet; ye also ought to wash one another's feet. For I have given you an example, that ye should do as I have done to you. Verily, verily, I say unto you, The servant is not greater than his lord; neither he that is sent greater than he that sent him.
John 13:13–16

588

Then cometh Jesus from Galilee to Jordan unto John, to be baptized of him. But John forbad him, saying, / **I have need to be baptized of thee, and comest thou to me?**

And Jesus answering said unto him, / **Suffer it to be so now: for thus it becometh us to fulfill all righteousness.** / Then he suffered him. And Jesus, when he was baptized, went up straightway out of the water: and, lo, the heavens were opened unto him, and he saw the Spirit of God descending like a dove, and lighting upon him: And lo a voice from heaven, saying, / **This is my beloved Son, in whom I am well pleased.**
Matthew 3:13–17

589

Come unto me, all ye that labor and are heavy laden, and I will give you rest. Take my yoke upon you, and learn of me; for I am meek and lowly in heart: and ye shall find rest unto your souls. For my yoke is easy, and my burden is light.

Matthew 11:28–30

590

Every man according as he purposeth in his heart, so let him give; not grudgingly, or of necessity: for God loveth a cheerful giver. And God is able to make all grace abound toward you; that ye, always having all sufficiency in all things, may abound to every good work.

2 Corinthians 9:7–8

591

Ye are the body of Christ, and members in particular.

1 Corinthians 12:27

And he is the head of the body, the church: who is the beginning, the firstborn from the dead; that in all things he might have the preeminence.

Colossians 1:18

And he gave some, apostles; and some, prophets; and some, evangelists; and some, pastors and teachers; for the perfecting of the saints, for the work of the ministry, for the edifying of the body of Christ: Till we all come in the unity of the faith; and of the knowledge of the Son of God, unto a perfect man, unto the measure of the stature of the fulness of Christ.

Ephesians 4:11–13

592

The Lord Jesus, on the night he was betrayed, took the bread, gave thanks to God, broke it, and said, / **"This is my body, which is for you. Do this in memory of me."**

In the same way, he took the cup after the supper and said, / **"This cup is God's new covenant, sealed with my blood. Whenever you drink it, do it in memory of me." For until the Lord comes, you proclaim his death whenever you eat this bread and drink from this cup.**

It follows, then, that if anyone eats the Lord's bread or drinks from his cup in a way that dishonors him, he is guilty of sin against the Lord's body and blood. / **So then, everyone should examine himself first, and then eat the bread and drink from the cup.**

1 Corinthians 11:23–28 (TEV)

593

Whosoever shall call upon the name of the Lord shall be saved. / **How then shall they call on him in whom they have not believed?** / and how shall they believe in him of whom they have not heard? / **and how shall they hear without a preacher?** / and how shall they preach, except they be sent?

Romans 10:13–15

Go ye therefore, and teach all nations, baptizing them in the name of the Father, and of the Son, and of the Holy Ghost: teaching them to observe all things whatsoever I have commanded you: and, lo, I am with you alway, even unto the end of the world.

Matthew 28:19–20

594

Thus it is written, and thus it behooved Christ to suffer, and to rise from the dead the third day: / **and that repentance and remission of sins should be preached in his name among all nations, beginning at Jerusalem. And ye are witnesses of these things.** *Luke 24:46–48*

Go ye therefore, and teach all nations, / **baptizing them in the name of the Father, and of the Son, and of the Holy Ghost:** / Teaching them to observe all things whatsoever I have commanded you: / **and, lo, I am with you alway, even unto the end of the world.** *Matthew 28:19–20*

But ye shall receive power, after that the Holy Ghost is come upon you: / **and ye shall be witnesses unto me both in Jerusalem, and in all Judaea, and in Samaria, and unto the uttermost part of the earth.** *Acts 1:8*

595

What use is it, my brethren, if a man says he has faith, but he has no works? Can that faith save him? If a brother or sister is without clothing and in need of daily food, and one of you says to them, "Go in peace, be warmed and be filled," and yet you do not give them what is necessary for their body, what use is that? Even so faith, if it has no works, is dead, being by itself.

But someone may well say, "You have faith, and I have works; show me your faith without the works, and I will show you my faith by my works." *James 2:14–18 (NASB)*

596

One of the scribes came, and . . . asked [Jesus], which is the first commandment of all? And Jesus answered him, The first of all the commandments is, Hear, O Israel; The Lord our God is one Lord: and thou shalt love the Lord thy God with all thy heart, and with all thy soul, and with all thy mind, and with all thy strength: this is the first commandment.

And the second is like, namely this, Thou shalt love thy neighbor as thyself. There is none other commandment greater than these. *Mark 12:28–31*

597

Come, ye blessed of my Father, inherit the kingdom prepared for you from the foundation of the world: / **for I was an hungered, and ye gave me meat:** / I was thirsty, and ye gave me drink: / **I was a stranger, and ye took me in:** / naked, and ye clothed me: / **I was sick, and ye visited me:** / I was in prison, and ye came unto me.

Then shall the righteous answer him, saying, Lord, when saw we thee an hungered, and fed thee? / or thirsty, and gave thee drink? / **When saw we thee a stranger, and took thee in?** / or naked, and clothed thee? / **Or when saw we thee sick, or in prison, and came unto thee?**

And the King shall answer and say unto them, Verily I say unto you, Inasmuch as ye have done it unto one of the least of these my brethren, ye have done it unto me. *Matthew 25:34–40*

598

Rejoice in the Lord alway: and again I say, Rejoice. / **Let your moderation be known unto all men. The Lord is at hand.** / Be careful for nothing; but in every thing by prayer and supplication with thanksgiving let your requests be made known unto God. / **And the peace of God, which passeth all understanding, shall keep your hearts and minds through Christ Jesus.**

Finally, brethren, whatsoever things are true, whatsoever things are honest, whatsoever things are just, whatsoever things are pure, whatsoever things are lovely, whatsoever things are of good report; if there be any virtue, and if there be any praise, think on these things.

Philippians 4:4–8

599

The fruit of the Spirit is love, joy, peace, longsuffering, gentleness, goodness, faith, meekness, temperance: against such there is no law. And they that are Christ's have crucified the flesh with the affections and lusts.

If we live in the Spirit, let us also walk in the Spirit. Let us not be desirous of vain glory, provoking one another, envying one another.

Galatians 5:22–26

600

But if any one has the world's goods and sees his brother in need, yet closes his heart against him, how does God's love abide in him? Little children, let us not love in word or speech but in deed and in truth.

1 John 3:17–18 (RSV)

601

I am the vine, ye are the branches: He that abideth in me, and I in him, the same bringeth forth much fruit: for without me ye can do nothing. If a man abide not in me, he is cast forth as a branch, and is withered; and men gather them, and cast them into the fire, and they are burned. If ye abide in me, and my words abide in you, ye shall ask what ye will, and it shall be done unto you. Herein is my Father glorified, that ye bear much fruit; so shall ye be my disciples.

As the Father hath loved me, so have I loved you: continue ye in my love. If ye keep my commandments, ye shall abide in my love; even as I have kept my Father's commandments, and abide in his love. These things have I spoken unto you, that my joy might remain in you, and that your joy might be full.

This is my commandment, That ye love one another, as I have loved you. Greater love hath no man than this, that a man lay down his life for his friends.

John 15:5–13

602

Therefore being justified by faith, we have peace with God through our Lord Jesus Christ: / **By whom also we have access by faith into this grace wherein we stand, and rejoice in hope of the glory of God.**

And not only so, but we glory in tribulations also: knowing that tribulation worketh patience; and patience, experience; and experience, hope: / **and hope maketh not ashamed; because the love of God** is shed abroad in our hearts by the Holy Ghost which is given unto us.

For when we were yet without strength, in due time Christ died for the ungodly. For scarcely for a righteous man will one die: yet peradventure for a good man some would even dare to die.

But God commendeth his love toward us, in that, while we were yet sinners, Christ died for us.
Romans 5:1–8

603

We know that all things work together for good to them that love God, to them who are the called according to his purpose.

If God be for us, who can be against us? / He that spared not his own Son, but delivered him up for us all, how shall he not with him also freely give us all things?

Who shall lay any thing to the charge of God's elect? It is God that justifieth. / Who is he that condemneth? It is Christ that died, yea rather, that is risen again, who is even at the right hand of God, who also maketh intercession for us. / **Who shall separate us from the love of Christ? shall tribulation, or distress, or persecution, or famine, or nakedness, or peril, or sword?**

Nay, in all these things we are more than conquerors through him that loved us. / **For I am persuaded, that neither death, nor life, nor angels, nor principalities, nor powers, nor things present, nor things to come, nor height, nor depth, nor any other** creature, shall be able to separate us from the love of God, which is in Christ Jesus our Lord.
Romans 8:28,31–35,37–39

604

Now the God of peace, that brought again from the dead our Lord Jesus, that great shepherd of the sheep, through the blood of the everlasting covenant, make you perfect in every good work to do his will, working in you that which is well-pleasing in his sight, through Jesus Christ; to whom be glory for ever and ever. Amen.
Hebrews 13:20–21

605

Grace and peace be multiplied unto you through the knowledge of God, and of Jesus our Lord.

His divine power hath given unto us all things that pertain unto life and godliness, through the knowledge of him that hath called us to glory and virtue: / Whereby are given unto us exceeding great and precious promises: that by these ye might be partakers of the divine nature, having escaped the corruption that is in the world through lust.

And beside this, giving all diligence, add to your faith virtue; and to virtue knowledge; and to knowledge temperance; and to temperance patience; and to patience godliness; and to godliness brotherly kindness; and to brotherly kindness charity. / For if these things be in you, and abound, they make you that ye shall neither be barren nor unfruitful in the knowledge of our Lord Jesus Christ.
2 Peter 1:2–8

606

In the year that king Uzziah died I saw also the Lord sitting upon a throne, high and lifted up, and his train filled the temple. / **Above it stood the seraphims: each one had six wings; with twain he covered his face, and with twain he covered his feet, and with twain he did fly.**

One cried unto another, and said, Holy, holy, holy, is the Lord of hosts: the whole earth is full of his glory. / **And the posts of the door moved at the voice of him that cried, and the house was filled with smoke.**

Then said I, Woe is me! for I am undone; because I am a man of unclean lips, and I dwell in the midst of a people of unclean lips: for mine eyes have seen the King, the Lord of hosts.

Then flew one of the seraphims unto me, having a live coal in his hand, which he had taken with the tongs from off the altar: / and he laid it upon my mouth, and said, Lo, this hath touched thy lips; and thine iniquity is taken away, and thy sin purged.

Also I heard the voice of the Lord, saying, Whom shall I send, and who will go for us? Then said I, Here am I; send me. / And he said, Go.

Isaiah 6:1–9

607

Though I speak with the tongues of men and of angels, and have not love, I am become as sounding brass, or a tinkling cymbal. / **And though I have the gift of prophecy, and understand all mysteries, and all knowledge; and though I have all** faith, so that I could remove mountains, and have not love, I am nothing. / And though I bestow all my goods to feed the poor, and though I give my body to be burned, and have not love, it profiteth me nothing.

Love suffereth long, and is kind; / love envieth not; / **love vaunteth not itself,** / is not puffed up, / **doth not behave itself unseemly,** / seeketh not her own, / **is not easily provoked,** / thinketh no evil; / **rejoiceth not in iniquity,** / but rejoiceth in the truth; / **beareth all things,** / believeth all things, / **hopeth all things,** / endureth all things.

Love never faileth: but whether there be prophecies, they shall fail: whether there be tongues, they shall cease; whether there be knowledge, it shall vanish away. / For we know in part, and we prophesy in part. / **But when that which is perfect is come, then that which is in part shall be done away.**

When I was a child, I spake as a child, I understood as a child, I thought as a child: but when I became a man, I put away childish things. / **For now we see through a glass, darkly; but then face to face: now I know in part; but then shall I know even as also I am known.** / And now abideth faith, hope, love, these three; but the greatest of these is love.

1 Corinthians 13

608

Honor the Lord with thy substance, and with the firstfruits of thine increase.

Proverbs 3:9

609

Blessed is the man that walketh not in the counsel of the ungodly, nor standeth in the way of sinners, nor sitteth in the seat of the scornful. But his delight is in the law of the Lord; and in his law doth he meditate day and night. And he shall be like a tree planted by the rivers of water, that bringeth forth his fruit in his season; his leaf also shall not wither; and whatsoever he doeth shall prosper.

The ungodly are not so: but are like the chaff which the wind driveth away. Therefore the ungodly shall not stand in the judgment, nor sinners in the congregation of the righteous. For the Lord knoweth the way of the righteous: but the way of the ungodly shall perish.

Lord, who shall abide in thy tabernacle? who shall dwell in thy holy hill? / **He that walketh uprightly, and worketh righteousness, and speaketh the truth in his heart.**

Psalms 1:1–6; 15:1–2

610

Ye are the salt of the earth: but if the salt have lost his savour, wherewith shall it be salted? it is thenceforth good for nothing, but to be cast out, and to be trodden under foot of men.

Ye are the light of the world. A city that is set on an hill cannot be hid. / Neither do men light a candle, and put it under a bushel, but on a candlestick; and it giveth light unto all that are in the house. / **Let your light so shine before men, that they may see your good works, and glorify your Father which is in heaven.**

Matthew 5:13–16

611

From the beginning of the creation God made them male and female. For this cause shall a man leave his father and mother, and cleave to his wife; and they twain shall be one flesh: so then they are no more twain, but one flesh. What therefore God hath joined together, let not man put asunder.

Mark 10:6–9

612

Seeing the multitudes, [Jesus] went up into a mountain: and when he was set, his disciples came unto him: and he opened his mouth, and taught them, saying, / **Blessed are the poor in spirit: for theirs is the kingdom of heaven.**

Blessed are they that mourn: for they shall be comforted. / **Blessed are the meek: for they shall inherit the earth.**

Blessed are they which do hunger and thirst after righteousness: for they shall be filled. / **Blessed are the merciful: for they shall obtain mercy.**

Blessed are the pure in heart: for they shall see God. / **Blessed are the peacemakers: for they shall be called the children of God.**

Blessed are they which are persecuted for righteousness' sake: for theirs is the kingdom of heaven. / **Blessed are ye, when men shall revile you, and persecute you, and shall say all manner of evil against you falsely, for my sake.** / Rejoice, and be exceeding glad: for great is your reward in heaven.

Matthew 5:1–12

613

Then said Jesus unto his disciples, If any man will come after me, let him deny himself, and take up his cross, and follow me. For whosoever will save his life shall lose it: and whosoever will lose his life for my sake shall find it. For what is a man profited, if he shall gain the whole world, and lose his own soul? or what shall a man give in exchange for his soul? For the Son of man shall come in the glory of his Father with his angels; and then he shall reward every man according to his works.

Matthew 16:24–27

614

Then came Peter to [Jesus], and said, Lord, how oft shall my brother sin against me, and I forgive him? till seven times? / **Jesus saith unto him, I say not unto thee, Until seven times: but, Until seventy times seven.**

Therefore if thou bring thy gift to the altar, and there rememberest that thy brother hath aught against thee; / **Leave there thy gift before the altar, and go thy way; first be reconciled to thy brother, and then come and offer thy gift. For if ye forgive men their trespasses, your heavenly Father will also forgive you: but if ye forgive not men their trespasses, neither will your Father forgive your trespasses.**

Matthew 18:21–22; 5:23–24; 6:14–15

615

Let love be genuine; / **hate what is evil,** / hold fast to what is good; / **love one another with brotherly af-**fection; / outdo one another in showing honor. / **Never flag in zeal,** / be aglow with the Spirit, / **serve the Lord.** / Rejoice in your hope, / **be patient in tribulation,** / be constant in prayer. / **Contribute to the needs of the saints,** / practice hospitality.

Bless those who persecute you; / bless and do not curse them. / **Rejoice with those who rejoice,** / weep with those who weep.

Live in harmony with one another; / do not be haughty, but associate with the lowly; / **never be conceited.** / Repay no one evil for evil, but take thought for what is noble in the sight of all. / **If possible, so far as it depends upon you, live peaceably with all.**

Romans 12:9–18 (RSV)

616

Do not let anyone look down on you because you are young, but be an example for the believers, in your speech, your conduct, your love, faith, and purity. / **Give your time and effort . . . to the public reading of the Scriptures, and to preaching and teaching.**

Do not neglect the spiritual gift that is in you, which was given to you when the prophets spoke and the elders laid their hands on you. / **Practice these things and give yourself to them, in order that your progress may be seen by all.** / Watch yourself, and watch your teaching. Keep on doing these things, because if you do you will save both yourself and those who hear you.

1 Timothy 4:12–16 (TEV)

617

The Lord God formed man of the dust of the ground, and breathed into his nostrils the breath of life; and man became a living soul. / **And the Lord God said, It is not good that the man should be alone; I will make an help meet for him.**

And the Lord God caused a deep sleep to fall upon Adam, and he slept: and he took one of his ribs, and closed up the flesh; and the rib, which the Lord God had taken from man, made he a woman, and brought her unto the man. / **And Adam said, This is now bone of my bones, and flesh of my flesh.**

Genesis 2:7,18,21–23

For this cause shall a man leave father and mother, and shall cleave to his wife: and they twain shall be one flesh. / **Wherefore they are no more twain, but one flesh. What therefore God hath joined together, let not man put asunder.** *Matthew 19:5–6*

618

Wives, submit yourselves unto your own husbands, as unto the Lord. / **For the husband is the head of the wife, even as Christ is the head of the church; and he is the savior of the body.** / Therefore as the church is subject unto Christ, so let the wives be to their own husbands in every thing.

Husbands, love your wives, even as Christ also loved the church, and gave himself for it. / So ought men to love their wives as their own bodies. He that loveth his wife loveth himself.

Children, obey your parents in the Lord: for this is right. / Honor thy father and mother. / **And, ye fathers, provoke not your children to wrath: but bring them up in the nurture and admonition of the Lord.**

Ephesians 5:22–25,28; 6:1–2,4

619

May the God of hope fill you with all joy and peace in believing, so that by the power of the Holy Spirit you may abound in hope.

Romans 15:13 (RSV)

620

How hard it is to find a perfect wife! She is worth far more than jewels! / **Her husband puts his confidence in her, and he will never be poor.** / As long as she lives, she does him good, and never harm.

She is a hard worker, strong and industrious. / She is generous to the poor and needy. / **She is strong and respected, and not afraid of the future.** / She speaks with a gentle wisdom.

She is always busy, and looks after her family's needs. / Her children show their appreciation, and her husband praises her. / **He says, "Many women are good wives, but you are the best of them all."**

Charm is deceptive, and beauty disappears, but a woman who fears the Lord should be praised. / **Give her credit for all she does. She deserves the respect of everyone.**

Proverbs 31:10–12,17,20,25–31 (TEV)

621

Do not lay up for yourselves treasures on earth, where moth and rust consume and where thieves break in and steal, / **but lay up for yourselves treasures in heaven, where neither moth nor rust consumes and where thieves do not break in and steal. For where your treasure is, there will your heart be also.**

No one can serve two masters; for either he will hate the one and love the other, or he will be devoted to the one and despise the other. You cannot serve God and mammon. / **But seek first his kingdom and his righteousness, and all these things shall be yours as well.**

Matthew 6:19–21,24,33 (RSV)

622

For unto us a child is born, unto us a son is given: / **and the government shall be upon his shoulder:** / and his name shall be called Wonderful, Counsellor, The mighty God, The everlasting Father, The Prince of Peace. / **Of the increase of his government and peace there shall be no end, upon the throne of David, and upon his kingdom, to order it, and to establish it with judgment and with justice from henceforth even for ever.**

With righteousness shall he judge the poor, and reprove with equity for the meek of the earth: / **and he shall smite the earth with the rod of his mouth, and with the breath of his lips shall he slay the wicked.**

Isaiah 9:6–7; 11:4

He shall judge among many people, and rebuke strong nations afar off; /

and they shall beat their swords into plowshares, and their spears into pruninghooks: / nation shall not lift up a sword against nation, / **neither shall they learn war any more.**

Micah 4:3

623

Glory and honor are in his presence; strength and gladness are in his place. Give unto the Lord, ye kindreds of the people, give unto the Lord glory and strength. Give unto the Lord the glory due unto his name: bring an offering, and come before him: worship the Lord in the beauty of holiness.

1 Chronicles 16:27–29

624

Upon the first day of the week let every one of you lay by him in store, as God hath prospered him.

1 Corinthians 16:2

I speak not by commandment, but by occasion of the forwardness of others, and to prove the sincerity of your love. For ye know the grace of our Lord Jesus Christ, that, though he was rich, yet for your sakes he became poor, that ye through his poverty might be rich.

This I say, He which soweth sparingly shall reap also sparingly; and he which soweth bountifully shall reap also bountifully. Every man according as he purposeth in his heart, so let him give; not grudgingly, or of necessity: for God loveth a cheerful giver. And God is able to make all grace abound toward you; that ye, always having all sufficiency in all things, may abound to every good work.

2 Corinthians 8:8–9; 9:6–8

625

Ask, and it shall be given you; seek, and ye shall find; knock, and it shall be opened unto you: for every one that asketh receiveth; and he that seeketh findeth; and to him that knocketh it shall be opened.

Matthew 7:7–8

Therefore I say unto you, What things soever ye desire, when ye pray, believe that ye receive them, and ye shall have them.   *Mark 11:24*

Be careful for nothing; but in every thing by prayer and supplication with thanksgiving let your requests be made known unto God.

Philippians 4:6

626

O give thanks unto the Lord; for he is good: / **for his mercy endureth for ever.** / O give thanks to the Lord of lords: / **for his mercy endureth for ever.** / To him who alone doeth great wonders: / **for his mercy endureth for ever.**

To him that by wisdom made the heavens: / **for his mercy endureth for ever.** / To him that stretched out the earth above the waters: / **for his mercy endureth for ever.** / To him that made great lights: / **for his mercy endureth for ever:** / The sun to rule by day: / **for his mercy endureth for ever:** / The moon and stars to rule by night: / **for his mercy endureth for ever.**

O give thanks unto the God of heaven: / **for his mercy endureth for ever.**   *Psalm 136:1,3–9,26*

627

At the same time came the disciples unto Jesus, saying, / **Who is the greatest in the kingdom of heaven?** / And Jesus called a little child unto him, and set him in the midst of them, and said, / **Verily I say unto you, Except ye be converted, and become as little children, ye shall not enter into the kingdom of heaven. Whosoever therefore shall humble himself as this little child, the same is greatest in the kingdom of heaven.**   *Matthew 18:1–4*

628

We give thanks to God and the Father of our Lord Jesus Christ, praying always for you, / **since we heard of your faith in Christ Jesus, and of the love which ye have to all the saints, for the hope which is laid up for you in heaven.**

For this cause we . . . do not cease to pray for you, and to desire that ye might be filled with the knowledge of his will in all wisdom and spiritual understanding; / **that ye may walk worthy of the Lord unto all pleasing, being fruitful in every good work, and increasing in the knowledge of God:** / strengthened with all might, according to his glorious power, unto all patience and longsuffering with joyfulness; / **giving thanks unto the Father, which hath made us meet to be partakers of the inheritance of the saints in light:** / who hath delivered us from the power of darkness, and hath translated us into the kingdom of his dear Son: / **in whom we have redemption through his blood, even the forgiveness of sins.**

Colossians 1:3–5,9–14

629

Bring ye all the tithes into the storehouse, that there may be meat in mine house, and prove me now herewith, saith the Lord of hosts, if I will not open you the windows of heaven, and pour you out a blessing, that there shall not be room enough to receive it.

Malachi 3:10

Moreover it is required in stewards, that a man be found faithful.

1 Corinthians 4:2

Therefore, as ye abound in every thing, in faith, and utterance, and knowledge, and in all diligence, and in your love to us, see that ye abound in this grace also.

2 Corinthians 8:7

630

Let not your heart be troubled: ye believe in God, believe also in me. / **In my Father's house are many mansions: if it were not so, I would have told you.** / I go to prepare a place for you. And if I go and prepare a place for you, I will come again, and receive you unto myself; that where I am, there ye may be also.

John 14:1–3

And I [John] saw a new heaven and a new earth: for the first heaven and the first earth were passed away; and there was no more sea. / And I . . . saw the holy city, new Jerusalem, coming down from God out of heaven, prepared as a bride adorned for her husband. / **And I heard a great voice out of heaven saying, Behold, the tabernacle of God is with men, and he will dwell with them, and they shall be his people,** and God himself shall be with them, and be their God.

And God shall wipe away all tears from their eyes; and there shall be no more death, neither sorrow, nor crying, neither shall there be any more pain: for the former things are passed away. / **And there shall be no night there; and they need no candle, neither light of the sun; for the Lord God giveth them light: and they shall reign for ever and ever.**

Revelation 21:1–4; 22:5

631

Let every soul be subject unto the higher powers. For there is no power but of God: the powers that be are ordained of God. / **Whosoever therefore resisteth the power, resisteth the ordinance of God: and they that resist shall receive to themselves damnation.** / For rulers are not a terror to good works, but to the evil. Wilt thou then not be afraid of the power? do that which is good, and thou shalt have praise of the same.

Romans 13:1–3

Blessed is the nation whose God is the Lord; and the people whom he hath chosen for his own inheritance.

Psalm 33:12

632

Do not lay up for yourselves treasures on earth, where moth and rust consume and where thieves break in and steal, but lay up for yourselves treasures in heaven, where neither moth nor rust consumes and where thieves do not break in and steal. For where your treasure is, there will your heart be also.

Matthew 6:19–21 (RSV)

633

If ye then be risen with Christ, seek those things which are above, where Christ sitteth on the right hand of God. Set your affection on things above, not on things on the earth. For ye are dead, and your life is hid with Christ in God.   *Colossians 3:1–3*

For the love of Christ constraineth us; because we thus judge, that if one died for all, then were all dead: and that he died for all, that they which live should not henceforth live unto themselves, but unto him which died for them, and rose again.

2 Corinthians 5:14–15

I am crucified with Christ: nevertheless I live; yet not I, but Christ liveth in me: and the life which I now live in the flesh I live by the faith of the Son of God, who loved me, and gave himself for me. But God forbid that I should glory, save in the cross of our Lord Jesus Christ, by whom the world is crucified unto me, and I unto the world.

Galatians 2:20; 6:14

634

[How] shall a young man cleanse his way? / **by taking heed thereto according to thy word.** / With my whole heart have I sought thee: / **O let me not wander from thy commandments.**

Thy word have I hid in mine heart, that I might not sin against thee. / **Blessed art thou, O Lord: teach me thy statutes.** / With my lips have I declared all the judgments of thy mouth. / **I have rejoiced in the way** of thy testimonies, as much as in all riches.

I will meditate in thy precepts, and have respect unto thy ways. / **I will delight myself in thy statutes: I will not forget thy word.**

Psalm 119:9–16

635

And God spake all these words, saying, I am the Lord thy God. Thou shalt have no other gods before me. Thou shalt not make unto thee any graven image.

Thou shalt not take the name of the Lord thy God in vain; for the Lord will not hold him guiltless that taketh his name in vain. Remember the sabbath day, to keep it holy.

Honor thy father and thy mother: that thy days may be long upon the land which the Lord thy God giveth thee.

Thou shalt not kill. Thou shalt not commit adultery. Thou shalt not steal. Thou shalt not bear false witness against thy neighbor. Thou shalt not covet . . . anything that is thy neighbor's.   *Exodus 20:1–4,7–8,12–17*

636

The steadfast love of the Lord never ceases, his mercies never come to an end; They are new every morning; great is thy faithfulness.

"The Lord is my portion," says my soul, "therefore I will hope in him."

Lamentations 3:22–24 (RSV)

637

To every thing there is a season, and a time to every purpose under the heaven: / **A time to be born, and a time to die;** / a time to plant, and a time to pluck up that which is planted; / **a time to kill, and a time to heal;** / a time to break down, and a time to build up; / **a time to weep, and a time to laugh;** / a time to mourn, and a time to dance;

A time to cast away stones, and a time to gather stones together; / a time to embrace, and a time to refrain from embracing; / **a time to get, and a time to lose;** / a time to keep, and a time to cast away; / **a time to rend, and a time to sew;** / a time to keep silence, and a time to speak; / **a time to love, and a time to hate;** / a time of war, and a time of peace.

He hath made every thing beautiful in his time: / also he hath set the world in their heart, so that no man can find out the work that God maketh from the beginning to the end. / **I know that there is no good in them, but for a man to rejoice, and to do good in his life.**

Ecclesiastes 3:1–8,11–12

638

I count everything as loss because of the surpassing worth of knowing Christ Jesus my Lord; . . . . / **that I may know him and the power of his resurrection, and may share his sufferings, becoming like him in his death,** / that if possible I may attain the resurrection from the dead.

Not that I have already obtained this or am already perfect; / but I press on to make it my own, because Christ Jesus has made me his own. /

Brethren, I do not consider that I have made it my own; / but one thing I do, forgetting what lies behind and straining forward to what lies ahead, / **I press on toward the goal for the prize of the upward call of God in Christ Jesus.**

Philippians 3:8–14 (RSV)

639

What shall I render unto the Lord for all his benefits toward me? I will pay my vows unto the Lord now in the presence of all his people.

Psalm 116:12,14

640

Let this mind be in you, which was also in Christ Jesus: who, being in the form of God, thought it not robbery to be equal with God: / **but made himself of no reputation, and took upon him the form of a servant, and was made in the likeness of men:** / and being found in fashion as a man, he humbled himself, and became obedient unto death, even the death of the cross.

Wherefore God also hath highly exalted him, and given him a name which is above every name: / that at the name of Jesus every knee should bow, of things in heaven, and things in earth, and things under the earth; / **and that every tongue should confess that Jesus Christ is Lord, to the glory of God the Father.**

Philippians 2:5–11

641

Set your minds on things that are above, not on things that are on earth. *Colossians 3:2 (RSV)*

INDEXES

Topical Index of Scripture Readings

Scriptural Index of Scripture Readings

Index of Scriptural Bases for the Hymns

Genesis
1—**154**
28:10–22—**421**

Leviticus
8:35—**407**

Deuteronomy
32:3—**22**

2 Chronicles
15:15—**457**

Job
19:25—**122**

Psalms
20:4—**26**
23—**215, 218, 341**
27:1–3—**343**
27:11—**330**
40:1–5—**402**
46—**37**
51:7—**185**
55:22—**203**
60:4—**387**
67—**297**
72—**282**
90:1–5—**223**
94:22—**163**
95:1–6—**21**
98—**88**
100—**17**
103—**29, 34**

103:1–6—**10**
104—**30**
113:1–2—**14**
118:24–29—**68**
119:105—**140**
136:1,2,7,25—**27**
139:23, 24—**266**
148—**11**
150—**23**

Isaiah
32:2—**195**
40:1–8—**77**

Jeremiah
8:22—**205**

Ezekiel
34:26—**273**

Daniel
6:16—**479**

Habakkuk
3:2—**263**
3:17,18—**221**

Zechariah
13:1—**107**

Matthew
5:8—**323**
6:9–13—**206**
6:25–34—**221**
16:18—**235**

16:24,25—**370**
22:9—**311**

Luke
2:8–14—**97**
12:32—**225**
12:49—**313**
15:1–7—**167**
15:10—**300**
23:12–46—**109**

John
3—**180**
3:16–18—**184, 445**
6:35—**138**
11:28—**188**
12:26—**367**
20:21—**280**
20:22—**131, 317**
20:27–29—**357**

Acts
2—**264**
6,7—**392**

Romans
6:4—**229**
10:13—**169**
14:7—**276**

1 Corinthians
2:2—**60**
16:13—**388**

Galatians
6:14—**60, 70, 111**

Ephesians
6:10–20—**389, 391**

Philippians
2:5–11—**43, 363**
2:9,10—**74**
4:4—**120**

1 Thessalonians
4:16—**503**

1 Timothy
1:12—**450**
1:17—**32**
6:12—**394**

2 Timothy
1:12—**344**

Hebrews
2:10—**125**
9:22—**158**
10:22—**352**

Revelation
3:20—**480**
4:8–11—**1**
5:11–13—**126**
11:15—**121**
22:1—**496**

Index of
Authors, Composers, and Sources

Alphabetical Index of Tunes

Precious to Me (11.11.11.8. w/ref), 449
Promised Land (C.M. w/ref), 490
Promises (11.11.11.9. w/ref), 335
Psalm 42 (8.7.8.7.7.7.8.8.), 77
Purer in Heart (6.4.6.4.6.6.4.4.), 323
Purpose (Irreg.), 509

Quebec (L.M.), 72

Rapture (9.6.9.8. w/ref), 160
Rathbun (8.7.8.7.), 70
Raymer (7.7.7.7.7.7.), 49
Reach Out (Irreg.), 314
Redeemed (9.8.9.8. w/ref), 446
Redeemer (9.9.9.9. w/ref), 109
Redeeming Love (10.8.10.8. w/ref), 471
Redentore (8.7.8.7.D.), 51
Redhead 76 (7.7.7.7.7.7.), 112
Regent Square (8.7.8.7.8.7.) 87
Reitz (9.9.9.9. w/ref), 399
Rescue (Irreg. w/ref), 283
Resolution (10.6.10.6. w/ref), 177
Rest (Elton) (8.6.8.8.6.), 270
Resurrection (Irreg. w/ref), 448
Retreat (L.M.), 244
Revive Us Again (11.11. w/ref), 263
Reynolds (L.M.), 248
Rhea (L.M. w/ref), 288
Richmond (C.M.), 460
Ring the Bells (11.9.11.9. w/ref), 300
Robertson (6.6.6.6.4.4.4.4.), 486
Robin (8.8.8.7.), 153
Roll Call (Irreg. w/ref), 503
Routh (8.7.8.7. w/ref), 455
Royal Banner (11.7.11.7. w/ref), 387

Safety (Irreg. w/ref), 462
St. Agnes (C.M.), 73, 133
St. Anne (C.M.), 223
St. Catherine (8.8.8.8.8.8.), 143, 201, 326
St. Christopher (7.6.8.6.8.6.8.6.), 360
St. Crispin (L.M.), 445
St. Denio (11.11.11.11.), 32
St. Dunstan's (6.5.6.5.6.6.6.5.), 384
St. Edmund (6.4.6.4.6.6.6.4.), 307
St. George's, Windsor (7.7.7.7.D.), 233
St. Gertrude (6.5.6.5.D. w/ref), 146, 393
St. Leonards (8.7.8.5.), 328
St. Louis (8.6.8.6.7.6.8.6.), 85
St. Magnus (C.M.), 125, 128
St. Margaret (8.8.8.8.6.), 368
St. Peter (C.M.), 249, 464
St. Petersburg (8.8.8.8.8.8.), 396
St. Theodulph (7.6.7.6.D.), 39
St. Thomas (S.M.), 240, 268
Salvation (C.M.D.), 320, 392
Salvationist (Irreg. w/ref), 459
Sankey (C.M.D. w/ref), 377
Satisfied (8.7.8.7. w/ref), 345
Savannah (7.7.7.7.), 227
Scales (11.11.11.11. w/ref), 302
Schuler (10.7.10.7. w/ref), 290
Scott (Irreg.), 358
Second Coming (Irreg. w/ref), 129
Seelenbräutigam (5.5.8.8.5.5.), 500
Seminary (8.4.8.4.8.8.8.), 414

Serenity (C.M.), 329
Serug (6.6.4.6.6.6.4.), 303
Seventh and James (11.10.11.10.), 239
Sewell (9.9.9.7.), 170
Sheltering Rock (9.9.8.9. w/ref), 195
Sheng En (9.8.9.9.), 250
Shere (S.M.), 286
Shout On (C.M. w/ref), 436
Showalter (10.9.10.9. w/ref), 254
Showers of Blessing (8.7.8.7. w/ref), 273
Sims (Abridged) (C.M.), 498
Sine nomine (10.10.10. w/Alleluias), 43,
    144
Skillings (8.8.12.8.), 259
Slane (10.10.10.10.), 212
Solid Rock (L.M. w/ref), 337
Somebody's Knocking (Irreg.), 480
Something for Jesus (6.4.6.4.6.6.6.4.), 418
Song 13 (7.7.7.6.), 241
Song of the Yangtze Boatman (5.5.6.5.), 332
Spanish Hymn (7.7.7.7.7.7.), 29, 427
Springbrook (C.M. w/ref), 119
Stanphill (Irreg. w/ref), 194
Stevens (S.M.D.), 224
Stille Nacht (Irreg.), 89
Stockton (C.M. w/ref), 183
Story of Jesus (8.7.8.7.D. w/ref), 437
Stuttgart (8.7.8.7.), 34, 36
Sullivan (Irreg.), 285
Sunlight (10.9.10.9. w/ref), 472
Sunshine (9.6.8.6. w/ref), 447
Surabaja (8.6.8.6.8.8.8.6.), 293
Surrender (8.7.8.7. w/ref), 347
Sweet By and By (9.9.9.9. w/ref), 495
Sweet Hour (L.M.D.), 401
Sweetest Name (9.7.9.7. w/ref), 435
Sweney (L.M. w/ref), 327

Tabernacle (8.8.8.6.), 186
Tabor (C.M.D.), 416
Tallis' Canon (L.M.), 443
Tallis' Ordinal (C.M.), 402
Terra Patris (S.M.D.), 155
The First Nowell (Irreg. w/ref), 91
Thompson (11.7.11.7. w/ref), 190
Tidings (11.10.11.10. w/ref), 295
Tillman (C.M. w/ref), 408
Times Like These (Irreg. w/ref), 469
To God Be the Glory (11.11.11.11. w/ref), 33
Toplady (7.7.7.7.7.7.), 163
Toronto (11.10.11.10. w/ref), 280
Travis Avenue (9.9.9.10. w/ref), 271
Trentham (S.M.), 317, 482
Truett (7.6.8.6. w/ref), 131
Trust and Obey (6.6.9.D. w/ref), 409
Trust in Jesus (8.7.8.7. w/ref), 375
Trusting Jesus (7.7.7.7. w/ref), 441
Tryggare kan ingen vara (L.M.), 207
Twenty-Fourth (C.M.), 504

Unafraid (Irreg.), 452

Valley (9.9.10.9.), 501
Varndean (7.6.7.6.7.7.), 38
Veni Immanuel (8.8.8.8.8.8.), 78
Vermont (C.M.), 412

Metrical Index of Tunes

Word of God, across the ages, 148

BLOOD OF CHRIST—(See *Atonement*)

BROTHERHOOD—(See *Social Concern*)

Christ is the world's true, 274
Christian hearts, in love, 253
Come, all Christians, 362
From every race, 247
In Christ there is, 258
One world, one Lord, 296
Rise up, O men of God, 268
We lift our hearts, 416
Where charity and love, 257
Where cross the crowded, 311

CALL OF CHRIST—(See *Discipleship, Invitation to Consecration, Commitment*)

CALLS TO WORSHIP

All people that on earth, 17
Come, Christians, join to sing, 61
Come, Holy Spirit, 134
Come, thou Fount, 12, 13
Glory be to the Father, 4, 5
God himself is with us, 16
Jesus, thou joy, 72
Let all the world, 24
O spirit of the living God, 264
O worship the King, 30
Our Father God, 206
Praise God from whom, 6, 7
Praise him, O praise him, 18
Praise the Lord who reigns, 23
Spirit of the living God, 136
Stand up and bless the Lord, 26
Sweet, sweet spirit, 255
The bond of love, 259

CHRISTIAN EXPERIENCE—(See *Testimony*)

CHRISTIAN HERITAGE

Faith of our fathers, 143
For all the saints, 144
Forward through the ages, 146
God of our fathers, 149
Lord of our life, 145
Lord, who dost give to thy church, 239
O God of our fathers, 507
O God, our help, 223
We are climbing Jacob's, 147
Word of God, across, 148

CHRISTIAN HOME—(See *Marriage and Family*)

CHRISTMAS—(See *Jesus Christ—Birth*)

CHURCH

Built on the Rock, 235
Christian hearts, in love, 253
For the beauty of the earth, 49, 54
I love thy kingdom, Lord, 240
Jesus, with thy church, 241
Lord, who dost give, 239
O church of God, 237
O Word of God incarnate, 140
Onward, Christian soldiers, 393
Stir thy church, O God, 269
The church's one, 236
To worship, work, 238

COMFORT—(See *Guidance and Care*)

COMMITMENT

A charge to keep I have, 407
All for Jesus, 485
All to thee, 346
At the name of Jesus, 363
Awake, awake to love, 413
Beneath the cross of Jesus, 360
Come, all Christians, 362
Follow on, 226
Footsteps of Jesus, 325
God of grace and God, 265
God's world today, 359
Have thine own way, Lord, 349
He who would valiant be, 384
Here is my life, 356
Hope of the world, 364
I am thine, O Lord, 352
I have decided to follow, 191
I surrender all, 347
I'll live for him, 189
Jesus calls us, 367
Jesus is Lord of all, 353
Jesus, keep me near, 351
Just as I am, thine, 243
Lead me to Calvary, 350
Let others see Jesus in you, 294
Living for Jesus, 348
Lord, speak to me, 276
Make me a blessing, 290
Make me a channel, 262
Make room within, 321
My heart looks in faith, 332
My singing is a prayer, 412
Near to the heart of God, 354
O gracious Lord, 19
O Jesus, I have promised, 365
O Love that wilt not, 368
O Master, let me walk, 369
Open my eyes that I, 358
Ready, 408
Search me, O God, 266
Send me, O Lord, send me, 293
Set my soul afire, 302
Speak to my heart, 355
Take my life, lead me, 366
Take my life, and let, 373, 374

Take up thy cross, 370
Walk ye in him, 279
We are called to be, 405
We walk by faith, 357
Where he leads me, 371
Wherever he leads I'll go, 361

CONFESSION—(See *Repentance and Confession*)

CONFLICT—(See *Loyalty and Courage*)

CONSECRATION—(See *Commitment*)

CONSOLATION—(See *Guidance and Care, Faith and Trust*)

CONVERSION—(See *Invitation and Acceptance*)

COURAGE—(See *Loyalty and Courage*)

CREATION

At the name of Jesus, 363
Declare, O heavens, 47
God of earth and outer space, 20
God, who stretched the, 150
He's everything to me, 463
How gracious are thy, 230
How great thou art, 35
I sing the almighty power, 154
Morning has broken, 151
My God is there, 153
Praise the Lord, the King, 46
Praise the Lord! Ye heavens, 11
Praise to the Lord, the, 10
The cattle on a thousand, 152
This is my Father's world, 155

CROSS—(See *Atonement*)

CRUCIFIXION—(See *Atonement, Jesus Christ—Suffering and Death*)

DEATH—(See *Future Life*)

A mighty fortress is our God, 37
Abide with me, 217
How gracious are thy, 230
My Jesus, I love thee, 76
Nearer, my God, to thee, 333
O God, our help, 223
Rock of ages, cleft for me, 163
The King of love, 215
The Lord's my shepherd, 341
What wondrous love, 106

DEDICATION OF BUILDING—(See *Church*)

DEDICATION OF CHRISTIAN WORKERS—(See *Commitment, Service, Discipleship*)

DEDICATION OF HOME—(See
Marriage and Family)

DEDICATION OF LIFE—(See
Stewardship, Commitment, Discipleship)

DEVOTION

All praise to thee, 43
All that thrills my soul, 434
Ask ye what great thing, 60
At the name of Jesus, 363
Be thou my vision, 212
Blessed be the name, 50
Children of the heavenly, 207
Come, Christians, join to sing, 61
Come, Holy Spirit, 134
Dear Lord and Father, 270
Fairest Lord Jesus, 48
Glorious is thy name, 59
Glorious is thy name, most, 419
God himself is with us, 16
God, our Father, we adore, 3
Great Redeemer, we adore, 51
Have thine own way, Lord, 349
His name is wonderful, 71
Holy, holy, holy, 1
How great thou art, 35
I am his and he is mine, 342
I love thee, 75
Immortal Love, forever full, 329
Jesus, lover of my soul, 172
Jesus, the very thought, 73
Jesus, thou joy of, 72
Joyful, joyful, we adore, 31
Lead me to Calvary, 350
More about Jesus, 327
My faith looks up to thee, 382
Near to the heart of God, 354
Nearer, my God, to thee, 333
O God of our fathers, 507
O Love that wilt not, 368
O thou, in whose presence, 372
Rock of Ages, cleft for me, 163
Turn your eyes upon Jesus, 198
We praise thee, O God, 15
What a friend we have, 403
What wondrous love, 106

DISCIPLESHIP

A charge to keep I have, 407
All to thee, 346
Awake, awake, to love, 413
Because I have been, 414
Dear Lord and Father, 270
Follow on, 226
Footsteps of Jesus, 325
God's world today, 359
He who would valiant be, 384
Here is my life, 356
His gentle look, 318
I gave my life for thee, 417
I have decided to follow, 191
I'll live for him, 189

Jesus calls us, 367
Just as I am, thine, 243
Let others see Jesus in you, 294
Living for Jesus, 348
Lord, I want to be, 322
Lord, lay some soul, 298
Lord, speak to me, 276
O Jesus, I have promised, 365
O Lord, who came, 309
Once to every man, 385
Onward, Christian soldiers, 393
Pass it on, 287
People to people, 308
Reach out and touch, 314
Ready, 408
Rise up, O men of God, 268
So send I you, 280
Strong, righteous Man, 101
Take my life, and let, 373, 374
Take up thy cross, 370
To worship, work, 238
Walk ye in him, 279
We are called to be, 405
When we walk with, 409
Where cross the crowded, 311
Where he leads me, 371
Wherever he leads I'll go, 361

EASTER—(See *Jesus Christ—Resurrection*)

ECOLOGY—(See *Creation, Nature*)

EDUCATION

Be thou my vision, 212
God, who stretched the, 150
Holy Bible, Book divine, 139
Lead on, O King eternal, 420
Lord, speak to me, 276
Lord, who dost give, 239
May the mind of Christ, 328
More about Jesus, 327
O Master, let me walk, 369
O Word of God incarnate, 140
Open my eyes, 358
Our Father God, thy, 206
Spirit of God, descend, 132
Teach me, O Lord, I pray, 406
Teach me thy way, O Lord, 330
Tell me the story of Jesus, 437
We praise thee with, 45

ENCOURAGEMENT—(See *Faith
and Trust, Guidance and Care*)

ETERNAL LIFE—(See *Future Life*)

EVANGELISM AND MISSIONS

Christ is the world's true, 274
Do you really care, 316
Draw thou my soul, 307
God is working his purpose, 509
God of mercy, God of grace, 297
I bless the Christ of God, 286
Jesus shall reign, 282

Let others see Jesus in you, 294
Let the song go round, 306
Lord, lay some soul, 298
Lord, speak to me, 276
Make me a blessing, 290
Make me a channel, 262
New life for you, 299
O God, we pray for, 305
O Zion, haste, 295
One world, one Lord, 296
Pass it on, 287
People to people, 308
Rescue the perishing, 283
Ring the bells of heaven, 300
Savior, teach me, 291
Send me, O Lord, send me, 293
Send the light, 304
Set my soul afire, 302
Share his love, 285
So send I you, 280
Spread, O spread, 284
Tell it out with gladness, 275
Tell the good news, 288
Thou, whose almighty, 303
Walk ye in him, 279
We have a gospel, 301
We have heard the, 277, 278
We've a story to tell, 281
Ye Christian heralds! 289
Ye servants of God, 292

EVENING

Abide with me, 217
God be with you, 261
Savior, again to thy, 65
Share his love, 285
Sweet, sweet spirit, 255
The bond of love, 259

EVERLASTING LIFE—(See *Future
Life*)

FAITH AND TRUST

Come, come, ye saints, 210
Faith is the victory, 377
Give to the winds, 224
God is my strong salvation, 343
God moves in a, 439
Have faith in God, 376
How firm a foundation, 383
I need thee every hour, 379
Lord, you bid us ever, 378
Moment by moment, 381
My faith has found, 380
My faith looks up to thee, 382
My God is there, 153
My heart looks in faith, 332
O thou, in whose presence, 372
'Tis so sweet to trust, 375
We walk by faith, 357

FAITHFULNESS—(See *Faith and
Trust, God—Faithfulness*)

FAMILY—(See *Marriage and
Family*)

FAREWELL

Blest be the tie, 256
God be with you, 261

FATHER'S DAY—(See *Marriage and Family*)

FELLOWSHIP OF BELIEVERS

Blest be the tie, 256
Brethren, we have met, 260
Christian hearts, in love, 253
God be with you, 261
In Christ there is, 258
Leaning on the everlasting, 254
Sweet, sweet spirit, 255
The bond of love, 259
Where charity and love, 257

FELLOWSHIP WITH GOD

All praise to thee, 43
Breathe on me, Breath, 317
Built on the Rock, 235
Day by day, 222
He's everything to me, 463
How firm a foundation, 383
In Christ there is, 258
In the garden, 428
Leaning on the everlasting, 254

FORGIVENESS—(See *Grace and Mercy*)

Blessed Redeemer, 109
Christ receiveth sinful men, 167
Dear Lord and Father, 270
Down at the cross, 454
Grace greater than our sins, 164
It is well with my soul, 339
No, not despairingly, 173
Since Jesus came into, 487
The great Physician, 102
There is a fountain, 107
"Whosoever" meaneth me, 169

FREEDOM—SPIRITUAL

Free from the law, 168
Free to be me, 331
New born again, 474
New life for you, 299
There is a name I love, 66
There is power in the blood, 159
"Whosoever" meaneth me, 169
Why do I sing about Jesus? 429

FUNERAL—(See *Death, Future Life*)

FUTURE LIFE

By and by, 506
Christ is the world's, 274
Day of judgment! Day, 502
Face to face with Christ, 489

Give me the wings of faith, 498
I know not what the, 492
Jerusalem, my happy home, 488
Jesus, still lead on, 500
Lead on, O King eternal, 420
Must Jesus bear the cross, 494
O that will be glory, 497
On Jordan's stormy banks, 490
Shall we gather at the river, 496
Sing we the King, 493
There is a land of, 504
There's a land that is, 495
We shall walk through, 501
We're marching to Zion, 505
When the morning comes, 499
When the roll is called, 503
When we all get to heaven, 491

GOD—CARE—(See *Guidance and Care*)

GOD—CREATOR—(See *Creation*)

GOD—FAITHFULNESS

Abide with me, 217
Children of the heavenly, 207
Day by day, 222
Great is thy faithfulness, 216
Have no fear, little flock, 225
Let us with a gladsome mind, 27
O God, our help, 223

GOD—FATHER

Be thou my vision, 212
Children of the heavenly, 207
Day by day, 222
God be with you, 261
God, our Father, we adore, 3
Great is thy faithfulness, 216
Have no fear, little flock, 225
If you will only let God, 203
Immortal, invisible, 32
In Christ there is, 258
Joyful, joyful, we adore, 31
O my soul, bless God, 34
Our Father God, thy name, 206
The cattle on a thousand, 152
This is my Father's world, 155
To God be the glory, 33

GOD—GLORY AND POWER

A mighty fortress is our God, 37
Declare, O heavens, 47
God is love, his mercy, 36
God is my strong salvation, 343
God is working his, 509
God of earth and outer space, 20
God who stretched the, 150
He's everything to me, 463
His gentle look, 318
Holy, holy, holy, 1
How great thou art, 35
I sing the almighty power, 154

Immortal, invisible, 32
Joyful, joyful, we adore, 31
Let us with a gladsome, 27
O my soul, bless God, 34
O worship the King, 30
Of the Father's love begotten, 62
Praise him, O praise him, 18
Praise the Lord who reigns, 23
Praise the Lord! Ye heavens, 11
Sing praise to God who, 22
To God be the glory, 33

GOD—LOVE—(See *Love—God's Love*)

GOD—MAJESTY—(See *God— Glory and Power*)

GOD—PRAISE—(See *Praise and Adoration*)

GOD—PROVIDENCE—(See *Guidance and Care*)

GOD—REFUGE—(See *Guidance and Care*)

GOD—TRINITY—(See *Trinity*)

GRACE AND MERCY

Amazing grace! 165
Are you washed in the, 162
As Jacob with travel, 421
At Calvary, 166
Christ receiveth sinful men, 167
Come, thou Fount, 12, 13
Day by day, 222
Free from the law, 168
God is love, his mercy, 36
God loved the world, 445
God moves in a mysterious, 439
Grace greater than our sin, 164
Great is thy faithfulness, 216
He included me, 170
How firm a foundation, 383
How gracious are thy, 230
I saw the cross, 483
In loving-kindness Jesus, 426
Jesus, lover of my soul, 172
Jesus paid it all, 156
Let us with a gladsome mind, 27
Majestic sweetness, 267
My song is love, 486
New born again, 474
No, not despairingly, 173
Nothing but the blood, 158
Redeemed, how I love, 444, 446
Rescue the perishing, 283
Saved, saved! 160
Since I have been redeemed, 442
Surely goodness and mercy, 228
The way of the cross leads, 161
There is power in the blood, 159
There's a wideness, 171
To God be the glory, 33
We have heard the, 277, 278

We praise thee, O God, 15
Whiter than snow, 185
"Whosoever" meaneth me, 169

GUIDANCE AND CARE

Abide with me, 217
All that thrills my soul, 434
All the way my Savior, 214
Be thou my vision, 212
Because I have been, 414
Children of the heavenly, 207
Come, come, ye saints, 210
Come, ye disconsolate, 211
Day by day, 222
Follow on, 226
Footsteps of Jesus, 325
Give to the winds, 224
God be with you, 261
God moves in a mysterious, 439
God of earth and outer space, 20
God of our fathers, 149
God will take care of you, 219
Great is thy faithfulness, 216
Guide me, O thou great, 202
Have no fear, little flock, 225
He leadeth me! 218
Heavenly sunlight, 472
He's everything to me, 463
I am his, and he is mine, 342
I will not be afraid, 452
If you will only let God, 203
In heavenly love abiding, 204
Jesus lives and Jesus leads, 38
Jesus makes my heart, 386
Jesus! What a friend, 64
Just a closer walk, 481
Just when I need him most, 220
Lead on, O King eternal, 420
Like a river glorious, 208
Moment by moment, 381
My Lord is near me, 209
No, not one, 478
O God, our help, 223
O the deep, deep love, 340
O thou, in whose presence, 372
O worship the King, 30
Our Father God, thy, 206
Our hope is in the, 201
Purer in heart, O God, 323
Savior, like a shepherd, 213
Show, O Lord, thy, 227
Sometimes a light surprises, 221
Spirit of God, our, 133
Strong, righteous Man, 101
Surely goodness and mercy, 228
The King of love, 215
The Lord's my Shepherd, 341
There is a balm in Gilead, 205
Trusting Jesus, 441
Walk ye in him, 279

HEAVEN

Come, come, ye saints, 210
Face to face with Christ, 489

Guide me, O thou, 202
How great thou art, 35
I know that my Redeemer, 122
I love thee, 75
Jerusalem, my happy home, 488
Must Jesus bear the cross, 494
O that will be glory, 497
On Jordan's stormy banks, 490
Saved, saved! 160
Shall we gather at the river, 496
Surely goodness and mercy, 228
The way of the cross leads, 161
There's a land that is, 495
We're marching to Zion, 505
When the morning comes, 499
When we all get to heaven, 491

HERITAGE—(See *Christian Heritage, Patriotic*)

HOLY SPIRIT

Alleluia! Alleluia! 117
Break thou the bread, 138
Breathe on me, 131
Breathe on me, Breath, 317
Built on the Rock, 235
Come, Holy Spirit, 134
Come, thou Almighty King, 2
God himself is with us, 16
Holy Spirit, Light Divine, 135
I surrender all, 347
Love divine, all loves, 58
O Breath of Life, 137
O spirit of the living God, 264
Open my eyes that I, 358
Pentecostal power, 130
Search me, O God, 266
Spirit of God, descend, 132
Spirit of God, our, 133
Spirit of the living God, 136
Sweet, sweet spirit, 255
There is a balm in Gilead, 205
Thou, whose purpose, 313
We bless the name, 244
We have a gospel, 301
We praise thee, O God, 15
We praise thee with, 45

HOME—(See *Marriage and Family*)

HOPE—(See *Peace—Inner, Faith and Trust, Guidance and Care*)

Come, thou Fount, 12, 13
Come, thou long-expected, 79
Come, ye disconsolate, 211
Great is thy faithfulness, 216
He lives, 438
Heaven came down, 425
Hope of the world, 364
If you will only let God, 203
Lord, you bid us ever, 378
Nothing but the blood, 158
O God, our help, 223
O thou, in whose presence, 372

Our hope is in the, 201
Take the name of Jesus, 473
The solid Rock, 337

HUMILITY

Amazing grace! 165
Beneath the cross of Jesus, 360
Blessed assurance, 334
He leadeth me! O blessed, 218
How great thou art, 35
I surrender all, 347
Just as I am, 186, 187
O sacred Head, 105
Rock of Ages, cleft for me, 163
Teach me to pray, 399
When I survey, 111
Whiter than snow, 185

INVITATION TO CONSECRA-TION

A charge to keep I have, 407
Beneath the cross of Jesus, 360
Breathe on me, 131
Come, all Christians, 362
Do you really care, 316
Follow on, 226
Footsteps of Jesus, 325
Have thine own way, Lord, 349
He who would valiant be, 384
Here is my life, 356
I am thine, O Lord, 352
I have decided to follow, 191
I surrender all, 347
Jesus calls us, 367
Jesus is Lord of all, 353
Make room within my, 321
Out of my bondage, sorrow, 178
Ready, 408
Rise up, O men of God, 268
Search me, O God, 266
Send me, O Lord, send me, 293
Something for thee, 418
Take my life, and let, 373, 374
Take my life, lead me, 366
Take up thy cross, 370
The time is now, 193
Turn your eyes upon Jesus, 198
When we walk with, 409
Where he leads me, 371
Wherever he leads I'll go, 361
Whiter than snow, 185

INVITATION AND ACCEPT-ANCE

Are you washed in the, 162
Come, ye sinners, 196, 197
I have decided to follow, 191
I hear thy welcome voice, 175
I'll live for him, 189
Jesus is tenderly calling, 188
Just as I am, 186, 187
Let Jesus come into, 179
Lord, I'm coming home, 174

My faith has found, 380
Satisfied with Jesus, 455
Search me, O God, 266
Turn your eyes upon Jesus, 198
We walk by faith, 357

PENTECOST—(See *Holy Spirit*)

**PRAISE AND ADORATION—
GOD THE FATHER**

All creatures of our God, 9
All people that on earth, 17
Come, thou Fount, 12, 13
God himself is with us, 16
God of earth and outer space, 20
I sing the almighty power, 154
Let all the world in every, 24
Let us with a gladsome mind, 27
Morning has broken, 151
O come, loud anthems, 21
O gracious Lord, accept, 19
O my soul, bless God, 34
O worship the King, 30
Praise God from whom all bless-
ings flow, 6, 7
Praise him, O praise him, 18
Praise, my soul, the King, 8
Praise the Lord, 14
Praise the Lord who reigns, 23
Praise the Lord! Ye heavens, 11
Praise to the Lord, the, 10
Rejoice, ye pure in heart, 28
Sing praise to God who, 22
Stand up and bless the Lord, 26
The God of Abraham praise, 25
We praise thee, O God, 15

**PRAISE AND ADORATION—
JESUS CHRIST**

All glory, laud, and honor, 39
All hail the power, 40, 41, 42
All praise to thee, 43
Alleluia, 422
Ask ye what great thing, 60
Blessed be the name, 50
Come, Christians, join to sing, 61
Crown him with many, 52
Declare, O heavens, 47
Fairest Lord Jesus, 48
For the beauty of the, 49, 54
Glorious is thy name, 59
Great Redeemer, we adore, 51
His name is wonderful, 71
How great thou art, 35
How sweet the name, 464
I love thee, 75
I stand amazed, 63
I will sing the wondrous, 53, 55
In the cross of Christ I glory, 70
Jesus lives and Jesus leads, 38
Jesus! Name of wondrous, 74
Jesus, the very thought, 73
Jesus, thou joy of loving, 72
Jesus! What a friend, 64

Love divine, all loves, 58
"Man of Sorrows," 56
My God, I love thee, 57
My Jesus, I love thee, 76
My song is love, 486
O for a thousand, 50, 69
Of the Father's love begotten, 62
Praise him! Praise him! 67
Praise the Lord, the King, 46
Savior, again to thy dear, 65
There is a name I love, 66
This is the day the Lord, 68
We praise thee with our, 45
When morning gilds, 44

PRAYER

I waited for the Lord, 402
Jesus, thou joy of loving, 72
Near to the heart of God, 354
Prayer is the soul's sincere, 400
Sweet hour of prayer, 401
Teach me to pray, 399
Tell it to Jesus, 404
What a friend we have, 403

PRIESTHOOD OF BELIEVERS

Jesus, lover of my soul, 172
Lord, speak to me, 276
Speak to my heart, 355
Spirit of God, descend, 132

PROVIDENCE—(See *Guidance and
Care*)

RACE RELATIONS—(See *Social
Concern*)

REDEMPTION—(See *Salvation,
Atonement, Grace and Mercy*)

REFUGE—(See *Guidance and Care,
Faith and Trust*)

RENEWAL AND REVIVAL

Awake, awake to love, 413
Christian men, arise, 141
Dear Lord and Father, 270
God of grace and God, 265
Lord, send a revival, 272
Lord, who dost give, 239
Majestic sweetness, 267
Make me a channel, 262
New life for you, 299
O Breath of Life, 137
O Jesus, I have promised, 365
O spirit of the living God, 264
Revive us again, 263
Rise up, O men of God, 268
Search me, O God, 266
Send a great revival, 271
Stir thy church, O God, 269
Sweet, sweet spirit, 255
Teach me to pray, 399
There is a balm in Gilead, 205

There shall be showers, 273
Thou, whose purpose is, 313
We are called to be, 405
We praise thee, O God, 15

**REPENTANCE AND CONFES-
SION**

I am resolved, 177
I hear thy welcome voice, 175
Jesus paid it all, 156
Lord, I'm coming home, 174
No, not despairingly, 173
Out of my bondage, sorrow, 178
Pass me not, O gentle, 176
Savior, like a shepherd, 213
Tell the good news, 288
Victory in Jesus, 475

RESURRECTION—(See *Jesus
Christ—Resurrection and Exalta-
tion*)

SALVATION—(See *Grace and
Mercy, Atonement*)

Are you washed in the, 162
At Calvary, 166
At the cross, 157
Christ is the world's, 274
Down at the cross, 454
Free from the law, 168
Glory be to God on high, 104
He is able to deliver, 479
Heaven came down, 425
Hope of the world, 364
I bless the Christ of God, 286
I love thee, 75
I saw the cross, 483
Jesus paid it all, 156
Love divine, all loves, 58
Love lifted me, 462
My faith has found, 380
My song is love, 486
New born again, 474
New life for you, 299
Nothing but the blood, 158
Now I belong to Jesus, 477
O gracious Lord, accept, 19
O thou, in whose presence, 372
Praise him! Praise him! 67
Praise the Lord! Ye heavens, 11
Ring the bells of heaven, 300
Rock of Ages, cleft for me, 163
Satisfied, 345
Saved, saved! 160
Since I have been redeemed, 442
Sing praise to God who, 22
Tell it out with gladness, 275
The church's one, 236
The way of the cross, 161
There is power in the blood, 159
To God be the glory, 33
Turn your eyes upon Jesus, 198
Victory in Jesus, 475
We have heard the, 277, 278
Wonderful words of life, 142

Ye must be born again, 180
Ye servants of God, 292

SCRIPTURES—(See *Bible*)

SECOND COMING—(See *Jesus Christ—Return*)

SERVICE

A charge to keep I have, 407
Christian men, arise, 141
Come, all Christians, 362
God's world today, 359
In Christ there is, 258
Jesus is Lord of all, 353
Lord, who dost give, 239
Make me a blessing, 290
Make me a channel, 262
New life for you, 299
O Lord, who came to, 309
O Master, let me walk, 369
Ready, 408
Rise up, O men of God, 268
Satisfied with Jesus, 455
Send me, O Lord, send me, 293
Serve the Lord with, 411
So send I you, 280
Stir thy church, O God, 269
Take my life, and let, 373, 374
Teach me, O Lord, I pray, 406
Tell it out with gladness, 275
To worship, work, 238
Walk ye in him, 279
We are called to be, 405
We lift our hearts in, 416
We thank thee that, 410
We would see Jesus; lo, 98
When we walk with, 409

SOCIAL CONCERN

Because I have been given, 414
Breathe on me, Breath, 317
Christ is the world's, 274
Do you really care, 316
Jesus, friend of thronging, 100
O church of God, 237
O God of every time, 320
O Lord, who came to, 309
Peace in our time, O Lord, 310
People to people, 308
Reach out and touch, 314
Soldiers of Christ, in truth, 315
Stir thy church, O God, 269
Teach me, O Lord, to care, 312
Thou, whose purpose is, 313
We lift our hearts, 416
We thank thee that, 410
When the church of Jesus, 319
Where cross the crowded, 311

SPACE

Declare, O heavens, 47
God of earth and outer space, 20
God, who stretched the, 150

Great is thy faithfulness, 216
How great thou art, 35
I sing the almighty power, 154
Praise the Lord! Ye heavens, 11
The cattle on a thousand, 152

SPECIAL OCCASIONS—(See *Patriotic, New Year*)

SPIRITUALS

By and by, 506
Go, tell it on the mountain, 82
Lord, I want to be, 322
New born again, 474
Somebody's knocking, 480
There is a balm in Gilead, 205
We are climbing Jacob's, 147
We shall walk through, 501
Were you there, 108

STEWARDSHIP

Awake, awake to love, 413
Because I have been given, 414
Come, all Christians, 362
Free to be me, 331
Give to the Lord, as he, 415
Glorious is thy name, 419
Here is my life, 356
I gave my life for thee, 417
Lead on, O King eternal, 420
My singing is a prayer, 412
O Zion, haste, 295
Ready, 408
Something for thee, 418
Take my life, and let, 373, 374
Teach me, O Lord, to care, 312
We lift our hearts, 416
We praise thee with, 45

SUBMISSION—(See *Humility, Commitment*)

SURRENDER—(See *Commitment*)

TEMPTATION—(See *Loyalty and Courage*)

TESTIMONY

All for Jesus, 485
All that thrills my soul, 434
Alleluia, 422
As Jacob with travel, 421
Ask ye what great thing, 60
At Calvary, 166
Because he lives, 448
Blessed Savior, thee I love, 427
Down at the cross, 454
Fill thou my life, O Lord, 460
God loved the world, 445
God moves in a mysterious, 439
He hideth my soul, 451
He is able to, 479
He is so precious to me, 449
He keeps me singing, 435

He lives, 438
Heaven came down, 425
Heavenly sunlight, 472
He's everything to me, 463
His name is wonderful, 71
How great thou art, 35
How sweet the name, 464
I am not skilled to, 433
I have decided to follow, 191
I know that my Redeemer lives, 436
I know that my Redeemer liveth, 122
I love to tell the story, 461
I saw the cross of, 483
I stand amazed, 63
I will sing of my Redeemer, 465
I'm not ashamed to, 450
In loving-kindness, 426
In the garden, 428
In times like these, 469
It's so wonderful, 467
I've found a friend, 423
I've got peace like a river, 458
Jesus is all the world to me, 424
Just a closer walk, 481
Just when I need him most, 220
Love is the theme, 453
Love lifted me, 462
Majestic sweetness, 267
More love to thee, 484
My blessed Savior, 431
My faith has found, 380
My Lord is near me, 209
My song is love, 486
My soul in sad exile, 338
New born again, 474
No, not one, 478
Now I belong to Jesus, 477
O for a thousand, 50, 69
O happy day, 457
O love of God, 482
O Teacher, Master, 443
O thou to whose, 470
One day, 127
Redeemed, how I love, 444, 446
Room at the cross, 194
Satisfied, 345
Satisfied with Jesus, 455
Saved, saved! 160
Since I have been redeemed, 442
Since Jesus came into my heart, 487
So let our lips and lives, 456
Somebody's knocking, 480
Sunshine in my soul, 447
Tell me the story of Jesus, 437
Thank the Lord with, 466
The Lily of the Valley, 459
The old rugged cross, 430
The Savior's wondrous love, 476
The solid Rock, 337
There is no name so sweet, 440
There's a glad new song, 471
Trusting Jesus, 441
Victory in Jesus, 475

Index of First Lines and Titles

Titles are in caps and small caps; first lines in lower case type